RESILIENCE AND FAMILISM

CONTEMPORARY PERSPECTIVES IN FAMILY RESEARCH

Series Editor: Sampson Lee Blair

Previous Volumes:

EDITORIAL BOARD

CONTEMPORARY PERSPECTIVES IN FAMILY
RESEARCH   VOLUME 23

RESILIENCE AND FAMILISM: THE DYNAMIC NATURE OF FAMILIES IN THE PHILIPPINES

EDITED BY

VERONICA L. GREGORIO
National University of Singapore, Singapore

CLARENCE M. BATAN
University of Santo Tomas, Philippines

and

SAMPSON LEE BLAIR
The State University of New York, USA

United Kingdom – North America – Japan
India – Malaysia – China

Emerald Publishing Limited
Howard House, Wagon Lane, Bingley BD16 1WA, UK

First edition 2023

Reprints and permissions service
Contact: permissions@emeraldinsight.com

British Library Cataloguing in Publication Data
A catalogue record for this book is available from the British Library

ISBN: 978-1-80455-415-9 (Print)
ISBN: 978-1-80455-414-2 (Online)
ISBN: 978-1-80455-416-6 (Epub)

ISSN: 1530-3535 (Series)

Printed and bound by CPI Group (UK) Ltd, Croydon, CR0 4YY

ISOQAR certified
Management System,
awarded to Emerald
for adherence to
Environmental
standard
ISO 14001:2004.

ISOQAR REGISTERED
Certificate Number 1985
ISO 14001

INVESTOR IN PEOPLE

CONTENTS

LIST OF FIGURES AND TABLES

ABOUT THE CONTRIBUTORS

Jeofrey B. Abalos is a postdoctoral fellow at the National University of Singapore Centre for Family and Population Research. His research interests include population aging and health, marriage and cohabitation, and divorce and separation.

Sunshine Therese S. Alcantara graduated with a bachelor's degree in Sociology, cum laude, in 2015 from the University of the Philippines Los Baños. She finished her master's degree in Sociology with a minor in Development Management and Governance from the same university in 2019. Upon completing her master's, she worked as a Research Associate at the Asian Institute of Management – Rizalino S. Navarro Policy Center for Competitiveness. Currently, she serves as an Assistant Professor at the University of the Philippines Los Baños, teaching various sociology courses. Her research interests include family, youth, remote work, and qualitative research.

Clarence M. Batan is a Professor and Head of the Department of Sociology, and former Director of the Research Center for Culture, Education, and Social Issues (RCCESI) from 2015 to 2016 at the University of Santo Tomas (UST), Manila, Philippines. He was instrumental in reorganizing the RCCESI which led to the establishment of two multi-disciplinal-based centers namely, the Research Center for the Social Sciences and Education and the Research Center for Culture, Arts, and Humanities in 2017. He was President of the Philippine Sociological Society (2017–2018) and Vice President for Asia in the Research Committee on the Sociology of Youth (RC34) (2014–2018) of the International Sociological Association. His research interests are the sociology of childhood and youth, sociology of work and employment, sociology of Filipino Catholicism, Global South scholarship, and qualitative and mixed methods. He obtained his AB in Sociology from UST; MA in Sociology from the University of the Philippines Diliman. Having completed his graduate studies in North America (including a PhD in Sociology at Dalhousie University in Canada and an international research fellowship at Brown University in the USA) he has been challenged through his involvement in the Global South youth studies project to center the works of Southeast Asian theorists and Filipino academics in his sociological research. He actively serves as a policy consultant in the Department of Education, and the Commission on Higher Education of the Philippine Government. He continues his istambay (on standby) research on the phenomenon of "waithood and precarity" through the project, Pilipinong Kabataang Naghahabi ng Buhay (Filipino Youth Weaving Lives) and leads The National Catechetical Study: Pastoral Action Research and Intervention Project in partnership with the Catholic Bishops' Conference in the Philippines – Episcopal Commission on Catechesis and Catholic Education, which allows him to investigate more closely the present-day dynamics of the Sociology of Catholicism in the Philippines.

Samuel I. Cabbuag is an Assistant Professor of Sociology at the University of the Philippines Diliman where he finished both his bachelor and master's degrees. He is also a PhD student in Sociology at Hong Kong Baptist University. His research interests include digital sociology, cultural sociology, media and cultural studies, digital cultures, popular culture, fan studies, and influencer cultures. He has published in the *Philippine Sociological Review*, *Asian Politics & Policy*, *Plaridel*, *Katipunan*, and *Southeast Asian Media Studies Journal*. His recent co-authored publication is about pseudonymous influencers and media manipulation in the Philippines in understanding the complicities of the influencer industry with disinformation.

Jerome V. Cleofas is an Associate Professor and the Graduate Program Coordinator of the Department of Sociology and Behavioral Sciences (DSBS), De La Salle University, Manila (DLSU), Philippines. He is a registered nurse and health social scientist with a BS Nursing degree from Far Eastern University, graduating cum laude. He earned his MA Nursing major in Clinical Management degree at St. Paul University Manila, where he previously worked as a Senior Research Associate and University Planning Coordinator. He earned his PhD in Sociology, majoring in Family, Health, and Population Dynamics at DSBS-DLSU, where he is currently a full-time Faculty handling social research and health-related courses. Currently, he is a member of the Research Capability Building Committee of the Metro Manila Health and Development Consortium and a member of the Board of Directors of the Philippine Sociological Society. His research interests and publications are in the fields of health social sciences, youth and emerging adulthood, family studies, gender studies, mixed methodology, nursing studies, and social media.

Carla Krishan A. Cuadro is a Medical Speech-language Pathologist at the Memory Center and the Voice and Swallowing Center at St. Luke's Medical Center in the Philippines. She is an adjunct Research Assistant Professor at the Institute of Aging, National Institutes of Health, University of the Philippines-Manila, where she conducts research on dementia care in the Philippines and aims to lend an anthropological eye to investigations on food (in)security among Filipino elderly, particularly in dysphagia management, dysphagia, and dementia, and the use of artificial feeding tubes. She collaborates with colleagues in the country and abroad on studies highlighting Filipino cultural considerations to the life participation approach in aphasia, the role of identity and personhood in the management of aphasia and dementia, and creating select, culturally appropriate testing material for local use. Her advocacy work sees her coordinate actively with the Dementia Society of the Philippines and the Philippine Association of Speech Pathologists. She is presently working on her dissertation investigating cultural concepts of death and dying in end-of-life conversations of older Filipinos with their families, leading toward a Doctorate in Philippine Studies, specializing in anthropology.

Tisha Isabelle M. de Vergara earned her Bachelor of Arts in Sociology (magna cum laude) from the University of Santo Tomas and is currently taking up a Master of Arts in Sociology at the University of the Philippines Diliman. Her research interests include the sociology of Catholicism and religion, social health, and environmental sociology.

Dennis Erasga is a Senior Faculty and Professor of Sociology at the Department of Sociology and Behavioral Sciences, De La Salle University, Manila, Philippines. He was a Visiting Professor at the Mahidol University, Department of Health and Society, Salaya Campus, Thailand (2014); a Salzburg Global Seminar Fellow in Austria (Biography as Mirror of Society, 2012), and a Lecturer in the Quality Management in International Health Program of the University of Heidelberg, Department of Tropical Health and Public Hygiene, Heidelberg, Germany (2017). His range of publications included topics in grassroots sociology, social theory, ecoconstructionism, sociology of literature, science/fiction, futures studies, as well as on qualitative research methodology. His forthcoming book explores (i) the formative issues, (ii) the phenomenological stance, and (iii) methodological affordances of an emerging nativist sociology by Filipinos, the Pilipinong Sosyolohiya. His notion of Pakiramdaman conceives the idiosyncratic features of Filipino interactions as constitutive of a "mutual sense of kapwa." His book – *From Grain to Nature* (2015) narrates an alternative genealogy of the environmental discourse in the Philippines through the biography of rice (palay). He is a Fellow of the university's Social Development Research Center, where several of his major field research was implemented. He is a member and once served as Board Secretary of the Philippine Sociological Society. He is currently a member of the Canadian Sociological Association, the American Sociological Association, the International Sociological Association, and the European Sociological Association. He obtained his BA and MA (Sociology) and PhD (Environmental Science) from the University of the Philippines at Los Baños. He was born in the historic town of Calamba (Laguna) where he lives and plans to spend the rest of his professional life.

Rizason L. Go Tian-Ng started her practice in 1998 as a play therapist under her former mentor, Dr Maria Lourdes A. Carandang. Her practicum work with children had opened her eyes to children who acted out family stresses or personal struggles. She then worked on her graduate thesis on the criterion validation of a Tagasalo personality using the Panunukat ng Pagkataong Pilipino by Dr Annadaisy J. Carlota, a personality test that assesses 19 traits in terms of various Filipino personality trait constructs. Many years later, she taught Theories of Personality to undergraduate students and realized that the Tagasalo personality is a good illustration of Sikolohiyang Pilipino as an indigenous psychology within the Filipino family. She thought of engaging her students on a small project that gave way to her chapter in this volume. As mentioned earlier, she is a part-time Faculty member of the Departments of Psychology at Ateneo de Manila University and at the University of the Philippines Diliman. Her interests in teaching are Theories of Personality, Developmental Psychology, Cognitive Psychology, and Introduction to Counseling. She is also invited to speak on topics on Parenting and on Child Development. She is also a Clinical Psychologist who works with the adolescent and up to middle adulthood group. In many of her cases, clients manifest Tagasalo behavior and this has inspired her to pursue writing about Tagasalo to give rise to this unique Filipino coping behavior and personality development.

Veronica L. Gregorio received her PhD from the Department of Sociology and Anthropology, National University of Singapore where she is currently a Teaching Assistant. Her research on rural transformation, gender and sexuality, and youth and family relations has been published in journals like the *Asia Pacific Social Sciences Review*, *Current Sociology*, *Review of Women's Studies*, and *Simulacra Jurnal Sosiologi*. In 2021, she was named Sociologist of the Month by the International Sociological Association. In 2018, she was named by the Philippine Sociological Society as the first awardee of the Gelia Tagumpay Castillo Research in Community Engagement. In 2015, she received the 5th Lourdes Lontok-Cruz Award for Best Thesis in Women and Gender Studies.

Carlo S. Gutierrez obtained his PhD in Comparative Asian Studies from the National University of Singapore in 2022. His current research interests include area studies, social theory, institutionalism, rural studies, semiotic analysis, and demography. His PhD dissertation tackles the interactions among institutional actors resulting in current policies (realities) in communities (broadly speaking). His chapter in this volume focused on the role of the family as an institutional actor in the community. He has a multicultural academic background. He obtained academic degrees from different countries: PhD (Singapore), MA (Japan), and BA (Philippines). Furthermore, he has almost a decade of formal experience as a faculty member before his PhD pursuit – teaching sociology and international studies courses. In the future, he wishes to engage in academic careers sharpening his competence in social theory and critical analysis of institutions.

Joselito G. Gutierrez, PhD, is a Faculty member of the University of Santo Tomas (UST) Institute of Religion (IR). He is a Research Associate of the UST – Center for Theology, Religious Studies, and Ethics and the Chair of the Certificate on Religious Education program of UST-IR, which gives free training for the catechists and religious educators of partner dioceses. He finished his PhD in Family Studies at Miriam College and obtained his MA in Theology, majoring in Pastoral Ministry from St. Vincent School of Theology, Adamson University. He is a Bachelor of Science in Management and Industrial Engineering graduate of Mapua Institute of Technology. He is also a Licensed Professional Teacher. Before joining UST, he was the Director of the Office of Student Affairs of Colegio De San Lorenzo. He is also a volunteer parish pastoral worker, marriage and family specialist, retreat facilitator, and resource person in various topics such as catechesis, parenting, leadership training, community organizing, and faith formation. His research interests include fatherhood, parenting, marriage, and family in the field of sociology, as well as Christology and Catholic social teaching in the field of theology.

Derrace Garfield McCallum is an Assistant Professor of English and Cultural Studies in the Department of Global Liberal Arts at Aichi University in Nagoya, Japan. His main research interests include migration, transnationalism, family life, race/ethnicity, multiculturalism, gender, care, and social policy. He is the author of several journal articles and book chapters that examine various aspects of social policy and the experiences of transnational families. He is also the co-editor of the recently published book entitled *Children and Youths' Migration in a Global Landscape*. He is currently conducting research regarding the transition of Japan into a more multicultural society, primarily focusing on the experiences of relatively new migrant groups. His current research focus also includes the individual and collective experiences of members of transnational families.

Belen T. Medina obtained her BA (cum laude) and MA from the University of the Philippines Diliman where she majored in Sociology, after which she took postgraduate courses in sociology/anthropology and Southeast Asian Studies at Cornell University as a Fulbright/Smith-Mundt scholar. She trained in the Sociology of Development at Delhi University as a UNESCO Fellow and obtained a Certificate in Social Research for Developing Societies (With Merit) at the University of London. With a Ford-Rockefeller Grant, she visited the University of California at Los Angeles and Irvine, Wright State University, University of Cincinnati, and Miami University for enrichment studies in the sociology of the family. She also visited the Chulalongkorn and Thammasat Universities, Rangoon University, the University of Malaya, the University of Singapore, and the University of Indonesia on an Asia Foundation Grant for Southeast Asian Studies. She taught for 53 years at the Department of Sociology of the University of the Philippines Diliman where she served as Chairperson twice. She is the recognized expert on the Filipino family and the author of the only textbook on the sociology of the family in the country, *The Filipino Family*, published by the UP Press (1st ed. in 1991, 2nd ed. in 2001, and 3rd ed. in 2015). She has published many articles and books and has read papers at conferences in the Philippines and abroad on this topic. She is an elected member of the Phi Kappa Phi International Honor Society and the Pi Gamma Mu International Honor Society in the Social Sciences. She is a founding member and now a recognized Honorary Member of the Philippine Sociological Society. She is also an elected Regular Member and awarded as Member Emeritus of the National Research Council of the Philippines.

Maria Cecilia T. Medina holds a bachelor's degree in Sociology, cum laude (1983) and Master of Arts in Asian Studies (1991) from the University of the Philippines. She also has a second master's degree in Religious Studies (2020) from the Maryhill School of Theology and a doctoral degree in Sociology from Xavier University (2004). She is an Associate Professor of Philippine and Asian Studies at the Asian Center, University of the Philippines, and previously served as Assistant to the Dean for Administration and Public Affairs, Coordinator of the Tri-College PhD Philippine Studies Program, and Editor-in-Chief of the *Asian Studies: Journal of Critical Perspectives on Asia*. She is currently an Associate Editor of *Social*

Science Diliman: A Philippine Journal of Society and Culture, the flagship journal for the social sciences at the University of the Philippines Diliman. She also served on the board of the Philippine Sociological Society and is an elected member of the International Honor Society of Phi Kappa Phi and the International Honor Society of Pi Gamma Mu for excellence in the Social Sciences. She is also a member of the Research Committee on Sociology of Religion (RC 22) and the Research Committee on the Sociology of Disasters (RC 39) as a member of the International Sociological Association. Her publications and research interests are on Asian religions, cultures, and development, indigenous peoples and ethnic relations, disaster studies, and Southeast Asian studies. She is also a regular member of the Division of Social Sciences of the National Research Council of the Philippines.

Romulo Nieva Jr. is a health sociologist, policy researcher, and public health advocate. He is a faculty member at the UP-Manila College of Public Health. His broad teaching and research interests are the intersectionality of health, biopower and health, gender, and health systems, health and social policy, and prison health. He holds a doctoral degree from the University of Otago in New Zealand on an Otago doctoral research scholarship. He also obtained a master's degree in Health Social Science from De La Salle University as a Ford Foundation scholar and a bachelor's degree in Nursing (cum laude graduate) from Bukidnon State University. His PhD research explores the nexus between women's imprisonment and reproductive well-being in the Philippines. In this qualitative study, he applied sociological and feminist criminological approaches to examine the lived experience of reproductive health among Filipino women in prison. Before pursuing a PhD, he worked as a Health Policy Research and Advocacy Officer for the Zuellig Family Foundation in the Philippines. He was chosen as the 2020–2021 Policy Fellow of the Population Reference Bureau (PRB), where he underwent policy development and advocacy training and worked with PRB for policy research and advocacy on the reproductive health of women in prison. He was a finalist in the 2022 International Sociological Association Worldwide Competition for Junior Sociologists engaged in social research for his academic paper discussing Filipino pregnant prisoners' childbearing experience.

Janus Isaac V. Nolasco is University Researcher IV at the Center for Integrative and Development Studies (CIDS), University of the Philippines, where he is also Deputy Editor in Chief of the *Philippine Journal of Public Policy*, which is published by UP CIDS. He dabbles in popular culture, philosophy, political thought, Asian/Area Studies, premodern West Asian history, and literary criticism. His writings have appeared in *Suvannabhumi: Multi-Disciplinary Journal of Southeast Asian Studies*, *Asian Politics & Policy*, *Pelikula: A Journal of Philippine Cinema*, *New Mandala*, *Inquirer*, and the *Kyoto Review of Southeast Asia*. He has a BA in Comparative Literature and an MA in Asian Studies (majoring on West Asia), both from the University of the Philippines Diliman.

Ryan Michael F. Oducado is a registered nurse, midwife, guidance counselor, and licensed professional teacher with a PhD in Education major in Psychology and Guidance. He is an Assistant Professor at the College of Nursing, West Visayas State University, Iloilo, Philippines. His research interests are in the fields of nursing education, public health, and mental health.

Enrique G. Oracion is concurrently Professor of Anthropology and Sociology and the Director for Research of Silliman University in Dumaguete City, Negros Oriental. He earned his Bachelor (1980, cum laude) and Master of Arts (1985) degrees majoring in Sociology from Silliman University while he completed his PhD in Anthropology (2006) from the University of San Carlos in Cebu City. He was also a United Board Fellow assigned at The Chinese University of Hong Kong (2011) and Baylor University, Texas, USA (2012). He is a regular member of the National Research Council of the Philippines and a past Board Member of the Anthropological Association of the Philippines or the Ugnayang PangAghamtao and the Philippine Sociological Society. He was a zonal and qualifier recipient of the REPUBLICA (Research and Publication Award) of the Commission on Higher Education in 2005 and 2016, respectively. He is the Community Specialist of the Silliman University South Negros BFAR-USAID Fish Right Program (2018–2023). Specifically, he coordinated the development of the Right Fishing Modules to augment science lessons in basic education, the Fish Tiangge initiative that introduces livelihood to women through fish consolidation and fish processing, and the rapid fish stock assessment tool based on fishers' perception. His disciplinal interest is environmental anthropology and he covers various issues and dimensions related to human–environment interaction. Related to his contribution to this book, he had published about child labor in fishing and intergenerational support to marine conservation. His other publications include Negrito adaptation, gender and women issues, education and service-learning, ecotourism and marine protected area management, cultural heritage management, aging and health, and culture of disaster and resiliency.

A. M. Leal Rodriguez is a PhD candidate currently affiliated with the University of Auckland as a Faculty of Arts doctoral scholar. A product of the Department of Sociology and the School of Critical Studies in Education, her PhD project focuses on masculinities in the global south, gender, and higher education, or universities (University of Auckland Doctoral Research Fund). Working as a feminist activist with almost 10 years of experience in the development and education sector led her to decolonial and post-structuralist theory. She has presented her work to numerous organizations across the globe (the New Zealand Association for Research in Education Conference, the Sociological Association of Aotearoa New Zealand, the Contacts and Continuities: 500 Years of Iberian-Asian Relations Conference, the American Education Research Association, and the Women's and Gender Studies Association of the Philippines). The textbook she co-authored, *Gender and Society: The Whys of Women, Their Oppressions,* *and Paths to Liberation*, is being used by higher education institutions for their curriculum on gender studies. She has also worked on projects focusing on ethnicity and youth achievement in education (Performance-Based Research Fund, Tertiary Education Union New Zealand) and exploring political gift-giving in the context of (Marsden Fund, Royal Society of New Zealand). She now resides in Aotearoa New Zealand where she burns rubber through cycling and touches rocks through climbing, to chase inspiration.

Tricia Olea Santos is an adjunct Professor at Baylor University, Robbins College of Health and Human Sciences, Department of Communication Sciences and Disorders. Her primary area of expertise is in healthy aging and adult cognitive-linguistic disorders. Over the past decade, she has been involved in research that explores discourse in healthy aging, dementia, and aphasia, cultural differences in illness narratives, renegotiating identity in aphasia, caregiving in dementia, health literacy in minority populations and stroke patients, and life participation after stroke. In addition to teaching at the undergraduate, graduate, and clinical levels, she also provides professional continuing education webinars for speech-language pathologists. She maintains a clinical caseload in acute care and inpatient rehabilitation hospital settings involving the assessment and intervention of adult neurogenic disorders. She has co-authored journal articles and a book chapter on topics pertinent to discourse in healthy aging, aphasia, and dementia. She has published her works in a variety of peer-reviewed journals, such as *Aphasiology*, *Folia et Phoniatrica*, *Topics in Stroke Rehabilitation*, *Journal of Aging and Social Change*, and *International Journal of Speech-language Pathology*. Her work has been presented nationally and internationally at speech-language pathology and gerontology conventions.

Hanna K. Ulatowska is Professor Emerita at the University of Texas at Dallas, School of Behavioral and Brain Sciences, Callier Center for Communication Disorders. Her primary area of research is neurolinguistics, and more specifically, investigations of discourse in aphasia, dementia, and advanced aging. The focus of her research is the characterization of the communicative competence of these populations and how it relates to preservations and impairments of both linguistic and cognitive functioning. Another research focus deals with the effects of different language types on the disruption of language in aphasia which stems from my investigations of aphasia in Polish. In the past, she has investigated discourse in African American, Hispanic-American, and Filipino American elderly. She has also been involved in studying the representation of camp experiences in narratives told by elderly camp survivors in Poland. Her recent research has involved how communication in testimonies from American World War II veterans can be used in collective memory by examining autobiographical memory, emotional memory, and life review of the veterans in evaluations of war experiences. She is presently studying patterns of recovery from aphasia in writers from different cultures.

Jofel D. Umandap was a marketing professional, with a Management undergraduate degree from Ateneo de Manila University and a post-graduate degree in Commerce from Macquarie University, before deciding to pursue a career as a psychologist. She completed her MA in Psychology from the Ateneo de Manila University and is currently pursuing her PhD in Clinical Psychology, also at the same university. Her areas of interest are marriage and family therapy, personal growth, mindfulness, and self-compassion. She is also involved in developing programs and modules, as well as in facilitating workshops for psychoeducation and brief intervention programs. She is currently a licensed psychologist practicing therapy and training at the Ateneo Bulatao Center for Psychological Services, the research and training arm of the Psychology Department, at UGAT Foundation, an organization with psycho-spiritual interventions for Filipino grassroots families, and at the Life Science Center for Health and Wellness. She is also a part-time Lecturer at the Department of Psychology at Ateneo de Manila University, teaching Abnormal Psychology, Developmental Psychology, and a core formation course, Understanding the Self.

FOREWORD

The evolving nature of families across the world is continuously subjected to social changes, cultural shifts, and global flows. In our contemporary world, the dynamics and confluence of factors shaping and influencing "families" remain an intriguing facet of both scholarship and policies. This sociological fascination roots in the central interest of/in knowledge and/or the lack of it in understanding the nature, contours, and textures of families, especially in societies that are historically colonized and persistently marred by problematic socio-political and economical tensions such as the Philippines.

The Philippines is a unique country, and its distinct history and culture provide an intriguing context for families. Comprising over 7,000 islands, the Philippines has been visited by numerous groups in its prehistoric times, while over the past five centuries, Spanish colonization influenced the course of Filipino culture, particularly regarding religion. Even after the formal establishment of the Republic of the Philippines in 1946, American cultural influence persisted. Its long history, coupled with its peculiar population distribution across thousands of islands, has resulted in a culture which is decidedly familistic. Filipino families maintain perhaps the strongest family bonds of any culture and have shown a unique ability to persevere, even when faced with the direst of circumstances.

This multidisciplinary volume of CPFR brings into focus a comprehensive collection of the dynamic nature of families in the Philippines. Generally, we ask: Why do Filipino families maintain perhaps the strongest family bonds of any culture? How has this shown a unique ability to persevere, even when faced with the direst of circumstances?

MAIN THEMES OF THE VOLUME

Our journey in soliciting academic responses to these questions led us to this collection covering a broad range of topics including Filipino family's social demography and various dimensions of "familism" in contemporary Filipino families such as parenthood, care provisions, families across sectors (overseas Filipino workers or OFWs, farmers, and fisherfolks), and emerging familial representations. By looking at census and survey data, Jeofrey B. Abalos details his findings in the lead chapter, "A Demographic Portrait of the Filipino Family: A Glimpse from the Recent Past." In this work, he examined the following: marriage, cohabitation, and other types of relationships, rise of non-marriage, fertility and fertility preferences, childlessness, attitudes toward the family and other relationships, and the living arrangements and exchange of support among the elderly. One of Abalos' fitting conclusions for this volume is that while the Filipino family may have changed in size and structure and how it is formed and dissolved, it has remained constant in how it values its members, particularly the young and the old.

Drawing from multidisciplinary views, the empirical descriptions in this collection also draw attention to the underlying "resilience" of/in Filipino families relative to the multifaceted issues explored in this volume. We will discuss the four themes in the succeeding subsections.

Narratives of Parenthood

Parenthood is one of the longest stages of one's life. Chapters 2–5 will explore the different experiences of parenthood in the Philippines. Samuel I. Cabbuag, in "The Road to Visibility: IVF and Motherhood Journey of Filipino Influencers," discusses the taboo topic of childbearing via in vitro fertilization (IVF). Through web scraping, he coded 438 comments from YouTube videos of Filipino influencers who opted to bear children via IVF. He argues that through the visibility labor of influencers, the phenomenon of childbearing via IVF is not only promoted as a viable, if not acceptable procreative process, but also perpetuated as an in/accessible procedure in the Philippines.

From YouTube influencers, the volume will then move to a different group in Chapter 3: incarcerated women. Romulo Nieva Jr's work, "Pregnancy, Motherhood, and Family: Stories Behind Bars," is based on his PhD project wherein he conducted face-to-face semi-structured interviews with women who had experienced pregnancy in prison. Nieva suggests that experiences of mothering and childbearing for incarcerated women are negative and complex. He finds that "women's institutionally imposed 'prisoner identity' overshadows their pregnancy status and mothering role, exacerbated by their experiences of systemic scarcity, restricted contact with family, and limited autonomy."

Partnership (or its absence) in connection to parenthood is also an important factor in family formation. In Chapter 4, "Acceptance Is Key: Toward a Framework for Understanding Serial Cohabitation," Veronica L. Gregorio explores how serial cohabiters with children, in response to social stigma, exhibit resiliency toward stepfamily formation and committed sexual relationships. She conceptualizes "family acceptance" which refers to embracing the fluidity, reconfigurations, and "imperfections" of cohabiters' newly formed family and "community acceptance" which covers the same affirmation from friends, neighbors, and extended relatives who are considered as relevant others by serial cohabiters.

The above chapters which focus on women's experiences will be complemented by Chapter 5, "Selected Cases of Teenage Fatherhood in the Philippines: An Analysis of Risks and Resilience," by Joselito G. Gutierrez, Tisha Isabelle M. De Vergara, and Clarence M. Batan. The authors interrogate the consequences of sexual behaviors on the well-being of teenage fathers in the contexts of their families of orientation and families of procreation. The authors argue that the risks of teenage fatherhood in the Philippines are relatively mitigated by conservative culture and religious orientation that leads to the experiences of "natauhan" (realization), "pinangatawanan" (accountability), and "pinanindigan" (owning responsibility).

Care Provisions in/From the Family

As lifespans continue to increase, the chances of facing shocks during middle and old ages also increase. Families face sudden shocks like losing jobs, natural calamities, and health issues, among others. In such times, how do Filipino family members take charge and continue with their lives? The second theme of the volume, Care provisions in/from the family, will explore this question.

In Chapter 6, "ICT-mediated Familial Care in Turbulent Times: Filipinos' Subjectivities, Virtual Intimacy, and Resilience amid Social Change," Derrace Garfield McCallum draws on data collected as part of a multi-sited transnational ethnography. The work revolves around the lives of Filipino migrants who live in Japan and their family members who live in the Philippines. McCallum explains how transnational families preserve and nurture their collective commitments using Information and Communication Technologies (ICTs). He argues that families maximize ICTs not just to (re)enact and (re)create mundane existences but also to recognize, celebrate, and display significant family milestones.

Is it possible to turn "caringness" and "responsibleness" into a personality? Rizason L. Go Tian-Ng and Jofel D. Umandap's chapter, "An Exposition of the Multidimensionality of the Tagasalo Personality," uses Philippine indigenous psychology literature to provide an in-depth theoretical-historical development of the Tagasalo personality. The Tagasalo is the family member who "catches" or "saves" the family from the different shocks as mentioned earlier. Using case study reviews and thematic analysis of reflective essays, Go Tian-Ng and Umandap propose new dimensions of internalizing and externalizing behaviors that serve to alleviate the distress experienced by the Tagasalo.

The next chapter, "Maintaining Personhood and Identity in Dementia: Families as Partners in Care," focuses on informal caregivers of persons with dementia. Tricia Olea Santos, Hanna K. Ulatowska, and Carla Krishan A. Cuadro's work probes into the characteristics and structure of the Filipino family, and the challenges in caring for a loved one with dementia. Aside from turning down career opportunities to stay at home full time, these family caregivers (mostly women) are also designing the day-by-day schedule of their elderly parents using family photo albums, TV shows, prayer meetings, gardening, and even music-related activities. The authors also analyze cultural and relational factors that influence dementia care and the preservation of identity in dementia.

Sexual identities in relation to health status are often analyzed in terms of individual well-being, coping mechanisms, and access to services. The work "Sexual Identity Visibility and Compounding Stigma in the Familial Context: Life Histories Among Filipino MSMs Living with HIV" by Jerome V. Cleofas and Dennis Erasga provides a different perspective by focusing on the family of men living with HIV. The authors partnered with The Project Red Ribbon, a community-based HIV organization, to recruit and conduct key interviews with 31 participants. Based on the results, Cleofas and Erasga conceptualized sexual identity visibility in the family (SIVF) as the nature of the family's consciousness and acceptance of the informants' sexual identity/ies and further posit that SIVF shapes an individual's sexual health across the lifespan.

The last work under the theme on care provisions is "Family Relationship, Mental Well-being, and Life Satisfaction During the COVID-19 Pandemic: A Mediation Study Among Filipino Graduate Students." With school and work moving online for long periods of time, the quality of life within households abruptly and steadily changed. Drawing from an online survey among 337 graduate students enrolled during the second year of the pandemic, Ryan Michael F. Oducado and Jerome V. Cleofas examined the three family relationship domains (cohesion, expressiveness, and conflict), their predictive relationships with life satisfaction, and the mediating role of mental well-being on these relationships.

Families of OFWs, Farmers, and Fisherfolks

The next theme is sectoral, with a focus on families of overseas Filipino workers or OFWs, farmers, and fisherfolks. In the exploratory work, "Response and Coping Mechanism of Overseas Filipino Workers (OFW) Children to Parents' Separation," Sunshine Therese S. Alcantara focused on the social and emotional costs of migration to Filipino families. She analyzed the experiences of OFW children with separated parents due to marital infidelity and found how they process their emotions to eventually accept their parents' decisions. Alcantara also emphasized the role of peers in OFW children's coping process. For future research on the same sample group, she recommends comparing mechanisms between male and female children.

As international migration continues, will farmers continue to work in the fields? In Chapter 12, the contribution of goods to the economy and the reproduction of the next generation of farmers was problematized by Carlo S. Gutierrez. His comparative work, "The Family as a Farm Institution: Cases in Japan and the Philippines," factors in the demographic changes, role of civil society organizations, and pluriactivity of households in the survival of smallholdings. More importantly, Gutierrez emphasized that in the Philippines, "the absence of an effort by the state for a farm industrialization project led to primarily family-based farming."

Fishing livelihood is as important as farming, especially in an island nation like the Philippines. The collective decision of rural families to maintain or sell their farms has similarities with the collective decision of fishing families to stay in the sector or to explore other options. Chapter 13, "Parental Livelihood Preference for Children Among Municipal Fishing Families in South Negros, Philippines" by Enrique G. Oracion, will focus on this issue. Using a survey covering 23 coastal barangays, he found that

> while fishing is perceived now as risky and hard because of the accumulated impacts of climate change and the persisting problem of illegal, unreported, and unregulated (IUU) fishing, it is always a ready option for the livelihood of their children if they would fail to get quality education and secure better employment opportunities.

Representations of the Filipino Family

The last theme in the volume will underscore representations of the Filipino family in three aspects: family-orientedness, masculinity vis-á-vis fatherhood, and filial piety toward the elderly.

The chapter of Janus Isaac V. Nolasco, "Self, Family, and Democracy: Individualism and Collectivism in Two Contemporary Filipino Family Films," provides a refreshing take on democracy and its political resonance in Filipino families. By analyzing hierarchical siblingship dynamics and family relations in the films *Kung Ayaw Mo, Huwag Mo* (1998) and *Four Sisters and a Wedding* (2013), Nolasco argues that such "films seek to articulate, manage, and resolve the tensions between self and family, autonomy and dependence, individualism and collectivism."

By engaging with Sikolohiyang Pilipino or Indigenous Filipino Psychology, A. M. Leal Rodriguez traced the construction of masculinity vis-á-vis fatherhood in the Philippines. The chapter, "*Tunay Na Lalaki*/True Manhood in the Philippines: Historical Development, Identity Formations, and Family Contexts," based on a critical review of literature, factored in colonial history and informal systems that form such manhood. Rodriguez proposes to explore Filipino manhood using the banig (woven mat) as representation. Through this banig, "one can dissect how different facets of manhood are woven together to further the country's machismo, one that pervades different powerful institutions."

Finally, the last and closing chapter of the volume discusses filial piety toward the elderly. The chapter is symbolic on its own as it was co-authored by pioneering Filipino family sociologist Belen T. Medina with her daughter, sociologist and Asian Studies expert Maria Cecilia T. Medina. Chapter 16, "The Elderly in the Filipino Family," reviews the importance of intergenerational solidarity (adult child and elderly parent) for the well-being of the elderly. The authors also explain in the chapter why and how institutionalization of the elderly appears to be a last resort, to complement rather than replace the welfare function of the family.

THE FUTURE OF THE SOCIOLOGY OF FAMILY IN THE PHILIPPINES

The first and sole book on *Filipino Family* (1991, with 3rd ed. in 2015) was written by Belen T. Medina. Prior to its launch, many scholars from various fields have also published articles and book chapters that touch on the issues and challenges that Filipino families have faced. This volume is however the first attempt to put together more recent works that highlight the complex changes and relationships among Filipino families, as mediated by technology, and influenced by cultural shifts, economic conditions, and even by the COVID-19 pandemic.

The collection is multidisciplinary but with most authors (15 out of 23) and all three editors coming from the field of sociology. The authors and editors also came from different academic stages – from graduate students, and recent PhD graduates, to postdoctoral fellows, and professors who are already established in their areas. Hence, the topics of interest are not just diverse but also fresh or even controversial. The empirical works, theoretical contributions, and critical reviews in this volume will be most useful if read as a whole collection. With that, we would like to thank all the contributors and anonymous reviewers for their commitment to this collection.

What do we have to say after the completion of this volume? First, parenting among Filipinos will continue to evolve and be increasingly resilient. Second, more work is needed about sexual minorities in family contexts. Third, generational perspectives in different sectors will persistently be tied to economic conditions. And lastly, while hierarchies and gender inequalities are recognized and questioned, familism among Filipinos is here to stay.

As reflected in this work, the future of the sociology of family in the Philippines is in good hands. There is a lot of work to do in enriching the field. We hope to invite more scholars to write, collaborate, and produce related works – looking forward to the next volume!

CHAPTER 1

A DEMOGRAPHIC PORTRAIT OF THE FILIPINO FAMILY: A GLIMPSE FROM THE RECENT PAST

Jeofrey B. Abalos

ABSTRACT

The Philippines experienced several demographic and socioeconomic changes in the past decades, such as rising urbanization, educational expansion, lengthening life expectancy, and increasing overseas labor migration. These changes will have significant ramifications for families and households. For example, educational expansion may delay union formation and accelerate union dissolution. Meanwhile, the joint effect of declining fertility and increasing life expectancy can lead to population aging, which has important implications for intergenerational support and the provision of care to older adults. Against this backdrop, this chapter aims to sketch a demographic portrait of the Filipino family in the past decades, using different sources, including census and survey data. Specifically, it examines trends in union formation (marriage and cohabitation) and union dissolution (divorce and separation) in the Philippines and explores Filipinos' attitudes toward these behaviors. It also describes trends in fertility, fertility preference, and childlessness among Filipino women. Finally, it investigates changes (or lack thereof) in household size and structure in the Philippines, including the living arrangements and intergenerational support among older Filipinos.

Keywords: Philippines; demography; family; marriage; fertility; aging

Resilience and Familism: The Dynamic Nature of Families in the Philippines
Contemporary Perspectives in Family Research, Volume 23, 1–18
ISSN: 1530-3535/doi:10.1108/S1530-353520230000023001

INTRODUCTION

The family is the most important, most valued, and most enduring institution in Philippine society (Asis, 1994). It offers

> social security, old age pensions ..., care for the sick, home for the aged, counsel for the troubled, and most of all, love, affection, emotional sustenance, and social stability without which a Filipino's life is meaningless. (Castillo, 1979, p. 103)

Data from the 2019 World Values Survey showed that almost all adult Filipinos regard their family as very important (98.2%) and agree that one of their main goals is to make their parents proud (97.2%) (Haerpfer et al., 2022). However, while the Filipino family may seem to have endured the test of time, it is not impervious to the waves of change (Asis, 1994). Over the last several decades, the Philippines has been confronted by several demographic and socioeconomic changes, such as rising urbanization, educational expansion, lengthening life expectancy, and increasing overseas labor migration. For example, the percentage of the urban population in the country increased from 51.2% in 2015 to 54.0% in 2020 (Philippine Statistics Authority, 2022b), while life expectancy at birth among Filipino men increased from 57.5 years in 1960 to 66.9 years in 2010, and from 59.0 years to 73.0 years among Filipino women (Cabigon, 2001; Philippine Statistics Authority, 2014). The increase in life expectancy, and to some extent, fertility decline, has contributed to the steady increase of older people in the Philippines from 4.5% in 1970 to 7.5% in 2015 (Abalos, 2020; Abalos & Booth, 2020). Another enduring feature of the Philippine demographic landscape is the intensification of international labor migration. Data from the Commission on Filipino Overseas showed that the stock estimate of overseas Filipinos increased from 6.97 million in 1997 to 10.24 million in 2013 or about 10% of the Philippine population. Consequently, the proportion of households in the Philippines with at least one overseas worker nearly tripled from 3.2% in 1990 to 8.0% in 2015. These changes will have significant ramifications for families and households. For example, educational expansion may delay union formation (Abalos, 2014) and accelerate union dissolution (Abalos, 2017). Meanwhile, overseas migration will lead to the physical separation of families, alter the household composition, and impact the availability of support, particularly for older adults.

Against this backdrop, this chapter aims to sketch a demographic portrait of the Filipino family in the past decades, using various sources, including census and survey data. Specifically, the study examines changes in union formation (marriage and cohabitation) and union dissolution (divorce and separation) in the Philippines and explores Filipinos' attitudes toward these behaviors. It also describes trends in fertility, fertility preference, and childlessness among Filipino women. Finally, it investigates changes (or lack thereof) in household size and structure in the Philippines, including the living arrangements and intergenerational support among older Filipinos.

MARRIAGE, COHABITATION, AND OTHER TYPES OF RELATIONSHIPS IN THE PHILIPPINES

Marriage is a highly revered institution in Philippine society (Gultiano et al., 2009). It is not only a union of two individuals but also a union of their respective families (Medina, 2015). Thus, parents try to influence their children's mate selection process to ensure the stability of the marriage and upward social mobility of the family, particularly among the more well-off segment of society (Kabamalan, 2006; Xenos & Kabamalan, 2007). Over time, parental influence on their children's choice of spouse persists, particularly among Filipino youth. Based on the 2002 Young Adult and Fertility Study (YAFS), a nationally representative survey of Filipino youth, 2.9% of currently married Filipino youth aged 15–24 years cited arranged marriage as their reason for getting married; this proportion increased to 9.1% in 2013. Parental involvement in selecting their children's spouse can also be gauged in the prevalence of elopement, which is associated with "escaping" or leaving the parental abode without permission (Xenos & Kabamalan, 2007). The YAFS data indicated that the proportion of those currently in union who eloped with their current spouse or partner declined from 20.1% in 2002 to 14.3% in 2013. Based on the 2013 YAFS, their reasons for elopement include "love each other" (43.5%), parents/guardians opposed to marriage/relationship/partner or "parents/guardians are strict" (38.3%), and "got pregnant/got girl pregnant" (10.5%).

The age of marriage among Filipinos is relatively high and has continued to increase over time (Abalos, 2014; Ogena et al., 2008). It increased from 22.8 years in 1970 to 24.6 years in 2015 among women and from 25.4 years to 27.2 years among men (United Nations, Department of Economic and Social Affairs, Population Division, 2019). Increasing educational attainment may be related to the rising marriage age among Filipinos (Abalos, 2014).

Not only is the timing of marriage formation in the country changing, but also its form. Marriage in the Philippines usually takes the form of legal marriage (through a church of civil wedding) or cohabitation, but the majority of marriages are legal (Gultiano et al., 2009; Xenos, 1997). According to the 2015 Philippine census, 81.7% of the population aged 10 years and over who were in union (e.g., legally married or living-in) were legally married, and 18.3% were living together (Philippine Statistics Authority, 2017). Data from the National Demographic Survey (NDS) and National Demographic and Health Survey (NDHS) showed that while the total proportion of Filipino women who are in union remains relatively stable at around 60% (except in 2003 and 2008), the proportion of Filipino women aged 15–49 years who are legally married steadily declined from 54.4% in 1993 to 42.4% in 2017 (National Statistics Office [NSO] & Macro International Inc. [MI], 1994; Philippine Statistics Authority [PSA] & ICF, 2018). In contrast, the corresponding share of women who are cohabiting increased from 5.2% to 17.5% (National Statistics Office [NSO] & Macro International Inc. [MI], 1994; Philippine Statistics Authority [PSA] & ICF, 2018).

What are the reasons Filipinos are cohabiting instead of formally marrying? Nearly half (47.8%) of the 2013 YAFS respondents who are currently living-in cited economic reasons for cohabiting. Previous research indicated that these economic reasons may include the expenses to cover the costs of the wedding reception and fees to secure a marriage license and other required documents (Kabamalan, 2004). It may also include the "donation"[1] to officiate the wedding ceremony, and in some cases, there is a minimum amount for this "donation' that is quite expensive and may not be affordable for the poor (Williams et al., 2007). Other reasons why Filipinos resorted to cohabitation include legal impediments, cultural traditions, and misinterpretation of marriage laws (Kabamalan, 2004, 2011). Some of these legal impediments could be the lack of divorce law in the country, preventing those previously married from marrying again, and the absence of laws that recognize the marriage of same-sex couples (Abalos, 2023).

With the growing phenomenon of cohabitation among Filipinos, the question arises whether cohabitation serves as another path to marriage or an alternative to marriage in the Philippines. Existing evidence implies that it is more of the former than the latter. For example, the 1994 International Social Survey Programme (ISSP) survey showed that 24.8% of married respondents aged 18 years and over lived with their spouse before marriage (ISSP Research Group, 1997). Meanwhile, the 2013 YAFS data showed that 62.3% of currently married non-Muslim respondents aged 15–24 years lived with their partner before formally marrying.

Aside from consensual union or living together, another form of cohabitation is the querida system or the keeping of a second wife (Xenos & Kabamalan, 2007). There is sparse literature on the querida system in the Philippines, but anecdotes about this phenomenon abound (Kabamalan, 2006). A proxy indicator for the prevalence of the querida system is the proportion of Filipinos who have had extramarital sex (EMS). An earlier study based on the 2003 NDHS revealed that 21.6% of Filipino men in 2003 have had EMS; of those who had EMS, 79.8% had regular partners only, 5.3% had occasional partners only, and 3.4% had regular and occasional partners (Abalos, 2011). Moreover, the 2003 NDHS data indicated that the prevalence of EMS among Filipino men was higher among those who are currently cohabiting, those who have no living children, those who are undecided about their fertility preference, or whose wife was sterilized or infecund, those who belong to religions other than Roman Catholic and Islam, and those who have been drunk in the past month.

Meanwhile, the 2013 YAFS data showed that 3.1% of Filipino youth have engaged in EMS; the prevalence of EMS is more than 10 times higher among males (10.1%) than females (0.6%) (Marquez, 2016). Having EMS is strongly frowned upon in Philippine society, with 84.1% of the 2008 ISSP respondents considering this behavior always wrong (ISSP Research Group, 2018). For comparison, 54.6% of respondents in the same survey considered premarital sex (PMS) always wrong (ISSP Research Group, 2018). The strong disapproval against EMS over PMS is because EMS not only disrupts a marriage but also impacts married couples, their children, and other family members (Medina, 2015). For example, the 2013 YAFS data revealed that 23.6% of Filipino youth cited extramarital affairs as the main reason their first marriage ended.

Accompanying the changes in the timing and type of unions in the Philippines is the shift in the type of wedding ceremonies. For example, the proportion of Catholic Church weddings declined from 70.0% in 1960 to 36.2% in 2019, while the corresponding proportion of civil ceremonies increased from 21.4% to 38.6% (Bureau of the Census and Statistics, 1962; Philippine Statistics Authority,

2022a). The cost of having a Church wedding compared to a civil wedding may have contributed to the growing popularity of civil weddings.

Aside from cohabitation, other alternative types of partnerships, such as living apart together (LAT) and commuter marriages that are documented in other countries, may also exist in the Philippines. Couples in a LAT relationship are viewed by themselves and their personal network as a couple, but they do not share a common residence, while those in commuting relationships live in one home, but one (or both of them) have a second apartment where he or she stays when away from home due, to employment or education reasons (Levin, 2004). Qualitative evidence revealed that some Filipinos are in a LAT relationship (Gregorio, 2020), but there are no national estimates of this phenomenon due to limited data. Similarly, estimates of commuter marriages in the Philippines are lacking, but based on the 2017 NDHS, about 8% of Filipino women in a union were not living with their spouse or partner for reasons other than international migration in the past 24 months.

Another emerging type of relationship that has been recently documented in the Philippines is "FUBU" ("fuck buddies") or "FB" ("friends with benefits"). This type of sexual relationship occurs when "two people who are not in a romantic relationship regularly engage in sexual intercourse" (Marquez, 2016, p. 102). Based on the 2013 YAFS data, 3.6% of Filipino youth have engaged in a FUBU; a higher proportion of males (6.6%) than females (0.7%) engaged in this sexual activity (Marquez, 2016). In addition, an earlier study by the University of the Philippines Population Institute in 2009 also showed that a significant proportion of call center (13.6%) and non-call center (7.9%) professionals with sexual experience have had a FUBU (University of the Philippines Population Institute, 2010).

THE RISE OF NON-MARRIAGE AMONG FILIPINOS

Along with the changing character and timing of union formation in the Philippines is the growing aversion toward marriage. This is evidenced by the increasing share of permanent celibacy, measured in terms of the proportion of never-married at ages 40–49 years. Census data indicated that the proportion of Filipinos who have never married in their 40s increased from 4.3% in 1970 to 11.3% in 2015 among men and from 7.0% to 8.8% among women (United Nations Statistics Division, 2022). Non-marriage in the Philippines is more prevalent among low-educated men and highly educated women (Abalos, 2023). These patterns where low-educated men and highly educated women experience difficulty finding partners suggest the presence of a "marriage squeeze" (Williams & Arguillas, 2012). The faster expansion of education among Filipino women relative to men and the cultural expectations that discourage women from "marrying down" or marrying someone with lower education than them may have contributed to this phenomenon. The presence of marriage squeeze, particularly among males, is also observed in China (Jiang et al., 2014). These men are referred to as "bare branches," a term for men in the countryside who are past a certain age and unable to get married, hence are forced to remain single (Jiang & Sánchez-Barricarte, 2013). However, research also showed that the proportion of unmarried Filipino men in their 40s is almost the same for men with primary and college education (Abalos, 2023). This Philippine pattern deviates from the pattern found in other Asian countries such as South Korea, China, and Singapore, where the share of tertiary-educated men who are unmarried in their 40s is much lower than their counterparts with less than tertiary level education (Jones, 2018).

UNION DISSOLUTION

Under the Family Code of the Philippines, divorce is illegal in the country, except for Filipinos who are married to foreigners and obtain a divorce in another country and Filipino Muslims who are governed by the Code of Muslim Personal Laws of the Philippines (Lopez, 2001). This makes the Philippines the only state in the world, aside from the Vatican City, where divorce is illegal (Emery, 2013). However, the Family Code offers three measures that permit spouses to seek relief from a marriage: (a) legal separation, (b) annulment of marriage, and (c) declaration of nullity of marriage (Gloria, 2007). Civil registration data from the Philippine Statistics Authority (PSA) indicated that of the 14,264 cases of marriage dissolution processed from 1968 to 2016, declaration of absolute nullity of marriage was the most common ground for dissolution (83.6%), followed by Islamic divorce (9.1%), foreign decree of divorce (6.3%), and annulment (1.0%) (De Guzman, 2017). However, despite the availability of a legal means to end a marriage in the Philippines, Filipinos seldom resort to them due to the high costs of the procedure, the lengthy legal process involved, and the uncertainty that they will be approved (Calonzo & Cayabyab, 2013; Emery, 2013; Lopez, 2001; Taylor, 1983). Given these constraints, some couples just informally separate and are reported as separated in surveys and official statistics.

Divorce and separation in the Philippines have become more common in recent years (Abalos, 2017). Census data showed that since 1960, the proportions for both men and women have more than trebled, while the absolute numbers have gone up by at least 14 times. Specifically, the number of divorced or separated Filipino men increased from 28,988 in 1960 to 466,953 in 2015, while the corresponding numbers among women were 52,187 in 1960 and 744, 309 in 2015. As in other countries (Dommaraju, 2016), the higher rates of re-partnering among men than women could explain the higher number of women than men who are divorced or separated in the Philippines. Survey data also revealed that the percentage of Filipino women aged 15–49 years who were divorced or separated increased from 1.8% in 1993 to 3.3% in 2017 (National Statistics Office [NSO] & Macro International Inc. [MI], 1994; Philippine Statistics Authority (PSA) & ICF, 2018). There are several reasons why Filipinos separate from their partners. As noted earlier, the extramarital affair was the most common reason cited by Filipino youth why their first marriage ended. Other reasons mentioned by the 2013 YAFS respondents include personality issues (10.8%), disapproval by the family (10.0%), physical and sexual abuse (6.6%), vices (5.3%), and financial matters (5.1%).

FERTILITY AND FERTILITY PREFERENCES

The total fertility rate (TFR), or the average number of children a woman would have by the end of her reproductive years if she bore children at the prevailing age-specific fertility rates (Philippine Statistics Authority (PSA) & ICF, 2018), remains to be one of the highest in Southeast Asia but has slowly declined from 4.1 children in 1993 to 2.7 in 2017 (Table 1.1). The TFR in the country is generally higher among women in rural areas and those with lower levels of education (Philippine Statistics Authority (PSA) & ICF, 2018). Moreover, fertility generally declined in all age groups, except among women aged 15–19 years, particularly between 1998 and 2013 (Philippine Statistics Authority (PSA) & ICF, 2018). This is consistent with the country's increasing trend of teenage pregnancy (Gregorio, 2018; Natividad, 2013). Based on the NDS and NDHS, the percentage of Filipino women aged 15–19 years who have begun childbearing rose from 6.5% in 1993 to about 10% in both 2008 and 2013 before dropping slightly to 8.6% in 2017 (National Statistics Office [NSO] & ICF Macro, 2009; National Statistics Office [NSO] & Macro International Inc. [MI], 1994; Philippine Statistics Authority & ICF International, 2014; Philippine Statistics Authority (PSA) & ICF, 2018).

However, not all births in the country are "wanted" or within Filipino women's reported ideal number of children. In 1993, only 2.9 children out of the TFR of 4.1 were considered ideal or "wanted" fertility, and 1.2 children were "unwanted" or above Filipino women's ideal number (National Statistics Office [NSO] & Macro International Inc. [MI], 1994). Over time, both wanted and unwanted fertility declined, so much so that in 2017, the total wanted fertility was 2.0 children, and unwanted fertility was 0.7 children (Table 1.1). This implies that the TFR in the Philippines would have declined to 2.0 children or slightly lower than the "replacement" fertility of 2.1 children if unwanted births were prevented (Philippine Statistics Authority (PSA) & ICF, 2018).

There is a consensus between couples regarding the number of children they would have. For example, in 2017, 69.0% of currently married women reported that they and their spouse want the same number of children, while 20.3% said that their spouse wants more children than they do, and another 7.5% stated that their spouse wants fewer children than they do (Philippine Statistics Authority (PSA) & ICF, 2018). Furthermore, regarding the preferred sex of children, 55.7% of Filipino

Table 1.1. Trends in Wanted and Actual Fertility of Women in the Philippines, 1993–2017.

	TFR	Wanted Fertility	Unwanted Fertility
1993 NDS	4.1	2.9	1.2
1998 NDHS	3.7	2.7	1.0
2003 NDHS	3.5	2.5	1.0
2008 NDHS	3.3	2.4	0.9
2013 NDHS	3.0	2.2	0.8
2017 NDHS	2.7	2.0	0.7

Source: Philippine Statistics Authority (PSA) and ICF (2018).
Note: NDS = National Demographic Survey; NDHS = National Demographic and Health Survey

women in 2008 had balanced gender preferences, and 8.9% had no gender preference, while 20.9% and 14.5% had daughter and son preferences, respectively (Fuse, 2010).

CHILDREN AND CHILDLESSNESS IN THE FILIPINO FAMILY

The Filipino family is child-centered, as indicated by the sacrifices and hard work parents make for their children (Castillo, 1979; Medina, 2015). Children are considered a source of joy and support in old age. For example, almost a universal proportion (95.4%) of adult respondents in the 2012 ISSP survey agreed that "watching children grow up is life's greatest joy," while 8 in 10 respondents agreed that "adult children are an important source of help for elderly parents" (ISSP Research Group, 2016). Despite the hardships and challenges associated with childbearing and child-rearing in Philippines, children are hardly considered burdens or obstacles to parents' freedom or career advancement. This is evidenced by a relatively lower proportion of respondents in the 2012 ISSP survey who agreed that "having children restricts the employment and career chances of one or both parents" (22.3%), "children are a financial burden on their parents" (21.5%), and "having children interferes too much with the freedom of parents" (18.6%) (ISSP Research Group, 2016).

The strong value placed on Filipino children begins even before the child is born. For example, the ISSP data indicated that the proportion who agreed that it is always or almost always wrong for a woman to have an abortion "if there is a strong chance of serious defect in the baby" increased from 75.9% in 1991 to 89.3% in 2008 (ISSP Research Group, 1993, 2018). Similarly, the share who agreed that it is always wrong or almost always wrong for a woman to have an abortion if "the family has a very low income and cannot afford any more children" increased from 82.9% in 1991 to 97.9% in 2018 (ISSP Research Group, 1993, 2020). The strong disapproval against abortion among many Filipinos may be due to the influence of the Catholic Church, which 80% of Filipinos adhere to.

While the presence of children is highly celebrated in most Filipino families, their absence can also be a great cause for concern. There is a common assumption that those who get married want to have children, and couples who are childless are considered unlucky and pitied upon because there must be something "wrong" with them (Castillo, 1979). The NDS and NDHS data revealed that the proportion of all Filipino women who are childless at ages 45–49 years slightly increased from 8.5% in 1993 to 9.8% in 2017 (National Statistics Office [NSO] & Macro International Inc. [MI], 1994; Philippine Statistics Authority [PSA] & ICF, 2018). Similarly, the corresponding proportions among women who are currently in union also modestly increased from 3.1% in 1993 to 4.2% in 2017 (National Statistics Office [NSO] & Macro International Inc. [MI], 1994; Philippine Statistics Authority (PSA) & ICF, 2018). Childless women in the survey may include those who voluntarily chose to be childless or childfree and those who are infecund or have health conditions that prevent them from getting pregnant.

ATTITUDES TOWARD MARRIAGE, COHABITATION, AND DIVORCE

Concomitant with the changes in the trends and patterns of union formation and dissolution are several changes in attitudes toward these behaviors. Having children born out of wedlock is common in the Philippines but having children within marriage is still generally preferred. Based on the ISSP data, the proportion of adult Filipinos who agreed that "people who want children ought to get married" remained unchanged at around 83% in 1994 and 2012, although it dropped to 75.9% in 2002 (Table 1.2). While formal or legal marriage remains the most common type of union in the Philippines, data suggest a growing acceptance among Filipinos of non-traditional arrangements, including non-marriage and cohabitation (Table 1.2). For instance, most Filipinos disagreed with the statement that "it is better to have a bad marriage than no marriage at all," while the proportion who agreed declined from 32.4% in 1994 to 27.4% in 2002. Table 1.2 shows that public approval for cohabitation, either as a precursor or as an alternative to formal marriage, has risen over time. The percentage of Filipinos who agreed that it is "all right for a couple to live together without intending to get married" nearly doubled from 17.9% in 1994 to 34.9% in 2012. Similarly, the proportion who believed that "it is a good idea for a couple who intend to get

Table 1.2. Trends in Attitudes Toward Marriage and Cohabitation: The Philippines, 1994–2012.

Attitudes Toward Marriage and Cohabitation	1994	2002	2012
"People who want children ought to get married"			
Agree	82.6	75.9	82.8
Neutral	8.0	10.9	9.1
Disagree	9.4	13.2	8.1
"Married people are generally happier than unmarried people"			
Agree	63.5	61.4	70.3
Neutral	20.0	20.0	16.1
Disagree	16.5	18.7	13.6
"It is better to have a bad marriage than no marriage at all"			
Agree	32.4	27.4	n.a.
Neutral	15.0	14.0	n.a.
Disagree	52.6	58.6	n.a.
"It is all right for a couple to live together without intending to get married"			
Agree	17.9	19.4	34.9
Neutral	8.8	12.5	18.8
Disagree	73.2	68.1	46.3
"It is a good idea for a couple who intend to get married to live together first"			
Agree	31.4	35.5	n.a.
Neutral	10.3	13.6	n.a.
Disagree	58.3	50.9	n.a.

Source: Author's calculation based on 1994, 2002, and 2012 ISSP Data (ISSP Research Group, 1997, 2013, 2016).

married to live together first" increased modestly from 31.4% in 1994 to 35.5% in 2002.

Stigma against people who are living together has also started to fade. Data from the World Values Survey showed that the percentage of Filipinos who disapproved of cohabiting couples as neighbors decreased from 21.6% in 2012 to 16.0% in 2019 (Haerpfer et al., 2022; Inglehart et al., 2014). The shift toward more liberal views on marriage and cohabitation may be due to the growing exposure of Filipinos to unconventional values and ideals through mainstream and social media. The increasing number of Filipino public figures (e.g., politicians and actors) who publicly admitted to be living together with their partner or had gone through cohabitation before marriage may have also contributed to the growing acceptance of cohabitation in the country. Finally, public approval of divorce has also grown over the years. The share of adult Filipinos who agreed that "married couples who have already separated and cannot reconcile anymore should be allowed to divorce so they can get legally married again" increased from 43% in 2005 to 53% in 2017 (Social Weather Stations, 2018b).

ATTITUDES TOWARD SEXUAL BEHAVIOR AND RELATIONSHIPS OF SEXUAL MINORITIES IN THE PHILIPPINES

Much of what we know about the Filipino family pertains to heterosexual couples, even though a significant proportion of the population belongs to the lesbian, gay, bisexual, and transgender (LGBT) community. The 2013 YAFS data show that 2.4% of Filipino male youth aged 15–24 years identified themselves as gay, while 1.9% considered themselves bisexual. Among female youths, 1.8% self-identified as lesbian and 1.6% as bisexual (Cruz, 2016). In addition, the YAFS data revealed that 15.9% and 9.8% of Filipino youth know of family members who are gay and lesbian, respectively, while less than 3% know of family members who are a bisexual man (2.3%) and bisexual woman (1.0%). Moreover, half of the Filipino youth disclosed that they have a close friend who is gay, while a third reported that they have a close friend who is lesbian. Prior research indicated that Filipino attitudes toward lesbians and gays were largely negative, and these heterosexist views were prevalent (Manalastas & Del Pilar, 2005). However, a 2019 survey data by the Pew Research Centre showed that 73% of Filipinos agreed that homosexuality should be accepted by society, which was the highest among the Asian countries included in the survey, such as Japan (68%), South Korea (44%), and India (37%) (Pew Research Center, 2020). While homosexuality is generally accepted in Philippine society, there is still strong disapproval of the sexual behaviors of people of the same sex. The ISSP data revealed that the proportion of adult Filipinos who responded that it is always wrong or almost always wrong to have sexual relations between two adults of the same sex slightly grew from 92.3% in 1991 to 94.4% in 2018 (ISSP Research Group, 1993, 2020). Similarly, the childrearing practice of homosexual couples is also not widely accepted in the country. Based on the 2012 ISSP data, less than half of adult

Filipinos agreed that same-sex female couples (40.8%) and same-sex male couples (32.9%) can raise a child as well as heterosexual couples (ISSP Research Group, 2016). Finally, legislating same-sex unions in the Philippines remains a considerable challenge. According to a 2018 survey, 61% of adult Filipinos disagreed, and only 22% agreed that "there should be a law that will allow the civil union of two men or two women" (Social Weather Stations, 2018a).

HOUSEHOLDS IN THE PHILIPPINES

The family is the "small world" of Filipinos, and it is hard to understand the way Filipinos behave unless we have some understanding of the family and household in which they live (Castillo, 1979). Therefore, this section documents some trends in household size and structure in the Philippines to improve our understanding of the immediate social environment of Filipinos.

The household size in the country steadily decreased from 5.2 household members in 1990 to 4.4 in 2015 (Abalos & Yeung, 2023) due in part to the fertility decline. In terms of structure, nuclear households, which have been the dominant form of households in the Philippines as early as the 1960s (Arce, 1994; Castillo, 1979; Go, 1994; Liu & Yu, 1968), continue to be the most common form of households in recent years, although its prevalence declined from 69.1% in 1990 to 64.9% in 2010 (Table 1.3). Nuclear households in this study can be in the form of (1) a married/cohabiting couple with no children, (2) a married/cohabiting couple with children, and (3) a single-parent family. Of these three types of nuclear households, the couple with children was most prevalent, but its share declined from 58.1% in 1990 to 51.5% in 2010. In contrast, the share of couple-only households increased from 5.2% in 1990 to 6.7% in 2010, while the proportion of single-parent family likewise increased from 5.8% to 6.7% between 1990 and 2010. Similarly, the proportion of extended households increased modestly from 22.9% in 1990 to 25.2% in 2010. An emerging trend in the Philippines is the consistent increase in the proportion of one-person households, from 2.9% in 1990 to 6.0% in 2010 (Abalos & Yeung, 2023).

Table 1.3. Household Structure in the Philippines, 1990–2010.

	1990	2000	2010
One-person households	**2.9**	**4.3**	**6.0**
Nuclear households	**69.1**	**68.5**	**64.9**
Married/cohabiting couple, no children	5.2	6.2	6.7
Married/cohabiting couple with children	58.1	56.2	51.5
Single-parent family	5.8	6.1	6.7
Extended family, relatives only	**22.9**	**22.3**	**25.2**
Composite household, family, and non-relatives	**4.3**	**3.9**	**3.2**
Non-family households	**0.4**	**0.5**	**0.6**
Unclassifiable	**0.3**	**0.5**	**0.1**
Total	**100.0**	**100.0**	**100.0**

Source: Author's calculation using Philippine census data from IPUMS International (Minnesota Population Center, 2020).

LIVING ARRANGEMENTS AND EXCHANGE OF SUPPORT AMONG OLDER FILIPINOS

Based on the 2015 census, there were 7.5 million older Filipinos, representing 7.5% of the total population (Abalos & Booth, 2020). By 2025, this number is expected to reach 11.5 million or 9.9% of the total population (Philippine Statistics Authority, 2019). Providing care and support for older people is one of the concerns of an aging population (Jones, 2012) since the prevalence of ill health increases at older ages (Cruz & Saito, 2019). As with most Asian countries, the Filipino family plays a critical role in providing care and support for older Filipinos. The importance of this family caregiving is reflected in older people's living arrangements (Medina, 2011). Table 1.4 shows that a large majority of older Filipinos live with at least one child, but the proportion in this arrangement declined from 70.4% in 1996 to 60.2% in 2018 after a slight increase to 73.9% in 2007. The decline in coresidence between 1996 and 2018 may be driven by many factors, including physical separation between children and their parents due to internal and international migration.

Meanwhile, the proportion of older adults who live with their spouse only slightly increased from 7.9% in 1996 to 9.3% in 2018. This pattern could be a reflection of the improvement in life expectancy (Abalos, 2020) that allows couples to have joint survivorship (Casper & Bianchi, 2002). Furthermore, living alone, especially at older ages, is frowned upon in Philippine society because it suggests that the family has reneged on its filial obligation to care for older people (Natividad & Cruz, 1997). Hence, the proportion of living alone among older people was relatively low at 5.5% in 1996, but it nearly tripled to 13.5% in 2018. Finally, it is worth noting that there are sex differences in the living arrangements of older Filipinos. Specifically, a higher proportion of older men than women live with their spouse only or with children, but there are more women than men who live alone. These differences could be due to sex differences in life expectancy, where women tend to outlive men, leaving women to live alone since they have no surviving spouse to live with.

In terms of actual provision of support, prior research indicated that the Filipino family, particularly spouses and daughters, assists older Filipinos who

Table 1.4.   Living Arrangements of Older Adults in the Philippines, 1996–2018.

Living arrangements	1996			2007			2018		
	Male	Female	Both Sexes	Male	Female	Both Sexes	Male	Female	Both Sexes
Living alone	4.3	6.4	5.5	3.3	5.3	4.5	11.3	15.0	13.5
Living with spouse only	8.9	7.2	7.9	9.9	6.8	8.1	11.8	7.7	9.3
Living with at least one child	72.6	68.8	70.4	74.5	73.4	73.9	63.7	57.9	60.2
Other types of arrangement	14.2	17.7	16.2	12.4	14.4	13.6	13.3	19.5	17.0

Sources: Cruz and Cru (2019), Cruz et al. (2009) and author's calculation based on the 1996 Philippine Elderly Survey.

need help in carrying out functional activities (Abalos et al., 2018). However, this provision of assistance follows a gendered pattern, with the spouse assisting older men, whereas daughters give assistance to older women (Abalos et al., 2018). In addition, children also provide other types of support aside from helping their parents who are in poor health. Specifically, the 2018 LSAHP data showed that a great majority of older Filipinos received emotional support (81.1%), material support (74.1%), and financial support (69.9%) from their coresident children (Marquez, 2019). However, the provision of support extends beyond the household, as non-coresident children also give support to their parents, notably emotional support (86.7%), financial support (86.1%), and material support (78.8%) (Marquez, 2019). Moreover, parents are not just passive recipients of support, but they also support their children. For example, 89.3% of older Filipinos gave emotional support to their coresident children, while 37.6% gave financial support to their non-coresident children (Marquez, 2019). In addition, the LSAHP data revealed that 24.2% of older Filipinos take care of their grandchildren, either partially or fully (Cruz & Cruz, 2019). The main reasons why older Filipinos fully take charge in taking care of their grandchildren include labor migration of the latter's parents (34.6%) and parents' union dissolution (33.3%) (Cruz & Cruz, 2019).

SUMMARY AND CONCLUSION

Against a backdrop of demographic and socioeconomic changes, this study sketched a demographic portrait of Filipino families in the past decades using census and survey data. Specifically, it examined broad aspects of family-related topics, including marriage and cohabitation, divorce and separation, fertility and fertility preferences, household structure, and living arrangements of older people. It also explored Filipinos' attitudes toward various aspects of the family.

Results showed that the timing and character of union formation in the Philippines have changed over the last few decades. Filipinos are postponing marriage to a later age, while some are forgoing marriage altogether. Some may delay entry into marriage until they can economically support their own family, while others choose to pursue higher education and career advancement over getting married. The rise of non-marriage in the country may be related to the lack of an available pool of potential partners for some segments of the population, particularly low-educated men and highly educated women. Preference for an alternative lifestyle may also contribute to this growing aversion toward marriage among highly educated Filipino men and women.

Legal or formal marriage in the Philippines has declined, while cohabitation has become more common, particularly among younger people. Economic factors were the primary reasons young Filipinos chose to cohabit and not formally marry. However, Filipinos are not entirely abandoning marriage in favor of cohabitation. Evidence suggests that cohabitation has become a pathway to marriage rather than an alternative to marriage, as a significant proportion of those who cohabit eventually marry their partner.

The changes in the timing and character of union formation in the Philippines are also accompanied by rising union dissolution cases. The increasing prevalence of cohabitation, on the one hand, and the rising cases of union dissolution, on the other hand, do not happen in isolation. Most Filipinos who have been estranged from their spouse do not have the means to end their marriage legally, so some choose a live-in arrangement with their new partner due to legal constraints. Meanwhile, the growing popularity of live-in arrangements may lead to more informal separations, as cohabiting people are more likely to separate than those legally married (Abalos, 2017). Urbanization and educational expansion may also contribute to the country's growing prevalence of union dissolution. Research showed that exposure to urban life and a higher level of education are associated with a higher likelihood of union dissolution among Filipino women (Abalos, 2017).

Regarding family-related attitudes, the study showed that Filipinos had become more accepting of cohabitation and divorce in the country. However, while Filipinos have become more tolerant of behaviors associated with heterosexual couples, sexual behavior and family formation of sexual minorities are not yet widely accepted. At least 9 in 10 Filipinos view sexual relations between people of the same sex as wrong, 61% disagree with having a law that legalizes same-sex unions, and less than half agree that homosexual couples can raise a child as well as heterosexual couples.

The fertility rate in the Philippines has declined in recent years but is still above the replacement rate of 2.1 children and beyond Filipino women's ideal or desired family size. This implies that some Filipino women's births were "unwanted" or more than their desired number. The inconsistency between Filipino women's actual and ideal number of children could be due to several factors, one of which is access to effective contraceptive methods. Based on the 2017 NDHS, only 54.3% of currently married women are using any contraceptive method, with 40.4% using any modern method and 13.9% using any traditional method.

Children are highly cherished in Filipino families. They are considered a source of joy and support in old age and are hardly viewed as a "burden," despite the hardships associated with childbearing and childrearing. Moreover, the high proportion of adult Filipinos who reject abortion, regardless of whether the baby has a serious defect or when the family is poor and cannot afford more children, also attest to the great importance of children in Philippine society. Meanwhile, childlessness in the country is relatively low, but its prevalence has slightly increased in recent years.

The impact of changes in union formation, dissolution, and fertility can be observed by examining the Filipino household. Over time, the Filipino household has become smaller, mainly due to fertility decline. In addition, nuclear households, the dominant form of household in the country, have declined, while one-person households or living alone have increased in recent years. Population aging and increasing union dissolution are associated with the increasing rates of one-person households in the Philippines (Abalos & Yeung, 2023).

The family remains an essential source of support among older people in the Philippines. The prominence of this family support is reflected in the high proportion of older Filipinos who live with their children, although the proportion in this arrangement has declined from 70.4% in 1996 to 60.2% in 2018. In contrast, there is a slight increase in the percentage of older Filipinos who live with their spouse only and a sharper increase in the proportion who live alone. These changes in living arrangements may be due to demographic and socioeconomic factors, such as the lengthening of life expectancy and increasing migration. Older Filipinos also received support from their coresident and non-coresident children. In turn, older Filipinos also support their children, including taking care of their grandchildren.

In conclusion, while the Filipino family may have changed in size and structure and how it is formed and dissolved, it has remained constant in how it values its members, particularly the young and the old. Moreover, the Filipino family will also continue to evolve in response to the country's continuing demographic and socioeconomic changes. Filipinos will continue to marry, but cohabitation will be essential in the union formation process. Although the evidence showed that cohabitation has become a pathway to marriage in the Philippines, it is not unlikely that it will become an alternative for some couples. Given the persistent poverty and the legal impediments in dissolving and forming a marriage in the country, cohabitation without marriage may become the only option for some Filipino couples, including homosexual couples, who wish to establish their own family.

Although the legalization of divorce in the country is less likely to happen in the next few years due to the strong opposition of the Catholic Church, we can expect the share of Filipinos who are divorced or separated to increase in the future. This increase can be related to the growing prominence of cohabitation, which is easier to dissolve than legal marriage, and the increasing economic independence of Filipino women, allowing them to leave a bad marriage or partnership.

Due to the steady fertility decline, the continuing improvement in life expectancy, and increasing international migration, Filipino households will be less nuclear and become more extended in the future. However, despite the changes in the structure and composition of Filipino households, family cohesion and intergenerational support will continue to persist due to the resilience of Filipino values and the growing importance of information and transportation technology.

NOTE

1. Giving of "donation" is mostly practiced in wedding ceremonies officiated by the Catholic Church.

ACKNOWLEDGMENT

This study uses data from the Philippine Population Data Archive of the University of the Philippines Population Institute (UPPI) and the Demographic Research and Development Foundation, Inc. (DRDF), as well as data from the Philippine Statistics Authority and IPUMS International.

REFERENCES

Abalos, J. B. (2014). Trends and determinants of age at union of men and women in the Philippines. *Journal of Family Issues, 35*(12), 1624–1641.

Abalos, J. B. (2017). Divorce and separation in the Philippines: Trends and correlates. *Demographic Research, 36*(50), 1515–1548.

Abalos, J. B. (2020). Older persons in the Philippines: A demographic, socioeconomic and health profile. *Ageing International, 45*, 230–254. https://doi.org/10.1007/s12126-018-9337-7

Abalos, J. B. (2023). Do Filipinos still say "I do"? The continuing increase in non-marriage and cohabitation in the Philippines. *Journal of Family Issues.*

Abalos, J. B., & Booth, H. (2020). Factors associated with regional variation in disability-free life expectancy based on functional difficulty among older persons in the Philippines. *Asian Population Studies, 16*(3), 1–23.

Abalos, J. B., Saito, Y., Cruz, G. T., & Booth, H. (2018). Who cares? Provision of care and assistance among older persons in the Philippines. *Journal of Aging and Health, 30*(10), 1536–1555.

Abalos, J. B., & Yeung, W.-J. J. (2023). Demographic, socioeconomic, and cultural factors for the rise in one-person households in developing countries: the case of the Philippines. *Journal of Population Research.*

Arce, W. F. (1994). The life cycle of the household and selected characteristics: A search and discussion. *Philippine Sociological Review, 42*(1–4), 119–141.

Asis, M. M. (1994). Family ties in a world without borders. *Philippine Sociological Review, 42*(1/4), 16–26.

Bureau of the Census and Statistics. (1962). *Vital statistics report: 1960.* Bureau of the Census and Statistics.

Cabigon, J. V. (2001). Complete life tables for the Philippines as a whole and Metro Manila for the years 1960, 1970, 1980, 1990 and 1995. *Philippine Quarterly of Culture and Society, 29*(1–2), 161–209.

Calonzo, A., & Cayabyab, M. J. (2013). *More Pinoy couples seeking annulment despite high cost.* http://www.gmanetwork.com/news/story/302435/news/nation/more-pinoycouples-seeking-annulment-despite-high-cost

Casper, L. M., & Bianchi, S. M. (Eds.). (2002). Changing families in a changing society. In *Continuity and change in the American family* (pp. 1–38). SAGE Publications, Inc.

Castillo, G. (1979). *Beyond Manila: Philippine rural problems in perspective.* International Development Research Centre.

Cruz, C. J. P. (2016). Gender identity and sexual orientation. In Demographic Research and Development Foundation Inc and University of the Philippines Population Institute (Ed.), *The 2013 young adult fertility and sexuality study in the Philippines* (pp. 154–168). Demographic Research and Development Foundation, Inc. and University of the Philippines Population Institute.

Cruz, C. J. P., & Cruz, G. T. (2019). Filipino older persons. In G. T. Cruz, C. J. P. Cruz, & Y. Saito (Eds.), *Ageing and health in the Philippines* (pp. 27–46). Economic Research Institute for ASEAN and East Asia (ERIA) & Demographic Research and Development Foundation, Inc.

Cruz, G. T., Abalos, J. B., Lavares, M., Natividad, J., & Saito, Y. (2009). Changing social structures and the well-being of the older Filipinos. *Transactions of the National Academy of Science and Technology (Philippines), 31*(2), 197–222.

Cruz, G. T., & Saito, Y. (2019). Functional health. In G. T. Cruz, C. J. P. Cruz, & Y. Saito (Eds.), *Ageing and health in the Philippines* (pp. 75–88). Economic Research Institute for ASEAN and East Asia (ERIA) & Demographic Research and Development Foundation, Inc.

De Guzman, E. T. (2017). Annulment and divorce statistics, Philippines: 1968–2016. Paper presented at the 10th National Convention of Solemnizing Officers, Atrium, Limketkai Mall Lapasan, Cagayan de Oro City.

Dommaraju, P. (2016). Divorce and separation in India. *Population and Development Review, 42*(2), 195–223.

Emery, R. E. (2013). *Cultural sociology of divorce: An encyclopedia:* SAGE publications.

Fuse, K. (2010). Variations in attitudinal gender preferences for children across 50 less-developed countries. *Demographic Research, 23*(36), 1031–1048.

Gloria, C. K. (2007). Who needs divorce in the Philippines. *Mindanao Law Journal, 1*(1), 18–28.

Go, S. P. (1994). The present and future of the family in the Philippines. *International Journal on World Peace, 11*(4), 61–75.

Gregorio, V. (2018). The only exception: Teenage pregnancy in the Philippines. *Review of Women's Studies, 28*, 1–28.

Gregorio, V. (2020). Living apart together: Debates, variations, and research opportunities. *Philippine Sociological Review, 68*, 55–74.

Gultiano, S., Hindin, M., Upadhyay, U., & Armecin, G. (2009). Marital status and psychological well-being of Filipino women. *Philippine Population Review, 8*(1), 16–33.

Haerpfer, C., Inglehart, R., Moreno, A., Welzel, C., Kizilova, K., Diez-Medrano J., M. Lagos, P. Norris, E. Ponarin & B. Puranen. (Eds.). (2022). *World Values Survey: Round Seven - Country-Pooled Datafile Version 5.0*. JD Systems Institute & WVSA Secretariat. doi:10.14281/18241.20

Inglehart, R., Haerpfer, C., Moreno, A., Welzel, C., Kizilova, K., Diez-Medrano, J., … Puranen, B. et al. (Eds.). (2014). *World values survey: Round six – Country-pooled datafile version*. JD Systems Institute. https://www.worldvaluessurvey.org/WVSDocumentationWV6.jsp.

ISSP Research Group. (1993). *International Social Survey Programme: Religion I – ISSP 1991*. GESIS Data Archive, ZA2150 data file version 1.0.0. https://doi.org/10.4232/1.2150

ISSP Research Group. (1997). *International Social Survey Programme: Family and changing gender roles II – ISSP 1994*. GESIS Data Archive, ZA2620 data file version 1.0.0. https://doi.org/10.4232/1.2620

ISSP Research Group. (2013). *International Social Survey Programme: Family and changing gender roles III – ISSP 2002* GESIS Data Archive, ZA3880 data file version 1.1.0. https://doi.org/10.4232/1.11564

ISSP Research Group. (2016). *International Social Survey Programme: Family and changing gender roles IV – ISSP 2012*. GESIS Data Archive, ZA5900 data file version 4.0.0. https://doi.org/10.4232/1.12661

ISSP Research Group. (2018). *International Social Survey Programme: Religion III – ISSP 2008*. GESIS Data Archive, ZA4950 data file version 2.3.0. https://doi.org/10.4232/1.13161

ISSP Research Group. (2020). *International Social Survey Programme: Religion IV – ISSP 2018*. GESIS Data Archive, ZA7570 Data file Version 2.1.0, https://doi.org/10.4232/1.13629.

Jiang, Q., Feldman, M. W., & Li, S. (2014). Marriage squeeze, never-married proportion, and mean age at first marriage in China. *Population Research and Policy Review, 33*(2), 189–204.

Jiang, Q., & Sánchez-Barricarte, J. J. (2013). Socio-demographic risks and challenges of bare-branch villages in China. *Asian Social Work and Policy Review, 7*(2), 99–116.

Jones, G. (2018). Changing marriage patterns in Asia. In Z. Zhao & A. Hayes (Eds.), *Routledge Handbook of Asian demography* (pp. 351–369). Routledge.

Jones, G. (2012). Changing family sizes, structures and functions in Asia. *Asia-Pacific Population Journal, 27*(1), 83–102.

Kabamalan, M. M. (2004). New path to marriage: The significance of increasing cohabitation in the Philippines. *Philippine Population Review, 3*, 111–129.

Kabamalan, M. M. (2006). *Cohabitation among youth in the Philippines* (Sociology). University of Hawai'i at Mānoa.

Kabamalan, M. M. (2011). Cohabitation and poverty in the Philippines. In G. W. Jones, T. H. Hull, & M. Mohamad (Eds.), *Changing marriage patterns in Southeast Asia: Economic and sociocultural dimensions* (pp. 205–217). Routledge.

Levin, I. (2004). Living apart together: A new family form. *Current Sociology, 52*(2), 223–240.

Liu, W. T., & Yu, S.-H. (1968). The lower class Cebuano family: A preliminary profile analysis. *Philippine Sociological Review, 16*(3–4), 114–123.

Lopez, J. V. (2001). *The Law on Annulment of Marriage: Rules of Disengagement: How to regain your freedom to re-marrying in the Philippines*: Published and exclusively distributed by Anvil Pub.

Manalastas, E. J., & Del Pilar, G. E. (2005). Filipino attitudes toward lesbians and gay men: Secondary analysis of 1996 and 2001 national survey data. *Philippine Journal of Psychology, 38*(2), 53–75.

Marquez, M. P. N. (2016). Sexual behavior. In Demographic Research and Development Foundation Inc and University of the Philippines Population Institute (Eds.), *The 2013 young adult fertility and sexuality study in the Philippines* (pp. 91–106). Demographic Research and Development Foundation, Inc. and University of the Philippines Population Institute.

Marquez, M. P. N. (2019). Family support and intergenerational exchanges. In G. T. Cruz, C. J. P. Cruz, & Y. Saito (Eds.), *Ageing and health in the Philippines* (pp. 161–172). Economic Research Institute for ASEAN and East Asia (ERIA) & Demographic Research and Development Foundation, Inc.

Medina, B. (2011). The family in the Philippines. In C. B. Hennon & S. M. Wilson (Eds.), *Families in a global context* (pp. 353–378). Routledge.

Medina, B. (2015). *The Filipino family* (3rd ed.). University of the Philippines Press.

Minnesota Population Center. (2020). *Integrated public use microdata series, International: Version 7.3* [dataset]. IPUMS. https://doi.org/10.18128/D020.V7.3

National Statistics Office [NSO], & ICF Macro. (2009). *Philippine National Demographic and Health Survey 2008*. NSO & ICF Macro.

National Statistics Office [NSO], & Macro International Inc. [MI]. (1994). *National Demographic Survey 1993.*: NSO and MI.

Natividad, J. N. (2013). Teenage pregnancy in the Philippines: Trends, correlates and data sources. *Journal of the ASEAN Federation of Endocrine Societies, 28*(1), 30.

Natividad, J. N., & Cruz, G. T. (1997). Patterns in living arrangements and familial support for the elderly in the Philippines. *Asia-Pacific Population Journal, 12*(4), 17–34.

Ogena, N., Kabamalan, M. M., & Sasota, R. (2008). Changing patterns and correlates of marriage in the Philippines. Paper presented at the 8th international conference on Philippine studies, Philippine Social Science Center, Quezon City, Philippines.

Pew Research Center. (2020). *The global divide on homosexuality persists*. Pew Research Center.

Philippine Statistics Authority. (2014). *Life table of the Philippines prepared by the interagency working group*. Philippine Statistics Authority.

Philippine Statistics Authority. (2017). 2015 *census of population, report no. 2 – Demographic and socio-economic characteristics: Philippines*. Philippine Statistics Authority.

Philippine Statistics Authority, & ICF International. (2014). *Philippines National Demographic and Health Survey 2013*. Philippine Statistics Authority & ICF International.

Philippine Statistics Authority (PSA), & ICF. (2018). *Philippines National Demographic and Health Survey 2017*. PSA and ICF.

Philippine Statistics Authority. (2019). *Updated population projections based on the results of 2015* POPCEN. Philippine Statistics Authority.

Philippine Statistics Authority. (2022a). *2019 Vital Statistics Report – Marriage Statistics Volume 1*. Philippine Statistics Authority.

Philippine Statistics Authority. (2022b). *Urban population of the Philippines (2020 census of population and housing)*. Philippine Statistics Authority.

Social Weather Stations. (2018a). *First quarter 2018 social weather survey: 61% of Pinoys oppose, and 22% support, a law that will allow the civil union of two men or two women*. Social Weather Stations.

Social Weather Stations. (2018b). *Fourth Quarter 2017 Social Weather Survey: 53% of Filipino adults agree to legalize divorce for irreconcilably separated couples*. Social Weather Stations.

Taylor, L. A. (1983). The querida: The surrogate divorce system in the Philippines. *Free Inquiry in Creative Sociology, 11*(2), 235–238.

United Nations, Department of Economic and Social Affairs, Population Division. (2019). World Marriage Data 2019 (POP/DB/Marr/Rev2019).

United Nations Statistics Division. (2022). *Population by marital status, age, sex and urban/rural residence*. United Nations Statistics Division.

University of the Philippines Population Institute. (2010). *Lifestyle, health status and behavior of young workers in call centers and other industries: Metro Manila and Metro Cebu*. Final report submitted by the University of the Philippines Population Institute to the Commission on Population.

Williams, L., & Arguillas, M. J. (2012). Correlates of non-marriage in the Philippines. *Philippine Population Review, 11*(1), 1–25.

Williams, L., Kabamalan, M., & Ogena, N. (2007). Cohabitation in the Philippines: Attitudes and behaviors among young women and men. *Journal of Marriage and Family, 69*(5), 1244–1256. https://doi.org/10.1111/j.1741-3737.2007.00444.x

Xenos, P. (1997). *Survey sheds new light on marriage and sexuality in the Philippines*. East West Center, Program on Population (Asia Pacific Population and Policy Paper, No. 42).

Xenos, P., & Kabamalan, M. M. (2007). Emerging forms of union formation in the Philippines. *Asian Population Studies, 3*(3), 263–286. https://doi.org/10.1080/1744173070

NARRATIVES OF PARENTHOOD

CHAPTER 2

THE ROAD TO VISIBILITY: IVF AND MOTHERHOOD JOURNEY OF FILIPINO INFLUENCERS

Samuel I. Cabbuag

ABSTRACT

Childbearing via in vitro fertilization (IVF) was taboo for a long time in the Philippines despite being available in the Philippines since 1996 and the signing of the Republic Health Law back in 2013 (Dupont, 2013). In this chapter, the author examines how IVF is imagined, presented, and accepted in the Philippine context by looking at selected case studies of Filipino influencers who opted to bear children via IVF. The author explores these through analyses of selected YouTube videos and Facebook posts through the lens of visibility labor which refers to the activities done by influencers to "the work enacted to flexibly demonstrate gradients of self-conspicuousness in digital or physical spaces depending on intention or circumstance for favourable ends" (Abidin, 2016). The author also examines the comments sections of these selected videos and posts through web scraping to get a glimpse of the reception to the journeys and struggles of these public figures. The author argues that through the visibility labor of influencers, the phenomenon of childbearing via IVF is not only promoted as a viable, if not acceptable procreative process, but also perpetuated as an inlaccessible procedure in the Philippines.

Keywords: Visibility labor; IVF; influencer cultures; motherhood journey; attention economy; digital cultures; Philippines

Resilience and Familism: The Dynamic Nature of Families in the Philippines
Contemporary Perspectives in Family Research, Volume 23, 21–34
Copyright © 2023 by Emerald Publishing Limited
All rights of reproduction in any form reserved
ISSN: 1530-3535/doi:10.1108/S1530-353520230000023002

1. INTRODUCTION

In November 2021, Journalist and YouTuber Karen Davila (2021) uploaded a 26-minute YouTube video featuring entrepreneur and "Lord of the Scents" Joel Cruz, and this vlog garnered around three million views on Davila's channel (as of February 2022) with around 800k subscribers. In this vlog, Cruz discussed with Davila his daily life and journey with his eight children, all healthy and all done through surrogacy, specifically through IVF, and he had spent nearly PhP 54 million (~$2.7 million[1]) for the procedures (GMA News, 2021). IVF, also known as "test-tube conception," refers to assisted reproductive technology (ART) wherein medical professionals retrieve egg cells and fertilized them with a sperm outside the body and then transfer the embryo back to the uterus either of the same or another woman for gestation (DeWeerdt, 2020). This procedure helps particularly those who are evaluated as infertile and thus could not proceed with a natural pregnancy, and therefore one of the first steps according to various sources states that the women need to be examined for infertility. The different types of IVF, among others, are the natural cycle where no medication is used, and the minimal stimulation wherein doctors used medication and injections to promote follicular development (Kato, n.d.).

All throughout Karen Davila's video with Joel Cruz shows the unfiltered side where all children are talking, playing, and running, and Davila (2021, 4:30) applauded that his children are kind and thoughtful. Cruz mentioned in the video that all his children came from one mother who is based in Russia (Davila, 2021, 8:52; 9:45). Cruz's engagement with IVF first came in 2013 when his first two children were announced (Enriquez, 2013). A cursory search through the comments section of Davila's YouTube video shows that the majority of the viewers posted positive feedback on Cruz's experiences with IVF. Aside from Joel Cruz, other celebrities have engaged in IVF treatment showing their healthy babies to the world (Eusebio & Quieta, 2021). One celebrated example is Scarlet Snow Belo, daughter of dermatologist Dr Vicki Belo and Hayden Kho (Inquirer Lifestyle, 2016). Fast forward now, Scarlet Snow, now aged 7 years, is well known in the Philippines with a large amount of following on social media and a dozen of brand endorsements (Godinez, 2021), and even a cover of the 30th anniversary of a fashion magazine (Acar, 2022).

These imaginaries are important because they afford viewers the necessary tools to spread awareness regarding IVF showing that children born from surrogacy and IVF are no different than those born of natural methods. However, not everyone still understands the concept, and some might even negatively react to the concept of childbearing as well as chiding Cruz's cosmopolitan lifestyle that he simply *can* afford to have all his children through IVF. This also begs the question of whether the reception that celebrities like Joel Cruz and Vicki Belo get is the same with influencers. Thus, this study asks the question: how is childbearing via IVF in the Philippines presented, made visible, and accepted in digital spaces?

I chose YouTube because it is the third most visited website in the Philippines, just next to Google and Facebook (Kemp, 2022). Additionally, the Global digital report for the Philippines also presented that one of the top reasons of using the internet in the country is to watch videos, TV shows, and movies with 74%. YouTube has been the platform for people, from simple users to experienced content creators, to showcase their stories and crafts to the public at large. As what will be presented in this chapter, pregnancy videos are usually shared on this platform. One example is Viy Cortez, a content creator with over 6 million subscribers. Cortez uploaded a YouTube video entitled "PLASWAN" (a play on "plus one") with over 6 million views on December 2, 2021, as well as on Instagram, announcing that she is pregnant after having a miscarriage previously (Cortez, 2021; Rappler, 2021). Her video started with her emotional after getting the positive result of her pregnancy test and then showed it to her husband and fellow vlogger Cong TV (Cortez, 2021, 00:10). Aside from the millions of views for this video, Cortez's video also garnered a plethora of comments to congratulate the couple. This video showcased the relatability of the pregnancy journey, the happy cries of the couple for a successful pregnancy, and hopes and plans for the future baby.

2. EXPLORING VISIBILITY OF IVF

This study is informed by the concept of *visibility labor* introduced by Anthropologist Crystal Abidin which refers to "the work enacted to flexibly demonstrate gradients of self-conspicuousness in digital or physical spaces depending on intention or circumstance for favourable ends" (Abidin, 2016, p. 2). Visibility labor is argued to be analog rather than algorithmic as it shows how influencers present themselves (Goffman, 1959) and curate their content to gather more currency in this attention economy (Goldhaber, 1997). Abidin (2016) introduced the concept of visibility labor in her study on advertorial campaigns on Instagram, specifically on their #OOTD posts on which followers of influencers are reposting posts in order to be noticed by influencers in Singapore.

Visibility labor is also explored in Abidin's (2021, p. 85) study on TikTok influencers and regular TikTokers in general focused on "repeated attempts, observed patterns, and gut feelings" as they navigate the platform and its algorithm, thus hoping to increase their visibility and popularity in the platform. In the case of TikTok, visibility labor comes in the form of (1) claiming ownership to videos, audios, and stories, among others; (2) algorithmic practices wherein TikTokers repeat their actions and behaviors to affect the algorithm of TikTok to their favor; (3) interactive practices wherein TikTokers engage in parasocial behavior to appeal to other users; and (4) legacy practices wherein users engage with activities outside of TikTok and thus maintaining their branding on other platforms (Abidin, 2021).

3. METHODS

To answer the research question, this study utilized digital methods, particularly content analysis of YouTube videos of influencers speaking about IVF childbearing, mostly of their success stories of their IVF treatments. The videos are chosen based on the first few videos that showed after searching for "IVF Philippines" on YouTube and it is also a good thing that their channels are both focusing on their motherhood journeys. The videos are then watched and analyzed and coded in two levels, and they will be described in the following section.

To supplement the analysis on the videos, the comments sections of these videos are also analyzed to provide a glimpse into the reaction and reception of the audiences. I used the website Netlytic (netlytic.org), a text and social network analyzer which can scrape publicly available posts on YouTube and Twitter, among others, to download the comments from the said videos in November 2021. As such, over 438 comments were coded. After analyzing the videos and comments, I will finish this chapter by dovetailing visibility labor and IVF. Both videos and the comments sections are coded in two levels to look at the different themes of reasons for doing IVF, costs and preparations before, during, and after IVF, stories of successes and failures, and issues and concerns experienced.

4. ANALYSIS OF YOUTUBE VIDEOS

In order to help in discussing the visibility of IVF, I chose two influencers whose channels discuss IVF treatment and their journeys to motherhood as case studies. I first discuss the two influencers, who can also be considered as "mommy bloggers" (Abidin, 2017) and then proceed to discuss the various themes from their videos.

The first influencer is Joyce Yeo, a mid-influencer with 122k subscribers on her YouTube channel. Yeo's channel is a mix of her motherhood journey and videos related to business. She has two videos discussing IVF: the first one was in 2019 where she discussed her infertility and the second was in 2020 discussing her IVF journey, focusing on the costs. She started her first video with a slideshow of her child Mira, a bible verse, and a message directed to her child as she presents her baby as a miracle baby done through IVF (Yeo, 2019, 00:01). After the slideshow, she started speaking that she was infertile but clarifying that while she is indeed barren and cannot bear a child, this condition does not make her less of a woman (Yeo, 2019, 02:57). Her situation was that she was considered infertile as she and her husband tried to have a baby but were unsuccessful in one year. She also mentioned that she had PCOS and when she consulted at the Kato Repro Biotech Center (KRBC, more known as "Kato" by influencers), an IVF clinic, she was advised for her fallopian tube to be removed (Yeo, 2019, 06:11; 06:41). She was then asked to take medicine for her eggs and eventually harvested some eggs and the sperms to generate embryos (Yeo, 2019, 07:25). Unfortunately, the first attempt of putting embryos to her failed (Yeo, 2019, 07:32). The doctors found that Yeo had autoimmune disease which blocks foreign objects put inside her body like the embryos since it has her husband's sperm (Yeo, 2019, 07:45). She had to undergo a procedure where they transfer husband's blood as white blood cells to her body (Yeo, 2019, 09:07). After the procedure they tried again inserting embryos and finally it was a success

(Yeo, 2019, 09:41). She sent a message to fellow women with similar situations that they are not alone as she felt giving up but pushed through with the help of her support group and her faith (Yeo, 2019, 11:10).

Her video focusing on her IVF journey was published in 2020, with over 17,000 views as of April 2022 (Yeo, 2020). This is an accompaniment to her blog back in 2018 which discusses more details about her IVF journey, particularly the costs (Gavia, 2018). She is not sure how much it costs during the time of filming the video, but she only discusses the costs she paid during her procedures (Yeo, 2020, 01:58). Similar to the first video, she discussed her medical history on PCOS and her check-up with the infertility clinic and her eventual consultation at Kato Center (Yeo, 2020, 02:28; 04:01). Because she was part of the research for medicine for the egg that was mentioned previously, some of the sessions were free. This second video is a run-through of the whole process of going through IVF specifically going on to the costs. She did not provide that many images let alone receipts to show the actual amounts as she only provided rough estimates per checkup, per operation, and the medicines she had to take.

The second mommy blogger is Welyn Mores, a nanoinfluencer with 5.8k subscribers as of April 2022. While Mores has fewer subscribers, she is an essential case of an influencer that focuses its channel on IVF and motherhood. A glance of her uploaded videos shows that she undergoes three rounds of IVF to have a successful pregnancy. This video wherein Mores (2020a) discussed the costs of the IVF treatment garnered over 38,000 views as of April 2022 and it shows the costs for her third IVF treatment cycle as the other two were unsuccessful. Like the previous influencer, Mores (2020a, 00:47) provided a caveat that the costs that she is sharing in the video are based on her experience at Kato Center and the expenses depend on how the body of the woman responds to the IVF treatment. Specifically, the whole IVF treatment costs PhP 358,044 which includes the medicines prescribed to her (Mores, 2020a, 01:12). As she itemized the specifics of the costs by looking at the notes she prepared, she showed some pictures of the medicine, tools like syringes and ultrasound tests (Mores, 2020a, 01:21). These images include screenshots of both pictures and video clips from her Instagram account. She also provided some caveat that she had difficulty breathing because she is 23 weeks pregnant as she is shooting this video (Mores, 2020a, 04:07).

She was not sure if they paid via cash or with a debit card, but she informed her viewers that they can also pay using a credit card (Mores, 2020a, 06:30). As she itemized the costs, she also itemized how many times she needs to do some procedures and take medicines (Mores, 2020a, 01:55). Aside from costs, she discussed the various steps she did as in the case of taking the other injections at home. One large amount was the harvesting of egg cells on cycle Day 12 which costs PhP 203,783 as the clinic was able to harvest six egg cells and they had to undergo freezing (Mores, 2020a, 03:27). She also expressed relief and thanked God (Mores, 2020a, 06:49) as the transfer was done right before the start of the COVID-19 quarantine in Metro Manila (CNN Philippines, 2020). As soon as the community quarantine started, all the harvesting and transferring of embryos stopped in her clinic. One highlight from her video was that they were supposed to do natural IVF back in January 2020 (Mores, 2020a, 09:10), of which no medication is used for the follicular growth (Kato Repro Biotech Center, n.d.). This attempt was unsuccessful as there were no egg cells harvested due to early ovulation. This procedure was supposed to be charged even if it is unsuccessful, but the doctor told them that they will not be charged so it lightened the couple's mood as they were expecting to harvest some eggs (Mores, 2020a, 09:55).

The other video which focuses on Mores' (2020b) preparation for the IVF treatment garnered 4,076 views as of April 2022. She recorded this video while she is 28 weeks pregnant, comparable to the first video, and in this video, she informed her viewers that she did a minimal stimulation IVF (Mores, 2020b, 00:31) which included medications (Kato, n.d.). Her intro montage included a clip from their "gender reveal" and she and her husband popped a black balloon with "It's a" in the balloon and pink confetti falls after popping, revealing that her child was a girl (Mores, 2020b, 00:23). With regard to the format of her vlog, the video is a simple sit-down video where the mommy blogger talks to her audiences with minimal pop-up texts and images. Her preparations were similar to her first two IVF cycles, but she added more steps in her preparations like maintaining a healthy diet, specifically doing a gluten-free diet, less eating outside, and increasing the vitamin intake (Mores, 2020b, 01:21). Her husband also did the same. Both took a healthier lifestyle, including doing sports and exercises, for 3 months and they both lost weight as they prepare for another set of extractions. Their immunologist suggested them to take medications to lessen their killer cells. Lastly, they also resorted to lots of prayers and faith – "total surrender" as per Mores (2020b, 08:51), which refers to total surrendering of the whole plan to God. Thankfully, she was not feeling any difficulty or encountering problems when she was 28 weeks pregnant during the recording of the video (Mores, 2020b, 08:59).

Both these two influencers have something in common – they all invite their viewers, either explicitly or implicitly via prompts on the video, to either like the video, subscribe to their channel, and follow them on other social media platforms.

4.1. Inspiration

YouTube vlogs, I argue, can be considered storytelling and thus tags YouTubers, and in this case, influencers as storytellers and YouTubers need to be innovators of the platform as they navigate its various affordances (Burgess & Green, 2018). Influencers thus have a role to smoothly narrate their stories in their content for their audience. Mommy bloggers became pillars of inspiration to all viewers, especially to women with similar experiences in infertility and having issues with bearing children *normally*. Their videos are stories of success as they presented that they have overcome the obstacles from before, during, and after the IVF treatment. To inspire their viewers, these mommy bloggers showcased a variety of images and video clips that tells a strong narration. Specifically, influencers would show the positive pregnancy test and eventually some sonogram pictures that indeed their IVF treatment worked for them after some tries. One mommy blogger started her video with her crying as she found out the positive pregnancy test while in Kato Center (Saril, 2022, 00:02). Another means to inspire viewers especially women who are interested in doing an IVF treatment was Bible verses. I noticed this especially in the case of Yeo's video where she started with a Bible verse and then proceed with a message to her baby (Yeo, 2019, 00:01). While subtle, this is also can be observed in Mores' (2020b, 09:04) case when she mentioned that she did a lot of praying and trusting with her faith to have a successful IVF treatment. They are all aware of the risks of doing such a procedure and it does take a toll on them.

Both these mommy bloggers have similar situations: they are all in their second, third, and last tries of IVF treatment. Statistically, the success rates of IVF depend on the age bracket with 32% for women younger than 35 years, 25% for women aged 35–37 years, and it continues to go down to 4% for women aged 44 years (National Health Service, n.d.). In the Philippine context, the success rate ranges from 30% to 50% depending on the clinic (Dupont, 2013). The Center for Advanced Reproductive Medicine and Infertility (CAMRI) of St. Luke's Hospital mentioned on their website that their overall pregnancy rate from their opening in October 2011 to February 2012 is 47% with 52% for women aged 32 years and younger, 46% for women aged 33–38 years old, and 45% for older than 39 years (CAMRI, "World-class Results from Initial Cases"). In another webpage, CAMRI ("IVF – In Vitro Fertilization") mentioned that the rate depends not just on the woman's age, but also on the presence of comorbidities and the quality of the husband's sperm. Victory A.R.T. Laboratory Philippines, Inc. (nicknamed Victory A.R.T.) posted on their website that their success rate is 40–50% per transfer (Victory A.R.T. Labs, "FAQ"). Mores (2020b, 09:39) also mentioned this rate of 40–50% chance of successful pregnancies but also expressed being overwhelmed with the procedure so she always thinks the process will work. Ultimately, she is ready for whatever happens in their attempts, and it is always up to God's will if she will get success from the procedure.

Therefore, while ultimately the IVF treatment worked for them, this information gives the viewers a hint that the treatment might not work in the first few tries. This realization makes stories of success more convincing as it shows these women overcome physical and emotional obstacles to have a child.

4.2. Money Matters

An article from Smart Parenting lists a rough estimate per IVF treatment according to each clinic: PhP 250,000–PhP 300,000 ($4,545–$5,454) at St. Luke's CARMI, around PhP 300,000 ($5,454) at Kato Repro Biotech Center, and PhP 250,000–PhP 500,000 ($4,545–$9,090) at Victory A.R.T. (Abrajano-Birate, 2020). While the doctor's consultation is PhP 560 ($10.18), Mores (2020a) had to consult more than once for the various days of monitoring the progress. It can be noted, as also in succeeding sections of this chapter, that most influencers can only give a rough estimate of their IVF treatment. Some do itemize the costs per consultations, medications, injections, and other procedures needed (Gavia, 2018; Mores, 2020a), but these are accompanied by a caveat that the items are only correct during the time they did the process of IVF treatment. As mentioned in the previous discussion, both Mores and Yeo are already on their third tries and thus this infers a lot of expenses on their part as there are additional costs per try and it also depends on the number of healthy egg cells harvested. If all the harvested eggs were unsuccessful, they had to repeat the whole process thus doubling and tripling the costs.

Thus, it is pivotal to highlight that this supposedly covert issue stands – that in order to have a successful IVF, one needs to have the capital to undergo all the procedures, undergo doctor's consultations from time to time, and purchase all the medicine that these doctors prescribe, and all these costs exclude the costs of maintaining optimal health from start to finish. Influencers had to buy fruits and maintain their diet to be healthy before and while undergoing the IVF treatment, and they continued to maintain a healthy lifestyle while already successful in the pregnancy to avoid any problems that might occur during the pregnancy (Mores, 2020b; Yeo, 2020).

4.3. Normalizing the Motherhood Journey

These videos not only aim to inspire people and shock them at the cost of prices, but these also help normalize the journey of their motherhood. Scholars have argued that IVF and "test tube babies" have become more normalized by the media (Dow, 2019; Franklin, 2013; van Dijck, 1995). In the case of YouTube vlogs, the mothers packaged themselves to be more appealing to their viewers and thus aim to be more normalized than ever as they are the ones telling their own stories without the help of mass media. As mentioned, these mothers have prayed for a successful IVF procedure and continued to pray when they got pregnant. Through the images and clips of their child, especially with the countless visits to the clinics and hospitals, these mothers presented that what they are doing is the same as any expecting mother would do. This echoes what Gregorio and Arguelles (forthcoming) argued in their study on #InstaMoms that mothers create content that unintendedly shape narratives on motherhood on Instagram. This also echoes our previous study on TikTok influencers and the curation of content to present the *baklang kanal* persona to their audience (Cabbuag & Benitez, 2022). In summary, this own labor of presenting themselves online through these vlogs does two things other than inspire others through their journey. One, these mothers invite the audience to respect their child as normal. Second, they want their audience to acknowledge them as legitimate mothers.

5. ANALYSIS OF YOUTUBE COMMENTS

Juxtaposing the analysis of the YouTube videos is this section which discusses the themes from the comments sections. As mentioned previously, 438 comments were coded into themes. The themes are as follows: (a) tackling health misinformation, (b) discussing successes and failures, and (c) to be old and gay. These themes can be argued as things that needed to be highlighted alongside the growing visibility of IVF as a form of childbearing. Through the visibility labor of these influencers (Abidin, 2016), these influencers were able to generate responses and feedback from their viewers. Their videos generated curiosity from their viewers especially for those who are looking for alternative means to bear children.

5.1. Tackling Health Misinformation

Both the videos and the comments section delve into one important thing: information. Influencers became key sources of information when it comes to IVF. Questions that are usually asked to the doctors and other medical professionals have been asked to these influencers. Some comments asked about if they could choose to have twins or even choose the sex of the baby if they will undergo IVF. While these are considered honest questions that people are curious about, it is also important to note here that there is an assumption that people can customize their pregnancies just because the procedure itself is *unnatural*. Another set of questions involves around medical matters. These questions asked for information on the clinics these influencers went to, the specific medicine they were prescribed to take, as well as questions regarding operations and consultations like how many times they had to go to the clinic for consultation and how many procedures are there in an IVF cycle. Interestingly, one specific question is about herbs or other alternative medicines used while undergoing IVF. There is an assumption that alternative medicine must be used alongside the usual medicine that doctors prescribe in order to have a successful pregnancy.

In this age of misinformation, especially health misinformation (Sylvia Chou et al., 2020; Wang et al., 2019), information has become a rare gem that influencers need to have and it is also easy to manipulate. Thus, the presentation of information especially in this situation where any miscalculation could afford a successful pregnancy let alone the overall health of the mother needs to be taken seriously. While pregnancy videos emphasize family formation and center on alternative motherhood journeys, these also serve another function in fighting health misinformation. The videos and comments section provide correct information not just about money which was previously mentioned but also about health and preparations before, during, and after a successful IVF operation. This is best observed in the earlier video of Yeo where she discussed what infertility is and some causes behind infertility through her experiences and her consultations with the doctor. This provides audiences with the information they need without having the need to pay for medical consultation. This can also be found in Mores' videos when she discussed the preparations during her IVF procedures especially in maintaining a healthy lifestyle. One interesting case is a question to Mores' video regarding the option to get pregnant even if the woman already got ligated. She replied by saying the only means to be pregnant once ligated is through IVF, otherwise, that woman needs to undergo reversal of tubes. What is interesting here is her advice to the woman to seek medical advice by contacting the fertility clinic to get the best option from them. This is interesting as she reiterates the authority that medical professionals have while also providing correct information herself.

5.2. Discussing Successes and Failures

The second pair of themes talks about how mothers were able to discuss success and failures. At the start of this chapter, I mentioned that the comments section of Karen Davila's visit to Joel Cruz's home has been flooded by positive and congratulatory comments. Similarly, the videos from influencers were also flooded with greetings and congratulations that these influencers had successful IVFs. Juxtaposing with these congratulations are aspirations to hopeful mothers. These women also wanted to have children but were unsuccessful via the normal childbearing method. Thus, they were curious to undergo IVF as well in order to have children of their own. Words like "soon," "someday," and "hopefully" are keywords in these comments that reflect the aspiration of these women.

On the other hand, comments were also flocked with frustrations. These frustrations come in the form of women who had unsuccessful IVF treatments. These women were happy that the videos had successful IVF treatments, but they also must express their frustrations that they had already gone once until thrice but still to no avail. As mentioned previously, the success rates of IVF treatments depend on the age of the woman, comorbidities, and the quality of the sperm (CAMRI, "IVF – In Vitro Fertilization"). Frustration also comes in the form of people being unable to do IVF due to the extreme costs it requires even just to harvest an egg cell. One commenter lamented they need to earn first as they are also interested in doing IVF but do not have the necessary capital to start an IVF. What is striking here is how money is added to the requirements – that truly, a barren woman needs money in order to have a child. Furthermore, this statement can be pushed further as one commenter in another video asked if she could undergo IVF while being a single mother.

The comments section has allowed both mothers and aspiring mothers to share their stories. While Mores and Yeo were not able to reply to all the comments on their videos, they were able to congratulate some of the mothers who commented they also had successful IVF procedures. What is more important to observe here was that these mothers were also able to provide comfort and prayers to grieving mothers who had failed IVF procedures. Some users also commented as well to send prayers while others ask some questions. The mothers have expressed that while God's will shall prevail in the end, they prayed for God to give them the blessing they are praying for and invite the commentors to put their trust in God.

5.3. To Be Old and Gay

The last theme of comments purported various intersectional issues. Intersectionality has been put upfront by many feminist scholars in analyzing digital cultures (Quan-Haase et al., 2021; Rogan & Budgeon, 2018). It shows that even with disembodied selves (Daniels, 2017; Hansen, 2006), intersectionality has a place in providing more nuance in digital cultures. In the context of YouTube comments, intersectionality comes in issues regarding age and gender. Age-related comments relate to people asking whether IVF is doable for those in the later stages of their lives. As mentioned previously, the success rate of IVF treatment is lower for older women with 45% for women aged 39 years and above as per CAMRI's website ("World Class Results from Initial Cases").

Conversations on gender are shown particularly from comments asking whether IVF treatment is open for same-sex couples. One commenter asked, "Hello, po. If both po kayo babae, pwede po ba na yung partner nyo is kadugo din nya yung batang dadalhin mo?" [Hello. If you are both women, is it possible that your partner will also be a blood relative of the child you'll bear?] This question can be interpreted as that the egg cell of the partner will be used to fertilize and then insert into the woman's body. This question is unfortunately unanswered by the influencer mother but as mentioned in the case of Scarlet Snow Belo (Inquirer Lifestyle, 2016), the doctors used Vicki Belo's egg cell, but it was placed in another woman's body. Thus, it can be inferred that the commenter's question can be done. However, what makes it complicated is the moral gray area with LGBTQ+ couples. There is no mention of information for single women nor LGBT+ couples on the websites of IVF clinics. Additionally, Joel Cruz is part of the LGBT community, and they did all their IVF transactions abroad.

Yeo (2019, 06:51), for example, was in her thirties in the videos and expressed hardships in the procedures because she is not getting younger and had to harvest eggs as soon as the doctors can. This is an additional layer to their miracles as success rates for IVF dwindle down with age (National Health Service, n.d.). Therefore, some mothers justify the use of IVF because of their age. However, it is more than that as discussed previously as these mothers experienced infertility and they need to disclose it in their videos. Both Yeo (2020, 02:30) and Mores (2020b, 04:17) discussed the challenges they faced with regard to health and thus the reason they could not conceive a child naturally. It can be inferred here that mothers who have undergone IVF had to justify to their viewers why they chose this route instead of just conceiving naturally.

6. VISIBILITY LABOR AND IVF

This section dovetails with visibility labor and IVF. Visibility labor is observable on two fronts: the visibility labor of influencers which is the main thrust, and the visibility labor of commenters. These two helped make IVF more visible and accepted in digital spaces, particularly on YouTube. YouTube as a platform is argued to be a "patron" of collective creativity and shaping of conditions whereby content is "produced, ordered, and re-presented for the interpretation of audiences" (Burgess & Green, 2018). YouTube therefore affords both content creators and their audiences to engage with topics and collectively shape discourses on these topics, and in this case IVF, in this participatory and convergence culture (Jenkins, 2006). YouTubers, like Yeo and Mores, are considered as "innovators" wherein the platform affords YouTubers to innovate from the features it offers (Burgess & Green, 2018). Innovation can be seen in the way these mommy bloggers create content and provide life updates, either through failed attempts, consultations, and even the positive result of their pregnancy proving the completed IVF treatment. Influencers, through their storytelling practices, present IVF to their audience in such a manner that would be accepted without any criticisms or backlash from the audience. On the other hand, the commenters contribute to the visibility labor through their replies especially with the way they reply to each other along with the interactions with the influencers in fostering a dialogue on IVF. These commenters forwarded important queries on IVF that are answered by those with actual experiences with IVF and might not have any resources to consult doctors.

One important outcome of visibility labor on IVF is that this labor opens opportunities for dialogue between the influencers and commenters who had practical experiences with IVF and the viewers who do not have that kind of information. This dialogue fosters an atmosphere of convergence that knits everyone interested in the topic at hand that is afforded by both the platform and the visibility labor. Aside from dialogue, visibility labor also spreads awareness not just on IVF as a viable option for childbearing for women but also the awareness about concerns such as infertility and the various causes that affects *normal* modes of pregnancy, and this also includes ideas about why there are certain procedures and medications that need to be bought. Thus, even without having an actual consultation, prospective clients already have a sense of what to do and prepare when they proceed with the treatment.

On the other hand, visibility labor on IVF also forwards a variety of issues. A very clear example from the analysis of both the videos and comments is the issue of the materiality of IVF. As I argued previously, one needs a lot of cash in order to bear a child with a risk of around 50% success rate, and thus the amount that the clinics have estimated might be doubled or tripled depending on the case. As a cosmopolitan practice of childbearing, IVF has become imaginary for displaying capital. Aside from economic capital is the information that potential clients need to research on before even contacting clinics for consultations. Of course, Frequently Asked Questions (FAQs) can be found on the websites of the clinics as in the case of Kato, but asking previous clients is also pivotal in informing new prospects.

Another issue that is exposed is issues on LGBT that seems to be missing from the narrative. Even on Kato's FAQs page, there is no mention of same-sex couples who might also be interested in getting a child of their own biologically or in cases like Belo's where her doctors used her egg cells, but in addition they used a surrogate mother instead of the two cases where they are the ones who gave birth themselves. What makes this missing picture in the narrative is that one of the biggest stories in the Philippines with regard to IVF is Joel Cruz, a member of the LGBT community. There needs to be an extension of the narrative with fertility clinics in the Philippines to include LGBT parenting.

7. CONCLUSION

This chapter is an attempt toward an understanding of childbearing via IVF in the Philippines by using two influencers as case studies and analyzing both videos and the comments sections. Throughout the chapter, I looked at how the visibility labor of influencers presented IVF to their viewers, how IVF is accepted by the viewers, but also how IVF is also made visible through the discussions in the comments sections. On the other hand, visibility labor also provided complexities to the phenomenon of IVF by putting forward issues that are less frequently discussed by the influencers but need further nuancing like materiality and intersectionality concerns. Through the visibility labor of these mother influencers, the videos and comments sections were able to tackle health misinformation, extend empathy to those who also experienced failed attempts, as well as open discussion for gender and age. Overall, visibility labor is pivotal in providing insights to analyze alternative forms of the Filipino family and help these mother influencers to push for the normalization not just of their motherhood journeys but also their identities as mothers.

What is missing from the whole discussion on IVF are alternatives to such an extravagant procedure. Surrogacy, while can be similar depending on the context, is one alternative, but it also has a great deal of, among others, legal and moral concerns in the Philippines as in the case of transnational transactions (Liamzon et al., 2021). Adoption, on the other hand, is legal in the Philippines with an act specifically for adoption (Salaverria, 2022) but it also brings notions of belongingness among other issues. Future research is recommended to explore visibility labors on surrogacy and adoption to provide nuance to the ever-changing Filipino family.

NOTE

1. $1 = PhP 55.

REFERENCES

Abidin, C. (2016). Visibility labour: Engaging with influencers' fashion brands and #OOTD advertorial campaigns on Instagram. *Media International Australia, 161*(1), 86–100. https://doi.org/10.1177/1329878X16665177

Abidin, C. (2017). #familygoals: Family influencers, calibrated amateurism, and justifying young digital labor. *Social Media + Society, 3*(2). https://doi.org/10.1177/2056305117707191

Abrajano-Birate, E. (2020). *Here's how much money you'll need if you're considering IVF.* Smart Parenting. https://www.smartparenting.com.ph/pregnancy/getting-pregnant/ivf-cost-philippines-a1846-20200208

Acar, A. (2022, February 5). *Scarlet Snow Belo is a 'lady' on the big 30th anniversary cover of a fashion magazine.* GMA Network. https://www.gmanetwork.com/entertainment/celebritylife/fashion/85367/scarlet-snow-belo-is-a-lady-on-the-big-30th-anniversary-cover-of-a-fashion-magazine/story

Britannica, The Editors of Encyclopaedia (2020, January 16). *In vitro fertilization.* Encyclopedia Britannica. https://www.britannica.com/science/in-vitro-fertilization

Burgess, J., & Green, J. (2018). *YouTube: Online video and participatory culture* (2nd ed.). Polity Press.

CARMI. (n.d.). *World class results from initial cases.* St. Luke's CARMI. http://www.stlukescarmi.com/about-us/success-rates-and-stories/92

Cabbuag, S., & Benitez, C. J. (2022). All hail, the Baklang Kanal!: Subversive frivolity in two Filipino influencers. *Plaridel, 19*(1), 55–89. https://doi.org/10.52518/2021-11cabben

CNN Philippines. (2020, March 12). *Metro Manila to be placed on 'lockdown' due to COVID-19.* CNN Philippines. https://www.cnnphilippines.com/news/2020/3/12/COVID-19-Metro-Manila-restrictions-Philippines.html

Cortez, V. (2021, December 2). *Plaswan* [Video]. YouTube. https://youtu.be/dLEro0SCek0

Daniels, J. (2017). Bodies in Code. In J. Daniels, K. Gregory & T. M. Cottom (Eds.), *Digital Sociologies* (pp. 335–338). Policy Press.

Davila, K. (2021, November 13). *Joel Cruz: Milyones ang binayad para magka-anak! | Karen Davila Ep28* [Video]. YouTube. https://youtu.be/YB2yy8o_ol8

DeWeerdt, S. (2020). How much should having a baby cost?. *Nature, 588*(7838), S174–S176. https://www.nature.com/articles/d41586-020-03536-2

Dow, K. (2019). Now she's just an ordinary baby: The birth of IVF in the British Press. *Sociology, 53*(2), 314–329. https://doi.org/10.1177/0038038518757953

Dupont, P. (2013). Life and death in the Philippines. *Facts, Views & Vision in ObGyn, 5*(4), 274. https://pubmed.ncbi.nlm.nih.gov/24753955/

Enriquez, M. (2013). How Joel Cruz planned his fatherhood. *Philippine Daily Inquirer.* https://lifestyle.inquirer.net/100265/how-joel-cruz-planned-his-fatherhood/

Eusebio, A. B. & Quieta, D. (2021, March 25). *IN PHOTOS: Celebrities who had children via IVF.* GMA Network. https://www.gmanetwork.com/entertainment/celebritylife/family/13774/in-photos-celebrities-who-had-children-via-ivf/photo/

Franklin, S. (2013). Conception through a looking glass: the paradox of IVF. *Reproductive Biomedicine Online, 27*(6), 747–755. https://doi.org/10.1016/j.rbmo.2013.08.010

Gavia, M. J. (2018, October 27). *Cost breakdown of our IVF journey.* MJPGJOYCE. https://mjpgjoyce.wixsite.com/mysite/post/how-much-did-ivf-costs-us?fbclid=IwAR0Ey46fC5fvfJju892Yc3w13ybXDVELGdlmIiUT1eWt0US6OCfDIYCCO_I

GMA News. (2021). *Joel Cruz spent nearly P54 million for the surrogacy of his 8 children.* GMA Network. https://www.gmanetwork.com/news/lifestyle/familyandrelationships/812199/joel-cruz-spent-nearly-p54-million-for-the-surrogacy-of-his-8-children/story/

Godinez, B. (2021, March 15). *Is Scarlet Snow aware of her celebrity status? Mom Vicki Belo answers.* GMA Network. https://www.gmanetwork.com/entertainment/celebritylife/family/75081/is-scarlet-snow-aware-of-her-celebrity-status-mom-vicki-belo-answers/story

Goffman, E. (1959). *The presentation of the self in everyday life.* Anchor Books

Goldhaber, M. H. (1997). The attention economy and the net. *First Monday, 2*(4). http://firstmonday.org/article/view/519/440

Gregorio, V. L., & Arguelles, C. V. (forthcoming). #InstaMoms: Filipina influencers on idealized contemporary motherhood. *Review of Women's Studies, 32*(2).

Hansen, M. B. N. (2006). *Bodies in code: Interfaces with dgital media.* Routledge.

Inquirer Lifestyle. (2016, June 22). Scarlet Snow is '100 percent our baby,' say Hayden and Vicki. *Inquirer.* https://lifestyle.inquirer.net/231342/scarlet-snow-is-100-percent-our-baby-say-hayden-and-vicki/

Jenkins, H. (2006). *Convergence culture: Where old and new media collide.* New York University Press.

Kato. (n.d.). *FAQs.* Kato Repro Bio Tech Center. https://www.katoreprobiotechcenter.com/faqs/

Kemp, S. (2022). *Digital 2022: The Philippines.* Datareportal.com. https://datareportal.com/reports/digital-2022-philippines

Liamzon, G. M. A., Santos, A. M. P., Tamayo, M. A. M. G., & Macapagal, M. E. J. (2021). Surrogacy among Filipinos who have struggled with infertility: A discourse analysis. *Journal of Pacific Rim Psychology, 15.* https://doi.org/10.1177/1834490921997933

Mores, W. (2020a, August 2). *IVF cost - Actual cost breakdown | IVF Philippines* [Video]. YouTube. https://youtu.be/_JEFV2IzFbo

Mores, W. (2020b, September 10). *Preparations I did for successful IVF/IVF Philippines* [Video]. YouTube. https://youtu.be/x0Zn4GwKYAo

National Health Service. (n.d.). *IVF.* NHS.uk. https://www.nhs.uk/conditions/ivf/

Quan-Haase, A., Mendes, K., Ho, D., Lake, O., Nau, C., & Pieber, D. (2021). Mapping #MeToo: A synthesis review of digital feminist research across social media platforms. *New Media & Society, 23*(6), 1700–1720. https://doi.org/10.1177/1461444820984457

Rappler. (2021, December 3). *Cong TV and Viy Cortez are expecting a baby.* https://www.rappler.com/entertainment/celebrities/cong-tv-viy-cortez-expecting-baby/

Rogan, F., & Budgeon, S. (2018). The personal is political: Assessing feminist fundamentals in the digital age. *Social Sciences, 7*(8), 132. https://doi.org/10.3390/socsci7080132

Salaverria, L. (2022, January 16). New adoption law welcomed: 'For families created by destiny'. *Inquirer.* https://newsinfo.inquirer.net/1540936/new-adoption-law-welcomed-for-families-created-by-destiny#ixzz7QAO0QPYJ

Saril, J. (2022, February 23). *My 3rd IVF transfer worked! Telling my family I'm pregnant* ❤ [Video]. YouTube. https://youtu.be/9GJwnI9xuVo

Sylvia Chou, W. Y., Gaysynsky, A., & Cappella, J. N. (2020). Where we go from here: Health misinformation on social media. *American Journal of Public Health, 110*(S3), S273–S275. https://doi.org/10.2105/AJPH.2020.305905

van Dijck, J. (1995). *Manufacturing babies and public consent: Debating the new reproductive technologies.* New york, NY: NYU Press.

Victory A.R.T. Labs. (n.d.), *FAQ.* https://victoryivfphilippines.com/

Wang, Y., McKee, M., Torbica, A., & Stuckler, D. (2019). Systematic literature review on the spread of health-related misinformation on social media. *Social Science & Medicine, 240,* 112552. https://doi.org/10.1016/j.socscimed.2019.112552

Yeo, J. (2019, February 22). *Our invitro journey. PCOS, autoimmune, blocked fallopian tubes some infertility causes* [Video]. YouTube. https://youtu.be/8_TmzckTGaw

Yeo, J. (2020, August 10). *My invitro fertilization journey in the Philippines* [Video]. YouTube. https://youtu.be/aNX74c3Rga0

CHAPTER 3

PREGNANCY, MOTHERHOOD, AND FAMILY: STORIES BEHIND BARS

Romulo Nieva Jr

ABSTRACT

Imprisonment can severely impact and disrupt women's childbearing and parenting experiences. Building on Sykes' (1958) "pains of imprisonment" and the expanded "gendered pains of imprisonment" proposed by feminist scholars, this chapter examines the pregnancy and mothering experiences of 18 Filipino incarcerated women. This study has illuminated women's diverse and distinct situations expressed in three broad themes: (a) lack of control and autonomy, (b) disrupted mothering role, and (c) social networks as coping resources. The findings demonstrated how women's institutionally imposed "prisoner identity" overshadows their pregnancy status and mothering role, exacerbated by their experiences of systemic scarcity, restricted contact with family, and limited autonomy. Finally, the results illustrated how emotional and material support from social networks (family and prison peers) helped women cope with the pains of imprisonment.

Keywords: Incarceration; pregnancy; family; mothering; Philippines; gender

Resilience and Familism: The Dynamic Nature of Families in the Philippines
Contemporary Perspectives in Family Research, Volume 23, 35–50
Copyright © 2023 by Emerald Publishing Limited
All rights of reproduction in any form reserved
ISSN: 1530-3535/doi:10.1108/S1530-353520230000023003

1. INTRODUCTION

Imprisonment can significantly change and disrupt mothering (Carlen, 1994; Genders & Player, 1990; Lockwood, 2018) and pregnancy experience (Wismont, 2000). Most incarcerated women globally are of reproductive age, and many are mothers (Moore & Elkavich, 2008; Sufrin et al., 2017). Although there is a small but growing body of research specifically focusing on mothering and imprisonment, little consideration has been given to analyzing Filipino women's mothering and pregnancy experiences in custody.

Women constitute between 2% and 9% of the whole prison population worldwide, either as sentenced or pre-trial detainees (van den Bergh et al., 2011; Walmsley, 2017). As a minority prison population, and despite the growing number in many counties, they are neglected to the detriment of their dignity, well-being, and fundamental human rights (Baker, 2014). Although women are a small group of the whole prison population, the number has risen dramatically over the last few decades and increased more than six-fold, outranking the growth rate of the male prison population (Bastick & Townhead, 2008; Van Hout & Mhlanga-Gunda, 2018; Walmsley, 2017). This growth has primarily been attributed to policy changes, including harsher drug-sentencing laws that profoundly impact women (Shlafer et al., 2019). For example, in the United States, it has been theorized that determinate and compulsory sentencing in parallel with "war on drugs" policies is the primary driver underpinning the growth (Bloom et al., 2004; Kruttschnitt, 2010).

Similarly, the Philippine correctional system is considered the most overcrowded globally, with an average congestion rate of 582 percent, including incarcerated women (World Prison Brief, 2018). Though it was already congested before President Rodrigo Duterte's "war on drugs," the prison population has increased by more than 67 percent from 120,000 in 2016 to 200,000 in 2018 (Narag & Jones, 2020). For example, as shown in Fig. 3.1, in 2018, 21,349 women were in custody (both in prisons and jails), which was 11 percent of the entire incarcerated population, a proportion higher than the global average of 6.9 percent (World Prison Brief, 2018). The significant increase in female prisoners between 2016 and 2018 could be attributed to the Duterte administration's "war on drugs" (Narag & Jones, 2020).

The Philippine government has further intensified its enforcement of Republic Act 9165 or the "Comprehensive Dangerous Drugs Act of 2002," which criminalizes various drug-related activities, including possessing, selling, and manufacturing (Panes, 2019). This "war on drugs" policy has significantly contributed to highly congested prisons in the country due to drug-related cases. Similar to the global pattern, punitive drug laws and the "war on drugs" approach have disproportionately impacted women and contributed to the rise in the number and proportion of Filipino incarcerated women. The Correctional Institution for Women, the largest women's prison in the Philippines, houses most women with long-term sentences (three years to life imprisonment). In February 2021, it was overcrowded, with 3,364 women in a space meant for only 1,500, which means it had a congestion rate of 234 percent (Bureau of Corrections, 2021). Of the

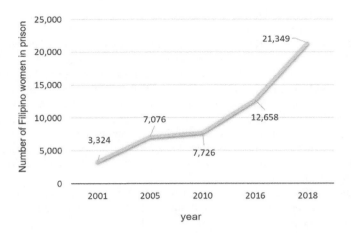

Fig. 3.1. The Number of Filipino Women in Custody over Time.

3,364 women, most were in the age groups 22–39 years ($n=1,001$) and 40–59 years ($n=1,799$).

Most incarcerated women come from the margins of society (van den Bergh et al., 2011). Global studies have shown that women involved in criminal activity share similar life experiences, such as poverty, underemployment, and poor education (Carlen & Worrall, 2013; Radosh, 2002). The profound economic inequity and unemployment have contributed to women's pathway to prison (Bastick & Townhead, 2008; Carlen, 1998). These pre-imprisonment circumstances profoundly impact women's capacity to sustain their distinct needs in prisons (Carlen & Worrall, 2013; Radosh, 2002).

2. PREGNANCY, MOTHERING, AND PAINS OF IMPRISONMENT

Prisons are total institutions where prisoners face numerous rules and regulations, strict prison schedules, almost constant monitoring and observation, and architecture and design that regulates movement and interaction to prioritize policing and surveillance (Goffman, 1961; Sykes, 1958). In his scholarly work, "Society of Captives," Gresham Sykes (1958, p. 417) coined the term "pains of imprisonment," arguing that "life in the maximum-security prison is depriving or frustrating in the extreme." He argues that the pains of imprisonment are best understood as a series of "deprivations and frustrations" that create severe psychological and social impacts on one's sense of self (Sykes, 1958, p. 64). Subsequently, generations of authors took up his work and applied it to various contexts and populations. Sykes (1958) identifies five pains of imprisonment: (1) deprivation of liberty, (2) deprivation of goods and services, (3) deprivation of heterosexual relationships, (4) deprivation of autonomy, and (5) deprivation of security. His theory accentuates the deprivation experiences among male inmates.

Since Sykes' work focused on adult male life prisoners in an American prison in the 1950s, critical and feminist criminologists have argued that Sykes' work should not be treated as a universal interpretation of prisoners' experiences. Multiple social circumstances and factors shape the experiences of prisoners. Several prison scholars and criminologists have argued that the prison experience is gendered (Bosworth, 2000; Carlen, 1983; Crewe et al., 2017; Genders & Player, 1990). Despite the diffuse discussion about the women-specific pain of imprisonment in the literature, most scholars have argued that women experience the pain of imprisonment differently compared to men (Carlen, 1983; Enos, 2001; Genders & Player, 1990).

Genders and Player's (1990) study of women lifers' experiences of the initial stages of an indeterminate sentence in an English prison revealed women-specific deprivations. These prison pains included the loss of liberty, possessions, autonomy, privacy, and heterosexual relations. Genders and Player (1990) argue that the most prominent deprivations experienced by women lifers were related to loss of freedom and limited privacy. Several women in their study described "graphically the feelings of claustrophobia and despair generated by the miniature scale of the prison unit," which permits few opportunities for privacy and liberty (Genders & Player, 1990, p. 52). Walker and Worrall's (2000) study of the "gendered pains of indeterminate imprisonment," involving interviews with 47 imprisoned women in English prisons, found women-specific prison deprivations concerning the impact of time and the constraints on their mothering role due to prolonged and severe surveillance. Walker and Worrall (2000, p. 28) conclude that women lifers suffer differently from the "pains of indeterminacy," such as the loss of control over fertility and disrupted relationships with children.

Crewe et al. (2017), building on earlier studies on the pains of imprisonment, took a comparative approach and explored the similarities and differences between male and female life-sentenced prisoners. They identify four "gendered pains of imprisonment" that are different from Syke's concept: (1) losing contact, (2) loss of power, autonomy, and control, (3) mental health and psychological well-being problems, and (4) loss of trust, privacy, and intimacy. Crewe et al. (2017) argue that women experience more distinct and severe "pains" than men. For example, Crewe et al. (2017) found that losing contact with family and friends impacted women more than their male counterparts. The main maternal pain of imprisonment includes removing women's role as a mother and their inability to fulfill their motherly responsibilities (Belknap, 2007; Crewe et al., 2017; Datesman & Cales, 1983). Imprisoned mothers tend to face more burden resulting from disrupted contact with their children than men (Belknap, 2007). This situation may be related to their role as primary and sole carers for their children before imprisonment (Berry & Eigenberg, 2003; Datesman & Cales, 1983). Berry and Eigenberg (2003) argue that while imprisoned women keep their "mother" status, they cannot fulfill their maternal responsibilities resulting in a disrupted and strained role. These disrupted maternal role and the sense of being a "failed mother" has been described as substantial sources of maternal suffering among incarcerated mothers (Belknap, 2007).

Imprisoned mothers and pregnant women are considered a vulnerable prison population. Pregnancy and motherhood experience, in general, is a significant psychosocial change for most women (McVeigh, 1997). Some mothers face substantial challenges, such as psychological and emotional distress and an inability to cope effectively (Razurel et al., 2013). Psychological, social, and material resources are important factors that enable a positive transition to a new mothering role (Glazier et al., 2004; Razurel et al., 2013). These social resources are protective by buffering the impact of life stress on the emotional well-being of pregnant mothers (Glazier et al., 2004). These facilitating transition and enabling environments are challenging for pregnant women and mothers in prison because they are detached from their psychosocial resources at home and in the community.

Outside social networks are hypothesized to "connect inmates to the free world, linking them to their previous lives" (Lindquist, 2000, p. 434). Gibbs (1982) argues that external social connections are critical for prisoners' emotional and mental well-being, particularly during early imprisonment. Additionally, maintaining ties to family and friends, mainly through visitation, improves inmates' well-being (Cochran & Mears, 2013). Social networks are resources that help prisoners cope with prison deprivations (i.e., deprivation of goods and services) through emotional comforts and material resources, such as food, toiletries, clothing, and money (Ditchfield, 1994; Noble, 1995). However, maintaining outside social connections in prisons is difficult because of the limited means and time to communicate (Bronson, 2008). Thus, prison peers are often the only directly available "interpersonal sources" to fulfill prisoners' basic and social needs. Kruttschnitt and Gartner (2005) add that social integration with peers lessens rejection, isolation, and marginalization. In addition, the nature of interpersonal resources in prison can be emotional (e.g., affection and caring) and instrumental (e.g., practical help and getting something done) (Sentse et al., 2019). A Philippine study provides additional features of community prison solidarity connected to Filipino norms and values, such as family-like and communal support networks (Narag & Jones, 2020). Narag and Jones, drawing on their study on Philippine men's prisons, argue that the distinctive coping strategies among male prisoners and prison dynamics develop a livable environment. The authors believe that the Filipino values and cultural norms of *padrino* (patron–client relationship), *bayanihan* (community spirit), and *damayan* (helping one another) are imported into the prisons. These Filipino values help the prisoners cope with prison deprivations (Narag & Jones, 2020).

For incarcerated women, themes from early research studies portray women's prisons as supportive, caring, and homelike (Giallombardo, 1966; Harner & Riley, 2013; Ward & Kassebaum, 1966). Giallombardo (1966) notes that women form family structures using traditional feminine roles, such as wives or mothers. These families are often referred to in the literature as family-like relationships or kinship networks (Giallombardo, 1966; Severance, 2005; Ward & Kassebaum, 1966). Incarcerated women establish these family-like relationships to fulfill lost familial roles, such as daughter, wife, father, cousin, grandmother, and partner (Giallombardo, 1966; Severance, 2005; Ward & Kassebaum, 1966). Several scholars contend that female inmates recreate family units in prisons to cope with the pains of imprisonment, particularly separation from families (Harner & Riley, 2013; Kruttschnitt et al., 2000; Severance, 2005).

Although Sykes' theory and the expanded "gendered pains of imprisonment" of several feminist and critical criminologists offer vital information about the deprivation encountered by prisoners and the specific experiences of women, little is known about the distinct and complex experiences of Filipino incarcerated women concerning childbearing and mothering in prison. In this chapter, drawing on key sociological and criminological perspectives, I examine Filipino incarcerated women's childbearing and mothering experiences.

3. MOTHERHOOD IN THE PHILIPPINES

The concept of motherhood in the Philippines has been shaped by historical intersections of colonialism, religion, economics, and globalization (Alampay & Jocson, 2011; Licuanan, 1979; Medina, 2015). Filipino women have been negotiating the patriarchal depictions of women rooted in their institutionalized faith as Catholics (Collantes, 2018). The idealization of Filipino women's roles as devoted mothers and wives has been linked to the symbolism of the Virgin Mary (Peracullo, 2017). Like Virgin Mary, Filipino women are expected to sacrifice for their families and obey their husbands (Collantes, 2018). The Philippines is family-oriented and pronatalist at normative and institutional levels, which mirrors the dominant Catholic influence over the social construction of motherhood (Alampay & Jocson, 2011; Licuanan, 1979). Grounded in the conservative Catholic teaching, motherhood is socially valued and regarded as a national mission in the wider Philippine society, reflecting the Virgin Mary's image and a colonial vestige burrowed in Filipino women's cultural psyche (Peracullo, 2017).

The country's social construction of motherhood and womanhood has significantly changed due to economic growth, global restructuring, domestic policies related to women empowerment, and changing social norms (Collantes, 2018; Parreñas, 2001). The national discourses on Filipino women's overseas labor highlight incongruities with traditional ideals of gendered domestic roles (Collantes, 2018). Parreñas (2007, p. 37) argues that "in the Philippines, the economy depends on the work of women outside the home, but at the same time, it must maintain the belief that women belong inside the home." The introduction of several policies and programs promoting women's empowerment and gender equality impacts Filipino women's social and economic status. For instance, Filipino women have achieved more significant gains in education than men, with female students now outranking their male counterparts in secondary education (UNESCO Institute of Statistics, 2017). In addition, the Philippines has shown improvement in women's political participation, and women are increasingly visible as leaders and decision-makers

(Asian Development Bank, 2013). In the household, Filipino women often decide on the household budget and how family expenses are managed (Ashraf, 2009). However, data indicate that Filipino women's power in these "public" spheres may not necessarily translate into "private" dimensions, such as reproduction and sex (Casterline et al., 1997; Medina, 2015; Reyes, 2008). These socio-economic changes have expanded the understanding of an ideal Filipina mother – someone who does care work, provides economically, is present (physical and emotional), and "have it all" (Ashraf, 2009; Gregorio & Arguelles, forthcoming; Medina, 2015; Parreñas, 2007).

4. METHODOLOGY

The data for this chapter were drawn from the analysis of 18 face-to-face semi-structured interviews with women who had experienced pregnancy in prison (Philippine women's prisons have no conjugal visits). These interviews were conducted as part of doctoral research, which examined the intersection of reproductive well-being and women's incarceration in the Philippines (Nieva, 2022). A qualitative inductive approach was undertaken to explore women's mothering and pregnancy experiences within women's prisons in the Philippines.

Eighteen participants aged 21–48 years participated in the interviews. The women were diverse in relation to age, educational attainment, number of children, length of sentence, and contact with their children. All had at least one child (ranging from 1 to 12). Most participants were imprisoned for drug involvement, theft, and property crime. The women were serving sentences ranging from 1 to 17 years. Most stated they had unstable jobs, were low-wage earners before imprisonment, and were entirely reliant on their husband's earnings.

The interviews were conducted face-to-face in a room assigned by the staff and lasted for an hour or more. The interviews, conducted in Tagalog, were audio-recorded and transcribed verbatim to capture the richness of the data. The interview extracts were translated into English by the researcher. Maintaining confidentiality and anonymity was a priority, not only to protect participants but also because of the sensitive nature of the topics. Pseudonyms were chosen to identify each participant; hence, interview transcripts were anonymized by removing real names.

A semi-structured interview was chosen for this study because it combines an open-ended exploration of an unstructured interview and pre-defined questions used in structured interviews (Wilson, 2014). Compared with the structured interview, the semi-structured approach allows interviewers to ask broadly the same questions with the flexibility to explore the response given (Dearnley, 2005). This approach allowed me to probe participants' answers to gain more depth. In semi-structured interviews, the sequence of the questions can vary between interview participants depending on the responses given (Dearnley, 2005).

A reflexive thematic analysis approach (Braun & Clarke, 2019) was used to analyze the data, and major themes were identified and organized to answer the main research question. Codes in the form of words or phrases were used to highlight words, phrases, sentences, or paragraphs that encapsulate key ideas and narratives. Line-by-line open coding was done to determine initial categories or subcategories. After coding, data identified with similar codes were grouped together. Transcript lines, sentences, and paragraphs were reviewed and matched with field notes to look for patterns. NVivo, a computer-assisted qualitative data management software package, supported early manual coding. Rigor in the analysis was attained by following Braun and Clarke's (2006, p. 87) six phases of thematic analysis: "familiarizing myself with the data, generating initial codes, searching for themes, reviewing themes, defining and naming themes, and producing the report."

5. FINDINGS AND DISCUSSION

This section details findings from the thematic analysis, whereby the Filipino women's accounts were drawn on to describe their mothering and childbearing experiences in prison. Participants' experiences of childbearing and mothering behind walls were reflected in three overarching themes: (a) lack of control and autonomy, (b) disrupted mothering role, and (c) social networks as coping resources.

5.1. Lack of Control and Autonomy

Participants' lack of control was described in their reliance upon the institution and other prisoners as gatekeepers to the programs and services for pregnant women in prison. The lack of control was most painfully experienced by the participants in the absence of opportunities to control pregnancy situations and make decisions.

The sense of powerlessness was profound among pregnant and lactating women due to the loss of autonomy. This absence of control over their pregnancies generated distress among participants.

> *Frany*: I felt sad when I learned I would not be allowed to go to the previous OB doctor. I was scared because I had no other experience with other doctors. I tried to ask them to reconsider my request, but I received no response. So I was sad when they brought us to a nearby public hospital for prenatal care.

> *Trisha*: When the prison staff confirmed I was pregnant, I asked God why it happened to me. Who will look after us [and baby] during the whole pregnancy?

Frany and Trisha's accounts illustrate the common experience of many women and how they described the feeling of being controlled by the institution. Although being confined is a general imprisonment experience, the disempowering feeling was distinct among pregnant women.

Many participants expressed the feeling of disempowerment because of experiences of being left unsupported and helpless in labor and not being transported early to the hospital. The environment was perceived as very hostile for women in labor in prison.

> *Leslie*: That was the most difficult part of my life. I felt helpless. I was alone. I could have saved my baby if I had not been imprisoned. I told them it was my first pregnancy and had no prior experience. They never listened to me. I rarely visited the hospital for my prenatal care.

Claire: I told the staff I had high blood pressure and that my pregnancy was high-risk, so Cesarean delivery was the better option. I told them about that information. [...] I felt labor pain at 9 pm and had extreme bleeding. But I was only brought to the hospital at 11 pm. When I arrived at the hospital, the staff could still hear my baby's heartbeat in the ER, but they could no longer hear the baby's pulse when I arrived at the operating room. I wish I had more control to decide to go to the hospital much earlier. That difficult situation made me helpless.

There was a sense of helplessness in Leslie and Claire's extracts due to a lack of control over their pregnancy condition. Apart from the sense of helplessness, a feeling of grief can be noted in the narratives of Leslie and Claire. They associated the loss of their baby with the lack of timely care from the staff and prison restrictions.

Apprehension concerning the baby extended beyond birth. The primary concern of the women was finding a caregiver for the newborn. In addition, many participants considered the impending separation from their newborn a substantial source of stress.

Trisha: I fear I have no family member who will look after my baby because of my strained relationship with them since I was imprisoned. [...] My baby might be placed in social welfare care [foster care].

Bianca: Yes, I am a prisoner; I am a criminal. But I am still a mother. I care about my kid, and it is difficult to be separated from my newborn baby. It is hard to be separated again from my kid like I was detached from other children.

How Trisha and Bianca expressed their apprehension of being separated from their newborns mirrors the feeling of anticipatory anxiety of all women interviewed who were pregnant in prison. This hopelessness was caused by their total lack of control, limited options, and difficult prison circumstances. The data are congruent with the literature indicating that hopelessness, apprehension, regret, and anger following the separation from newborns are common emotions of mothers in prison and exemplify the distinct maternal pains of imprisonment (Belknap, 2007; Crewe et al., 2017; Datesman & Cales, 1983; Walker & Worrall, 2000).

Participants' experiences of disempowerment were significantly linked to their limited autonomy over their mothering role, and pregnancy needs in prison. The lack of autonomy was most painfully experienced by women concerning enforced dependence and infantilization (Carlen, 1983; Crewe et al., 2017; Genders & Player, 1990). Furthermore, Irwin and Owen (2005) argue that prison life is completely routinized, with limited opportunities to make decisions over prisoners' daily routine, space, and time. Their argument resonates with the present study because several women described how the prison reinforced a feeling of disempowerment.

5.2. Disrupted Mothering Role

Several participants expressed the impact of imprisonment on their mothering role and childbearing experience. They also described the loss of their mothering role and expressed guilt about leaving their other children. For example, Jenky expressed concern about leaving her other three children behind, "To be honest,

I feel bad because I left my children behind, and they will grow up without their parents." Similarly, Kim stated her perception of being an "incomplete" mother because of her inability to support her family, particularly her children, "Sometimes I couldn't help but think of my family's current situation. I used to be the primary carer of the family, but my imprisonment changed our lives. [...] It feels *parang hindi kana kompletong ina* (incomplete mother)." She noted that it was a difficult situation because she used to be the family's breadwinner. Like Jenky and Kim, several participants stated how imprisonment interrupted their ability to fulfill their parental roles. The participants' accounts reflect the significant maternal pains of imprisonment concerning women's inability to retain their pre-incarceration mother's status. The primary maternal pain of imprisonment includes removing women's role as a mother and their failure to fulfill their motherly responsibilities (Belknap, 2007; Crewe et al., 2017; Datesman & Cales, 1983). Berry and Eigenberg (2003) argue that while imprisoned women keep the status of the mother, they cannot fulfill their maternal responsibilities resulting in a disrupted and strained role. These disrupted maternal status, and the sense of being a "failed mother" has been described as substantial sources of maternal suffering among incarcerated mothers (Belknap, 2007; Shamai & Kochal, 2008).

The disrupted mothering role was painfully experienced by the participants, as reflected in the narratives of Jenky and Kim, because it intertwines with the Filipino normative construction of motherhood. Although the normative parental role around child-rearing, discipline, and managing the home in the Philippines has significantly changed over the years, this traditional family role has remained predominantly women-centered, considerably shaping the Filipino women's mothering role (Alampay & Jocson, 2011; Licuanan, 1979). The dominant expectations for Filipino mothers are to do care work, provide economically, be present (physical and emotional), and "have it all" (Ashraf, 2009; Gregorio & Arguelles, forthcoming; Medina, 2015; Parreñas, 2007). However, these mothering expectations are disrupted or halted in prison. As a result, this parental role disruption created despair among the participants in the current study.

For first-time mothers, their first pregnancy in prison caused a turbulent and ambiguous experience of motherhood. Jeanneth explained that she could not clearly describe her emotions when she knew she was pregnant. It was an ambivalent feeling of excitement as a first-time mother and a fear for her baby because of imprisonment. She added that she was scared and anxious during labor because she felt alone and vulnerable. Similarly, Ada reported being clueless for several months about what to expect. She indicated she had no childbearing experience and received no support from the institution about pregnancy expectations. Ada said that "prison is not for pregnant mothers," and they should not be imprisoned. The storylines of Jeanneth and Ada demonstrate how their inmate status altered their new identity as first-time mothers. For first-time mothers, pregnancy and motherhood experience is a significant psychosocial change for most women (McVeigh, 1997). Emotional, social, and material resources are critical factors that enable a positive transition to a mothering role (Glazier et al., 2004; Razurel et al., 2013). This enabling transition appears impossible for first-time mothers in prison, who are detached from psychosocial resources. Lack of social support and absence of prison psychosocial programs for first-time mothers were apparent in the accounts of Jeanneth and Ada.

5.3. Social Networks as Coping Resources

This theme encapsulates how the incarcerated women's social networks (i.e., family and prison peers) serve as resources to cope with the pains of imprisonment concerning their pregnancy and mothering needs. These pains due to incarceration included loss of mothering role, limited prison resources, and disrupted contact with family.

Many participants indicated that their social networks' financial and material support helped them cope with challenges concerning pregnancy and mothering. Families were one of the largest financial and material support sources. This material support included money, medicines, food, and hygiene items.

Elmarie: My family has been the source to sustain my basic needs. They sometimes provide hygiene items like soap, shampoo, and toothpaste.

Angelie: Currently, my parents and kids are in my home province, and I am in [name of prison] in Metro Manila, so we are like islands away. But despite our distance, my mother has been sending money to help me with my everyday needs. Without my family support, it would be difficult on my part to sustain those needs as the resources in prisons are extremely limited.

Apart from being a significant source of financial and material support, many participants considered families their source of emotional support. Specifically, they discussed their families' support, love, and time as "enablers" that helped them cope with their prison adjustment.

Jenky: My family, especially my mother, has been very supportive. They always check in to see if I am okay. They bring food and supplements every time they visit.

Camille: When I heard that I was pregnant, I cried so much. I had difficulty telling my husband about it. During his visit, I told him about my situation, and he reassured me that everything would be okay. During those difficult moments, he never left me. He frequently visited and checked my situation. He bought things I need, and I am thankful for his support, presence, and not giving up.

The accounts above show how incarcerated women's families acted as a "buffer" when they coped with prison deprivations. Consistent with previous studies, family members' emotional, instrumental, and financial supports serve as a buffer against the pains of imprisonment (Ditchfield, 1994; Noble, 1995).

Maintaining external social relationships is challenging because of the limited means and time to communicate with the outside community (Bronson, 2008). As a result, prison peers are often the only directly available "interpersonal sources" to fulfill their basic and social needs.

Arbe: I do not know how to describe the challenge I experienced as a pregnant prisoner because your family is not present physically. I am grateful as many of my cellmates have been helping and supporting me in many ways. They are like my *pamilya* (family) to me. The presence of other women is a big boost to my spirit. It is comforting to see other pregnant women, and you realize that you are not alone, and they are there giving me advice and encouragement.

Jeanneth: As a first-time mom, I am so inexperienced and scared about pregnancy. But I managed the difficult time through the help and support of other women in the mother's ward. Without the big help from other women, who are like my *kapatid* (siblings) to me, I would not get through those tough times. They always remind me to look after myself and be brave for myself and my family.

The extracts of Jeanneth and Arbe show that peer and companion support alleviated the absence of their partner or family members throughout their pregnancy. This peer support lessened participants' anxiety and isolation during pregnancy in prison. The data above validate the findings of earlier research studies, showing the existence of family-like kinship networks formed by women to fulfill lost familial roles, such as daughter, mother, and partner (Giallombardo, 1966; Severance, 2005; Ward & Kassebaum, 1966). Additionally, several scholars have argued that involvement in family-like relationships is a women's way of coping with the pains of imprisonment, particularly separation from families (Harner & Riley, 2013; Kruttschnitt et al., 2000; Severance, 2005). The use of Filipino terms like *kapatid* (siblings), *pamilya* (family), and *nanay* (mother) mirrors the Filipino cultural norms of family-like, communal living, and friendship support networks in the wider Filipino society. These accounts illustrate Sykes' (1958) notion of how prisoners adapt to the "pains of imprisonment" by fostering shared solidarity by helping other inmates in need. This adaptation is known to minimize the deprivations and resist institutional dehumanization (Sykes, 1958).

6. CONCLUSION

This research project has illustrated the continued resonance of Sykes' (1958) concept and the "gendered pains of imprisonment" developed by critical and feminist criminologists (Crewe et al., 2017; Genders & Player, 1990; Owen, 1999; Walker & Worrall, 2000). The current study found that participants commonly described experiences of mothering and childbearing as negative and complex as they negotiated their entitlements and needs. The interviews revealed how the painful prison deprivations negatively impacted the participants' childbearing and mothering experiences, including deficiencies in accessing quality pregnancy care, comfort, and well-being support. The current research has extended the frameworks to encompass the pains associated with Filipino incarcerated women's childbearing experiences. In the present study, these prison deprivations concerning women's pregnancy characterize and extend Syke's (1958) pain of imprisonment, wherein prisoners experience significant restrictions in accessing services and goods. For instance, most participants did not obtain quality pregnancy care and support (i.e., regular prenatal care and timely professional care).

Several feminist and critical criminologists have outlined various gendered and women-specific pains of imprisonment (Crewe et al., 2017; Genders & Player, 1990; Owen, 1999; Walker & Worrall, 2000). The present study's incarcerated women's pregnancy, and mothering experiences were also strongly gendered, complementing the earlier analysis. The participants' painful loss of autonomy and control over their pregnancy and mothering role in prison reflects the significant "gendered pains of imprisonment" experienced by women (Crewe et al.,

2017; Genders & Player, 1990; Owen, 1999; Walker & Worrall, 2000). In the current project, the participants' limited autonomy and control over their pregnancy and mothering situations contributed to their experiences of disempowerment.

Several scholars have argued that the primary maternal pain of imprisonment includes removing women's role as a mother and their inability to fulfill their motherly responsibilities (Belknap, 2007; Crewe et al., 2017; Datesman & Cales, 1983; Enos, 2001). All participants in the current study experienced the burden due to disrupted contact with their children and constrained mothering roles. The present study also found that participants' inability to support and fulfill their mothering responsibilities and limited contact with children were expressed as deviation from their traditional mothering role, the symbolic loss of a salient characteristic of the Filipino mother's identity. Their experience is perhaps a culture-bound phenomenon given that Filipino mothers are expected to do care work, provide economically, be present (physical and emotional), and "have it all" (Ashraf, 2009; Gregorio & Arguelles, forthcoming; Medina, 2015; Parreñas, 2007).

The current study revealed the enabling function of women's social networks as their resources to cope with the pains of imprisonment. In particular, participants' families served as their significant outside social supports (i.e., material and emotional). Earlier studies have shown that external social connections, mainly through family visits, are critical for the prisoners' emotional and mental well-being (Cochran & Mears, 2013; Gibbs, 1982). These social networks are resources that help prisoners cope with prison deprivations through emotional support and material resources, such as clothing and money (Cochran & Mears, 2013; Gibbs, 1982; Sentse et al., 2019). The participants' accounts in the present study exemplify how women's families act as a "buffer" when they cope with the pains of imprisonment.

Prison peers played a family-like role in fulfilling the lost familial roles for women with limited family support. The current study validates the findings of earlier research studies, showing the existence of family-like kinship networks established by women to fulfill lost familial roles, such as daughter, wife, father, cousin, grandmother, and partner (Giallombardo, 1966; Severance, 2005; Ward & Kassebaum, 1966). These family-like relationships help women cope with the pains of imprisonment (Harner & Riley, 2013; Kruttschnitt et al., 2000; Severance, 2005). In the present study, Filipino terms like *kapatid* (siblings) and *pamilya* (family) reflect the Filipino cultural norms of communal living, family, and support networks in the broader Filipino society. These Filipino cultural norms were found to contribute to participants' coping strategies with prison deprivations in the present study.

ACKNOWLEDGMENTS

The author would like to thank the University of Otago for the Ph.D. scholarship. Furthermore, the author is grateful to the participants for sharing their experiences.

48

REFERENCES

Alampay, L. P., & Jocson, M. R. M. (2011). Attributions and attitudes of mothers and fathers in the Philippines. *Parenting, 11*(2–3), 163–176.

Ashraf, N. (2009). Spousal control and intra-household decision making: An experimental study in the Philippines. *American Economic Review, 99*(4), 1245–1277.

Asian Development Bank. (2013). *Gender equality in the labor market in the Philippines.* https://www.adb.org/publications/gender-equality-labor-market-philippines

Baker, J. (2014). *Conditions for women in detention in the Philippines: Needs, vulnerabilities and good practices.* https://stoptorture.today/wp-content/uploads/pubseries_no11.pdf

Bastick, M., & Townhead, L. (2008). *Women in prison: A commentary on the UN standard minimum rules for the treatment of prisoners.*https://www.peacewomen.org/sites/default/files/HR_Prisoners_QUNO_2008_0.pdf

Belknap, J. (2007). *The invisible women: Gender, crime and justice* (3rd ed.). Wadsworth Publishing Co.

Berry, P. E., & Eigenberg, H. M. (2003). Role strain and incarcerated mothers: Understanding the process of mothering. *Women & Criminal Justice, 15*(1), 101–119.

Bloom, B., Owen, B., & Covington, S. (2004). Women offenders and the gendered effects of public policy *Review of Policy Research, 21*(1), 31–48.

Bosworth, M. (2000). Confining femininity: A history of gender, power and imprisonment. *Theoretical Criminology, 4*(3), 265–284.

Braun, V., & Clarke, V. (2006). Using thematic analysis in psychology. *Qualitative Research in Psychology, 3*(2), 77–101.

Braun, V., & Clarke, V. (2019). Reflecting on reflexive thematic analysis. *Qualitative Research in Sport, Exercise and Health, 11*(4), 589–597.

Bronson, E. F. (2008). He ain't my brother… he's my friend'friendship in medium security prison. *Critical Issues in Justice and Politics, 1*(1), 63–74.

Bureau of Corrections. (2021). *Statistics on prison congestion.* http://www.bucor.gov.ph/inmate-profile/Congestion06112019.pdf

Carlen, P. (1983). *Women's imprisonment: A study in social control.* Routledge & K. Paul.

Carlen, P. (1994). Why study women's imprisonment? Or anyone else's?. *The British Journal of Criminology, 34*, 131–140.

Carlen, P. (1998). *Sledgehammer: Women's imprisonment at the millennium.* Macmillan.

Carlen, P., & Worrall, A. (2013). *Analysing women's imprisonment* (1st ed.). Willan.

Casterline, J. B., Perez, A. E., & Biddlecom, A. E. (1997). Factors underlying unmet need for family planning in the Philippines. *Studies in Family Planning, 28*(3), 173–191.

Cochran, J. C., & Mears, D. P. (2013). Social isolation and inmate behavior: A conceptual framework for theorizing prison visitation and guiding and assessing research. *Journal of Criminal Justice, 41*(4), 252–261.

Collantes, C. F. (2018). *Reproductive dilemmas in metro Manila: Faith, intimacies and globalization.* Palgrave Macmillan.

Crewe, B., Wright, S., & Hulley, S. (2017). The gendered pains of life imprisonment. *British Journal of Criminology, 57*(6), 1359–1378.

Datesman, S. K., & Cales, G. L. (1983). "I'm still the same mommy": Maintaining the mother/child relationship in prison. *The Prison Journal, 63*(2), 142–154.

Dearnley, C. (2005). A reflection on the use of semi-structured interviews. *Nurse Researcher, 13*(1), 19–28.

Ditchfield, J. (1994). Family ties and recidivism. *Home Office Research Bulletin, 36*, 3–9.

Enos, S. (2001). *Mothering from the inside: Parenting in a women's prison.* SUNY Press.

Genders, E., & Player, E. (1990). Women lifers: Assessing the experience. *The Prison Journal, 70*(1), 46–57.

Giallombardo, R. (1966). *Society of women: A study of a women's prison.* Wiley.

Gibbs, J. (1982). Disruption and distress: Going from the street to jail. In N. Parisi (Ed.), *Coping with imprisonment* (pp. 29–44). Sage.

Glazier, R., Elgar, F., Goel, V., & Holzapfel, S. (2004). Stress, social support, and emotional distress in a community sample of pregnant women. *Journal of Psychosomatic Obstetrics & Gynecology, 25*(3–4), 247–255.

Goffman, E. (1961). On the characteristics of total institutions. In E. Goffman (Ed.), *Asylums: Essays on the social situation of mental patients and other inmates* (1st ed., pp. 3–124). Anchor Books.

Gregorio, V. L., & Arguelles, C. V. (forthcoming). #InstaMoms: Filipina influencers on idealized contemporary motherhood. *Review of Women's Studies, 32*(2).

Harner, H. M., & Riley, S. (2013). The impact of incarceration on women's mental health: Responses from women in a maximum-security prison. *Qualitative Health Research, 23*(1), 26–42.

Irwin, J., & Owen, B. (2005). Harm and the contemporary prison. In A. Liebling & S. Maruna (Eds.), *The effects of imprisonment* (1st ed., pp. 94–117). Willan.

Kruttschnitt, C. (2010). The paradox of women's imprisonment. *Daedalus, 139*(3), 32–42.

Kruttschnitt, C., & Gartner, R. (2005). *Marking time in the golden state: Women's imprisonment in California*. Cambridge University Press.

Kruttschnitt, C., Gartner, R., & Miller, A. (2000). Doing her own time? Women's responses to prison in the context of the old and the new penology. *Criminology, 38*(3), 681–718.

Licuanan, P. B. (1979). Aspects of child rearing in an urban low-income community. *Philippine Studies, 27*(4), 453–468.

Lindquist, C. H. (2000). Social integration and mental well-being among jail inmates. *Sociological Forum, 15*(3), 431–455.

Lockwood, K. (2018). Disrupted mothering: Narratives of mothers in prison. In T. Taylor & K. Bloch (Eds.), *Marginalized mothers, mothering from the margins* (pp. 157–173). Emerald Publishing Limited.

McVeigh, C. (1997). Motherhood experiences from the perspective of first-time mothers. *Clinical Nursing Research, 6*(4), 335–348.

Medina, B. (2015). *The Filipino family*. University of Philippines Press.

Moore, L. D., & Elkavich, A. (2008). Who's using and who's doing time: Incarceration, the war on drugs, and public health. *American Journal of Public Health, 98*(5), 782–786.

Narag, R. E., & Jones, C. (2020). The Kubol effect: Shared governance and cell dynamics in an overcrowded prison system in the Philippines. In J. Turner & V. Knight (Eds.), *The prison cell: Embodied and everyday spaces of incarceration* (pp. 71–94). Palgrave Macmillan.

Nieva, R. J. F. (2022). *Contextualising the intersection of reproductive well-being and incarceration: The case of Filipino women in prison* [Doctoral Thesis]. University of Otago, Dunedin, New Zealand. http://hdl.handle.net/10523/13480

Noble, C. (1995). *Prisoners' families: The everyday reality: An account of the experience of thirty people in Cambridgeshire with close relatives in prison*. Ormiston Charitable Trust.

Owen, B. (1999). The gendered consequences of the US imprisonment binge. In S. Cook & S. Davies (Eds.), *Harsh punishment: International experiences of women's imprisonment* (pp. 81–90). Northeastern University Press.

Panes, D. J. E. (2019). *War on drugs: Critical analysis of the legislation of other countries and their implication to Republic Act Number 9165 or the Comprehensive Dangerous Drugs Act of 2002*. [Unpublished postgraduate thesis]. Central Philippine University, Jaro, Iloilo City.

Parreñas, R. S. (2001). Mothering from a distance: Emotions, gender, and intergenerational relations in Filipino transnational families. *Feminist Studies, 27*(2), 361–390.

Parreñas, R. S. (2007). The gender ideological clash in globalization: Women, migration, and the modernization building project of the Philippines. *Social Thought & Research, 28*, 37–56.

Peracullo, J. C. (2017). Maria Clara in the twenty-first century: The uneasy discourse between the cult of the Virgin Mary and Filipino women's lived realities. *Religious Studies and Theology, 36*(2), 139–154.

Radosh, P. F. (2002). Reflections on women's crime and mothers in prison: A peacemaking approach. *Crime & Delinquency, 48*(2), 300–315.

Razurel, C., Kaiser, B., Sellenet, C., & Epiney, M. (2013). Relation between perceived stress, social support, and coping strategies and maternal well-being: A review of the literature. *Women & Health, 53*(1), 74–99.

Reyes, R. (2008). *Love, passion and patriotism: Sexuality and the Philippine propaganda movement*. Singapore National University of Singapore Press.

Sentse, M., Kreager, D. A., Bosma, A. Q., Nieuwbeerta, P., & Palmen, H. (2019). Social organization in prison: A social network analysis of interpersonal relationships among Dutch prisoners. *Justice Quarterly, 38*(6), 1–23.

Severance, T. A. (2005). "You know who you can go to": Cooperation and exchange between incarcerated women. *The Prison Journal*, *85*(3), 343–367.

Shamai, M., & Kochal, R.-b. (2008). "Motherhood starts in prison": The experience of motherhood among women in prison. *Family Process*, *47*(3), 323–340.

Shlafer, R. J., Hardeman, R. R., & Carlson, E. A. (2019). Reproductive justice for incarcerated mothers and advocacy for their infants and young children. *Infant Mental Health Journal*, *40*(5), 725–741.

Sufrin, C., Baird, S., Clarke, J., & Feldman, E. (2017). Family planning services for incarcerated women: Models for filling an unmet need. *International Journal of Prison Health*, *13*(1), 10–18.

Sykes, G. (1958). *The society of captives: A study of a maximum security prison*. Princeton University Press.

UNESCO Institute of Statistics. (2017). *Philippines*. http://uis.unesco.org/en/country/ph

Van den Bergh, B. J., Gatherer, A., Fraser, A., & Moller, L. (2011). Imprisonment and women's health: Concerns about gender sensitivity, human rights and public health. *Bulletin of World Health Organization*, *89*(9), 689–694.

Van Hout, M. C., & Mhlanga-Gunda, R. (2018). Contemporary women prisoners health experiences, unique prison health care needs and health care outcomes in sub Saharan Africa: A scoping review of extant literature. *BMC International Health and Human Rights*, *18*(1), 31.

Walker, S., & Worrall, A. (2000). Life as a woman: The gendered pains of indeterminate imprisonment. *Prison Service Journal*, *132*, 27–36.

Walmsley, R. (2017). *World female imprisonment list*. http://www.prisonstudies.org/sites/default/files/resources/downloads/world_female_prison_4th_edn_v4_web.pdf

Ward, D. A., & Kassebaum, G. G. (1966). *Women's prison: Sex and social structure*. Transaction Publishers.

Wilson, C. (2014). Semi-structured interviews. In C. Wilson (Ed.), *Interview techniques for UX practitioners* (pp. 23–41). Morgan Kaufmann.

Wismont, J. M. (2000). The lived pregnancy experience of women in prison. *Journal of Midwifery & Women's Health*, *45*(4), 292–300.

World Prison Brief. (2018). *World prison brief data: Philippines*. http://www.prisonstudies.org/country/philippines

CHAPTER 4

ACCEPTANCE IS KEY: TOWARD A FRAMEWORK FOR UNDERSTANDING SERIAL COHABITATION

Veronica L. Gregorio

ABSTRACT

Demographic and health surveys in the Philippines have shown a rise in cohabitation among young people. This chapter aims to provide an in-depth sociological understanding of a more specific phenomenon called serial cohabitation – referring to the dissolution of current cohabitation and entering a new one, and the continuation of the cycle if the new one ends again. By developing the framework of undisplaying and re-displaying family from Janet Finch's displaying family, this study posits that serial cohabiters experience a cycle of wanting to display an ideal family and having to undisplay every time the dissolution of the cohabiting relationship happens. This study demonstrates how serial cohabiters with children, in response to social stigma, exhibit resiliency toward stepfamily formation and committed sexual relationships. This chapter, therefore, conceptualizes "family acceptance" which refers to embracing the fluidity, reconfigurations, and "imperfections" of their newly formed family and "community acceptance" which covers the same affirmation from friends, neighbors, and extended relatives who are considered as relevant others by serial cohabiters. Family acceptance comes in three forms: first is the acceptance of/by children, second is the acceptance by the parents to the repeated stepfamily formation within their own homes, and third is the acceptance of

Resilience and Familism: The Dynamic Nature of Families in the Philippines
Contemporary Perspectives in Family Research, Volume 23, 51–64
ISSN: 1530-3535/doi:10.1108/S1530-353520230000023004

the woman herself to the possibility that cohabitation is the "happy ever after."
This study argues that once these forms are achieved, serial cohabiters become
more capable of undisplaying their previous family and displaying their new
family.

Keywords: Family; gender; serial cohabitation; stepfamily; Philippines;
motherhood

INTRODUCTION

The global increase in cohabitation and divorce is continuously threatening marriage as an institution. Cohabitation refers to a non-marital union wherein the couple is in a sexual relationship and living in the same residence. There are two distinguishable patterns of cohabitation: first is cohabitation as a prelude to marriage and second is cohabitation as an alternative to marriage (Macklin, 1980). The former sees cohabitation as a transitional stage, which will eventually lead to legal marriage while the latter views cohabitation as a form of rejection of the institution of marriage itself. The subjective meaning of cohabitation in Europe and Australia is linked to three concepts: commitment, testing, and freedom (Perelli-Harris et al., 2014). Marriage is continuously viewed as a form of union with higher commitment. Testing is seen as a necessary step for couples to "make sure that their commitment is high enough for marriage" (Perelli-Harris et al., 2014, p. 1066). The last concept of freedom relates to the freedom to choose marriage or not, and other forms of freedom such as financial expenditure and time use.

Individualism and secularism have also been linked to the rise of cohabitation. Covre-Sussai et al. (2015) found that while the traditional type of cohabitation in Latin America is practiced by youth (before they reach 20) as a strategy to cope with poverty and adolescent pregnancy, there are modern types of cohabitation that include higher educated women in their mid-twenties and older. A huge part of the "cohabitation boom" in the region, more specifically in Chile, Brazil, and Argentina, is due to the said new or modern type of cohabitation (Esteve et al., 2016). As Latin American women get more jobs, they delay marriages for their career stability but at the same time remain interested in testing out a romantic relationship by living together.

The provision of legal recognition to cohabiting couples so that they have the same rights and benefits as those of married couples is another factor that has led to the blurring of lines between the two forms of union. For instance, cohabitation in the Scandinavian region as a well-established practice since the 1960s has become a norm to the point that almost all marriages have gone through cohabitation for some time (for more details see Trost, 1975, 1981). Courts and family laws in the said region revised and adjusted their rules to accommodate issues of cohabiting couples with emphases ranging from access to welfare (pension and social security) to economic matters such as division of assets and properties in case of separation (Danielsen, 1983; Noack, 2001).

In the American context, intimate relationships are becoming difficult to maintain because it is highly dependent on the efforts of the couples, unlike in the 1950s when strict rules were provided by different institutions (Giddens, 1991). Cohabitation trends show that: first, it is a short-lived experience which ends mostly in the dissolution of relations instead of marriage. Second, poor women are more likely to use cohabitation as an alternative to marriage, and lastly, more children are being born from this union (Lichter et al., 2006; Smock, 2000). These trends point to the fact that, between men and women who enter and leave a cohabitative union, it is women who are more affected. Women are more likely to end up as a single mother and the ex-partner can choose not to support the child, depending on how the law will interpret his responsibilities and whether it will enforce them. This gender aspect is also underscored in the case of West Africa, where child marriage and cohabitation with a child are rampant. Parents marry off or give away their daughters in exchange for a dowry (Avogo & Somefun, 2019).

In the next sections, cohabitation in wider Asian contexts will be discussed and the specific sub-phenomenon called serial cohabitation will be further analyzed. With a focus on family and gender relations, the study will demonstrate how Filipina serial cohabiters with children, in response to social stigma, display a form of resiliency toward stepfamily formation and committed sexual relationships.

COHABITATION IN ASIA

While most scholarship on cohabitation tends to focus on Western countries, attention to the phenomenon has also been expanding in Asia. In the Islamic Central Asia, the practice is still relatively less prevalent (Dommaraju & Agadjanian, 2008) whereas in the Greater Middle East (which includes North Africa), cohabitation is increasing but remains illegal and is looked down upon by family and friends (Gebel & Heyne, 2014). Iranians have been more expressive in their position about cohabitation to the point that they even have a colloquial term for it: white marriage (see Rodziewicz, 2020). Similarly, in Muslim-majority countries in Southeast Asia such as Malaysia, cohabitation among Muslims is against the law but is becoming more common (Abdul Malek, 2016). There are no clear cohabitation statistics in the abovementioned regions because couples rarely declare, if at all, that they are cohabitating for fear of criminal sanctions.

In the largest countries in Asia, India, and China, cohabitation is also gaining popularity. For the former, although the complexity of the caste system continues to play a role in the family formation options of the individual, the globalizing economy has given way to the acceptance of cohabitation (Agrawal & Sengupta, 2013; Mishra, 2019). As a matter of fact, legal changes were also implemented in recognition of the union. The Protection of Women from Domestic Violence Act of 2005 used the term "shared household" instead of "marital relationship" in order to protect women who are in cohabiting unions, or more commonly referred to as "live-in couples" (Anuja, 2012). As for China, descriptive studies reveal that cohabitation rates tend to be higher in cities such as Shanghai as compared to Gansu, which is an interior province. Rates are also higher among non-communist party members, pointing out the impact of surveillance among individuals (Yu & Xie, 2015). By looking more particularly at the migration aspect, Mu and Yeung (2017) found that rural and urban migrants are more likely to experience cohabitation and longer migration leads to more cohabitation. Additionally, those who have ever cohabited are more likely to get married at the end. They found three factors that lead to cohabitation: more liberal attitudes toward cohabitation in the receiving community, less parental supervision, and lighter financial pressures associated with cohabitation as compared to marriage jointly contribute to migrants' choices of cohabitation (p. 22).

Migration is also examined vis-á-vis cohabitation trends in Thailand. Using surveys/survey data between 1978 and 1979, Cherlin and Chamratrithirong (1988) found that cohabitation was more widespread in rural regions and in slums compared to a proper Bangkok neighborhood. Esara (2012) also conducted an ethnographic research among cohabiting couples living in a Bangkok slum and found that while marriage was still an ideal goal, economic difficulties prevented them from doing so. In a different aspect, a study revealed that university students in Northern Thailand cohabit with their partners as they have relatively more freedom because they lived far from their families and were mostly staying in dormitories (Mukaew, 2000). To complement the previous study, Samart (2007) focused her work on migrant workers from villages who reside in Bangkok. The works of Mukaew (2000) and Samart (2007) highlight the geographical location of cohabiters as a factor in making the choice of living together. Samart's work is of particular importance in this chapter as her interview participants are serial cohabiters. Out of the 11 participants, 4 were married and with a child/children while the rest have previous cohabiting experiences.

Philippine Context

Cohabitation is not a new practice in the Philippines, although it has been slowly increasing overtime. Abalos (2017) pointed out that

> the lack of a divorce law in the Philippines and the prohibitive cost of obtaining legal separation or annulment may have contributed to the rise of cohabitation in the country. (p. 1537)

The increase is comparable to Latin America with similar colonial legacies and religious influences. Hence, in the Philippines, there also exists an old and new form of cohabitation. Earlier studies on cohabitation focus on the new form relating the phenomenon to liberal attitudes, secularism, higher access to education, and urbanization (Kabamalan, 2004; Williams et al., 2007; Xenos & Kabamalan, 2007). However, more recent work by Kuang et al. (2019), related to old forms of cohabitation, suggested that rising cohabitation is more linked to socio-economic disadvantage and instability among the younger population.

Stigma against cohabitation in the Philippines is present, although fading (Abalos, 2023a). Cohabitation still is deemed as "incomplete institution" (Nock, 1995) and marriage is popularly known as the end goal in traditional Filipino family formation (Roces, 2014). Women are nudged more often than men when it comes to questions on settling down and those who cohabit are usually warned. In recent years, public figures who admitted to being in a cohabiting relationship received mixed comments of support/criticism but mostly the latter. For instance, when Nadine Lustre (Filipino actress) described cohabiting relationships as "It's normal naman na (it's just normal now), come on guys! It's 2017!" a quick scan on Facebook and YouTube comments show statements such as "lugi ka dyan" (your losing in that set up), "baka hindi ka na pakasalan" (there's a chance he will not marry you anymore), or "wala ka na pag naghiwalay kayo" (you will be left with nothing when you break up), among many others. This is due to the strong social construct that links women's worth to virginity (Delgado-Infante & Ofreneo, 2014; Manalastas & David, 2018). If stigma is already present in the first instance of a cohabitative union, what more if these unions are repeatedly occurring? Following the social construction of virginity that is to be "given" to a man after marriage, cohabitation is seen as "giving" a gift without assurance (marriage). Serial cohabitation in this line is "repeatedly giving" sex to different men, and unfortunately, the woman's value decreases as sexual partners increase. In addition to such problematic lowering of value stigma to serial cohabitation, what would be the case if there are children involved? Most cohabiting union do not end in marriage (Lichter et al., 2016) but it does not guarantee that cohabiting couples will not have children – especially in the Philippines where abortion has always been illegal.

In a society where most people tend to question women about their plans for settling down, how are women who frequently disrupt the conventional linear pattern of family formation perceived and treated? This study focuses on serial cohabitation by women with children, their families, and communities where they belong to. While serial cohabiters in Bangkok, as shown by Samart (2007), are living away from their families, hence have more sexual and physical freedom from their local community's surveillance, the current study will reveal the experiences of serial cohabiters who live in their hometowns together with their parents and extended kin.

This chapter conceptualizes two types of acceptance: "family acceptance" and "community acceptance." The former refers to embracing the fluidity, reconfigurations, and "imperfections" of their newly formed family. Family acceptance comes in three forms: first is the acceptance by the children of the new partner. Second is the acceptance by the parents to the repeated stepfamily formation within their own homes. Third is the acceptance of the woman herself to the possibility that marriage can be out of the long-term plans. Community acceptance covers the same affirmation from friends, neighbors, and extended relatives who are considered as relevant others by serial cohabiters. This study argues that once these types and forms are achieved, serial cohabiters become more capable of undisplaying their previous family and re-displaying their new family.

Theoretical Approach: Undisplaying and Re-displaying Family

"Doing family" as a sociological frame developed from the concept of family practices (Morgan, 1996, 2011). Family practices put emphasis on the everyday activities to reproduce a set of relationship and derive meanings and expectations. In extending the said framework, Sociologist Janet Finch (2007) suggested that while families include a set of practices or activities that helps in "doing family," and the said doing should also be seen by others – in short, it needs to be "done" and "displayed." Displaying

> emphasizes the fundamentally social nature of family practices, where the meaning of one's actions has to be both conveyed to and understood by relevant others if those actions are to be effective as constituting "family" practices. (Finch, 2007, p. 66)

Hence while doing family is more focused on the family members themselves, displaying family incorporates both family members and relevant others/audience to let the latter know the existence of the said family.

"Displaying family" is necessary in today's context where transnational households are increasing, where additional forms of families are developing through new technologies (assisted reproductive technologies) or changes in legal processes (same-sex marriages, adoption, co-parenting, etc.). Displaying the family relationship to others is a way to ask for recognition and acknowledgment that, "hey we are not your usual/ideal family type but here we are doing things that you also do, and it works for us too." Tools for displaying family include hanging of photos, passing down of mementos, communicating family narratives, and doing family activities (for elaborate discussion see Finch, 2007). Establishing and reinforcing family practices, doing them, and displaying them entails invisible labor, mostly for women. Because of the gender roles and norms associated with femininity, motherhood, and the notion of home, women are expected to think about and carry most if not all of the necessary displaying to have the family acknowledged, may it be by the extended kin, neighborhood, or institutions like school or state.

In the context of this study, serial cohabitation among women with children suggests the need to display, undisplay, and re-display their families. Undisplaying and re-displaying family as a developing framework for family research highlights family members' actions toward each other and for the relevant others to know the status of the family relationship. Undisplaying by slowly or abruptly untying family relations with someone and re-displaying by slowly or abruptly introducing someone new until they are acknowledged (again) by relevant others. Compared to the dissolution of cohabitation for couples without children, undisplaying and re-displaying are important in serial cohabitation and remarriages for couples with children because new people are joining the family to attempt to rebuild the previous one and to "do" family in ways the children would also accept and understand.

Undisplaying and re-displaying family is a way to let people know that "something happened, it did not work out, and now I am trying again." The expressions for undisplaying and re-displaying can be verbal (by directly explaining that the relationship has ended), physical (by appearing in church/school with the children but without the partner), or visual/written (by slowly posting photos, videos, or text statuses on social media).

METHODOLOGY

Drawing from ethnography (2014–2019) and netnography (2020–present) with Filipino families, this study grasps the views on romantic partnerships not just of the women and their partners, but also that of their families and neighbors. The data are based on the author's graduate research projects (for details see Gregorio, 2015, 2018, 2020b). During the duration of the research fieldwork, the author engaged with about 45–60 families using formal key interviews, focused group discussions, and ethnography. The author kept in touch with these families and communities since 2015, and while actual or personal visits became impossible due to the COVID-19 pandemic, "ongoing and mediated fieldwork" (Gregorio, 2020a) was used to stay updated with 10 families.

There are three field sites for the current study: Manila, Davao del Sur, and Facebook. First in Manila where the author conducted a semester of internship and another semester of data gathering in an urban poor community. The hosts include the Center for Women's Resources and Samahan ng Maralitang Kababaihang Nagkakaisa (SAMAKANA) or Organisation of United Urban Poor Women. As the author is also from Manila (5.4 km away), and SAMAKANA cannot find a host family who can take the author in to stay in the community during the research, the author traveled daily to do ethnography. The second site is a farming community in Davao del Sur where the author was supported by the Ateneo de Manila Institute of Philippine Culture and the local barangay officials. The author stayed in the village with one research assistant hosted by one family for the whole duration of the data gathering. Lastly, limited but direct communication was done through Facebook messenger and regular interactions were done through Facebook. Interactions include liking posts, reacting to them, and commenting. In the same manner, they also interact with the author's posts. While some netnographers choose to create a separate social media for research, my account is both for personal use and for the said ongoing and mediated fieldwork.

One limitation of this work is that partners of women serial cohabiters either do not have social media or they used to have multiple accounts. This is because they tend to buy and sell their mobile phones where their Facebook is logged in and they cannot retrieve the same account on the next mobile phone. Hence, when tagged on photos or videos, old accounts are showing up, except for Rose's partner who is consistently active on Facebook.

Acceptance of/by Children

Dalawa pala anak ninyo! (So you have two kids!), *Ay hindi po ate, sa una po yan pero anak ko na rin* (No sister, that's from the first (partner) but he is like my child too). Ryan was waiting for Judy when he explained that the child he was holding was "from the first (partner)" and technically not his, but "he is like his child too." During the early part of the study (2015), Judy had two daughters, the eldest is with a previous cohabiting partner of two years and the second child is with Ryan. The two live at Judy's parents' home. The couple were both in their early twenties and hence could get married if they wanted to. However, Judy shared that they might wait for a few more years until they were financially capable of marrying and having their own home.

In the succeeding visits to the community toward the end of 2018, Judy mentioned that their children are already attending nursery and primary school. In 2020, I saw on Judy's Facebook update that she is pregnant with her third child (second with Ryan). In a personal message through Facebook, she told me that they plan to get married (at the Mayor's office) after the pandemic. They continue to stay with Judy's parents and have no plans to move out any time soon.

The case of Judy is not uncommon in the community. In one instance, a parent (mid-40s) of another teenage mother confided, "Why will I expect them to get married? I am not married myself!" She is currently living with her cohabiting partner (which she calls husband despite not being married) and six children (with two different fathers). Her husband also has children from a different woman but he does not see them regularly and they are also not married. In the early stages of the fieldwork on teenage pregnancy, older women would also ask the author, "Anak, are you looking for married pregnant or just pregnant? Because most of our daughters are not married but the boyfriends are living with us!" There is no available data about the number of actually married couples and cohabiting ones in Tondo Manila, but for almost a year of house-to-house visits, there are very few households with a displayed wedding or civil union photo in their living room area. As a wedding ceremony is seen as a mark of social status (Esara, 2012), Filipino families usually display proof of the ceremony in the form of a picture. The lack of it is indicative of the potential dominant union formation in the urban poor community which is cohabitation.

This work posits that "active anonymizing"[1] of the names of the first or previous cohabiting partners is a way of undisplaying family. "Sa una" (the first) or "Yung mga una ko" (my firsts) are used by serial cohabiters to let the relevant others know that "the first" or "firsts" are no longer present and longed for. Moreover, it is done in front of the children so that they would also be aware of the status of their father who is no longer around, and whose name their mother does not even want to mention. Re-displaying on the other hand is led by Judy as she posted her pregnancy update on Facebook, tagging Ryan as the father and by updating on messenger that they also have plans to get married. The photo she posted also includes all the children. The re-displaying of the whole family shows an "ideal" family with mother, father, and children and the likes and congratulatory comments by her friends and relatives indicate a sign of acknowledgment.

Acceptance by the Parents

Naku, buntis na naman siya! (Oh my, she is pregnant again!) *Doon po sa pangalawa?* (With the second partner?) *Hindi, pero mas okay 'to!* (No! This is a different guy but he is better (than the second)!) Clara is sharing the news about the second pregnancy of her youngest daughter, Rose, during my 2019 fieldwork in Davao del Sur. Rose got pregnant with her first boyfriend in 2015. She was only 17 then and could not marry yet. They lived together with the parents of the guy in the next village. However, things got out of hand after she gave birth and she did not feel welcomed at her parents-in-law's house. The couple then moved to Rose's parents' house but eventually broke up. Sometimes the guy will visit the son and take him to his parents' home for family occasions then return him after a week. In her next relationship, Rose cohabited again. Clara mentioned that she is actually thankful that Rose did not get pregnant with the second boyfriend because he seems to be close-fisted with the eldest son.

When Rose introduced the third boyfriend and asked if he could live in their house, Clara and her husband agreed. Not all parents will support such a decision, but according to Clara, "This one is mature and very caring with my grandson. I can see it. Maybe things will be okay." Rose's parents treat her previous and current partners as their own son too. Clara calls them "anak" (gender neutral for son/daughter) and "manugang" (gender neutral for in-law) interchangeably when speaking about them. She uses "yung una/pangalawa kong manugang" (my first-/ second-in-law ...) to narrate stories with the author and the neighbors. To some extent, while the neighbors are not very supportive of Rose's serial cohabitation, they gradually learned to be open to it. To illustrate, during the annual fiesta (community event), the neighbors gathering led to talking about Rose, and one of Clara's friends interjected, "Kung yung magulang nga natanggap, e bakit tayo hindi? Sino ba tayo sa buhay niya?" (If Rose's parents accept her decisions, why can't we? Who are we in her life?)

In Philippines, where generational hierarchies exist, acceptance by the parents will eventually lead to acceptance by the community. The "public labelling" as son and first-/second-in-law is a way of re-displaying family. As revealed, without Clara's effort to talk about her daughter's partners this way, the community will most likely not recognize the family. It has to be noted that while Clara's husband is doing the same labeling, it is not as active as Clara's actions. Women's invisible labor in displaying, undisplaying, and re-displaying family is obvious in this case. The labor did not end during Clara's motherhood, as discussed, it is continuing during her life stage as a grandmother.

Acceptance of Cohabitation as the Happy Ever After

Judy and Ryan have been cohabiting for 7 years now. Will they ever get married? Perhaps. As of our last conversation (2022), it sounded that Judy is still positive about getting married. She shared, "we are saving money now and I am a regular cleaner again because I got vaccinated already," referring to being a regular on-call house helper again since she lost her job during the pandemic. She did not give any updates about Ryan's work though. Last time I was at their home, he was working as *palero* (scavenger) with his father and brother. Since he is not active on Facebook, there is no way for me to know if he is also thinking the same about marriage. In spite of the fact that community members and neighbors are recognizing Judy, Ryan, and her children as a family unit, and no longer expecting them to get married, it is not the happy ever after that Judy is imagining. This complements studies which show that Filipinos still do not see cohabitation as an alternative but rather a pathway to marriage (Abalos, 2023b). However, as wedding ceremonies entail logistical preparation and expenses, Judy is aware that their wedding might not happen.

As for Rose, she gave birth to her third child (second with the third cohabiting partner) and asked me to be a godmother. Unfortunately, I was not able to attend the Christening due to the pandemic. More recently on Facebook, she changed her profile photo to a studio family portrait with her partner and the two children. The following week, she also changed her last name on Facebook to that of her current partner. When I asked through Facebook messenger if she got married already, she said "No, Ate. But we are one happy family and it's basically the same. Acceptance is key!" The last line is an inside joke because she started selling beauty products online and she keeps on posting: "DM (direct message) is key."

Such "self-announcement," referring to Rose's act of changing of her last name into her partner's last name and calling him "*asawa ko*" (my husband), both on Facebook and in person interaction with others, despite not being married shows that she has accepted their cohabiting set up as the happy ever after of her story. The fluidities and complexities of relationship and family formation processes will only appear once the researcher learns how referring to "asawa ko" does not necessarily mean being legally married – sometimes it means, "in my mind, we are married."

CONCLUSION

This study has shown how the family acceptance of repetitive cohabiting unions happens in three forms. First is the acceptance of/by children (from the previous partner) by the new partner and the other way around for the children. This is shown in how new partners acknowledge the children of the women and call them "anak/child" in the most standard manner. The children being comfortable with the new cohabiting partner of their mother, in photos or meal time or during activities like going to the farm or hanging out in the common areas of the community, is a sign of their acceptance.

The second form is the acceptance of the woman's parents to the repeated stepfamily formation within their own homes. Parents of the serial cohabiters do not show strong approval or disapproval of the cohabitation, but they shared in similar ways that it is important for them to know the guy closely. In this sense, while cohabiting couples use the union to "know the partner better" or to "test compatibility," it shows here that even the parents are thinking the same way. Once parents start publicly labeling their child's partner as anak and/or manugang, it marks the acceptance of his status as part of the family. The label does not disappear once the relationship ends, especially if there are children involved.

The third form is the acceptance of the woman herself to the possibility that marriage can be out of the long-term plans. Rose made a strong stance on this, as she announced on social media that she has a whole family and that for her, her family name has already changed. Neighbors and cousins commented and congratulated her on the photo and the support of her partner was expressed further when they both changed their Facebook status from single to married. It should be noted that Rose initiated that the family goes to a studio for a formal/proper photoshoot. Such visual imagery is strong because photoshoot is commonly done by families when there is a celebratory event.

Moreover, community acceptance is seen in the improving interactions between cohabiters and their friends, neighbors, and extended relatives who they consider as relevant others. The reference to cohabiters' families as family, the open discussion and defense of Clara's friend toward her choices, and the similar use of labels (in-law and son) by the neighbors show this form of acceptance. Overall, undisplaying and re-displaying of a family as a framework uncovers how "active anonymizing," "public labeling," and "self-announcement" allow serial cohabiters with children to proceed with their everyday lives, despite the stigma. As researchers continue to explore the family and community interactions of unconventional family forms, other ways of undisplaying and re-displaying of the family will be observed.

RECOMMENDATIONS

This work highlights the role of parents in the cohabiting and stepfamily formation and therefore invites family scholars of the Philippines to explore the adjustment process of aging parents to the serial cohabitation of their adult children. Unlike the studies in Western contexts that are focused on the individual's and couples' decision-making processes, the discussions above illustrate how serial cohabitation in the Philippine context is enmeshed with the lives of the couple's respective families and communities, especially in households with three or more generations of families.

Additionally, the roles of changing representations in relationship and family formation in popular media should also be examined. Nadine Lustre and James Reid in their 2018 movie, *Never Not Love You*, represents a couple who then decides to cohabit, using the line "marry without a ring," and later migrate and live together overseas without getting married. In the same year, Kathryn Bernardo and Daniel Padilla's *The How's of Us* also featured a story about a young couple who also cohabited in their family's ancestral house. There are various aspects that need to be explored in studying cohabiting partnerships in order to understand how couples perceive themselves and how these perceptions remain or change in the future.

ACKNOWLEDGEMENTS

The first version of this paper was presented at the 13th Next Generation Global Workshop: New Risks and Resilience in Asian Societies and the World, hosted by the Kyoto University Asian Studies Unit (KUASU) and the Vietnam Academy of Social Science (VASS) in 2020. Critical engagements from the facilitators and participants helped in shaping the arguments and framing of the paper. The author would also like to thank the members of the Gender and Sexuality Research Cluster (GSRC) writing group of the NUS Faculty of Arts and Social Sciences for the support and feedback during the workshops in 2021.

NOTE

1. I thank the reviewer for pointing out that not mentioning the name of another person is not entirely unique to serial cohabiters. For example, mothers refer to their children as "panganay," "bunso," etc. when recounting stories about them to other people. However, it is different in this context as "active anonymizing" is deliberately being done to respect the current partner and for children to be more familiar with the family situation (where the current partner is the one acknowledged as part of the family).

REFERENCES

Abalos, J. B. (2017). Divorce and separation in the Philippines: Trends and correlates. *Demographic Research, 36*(50), 1515–1548.

Abalos, J. B. (2023a). Do Filipinos still say "I do"? The continuing increase in non-marriage and cohabitation in the Philippines. *Journal of Family Issues*.

Abalos, J. B. (2023b). A demographic portrait of the Filipino family: A glimpse from the recent past. In *Resilience and familism: The dynamic nature of families in the Philippines*. Contemporary Perspectives in Family Research. Emerald.

Abdul Malek, N. B. (2016). Is cohabitation an alternative to marriage? *Procedia – Social and Behavioral Sciences, 219*, 12–18.

Anuja, A. (2012). Law and 'live-in' relationships in India. *Economic and Political Weekly, 47*(39), 50–56.

Agrawal, A., & Sengupta, P. (2013). Globalization and live-in relations: From immortality to acceptability. *Journal of Politics and Governance, 2*(3 and 4), 256–261.

Avogo, W. A., & Somefun, O. D. (2019). Early marriage, cohabitation, and childbearing in West Africa. *Journal of Environmental and Public Health, 2019*(June), 1–10. https://doi.org/10.1155/2019/9731756.

Cherlin, A., & Chamratrithirong, A. (1988). Variations in marriage patterns in central Thailand. *Demography, 25*(3), 337. https://doi.org/10.2307/2061536.

Covre-Sussai, M., Meuleman, B., Botterman, S., & Matthijs, K. 2015. Traditional and modern cohabitation in Latin America: A comparative typology. *Demographic Research, 32*(May), 873–914. https://doi.org/10.4054/DemRes.2015.32.32.

Danielsen, S. (1983). Unmarried partners: Scandinavian law in the making. *Oxford Journal of Legal Studies, 3*(1), 59–76.

Delgado-Infante, M. L., & Ofreneo, M. A. P. (2014). Maintaining a 'Good Girl' position: Young Filipina women constructing sexual agency in first sex within Catholicism. *Feminism & Psychology, 24*(3), 390–407. https://doi.org/10.1177/0959353514530715.

Dommaraju, P., & Agadjanian, V. (2008). Nuptiality in Soviet and Post-Soviet Central Asia. *Asian Population Studies, 4*(2), 195–213. https://doi.org/10.1080/17441730802247463.

Esara, P. (2012). Moral scrutiny, marriage inequality: Cohabitation in Bangkok, Thailand. *The Asia Pacific Journal of Anthropology, 13*(3), 211–227. https://doi.org/10.1080/14442213.2012.680486.

Esteve, A., Lesthaeghe, R. J., López-Gay, A., & García-Román, J. (2016). The rise of cohabitation in Latin America and the Caribbean, 1970–2011. In A. Esteve & R. J. Lesthaeghe (Eds.), *Cohabitation and marriage in the Americas: Geo-historical legacies and new trends* (pp. 25–57). Springer International Publishing. https://doi.org/10.1007/978-3-319-31442-6_2

Finch, J. (2007). Displaying families. *Sociology, 41*(1), 65–81. https://doi.org/10.1177/0038038507072284

Gebel, M., & Heyne, S. (2014). *Transitions to adulthood in the Middle East and North Africa young women's rising?* Palgrave Macmillan.

Giddens, A. (1991). *Modernity and self-identity: Self and society in the late modern age.* Stanford University Press.

Gregorio, V. (2018). The only exception: Teenage pregnancy in the Philippines. *Review of Women's Studies, 28,* 1–28.

Gregorio, V. L. (2015). *Maagang Pagbubuntis: Mga Kwento Sa Likod Ng Kwenta.* University of the Philippines.

Gregorio, V. L. (2020a). *Farm and familialism in Southeast Asia: Gender and generational relations in Malaysian and Philippine villages* [Ph.D. thesis]. National University of Singapore, Singapore.

Gregorio, V. L. (2020b). Isolation and immunity within the family: Commuter marriages in Southeast Asia. *Current Sociology, 70*(5 November), 703–719. https://doi.org/10.1177/0011392120972143.

Jones, G. W., & Yeung, W.-J. J. (2014). Marriage in Asia. *Journal of Family Issues, 35*(12), 1567–1583. https://doi.org/10.1177/0192513X14538029.

Kabamalan, M. M. M. (2004). New path to marriage: The significance of increasing cohabitation in the Philippines. In *7th international conference on Philippine studies,* June 16–19, 2004, Leiden.

Kuang, B., Perelli-Harris, B., & Padmadas, S. (2019). The unexpected rise of cohabitation in the Philippines: Evidence of socioeconomic disadvantage or a second demographic transition? *Asian Population Studies, 15*(1), 8–27. https://doi.org/10.1080/17441730.2018.1560664.

Lichter, D. T., Qian, Z., & Mellott, L. M. (2006). Marriage or dissolution? Union transitions among poor cohabiting women. *Demography, 43*(2), 223–240. https://doi.org/10.1353/dem.2006.0016.

Lichter, D. T., Michelmore, K., Turner, R. N. & Sassler, S. (2016). Pathways to a stable union? Pregnancy and childbearing among cohabiting and married couples. *Population Research and Policy Review, 35*(3), 377–399. https://doi.org/10.1007/s11113-016-9392-2.

Macklin, E. D. (1980). Nontraditional family forms: A decade of research. *Journal of Marriage and the Family, 42*(4), 905. https://doi.org/10.2307/351832.

Manalastas, E. J., & David, C. C. (2018). Valuation of women's virginity in the Philippines. *Asian Women, 34*(1), 23–48. https://doi.org/10.14431/aw.2018.03.34.1.23.

Mishra, S. (2019). Grappling with live-in-relations: Respectability, dutifulness, and sexual desire among migrant young middle class women in Bangalore. *OMNES: The Journal of Multicultural Society, 9*(1), 110–147. https://doi.org/10.14431/omnes.2019.01.9.1.110.

Morgan, D. H. J. (1996). *Family connections: An introduction to family studies.* Polity Press; Blackwell Publishers.

Morgan, D. H. J. (2011). Rethinking family practices. In *Palgrave Macmillan studies in family and intimate life.* Palgrave Macmillan.

Mu, Z., & Yeung, W. J. J. (2017). How migration influences cohabitation and divorce: A mixed-method study in China. *Annual Meeting of the Population Association of America.* Chicago.

Mukaew, S. (2000). *Non-marital cohabitation: The case of university students* [MA thesis]. Thammasat University, Thailand.

Noack, T. (2001). Cohabitation in Norway: An accepted and gradually more regulated way of living. *International Journal of Law, Policy and the Family, 15*(1), 102–117. https://doi.org/10.1093/lawfam/15.1.102.

Nock, S. L. (1995). A comparison of marriages and cohabiting relationships. *Journal of Family Issues, 16*(1), 53–76.

Perelli-Harris, B., Berrington, A., Berghammer, C., Keizer, R., Lappegård, T., Mynarska, M., Evans, A., Isupova, O., Klaerner, A., & Vignoli, D. (2014). Towards a new understanding of cohabitation: Insights from focus group research across Europe and Australia. *Demographic Research, 31*(November), 1043–1078. https://doi.org/10.4054/DemRes.2014.31.34.

Roces, M. (2014). Migration and the rethinking of the Filipino family over one-hundred years, 2006–2010. Paper presented at the 3rd Philippine Studies Conference of Japan.

Rodziewicz, M. (2020). The legal debate on the phenomenon of 'white marriages' in contemporary Iran. *Anthropology of the Middle East, 15*(1), 50–63. https://doi.org/10.3167/ame.2020.150105.

Samart, S. (2007). *Unmarried cohabitation in Thailand: The case of migrant workers in Bangkok* [MA thesis]. Lund University, Sweden.

Smock, P. J. (2000). Cohabitation in the United States: An appraisal of research themes, findings, and implications. *Annual Review of Sociology, 26*(1), 1–20. https://doi.org/10.1146/annurev.soc.26.1.1.

Trost, J. (1975). Married and unmarried cohabitation: The case of Sweden, with some comparisons. *Journal of Marriage and the Family, 37*(3), 677. https://doi.org/10.2307/350532.

Trost, J. (1981). Cohabitation in the Nordic countries: From deviant phenomenon to social institution. *Alternative Lifestyles, 4*(4), 401–427. https://doi.org/10.1007/BF01094175.

Williams, L., Kabamalan, M., & Ogena, N. (2007). Cohabitation in the Philippines: Attitudes and behaviors among young women and men. *Journal of Marriage and Family 69*(5), 1244–1256. https://doi.org/10.1111/j.1741-3737.2007.00444.x.

Xenos, P., & Kabamalan, M. M. M. (2007). Emerging forms of union formation in the Philippines: Assessing levels and social distributions. *Asian Population Studies, 3*(3), 263–286. https://doi.org/10.1080/17441730701746417.

Yu, J., & Xie, Y. (2015). Cohabitation in China: Trends and determinants. *Population and Development Review, 41*(4), 607–628. https://doi.org/10.1111/j.1728-4457.2015.00087.x.

CHAPTER 5

SELECTED CASES OF TEENAGE FATHERHOOD IN THE PHILIPPINES: AN ANALYSIS OF RISKS AND RESILIENCE

Joselito G. Gutierrez, Tisha Isabelle M. De Vergara and Clarence M. Batan

ABSTRACT

This chapter examines the life histories of selected teenage Filipino fathers relative to their experiences of dating, courtship, and the discovery, engagement, and experimentation with risk-taking behaviors such as smoking, drinking alcohol, and premarital sex. Using an interpretative phenomenological analysis (IPA), this study conducts family genogram and in-depth semi-structured interviews among eight teenage fathers. In so doing, it interrogates the consequences of sexual behaviors to the well-being of their respective families of orientation as well as the future of their expected family of procreation. The chapter argues how the risks of teenage fatherhood in the Philippines are relatively mitigated by the general conservative culture of Filipino families and the Catholic sense of religious orientation that seems to provide resilience captured in three themed experiences of "natauhan" (realization), "pinangatawanan" (accountability), and "pinanindigan" (owning responsibility). Thus, this chapter unravels the voices of young Filipino teenage fathers who straddles, on the one hand, the risk of premarital sex and pregnancy, and on the other hand, the challenges of responsible parenthood. In conclusion, the chapter provides

Resilience and Familism: The Dynamic Nature of Families in the Philippines
Contemporary Perspectives in Family Research, Volume 23, 65–81
Copyright © 2023 by Emerald Publishing Limited
All rights of reproduction in any form reserved
ISSN: 1530-3535/doi:10.1108/S1530-353520230000023005

policy insights on sex education and gender equality training for the vulnerable Filipino youth in the country.

Keywords: Teenage fatherhood; risk-taking behaviors; premarital sex; responsible parenthood; gender equality; life history

INTRODUCTION

In the Philippines, the issue of teenage pregnancy and sexual promiscuity (i.e., premarital sex) often directs attention to socio-cultural considerations linked with Filipinos' adherence to religious values and conservative culture of marriage and family life. Traditionally, Filipinos espouse sexual intercourse only within the context of marriage wherein women are expected to remain chaste, pure, and untouched for their future husband. On the other hand, Filipino males are allowed to engage in sexual activities outside of marriage. For many males, dating is perceived as a way "to satisfy sexual desires" while for many females, it is a way "to get to know the person better" and assess him as a possible partner in the future (Tan et al., 2001).

The culture of sexual promiscuity among males is highly linked with machismo and they are even expected to engage in premarital sex (Medina, 2015). Their first sexual encounter is called "binyag" (baptism). In fact, an adolescent male can only be called "tunay na lalake" (true man) after he experienced his first sex (Tan et al., 2001). This cultural practice is coming from the idea that single males have nothing to lose.

As observed, for Filipinos, learning about sex and sexual acts is often perceived as bad and is not to be discussed. For instance, Batangan (2006) found out that for many Filipinos, talking about sex is considered taboo. Parents and children avoid talking about sex for it is perceived as *bastos* (disrespectful). At the same time, it is also sacred as the passage way to conceiving life, sex should only be discussed in a reverent manner. Utmost care and respect in discussing sex also lead to a culture of not talking about it in a more detailed way especially in the family.

Accordingly, engaging with sexual behaviors at a young age may lead to unwanted pregnancies. While many studies are already available concerning the risks of early pregnancies, teenage mothers, and the like, very little are available when it comes to teenage fatherhood. In the Philippines where fathers are expected to fulfill the roles of provider and protector, it also becomes complex when a young man is faced with the challenge of taking on these roles and responsibilities of being a father. This emphasizes the need to include teenage fatherhood in the discussions of early and unwanted pregnancies. This imbalance in the number of studies led this study to focus on the experiences of Filipino teenage fathers, particularly the antecedent events that lead them to become young fathers, their resilience, and their experiences of withstanding challenges in their attempts to prove themselves become responsible fathers. Thus, this chapter unravels the voices of young Filipino teenage fathers who straddle, on the one hand, the risk of pre-marital sex and pregnancy, and on the other hand, the challenges of responsible parenthood.

LITERATURE REVIEW

Teenage Fatherhood in the Philippines

In attaining manhood, one is considered capable of fathering once he becomes a "man." Accordingly, manhood (*pagkalalake*) is considered as both sexual prowess and being responsible for the family. Teenage males feel like a man by achieving financial independence even at a young age, and should they father a child, having the capability in becoming a provider and a protector of a family. Teenage males feel validated as they transition to become young fathers when they can independently provide for the needs of their families, though this is rare since they are still young and most of them are still studying (Kirven, 2014). For others, they identified events such as circumcision; sexual prowess such as exposure to adult films and magazines, masturbation, first dating, and first coitus experience; and various sports, and risk-taking activities such as smoking, drinking alcohol, drug use, dating, necking, and oral sex. However, teenage fatherhood may be considered unacceptable because teenagers are ste-reotyped as irresponsible and are not yet prepared for parental responsibility. Interestingly, teenage mothers are usually stigmatized as careless by "more care-ful" youth while teenage fathers are deemed responsible for their own family (Gregorio, 2018).

Role of Family and Culture

An individual is greatly influenced by family traditions and practices where behaviors, values, and attitudes are first learned (Laigo et al., 2009). Parents are a child's first teachers as they influence the child's behavior and the way the child thinks and rationalizes. Accordingly, a father's involvement in his child's life is directly connected to an increase in cognitive functioning, greater internal locus of control, greater empathy, and less sex role stereotyping (Lamb, 2004 cited in Long et al., 2014). At the same time, his involvement is explicitly connected to his increased confidence, lower psychological distress, and increased life satisfac-tion (Daly et al., 2009 as cited in Long et al., 2014). However, Casselman and Rosenbaum (2014) claimed that young males' aggressive behaviors are associ-ated with their own father's aggressive behaviors. On the other hand, a father's absence limits the male child's identification of a masculine role model (Aguiling-Dalisay et al., 2000). It is also seen as detrimental as many of the economic, social, and emotional aspects of the father's role will go unmet (Lamb, 1996 cited in Aguiling-Dalisay et al., 2000).

For many families in the Philippines, a man who has impregnated a woman, whether engaged or not, is pressured to marry the woman. Marriage is expected to save the female's honor and provide legitimacy to the child. Further, a male must be "man enough" to take the responsibility of becoming a father to his child. The Filipino value of *hiya* (shame) motivates a man to take responsibility for his ego and because his family's reputation is at stake (Bulatao & Gorospe, 1966). On the other hand, a pregnant woman out of wedlock must get married immediately to avoid shame and to avoid becoming the subject of gossip in her neighborhood (Medina, 2015). This cultural rule is very much true of teenagers. Thus, while psycho-emotional maturity is still lacking at their early age, many adolescents get married despite the absence of meaningful love and preparedness for family life.

Sex Education and Role of Media

Information about sex and sexuality is usually acquired from parents, teachers, as well as friends. Even if R.A. 9710 or the Magna Carta of Women (2010) encourages sex education to start at home, parents are seen as limited in their ability to offer this sensitive information due to conservatism. On the other hand, the school provides clinical and scientific information as part of the curriculum (Conaco et al., 2003). Generally, boys are not taught adequately about the anatomy of their reproductive organs. More often, mothers closer to their sons have inadequate information on male sexuality, leading the boys to get information from peer groups (Wormer, 2017).

Likewise, mass media is another sector that fills in the void for proper information about sex. At the same time, it is often blamed for teens' early exposure to sexuality. In fact, studies say that it has the most pervading influence on today's youth (Agarwal & Dhanasekaran, 2012). In the United States, the youth engage in sexual activity at an early age and with different partners (Chaves et al., 2005), blaming mass media as the culprit due to its strong influence to them. Straubhaar et al. (2014) attributed males' indiscreet behaviors and attitudes toward women to too much exposure to pornography. Another study depicted how young men's monopoly in sexual knowledge (i.e., watching videos and engaging in sexual activities) significantly influences how their female partners perceive sex and make sense of their sexual experiences (Gregorio, 2018).

Adolescence and Risky Behaviors

In many societies, adolescence is acknowledged as the most troublesome and stressful stage since it bridges the gap from childhood to adulthood (Papalia et al., 2009). Hence, being at the transitional stage of "unbecoming of a child – becoming an Adult" meant a period of undergoing big adjustments in all three domains – the physical, cognitive, and psychosocial. In physical development, the rate of increase in height is at its peak at 12.5–14 years of age while muscle strength develops at 15–16 years of age (Wormer, 2017). Cognitive skills were also directly associated with pubertal development (Koerselman & Pekkarinen, 2017). A related study pointed out that teenage males were relatively more emotionally stable, emotionally progressive, socially adjusting, have adequate personalities, and were more independent due to the patriarchal system, gender bias, family climate, and traditions among others (Rawat & Singh, 2017). This thinking leads to their own beliefs that they are special, unique, safe, and protected, resulting in carelessness in their doings.

Adolescence is a time in human development when many individuals are compelled to try on new roles, behaviors, and attitudes in life including building relationships with other individuals (Alampay et al., 2009; Papalia et al., 2009). Thus, this is the period for many young people who try to take risks in health-compromising activities such as taking illegal drugs, drinking, smoking, extreme sports, and engaging in sexual activity. Risk-taking is an important component of adolescence, it is a thrill-seeking stage necessary for the acquisition of adult behaviors, skills, and self-esteem (Hendry & Kloep, 2002).

In the Philippines, adolescence is a period of blossoming or more popularly known to Filipinos as *pagbibinata or pagdadalaga* (Batangan, 2006). Accordingly, it is not only referred to as a period in an individual's life but also a route wherein a person is entering the process of becoming a young adult. Development involves two processes – maturation and learning. It is a transitional stage where one evolves to full sexual and psychological maturity and from the state of total dependence to relative independence (Conaco et al., 2003). It also marks the onset of deliberate sexually motivated behavior – for girls, sex is motivated by love and a desire for a serious relationship and for boys, sex is motivated by the desire to enhance their status with peers (Steinberg, 2012). For Alampay et al. (2009), influences that contribute to family success are family structure, parental influence, perceptions of parental control or discipline, family dynamics, and family religious practices. Accordingly, adolescents with strong attachments to their family members are more likely to avoid risky behaviors compared to those who are in a family that lacks attachment.

Adolescents' risky and careless decisions are usually attributed to peer pressure. Studies showed that teens follow peer influence simply because of parental absenteeism. Teenagers turn to their peers not only for friendship and companionship but for nurturing, intimacy, security, and guidance as well (Conaco et al., 2003). Also, teenagers choose friends of similar interests or they want to be in a group with the people they admire. On the other hand, adolescents are more likely to engage in premarital sex when their peers are open to it and doing it (Zimmer-Gembeck & Helfand, 2008 cited in Kail, 2010).

Parenthood and Difficulties of Becoming Fathers

Teenage fathers use different styles in order to cope with the challenges of fatherhood. In the Philippines, Arca (2002) found out that becoming a father at an early age is a major challenge to overcome because it happened during a stage of transition where one is not yet prepared. For instance, Filipinos' patriarchal values put high regard on the role of fathers as an economic provider. Given this, teenage fathers are often afraid of their financial responsibility to both their child and their child's mother. If he is the eldest in the family, he may have responsibilities not only to his parents but also to his other siblings who are in need (Aguilar, 2009 cited in Medina, 2015).

The challenges also include emotional stability for the relationship, a sense of stability in the place where the baby will be raised in, the burden of marrying the mother of his child, and the pressure to work hard in order to offer a bright future for his child. Their fears associated with dealing with teenage pregnancy include fear of their family's anger, fear of the girl's family's reaction, fear of lack of resources to support a family, and lastly, the fear for the child's future.

Adolescents abrupt transitioning to fatherhood is inevitable. Teenage fathers utilize different styles in order to deal with the challenges brought by young parenthood. To cope with the changes, Guillermo and de Guzman (2007) enumerated varied sources of strengths such as self-confidence, supportive and stable family, responsible parents, caring classmates and teachers, genuine friends, student-friendly schools, and a committed church and community. Other modes of coping include praying, keeping feelings to oneself, redirecting self to other pleasurable things, and recreation.

In the Philippines, coping mechanisms are usually connected to religion and spirituality. Religion really runs in the blood of Filipinos and innate religiosity enables them to comprehend and accept challenges in the context of faith (Palispis, 2007). Filipinos, being God-centered and God-fearing people, always rely on God especially during heavy times. It explicitly expressed the Filipino attitude "bahala na" in which it has both positive and negative connotations. It is interpreted as the Filipino attitude of accepting suffering and problems and leaving everything to God.

This literature review directs attention to some research gaps which this chapter intends to respond to particularly about the nature and characteristics of Filipino teenage fatherhood as a social phenomenon in terms of roles, influences, demands, and coping social mechanisms. In so doing, this chapter intends to describe the "inner view," inner dynamics, and experiences of selected Filipino teenage fathers.

METHODS

This qualitative research study used the IPA method composed of two parts: phenomenology and interpretation. It reports the participants' reflection of their own lived experiences based on the researcher's personal interpretations: conceptions, beliefs, expectations, and experiences (Rafique & Hunt, 2015). Qualitative research was used in the study to elicit substantial information from teenage fathers' own experiences. Participants provided deep and meaningful information through careful and open-ended questions.

Participants were selected through purposive sampling. During the conduct of the study, except for one, all were unmarried teenage fathers, six were cohabiting and two were still living with their families of procreation. The two who were not cohabiting were no longer in good relationships with the mothers of their children. All participants have a 2-year old child, are 15–19 years of age at the time of interviews, and residents of Quezon City. Participants have common circumstances – seven of them were working while one was relying on his parent's support, three are still studying and two were working students.

The data gathering and data analysis procedures are summarized into four stages. The first stage was a nonstructured casual conversation to build rapport with the participant and followed by the interview proper. The second stage was the documentation procedure of the interview when a professional transcriber transferred the recorded information into a word document. There were two ways of gathering information from the participants. The first was by asking them to create their own family genogram and the second was through a one-on-one interview. Follow-up interviews were conducted to elicit further information and to validate previously gathered data.

From the interview transcripts, the analysis focused on how the participants made sense of their experiences. The data gathered were clustered into convergences and divergences, as well as emerging themes. These identified themes were then analyzed and presented in the results and discussion. The themes were reexamined in the fourth and final stages.

FINDINGS AND DISCUSSION

Family History and Dynamics

This study examines the life histories of selected teenage Filipino fathers in terms of their family life, premarital sexual behaviors, and parenthood. First, this traces how teenage fathers make sense of their own families and their dynamics (see Table 5.1). It centers on the life of Rodel who narrated that teenage parenthood is very common in their family. Accordingly, two subthemes emerged namely, history repeats itself and the impact of family dynamics. Most teenage fathers revealed that they have relatives from their older generations who also became teenage parents. For instance, one of the participants said some of his relatives became parents between the ages of 17 and 19 years. Some developed the courage to have a family at a young age because they copied their relatives who became early parents too.

Making sense of their family genogram, some of the participants attributed their teenage fatherhood to unpleasant family dynamics. For example, two of the participants noticed the estranged relationship between their mother and father. They were no longer together because each one now has their own family. Another participant noticed his aunt on his father's side who had two common law husbands. For him, his experience directly or indirectly contributed to his curiosity and openness to sex. Another participant claimed that the possible reason why his relatives got married at an early age was because of his grandfather's negative style of disciplining, and authoritarian parenting.

Premarital Sex as an Expression of True Love

In a one-on-one interview, when the participants were asked their reason why they engaged in premarital sex, all of them claimed that it was their way of expressing love. However, they gave different explanations when they were asked to give meaning to premarital sex as an expression of true love. As explained, the

Table 5.1.   Selected Quotations on Family History and Dynamics Among
Selected Filipino Teenage Fathers.

Dimensions	Selected Quotations
Making Sense of His Family Genogram	Napansin ko po na sa pamilya po ng Papa ko maaga po sila nagsipag-asawa. Sa side ng Mama ko, maaga din po sila nagsipag- asawa. Sa magkakapatid naman po, parang kaming dalawa naman po ng kuya ko, maaga po kami nagka-anak sa pamilya.
	Siguro po ang dahilan po ay nakikita rin po sa paligid. Nagagaya.'Yun po. Tulad po ng maagang pag-aasawa ng pamangkin ng step father ko. Isa pa po, baka nagaya din sa mga pinsan po naming babae doon tapos lalaki po, nag-aasawa agad, may isang 15, 16, meron pa pong 14.
	(I noticed with the family of my father, they all married at a young age. On my mother's side, it is the same. Among my siblings, my older brother and I both have children at a young age. I think the reason for that is because we see it and we adopt it. Another example is the nephew of my step father who also married early. Even our cousins, both male and female, even as early as 14, 15, and 16 years old.)
	(Rodel)
Family dynamics	Opo, dahil sa sobrang pagiging matapang at mabagsik ng aking lolo, at sa sobrang pananakit niya sa kanyang mga anak, ang kanyang mga anak ay naisip na lang na lumisan sa kanilang bahay, sumama sa kanilang mga kasintahan at bumuo ng sariling pamilya.
	(Yes, because my grandfather is too strong, strict, and even violent to his own children, they just decided to move out from their home, elope and start their own families.)
	(Rodel)

respondents are exposed to premarital sexual behaviors due to their own family
and peers (see Table 5.2). It is also where they develop certain perceptions about
sex and relationships. For Joel, having sex is not a big deal especially for individuals in a relationship.

Table 5.2.   Selected Quotations on Perceptions About Sex Among Selected
Filipino Teenage Fathers.

Dimensions	Perceptions About Sex
Sex as part of relationships	Ano lang po, kasi pag mag-girlfriend o boyfriend po kayo, kapag sa sobrang tagal ninyo na po, doon na po napupunta iyon. Parang doon nababase kung gaano mo siya kamahal.
	(It has no meaning to me. If you are in a long relationship, it is expected to lead to sex already. That also becomes a basis how much you love your partner.)
	(Joel)
Happiness and pleasure	Para sa 'kin Sir, parang nandiyan po yung kaligayahan kasi minsan naguusap-usap kaming mga tropa kapag nangyayari sa kanila 'yung pagse-sex 'yung pakiramdam daw po masarap ganun.
	(For me, we find happiness in it. When our friends talk about their sexual activities, they describe it as pleasurable.)
	(Jerry)

Another participant narrated that he was aware that it is hard to bear a family. However, he was certain that if he accidentally got his girlfriend pregnant, he would never think twice. He would definitely take responsibility for the consequences. The third teenage father said that premarital sex was a way of attaining happiness. The feeling was pleasurable and an effective way in releasing some stress. But he expressed his negative impression of a girl who engages in premarital sex with a man who is not her boyfriend.

At the same time, teenage fathers consider their romantic or sexual partners as a source of inspiration and a sign of manhood (Table 5.3). For instance, one of the respondents sees having a girlfriend as a motivation to go to school while Ariel makes sure to avoid hanging out and meeting other people. Meanwhile, peer pressure among male friends has also been a contributing factor in engaging to premarital sexual behaviors.

As the respondents became more aware and engaged in having relationships, they also experience risky sexual behaviors (see Table 5.4). This involves having sexual encounters under the influence of alcohol and risking unwanted pregnancy.

Table 5.3. Selected Quotations on Perceptions About Romantic/Sexual Partners Among Selected Filipino Teenage Fathers.

Dimensions	Selected Quotations
Source of inspiration	Noong una po akong magka-girlfriend, gusto ko lang po. Kasi sa magkakaibigan, kailangan po may ganoon. Kasi pag wala kang girlfriend, 'di naman sa nagpapasikat, inspirasyon na lang din po. (When I first had a girlfriend, I just wanted it because among friends, that is important. If you do not have a girlfriend, it's not about bragging, but more of a source of inspiration.) (Joel) Sa tingin ko parang gusto kong subukan (mag-girlfriend). Parang masaya po kasi meron kang inspirasyon. Mukhang mas ganado pong pumasok. Mas masaya pong pumasok pag meron ka inspirasyon. (I think I want to try having a girlfriend. It seems happy to have a source of inspiration. You become more motivated to go to school.) (Mar)
Sign of true manhood	"Masaya po kasi nakakabuo ng pagiging isang lalaki." (I am happy because it makes me feel whole as a man.) (Mar) *Pag*-uusapan ka niyan sir. Kunwari, nag-uusap kayong *magkakaibigan* na lalake, tapos ikaw wala ka pa, siempre po sir tatawagin ka nilang mahina. Mahina sa mga babae, mahina 'yung diskarte, parang torpe! (They will talk about you. For example, when you are talking with your guy friends and you still do not have a girlfriend, they would call you weak. You are weak when it comes to women.) (Peter)

Table 5.4.   Selected Quotations on Risky Sexual Behavior Among Selected
Filipino Teenage Fathers.

Dimensions	Selected Quotations
Risky sexual behavior	*Bale po noong ano, nag-sex po kami sa bahay nila, madaling araw po, bale doon ko na po talaga inano,...sinadya ko po talaga, pero 'di ko po sinabi sa kanya na pinutok ko po talaga sa loob.* (When we had sex at my girlfriend's house, that's when I intentionally tried to impregnate her without telling her.) (Ariel) "*... Nung last na ano po, 'yung birthday nung barkada ko. Na ano po, lasing, nalasing po'yung bisita nilang babae na dalawa, bale 'dun na po namin inano ng barkada ko.*" (During my friend's birthday, two of their female guests got drunk, and that's when my friend and I had sex with them.) (Ariel)

CHALLENGES AND EFFECTS OF TEENAGE FATHERHOOD

Different teenage fathers encountered different challenges brought by teenage fatherhood. Some of the common challenges they encountered were how to tell their parents, the cost of childbirth, and how to provide for the needs of the baby. The following discussions were divided into two: the challenges encountered by teenage fathers and the effects of early fatherhood to the teenage fathers' lives.

One of the key realizations of the respondents is having a stable work and source of income to provide for their families (see Table 5.5). As they have not completed their schooling yet, they consider it difficult to do their responsibility.

Teenage fathers reacted negatively when they discovered that they got their girlfriends pregnant. One participant said he became happy and at the same time afraid because he did not know how to tell this to his parents. Another participant said that it took him some time before he finally accepted that he will soon become a father. One teenage father's fear was how he will support his child, find a job, a place to stay, and many more. However, the disappointment was immediately replaced by acceptance of his fate for he had no other choice but to accept it.

Consequently, this study highlights *natauhan* or realization among the selected Filipino teenage fathers. For the first participant, teenage fatherhood made him realize that life should be treasured. Before, he was an easy-go-lucky person. Now, he is doing house chores like cooking, washing clothes, taking care of his child, and many more. Giving meaning to all these life experiences, he narrated that these events made him a more mature person and a responsible father. For another participant, when his girlfriend's abdomen was expanding in size, it meant that he should strive and work hard. He admitted that his girlfriend's pregnancy increased his self-confidence because he can show other people that he was a true man.

In addition, the realization is followed by a sense of accountability (see Table 5.6). One of the respondents emphasizes the importance of being able to graduate from school and find a stable work in order to set a good example for his children.

Table 5.5. Selected Quotations on Work and Income Realizations Among Selected Filipino Teenage Fathers.

Dimensions	Selected Quotations
Work and income	Ang pakiramdam ko po, halo-halo po eh. Parang masaya din po kaso natatakot din po...natatakot din po kasi hindi ko po alam kung paano sasabihin sa mga magulang ko pati sa mga magulang niya, takot po ako dahil syempre po... balak ko rin po kasi talaga mag aral nun eh tas 'yun nga po nabuntis ko nga siya. Wala rin akong trabaho tas ano...natatakot po ako dahil sa responsibilidad na darating sa kin...tulad ng paano ko bubuhayin pamilya ko,
	(I have mixed feelings. I feel happy but I am also afraid because I do not know how to tell my parents and her parents... I am scared because I intended to study but I impregnated her. I have no work and I am scared because of the responsibilities including how I can provide for my family.)
	(Jerlin)
	Yung girlfriend ko namumutla tapos ang una kong sinabihan ay 'yung brother-in-law ko na naging kadikit ko sa lahat ng family members kahit hindi ko siya kadugo. Ang sabi niya sa akin hindi ko pwedeng ipabukas-bukas yung ganun dahil kailangan ng vitamins, check-up ng mag ina ko.
	(I first informed my brother-in-law who is my closest among her family members. He told me that it is urgent for my girlfriend and our unborn child to get checked because they need vitamins.)
	(Peter)

Table 5.6. Selected Quotations on Accountability of Selected Filipino Teenage Fathers.

Dimensions	Selected Quotations
Sense of accountability	*Pagsisikap* sir eh. Laging tumatatak sa isip ko na kailangan kong magsikap. Magsikap. Magsikap. Laging sinasabi sa akin ng partner ko na hindi habang-buhay nandyan ang magulang namin.
	(Perseverance. I always instill in my mind to persevere and work hard. My partner always reminds me that our parents will not always be there for us.)
	(Peter)
	Hindi po, siguro tatapusin ko muna ang pag-aaral ko kasi po maganda po kung makatapos ka muna ng college kasi ngayon po hindi madaling makahanap ng trabaho.
	(I think I want to finish my education first because it is important in finding job.)
	(Peter)

One of the respondents explained that responsible fatherhood is "mabuti, responsable, mapagmahal sa anak at sa asawa, may paninindigan at sipag sa paghahanap-buhay" which means kind, responsible, loving to his child and wife, firm to his decision and diligent and hardworking. Teenage fatherhood brought new meaning to the lives of teenage fathers. In one way or the other, their experience of early parenthood gave them the opportunity to move forward and advance into maturity.

As narrated by one of the participants, he will persevere in his work to be able to provide the needs of his family. He only wanted to at the least provide three meals a day and to be able to send his child to school and finish his/her education.

He explained that all his dreams will come true by working hard, saving a lot and, if God will allow, work abroad. The fourth participant admitted that he encountered difficulties in managing his limited income but he said that he felt grateful whenever he was able to support his child.

With accountability, the selected Filipino teenage fathers also exemplify *paninindigan* or owing up to their responsibility (see Table 5.7). As teenagers, the respondents have engaged in various risky behaviors and vices. For instance, Ariel admitted that he uses cigarettes and drinks alcohol and he willingly stopped all his vices when he became a father. Consequently, some of the respondents consider fatherhood as a responsibility to protect their children and provide for the needs of their families.

Table 5.7. Selected Quotations on Owning Responsibility Among Selected Filipino Teenage Fathers.

Dimensions	Selected Quotations
Developing a sense of responsibility	*Sobrang* laki po (ng pagbabago). Since syempre po ngayon may *anak* na po ako, 'nung binata po ako dati, aminin ko po may bisyo po ako. Pero 'di po alam ng mga magulang ko, pero hindi po nila ako nahuhuli. Okay 'yung alak po legal na po ako sa magulang ko, 'yung sigarilyo po hindi yun. 'Yun itong nagkapamilya na po ako ngayon, bihira na po ako magganyan po, tapos alas-siete palang nandun na po ako sa bahay, pero dati po ala-una, alas-dos nandun pa po ako sa ano (labas).
	(There are many changes now that I have a child. Before, I really had vices and my parents had no idea. They are okay with me drinking alcohol, but cigarettes are not. Now that I have a family, I seldom do those vices. At 7 in the evening, I am already at home. Unlike before that I stay out until 2 am.)
	(Ariel)
	Ngayon sir… parang mas lalo akong ginaganahan, na pumasok, mag-aral kasi may inspirasyon na ako sir, parang gusto kong patunayan sa anak ko na magiging maganda buhay namin, na mapag-aaral ko siya sa magandang paaralan, na magiging maayos din ang lahat sa amin.
	(I became more motivated to go to school and study because I have an inspiration. I want to prove to my child that I can give us a good life and that I can also send him to school.)
	(Jerry)
Being a father	Ang isang mabuting ama ay itinuturo ang tama at mali sa anak, binibigyang direksyon, ilalapit sa Diyos, pinoproteksyonan ang anak, nagbibigay ng pangangailangan at higit sa lahat, di sinasaktan ang mga anak.
	(A good father teaches right and wrong, gives direction in life, helps his child to know God, gives protection, provides their needs, and above all, do not inflict harm to his children.)
	(Rodel)
	Para po sa'kin ah..ang pagiging isang responsableng ama syempre yung pagtatrabaho mo kailangan ah.. control ah.. nakadipende ka na sa trabaho mo hindi mo na kailangang magloko, nakatuon na lang yung buhay mo sa mga anak mo syempre at sa asawa mo.
	(For me, being a responsible father, you need to focus on your work and not engage in risky teen behaviors anymore. You should focus on your children and wife too.)
	(Mar)

The Three-Stage Processes of Teenage Fatherhood: "Natauhan (The Realization), Pinangatawanan (Accountability), and Pinanindigan (Taking Responsibility)"

In an attempt to make meaning of the participants' experiences, three key processes are identified: "Natauhan (the realization), Pinangatawanan (accountability), and Pinanindigan (taking responsibility)." The discussion starts from the antecedent events leading to impregnation or when an adolescent male got a girl pregnant to "natauhan" which means the realization of what he did and the challenges the young father must face. The next phase is "pinangatawanan," the moment when the teenage father accepts fatherhood; and the final phase is "pinanindigan" or when the adolescent father performs his responsibilities for the child and the family. The discussion highlights each process reflecting and drawing meaning on each of the participants' reflections of their experiences as well as from their own meaning of these experiences.

The framework starts on how the adolescent males in the study are surrounded by influences that encourage sexual risk-taking behavior that leads to getting a woman pregnant. Premarital sex is an attractive adventure. The prospect of having a sexual experience with someone with whom the teenage male is comfortable with is tolerated by the Filipino culture. The innate desire to experience life's firsts and the permissive environment, where adolescent men feel entitled to exercise their sexual prowess believing that they "have nothing to lose," where members in their ascendant generations were not sanctioned for their sexual behavior, where family dynamics are far from ideal – all these contribute to the risk-taking behavior that led them to engage in premarital sex that ends up in unplanned pregnancy to teenage fatherhood.

Natauhan (The realization). This process is the turning point. Upon learning that they got their girlfriend pregnant, teenage males experience some of life's challenges. Such challenges include how to tell their parents, how to support their girlfriend and soon-to-come child, where to get money for maternity expenses, where to stay, and many more.

All narrated that they have felt some fear – two felt disappointed since they were too young to become fathers and that they had to stop studying, find a job, earn a living, to stop thinking of themselves and place their child above everything else. However, they later realized that a child's life was soon to be dependent on them leading them to refocus and find a job.

Pinangatawanan (Accountability). All the teenage father participants knew that when they engage in sexual activity, pregnancy was a possibility as well as becoming an adolescent father. However, when fatherhood occurred, all of them admitted that, at first, they went through the denial stage wherein they refused to accept that they will soon become a father at a young age. They could not accept that they have to bear a serious responsibility as a consequence of their curiosity and adventurism.

They realized later that they have no other choice but to bear the consequence of their previous action brought by the risk-taking behavior of premarital and unsafe sex.

Pinanindigan (Taking responsibility). The last stage happens when teenage fathers decide to rise above the challenge of teenage fatherhood and take the responsibility that is expected from them. The characteristics of teenage fathers who are able to rise above the challenges brought by early parenthood are personal maturity, clearer personal and family goals, improved family dynamics, and stronger support system. Finally, a new meaning in life is found by putting their trust in God.

After getting their girlfriends pregnant, teenage fathers went beyond what was expected from them to prove to their families as well as to the family of their girlfriends that they were "man enough" to support their family. This is the meaning of *pinanindigan,* when a man decides to bear his responsibility to his girlfriend and child.

Making Sense of Teenage Fathers' Experiences

In trying to make sense of their experience, participants were asked on how they currently viewed teenage fatherhood. The following are participants' recommendations when asked if they will recommend their past actions to fellow teenage males who are in the stage of adolescence.

All eight participants agree that teenage fatherhood was an event that they did not wish to happen in their lives. Although two of the participants claimed that they intentionally impregnated their girlfriends, it was clear to all of them that at the age of adolescence, one is not yet capable of becoming a good and responsible father particularly when it comes to making serious decisions in life. Some teenage fathers were not reluctant in engaging in premarital sex even when they were aware that they could impregnate their girlfriends. They still engaged in sexual activities because becoming a teenage father and starting a new family could mean an escape from one's loose family ties. In their family of origin, they had parents who were far too preoccupied in their work or businesses that they failed to give quality time to their offspring. However, their risk-taking action can be interpreted as escaping from a dysfunctional family to form another new unplanned family.

Another important insight is that the events and circumstances tempted adolescent males to engage in risky sexual activities. Culture dictates that a true man must engage in risky sexual activities because it is the only way to be called macho or a true man. These events and circumstances contribute to the young males' curiosity and adventurism that lead to premarital sex and eventually to teenage fatherhood.

When the participants were asked what advise they can give to teenagers who wanted to marry or cohabit at an early age, two different points of view arose. First, is their direct objection to getting married or cohabitation at a young age. Second, is their suggestion not to get married or cohabit early but they did not explicitly say that getting married at a younger age is completely wrong. The advice is meant to discourage a teenage male from experiencing a risk-taking activity such as premarital sex.

The above insight is parallel to existing studies on adolescents. Teenage fathers were unable to make mature, moral, and rational decisions. They only based their actions using their personal feelings and not on the principles of rightness, fairness, or justice (Papalia et al., 2009). This also affirms that adolescents' lack of formal and abstract thinking is the reason why they could hardly arrive at a wise decision in their lives (Alampay et al., 2009). These could help us understand the reasons why teenage fathers have carried out immature decisions in the past.

CONCLUSION

Teenage fatherhood is brought about by several influences both internal and external from the person involved. The study indicated that teenage fathers became biological fathers because of internal influence such as adolescent risk-taking behaviors that include curiosity, adventurism, and the innate desire to explore new things. The attempt to experience life's firsts leads them to try risk-taking activities like engaging in sex. Unfortunately, sexual experiments can eventually lead to teenage pregnancy for the female and teenage fatherhood for the male. On the other hand, external influences instigating adolescent males to engage in risky sexual behaviors are Filipino culture and family dynamics such as the parents' modeling, marital relationship, and parenting style.

The study revealed the pattern of early parenthood from the past generations to the present. In this study, teenage fathers narrated that they had ascendant generations: grandparents, parents, parent's siblings, and other relatives, who became teenage parents like them. Seeing the patterns in the different family genograms produced during the first interview and then hearing how each of the teenage participants brought meaning to these patterns and their experiences within their families, this observes a continuing pattern that motivated individuals to follow the same path their older generations took.

Some Filipino cultural practices directly encourage male adolescents to engage in sex. As stated, Filipino males are given special privileges because they are perceived as invulnerable and have nothing to lose. The notion of invulnerability of Filipino males is ascertained in the tradition of "binyag" (baptism) wherein they are urged to experience sexual activity at an early age. This opens the door to risky sexual activities, sexual promiscuity, and premarital sex that may result in the early pregnancy of their partners and teenage fatherhood.

This also highlights some implications of youth's exposure to media with sexual content. Accordingly, aside from peer groups, male adolescents get their information about sex from media and these young people have the impression that information coming from media is always correct, reliable, and applicable to their own lives. In this study, knowledge of sex picked up from the media further triggered adolescents' curiosity and adventurism to engage in sex which eventually led to early pregnancy and teenage fatherhood.

In conclusion, this study directs attention to some policy insights on sex education and gender equality training for the vulnerable Filipino youth in the country. Current national strategies addressing teenage pregnancy and early family life give importance to women's rights and health education. The Magna Carta of Women asserts that "no school shall turn out or refuse admission to a female student solely on account of her being pregnant outside of marriage during her term in school." However, pregnant teenage women from resource-poor settings are not fully aware of their rights (Gregorio, 2018). Thus, it is crucial to provide proper sex education and gender equality training to Filipino youth in order to prevent unwanted pregnancies, teenage fatherhood, and/or better prepare them for parenthood and family life. Using an empowerment approach, it is important for teenage parents to recognize themselves as equals in their relationships, capable of protecting their own health and well-being.

For the parents, schools, and religious and government institutions, this study recommends a further increase of valuable groups, clubs, or worthwhile activities such as community involvement, tourism development, environmental protection, sports tournament, student exchange program, religious organization, support groups, among others in order to engage youth as active members of society.

REFERENCES

Agarwal, V., & Dhanasekaran, S. (2012). Harmful effects of media on children and adolescents. *Journal of Indian Association of Child Adolescents' Mental Health, 8*(2), 38–45. http://files.eric.ed.gov/fulltext/EJ989518.pdf

Aguiling-Dalisay, G. (1983). *Fathers as parents: An exploratory study* [Master's thesis]. University of the Philippines, Quezon City.

Aguiling-Dalisay, G., Mendoza, R., Miraflex, E., Yacat, J., Sto Domingo, M. R., & Bambico, F. R. (2000). *Pagkalalake: Men in control?* Pambansang Samahan sa Sikolohiyang Pilipino.

Alampay, L. P., Liwag, M. D., & Dela Cruz, A. S. (2009). Risk-taking among Filipino adolescents: A review with implications for research. *Philippine Journal of Psychology, 42*(1), 97–116.

Arca, J. R. A. (2002). *On disgrasyas and kati: Talk of Filipino boys on teenage pregnancy*. University of Amsterdam. http://amma.socsci.uva.nl/theses/arca%20(2002).pdf

Batangan, M. T. D. U. (2006). *Pagdadalaga at pagbibinata: Developmental contexts of adolescent sexuality*. University Center for Women's Studies.

Bulatao, J., & Gorospe, V. (1966). *Split-level Christianity. Christian renewal of Filipino values*. Ateneo de Manila University.

Casselman, R., & Rosenbaum, A. (2014). Fathers, sons, and aggression: A path model. *Journal of Aggression, Maltreatment & Trauma, 23*(5), 513–531.

Chaves, L., Tortolero, S., Markham, C., Low, B., Eitel, P., & Thickstun, P. (2005). Impact of the media on adolescent sexual attitudes and behaviors. *Pediatrics, 116*(1). http://pediatrics.aappublications.org/content/116/Supplement_1/303.short

Conaco, M. C. G., Jimenez, M. C. C., & Billedo, C. J. F. (2003). *Filipino adolescents in changing times*. U.P. Center for Women's Studies and Philippine Center for Population Development.

Gregorio, V. (2018). The only exception: Teenage pregnancy in the Philippines. *Review of Women's Studies, 28*, 1–28.

Guillermo, M. L., & de Guzman, A. B. (2007). *The Filipino Family in Constant (R)evolution*. Rex Bookstore.

Hendry, L., & Kloep, M. (2002). *Lifespan development: Resources, challenges and risks*. Thomson Learning.

Kail, R. V., & Cavanaugh, J. C. (2010). *Human development: A life-span view* (5th ed.). Cengage Learning.

Kirven, J. (2014). The reality and responsibility of pregnancy provides a new meaning to life for teenage fathers. *International Journal of Choice Theory and Reality Therapy, 33*(2), 24. http://www.wglasserinternational.org/wp-content/uploads/bsk-pdf-manager/19_IJCTRTSPRING2014.PDF

Koerselman, K., & Pekkarinen, T. (2017). *The timing of puberty and gender differences in educational achievement*. Institute of Labor Economics. https://docs.iza.org/dp10889.pdf

Laigo, L. B., Cura, N. M., Oreta, J. S., & Galang, G. P. (2009). *The Filipino family: Indicators of well-being*. PWU Publishing House.

Long, E., Fish, J., Scheffler, A., & Hanert, B. (2014). Memorable experiences between fathers and sons: Stories that shape a son's identity and perspective of his father. *Journal of Men's Studies, 22,* 122–139.

Medina, B. T. G. (2015). *The Filipino family*. The University of the Philippines Press.

Palispis, E. (2007). *Introduction to values education*. Rex Printing Company.

Papalia, D. E., Olds, S. W., & Feldman, R. D. (2009). *Human development* (11th ed.). The McGraw-Hill Companies, Inc.

Rafique, R., & Hunt, N. (2015). Experiences and coping behaviours of adolescents in Pakistan with alopecia areata: An interpretative phenomenological analysis. *International Journal of Qualitative Studies on Health and Well-being, 10,* 26039. http://dx.doi.org/10.3402/qhw.v10.26039

Rawat, C., & Singh, R. (2017). The paradox of gender difference on emotional maturity of adolescents. *Journal of Human Ecology, 58*(3), 126–131. http://dx.doi.org/10.1080/09709274.2017.1305610

Steinberg, L. (2012). *Adolescence* (12th ed.). McGraw Hill Education.

Straubhaar, J., La Rose, R., & Davenport, L. (2014). *Media now: Understanding media, culture, and technology* (8th ed.) Cengage Learning.

Tan, M. L., Batangan, M. T. U., & Cabado-Española, H. (2001). *Love and desire: Young Filipinos and sexual risks*. UP Center for Women's Studies.

Wormer, K. (2017). *Human behavior and the social environment (individuals and families)* (3rd ed.). Oxford University Press.

CARE PROVISIONS IN/FROM THE FAMILY

CHAPTER 6

ICT-MEDIATED FAMILIAL CARE IN TURBULENT TIMES: FILIPINOS' SUBJECTIVITIES, VIRTUAL INTIMACY, AND RESILIENCE AMID SOCIAL CHANGE

Derrace Garfield McCallum

ABSTRACT

Since the COVID-19 pandemic started and intensified over two years ago, constant lockdowns and social distancing measures have left many people feeling disconnected and disoriented. To recapture and sustain a semblance of normalcy and connected co-existence, online platforms, and various communication media have become indispensable. However, this mode of social connectedness while being physically separated is nothing new to Filipino transnational families who have persevered and kept their familial bonds alive and well across time and space.

Based on findings from an ongoing ethnographic study that started in 2016, in this chapter, the author engages with critical issues regarding how communication technologies shape the exchange of familial care and intimacy within contexts of geographical dispersion. Through a discussion of the ways in which new forms of communication reconstruct the temporal and spatial aspects of Filipino transnational family life, the author explains how families preserve and nurture their collective commitments to the maintenance of kinship by using information and communication technologies (ICTs) to (re)enact and

Resilience and Familism: The Dynamic Nature of Families in the Philippines
Contemporary Perspectives in Family Research, Volume 23, 85–101
Copyright © 2023 by Emerald Publishing Limited
All rights of reproduction in any form reserved
ISSN: 1530-3535/doi:10.1108/S1530-353520230000023006

(re)create mundane existences but also to recognize, celebrate, and display significant milestones along the family life course. One of the key questions raised is how effective technology-mediated exchanges are in substituting for physical co-presence, which is widely accepted as the foundation of strong and healthy family relationships. By interrogating these issues, the author builds on a valuable body of research which theorizes how ICTs facilitate new forms of intimacy and virtual togetherness; but also contentious relations and emotional burdens that test the Filipino family's resilience in turbulent times.

This chapter is a potent elaboration of how Filipino transnational family members adopt creative strategies to integrate their fragmented existences and (re)embed themselves into each other's temporalities and subjectivities.

Keywords: Philippines; family life; pandemic; COVID-19; resilience; communication technologies

INTRODUCTION

Migration scholars have often focused on the dislocations, disconnections, and disruptions that may take place in families that are dispersed across borders. Until more recently, it was assumed that the transnational mobility of family members resulted in increased fragility of familial bonds and intimate relations. More alarming was the perceived imminent demise of the family, as it were. It is true that this increased human mobility has transformed our socialities and the way that we understand and "do family" but, as recent studies have shown, the assumption that physical proximity is required for the maintenance of meaningful social ties must be reconsidered (Locke et al., 2014).

Over the last few years, the proliferation of information and communication technologies (ICTs) and the creation of new media environments have challenged the proposition that robust intimate relationships are predicated on face-to-face exchanges. While fast and affordable international transportation has enhanced transnational family life and remains crucial for these families, it is the significant changes that have taken place in communication technologies, primarily internet-based, that have truly transformed how family members interact and connect with geographically dispersed kin (Baldassar et al., 2016; Francisco-Menchavez, 2018; Madianou & Miller, 2012; Robertson, 2014). With these developments in media and communication technologies, it is now possible to consider that transnational migration does not inevitably result in disconnections with family members, friends, or even the homeland. At the bare minimum, constant instantaneous communications between migrants and their loved ones are possible.

Despite the foregoing, since the COVID-19 pandemic started and intensified over a year ago, constant lockdowns and social distancing measures have left many people feeling disconnected and disoriented. To recapture and sustain a semblance of normalcy and connected co-existence, online platforms and various communication media have become indispensable. However, these modes of social connectedness while being physically separated are nothing new to Filipino transnational families who have persevered and kept their familial bonds alive and well across time and space.

In contextualizing the increased dispersion of Filipino families, it is necessary to recognize that the Philippines is one of the most prolific migrant-sending countries in Asia with a highly institutionalized migration machinery. The state is integrally involved in the recruitment, deployment, and repatriation of what Rodriguez (2010) calls "migrants for export"; even as it encourages national discourses surrounding perceived detrimental social impacts on the family in the absence of women. In much of Rhacel Parreñas' work (see Parreñas, 2001, 2005, 2008, 2010, 2012 among others), she interrogates the local impacts of global economic activities and argues that the development of a labor export-oriented economy in the Philippines leads to a clash of competing gender ideologies regarding female domesticity. This clash arises from the state's economic dependence on women's work outside the country while simultaneously embracing a traditional gender ideology regarding family life that locates women's gendered obligations inside the domestic space.

In this larger context of national, regional, and international mobility, where wealth and economic opportunities are unevenly distributed and ambivalent dynamics surrounding gender, family, and social reproduction are obvious, sustained emigration of Filipinos has significantly affected institutions, social relations, and social norms in the communities of migrants. For instance, many scholars contend that while women's role has been expanded to include breadwinning, there has not been a concomitant expansion of men's role to include caregiving and nurturance. This creates what is often referred to as a "crisis of care," grounded in the care chains analysis, which has implications for the sustenance of good family life. Therefore, an exploration of these family dynamics and the possible implications becomes necessary. These contextual factors that mediate the negotiation of care obligations among migrants and their family members make the Philippines a fertile site for studying care not only at the micro-, but also at the meso- and macro-levels. A nuanced interrogation of these issues aids our understanding of Filipino family culture, gender relations, and familial separation; as well as increased international mobility precipitated by rising global demand and supply.

In this chapter, I engage with critical issues related to how communication media technologies shape the exchange of care and intimacy within contexts of geographical dispersion. I also discuss the ways in which new forms of communication shape intimate interactions and reconstitute the temporal and spatial aspects of Filipino transnational family life. One of the key questions raised is how effective technology-mediated transnational exchanges are in substituting for physical co-presence, which is widely accepted as the foundation of strong and healthy family relationships. By interrogating these issues, I build on a valuable body of research which theorizes how ICTs facilitate new forms of intimacy and virtual togetherness in families; and how the Filipino family has managed to remain resilient in turbulent times. This chapter is a potent elaboration of how Filipino transnational family members adopt creative strategies to integrate their fragmented existences and (re)embed themselves into each other's temporalities and subjectivities.

Following this introduction, I provide an explanation of the research methods adopted for this study and the reasons such methods are suitable in this context. The next section presents a brief discussion of existing literature regarding the proliferation of internet-based communication media and how its ubiquitous nature and saturation of contemporary life have transformed the concept of "presence" and the way people interact with each other. Based on empirical data, I then explain how families preserve and nurture their collective commitments to the maintenance of kinship by using ICTs to (re)enact and (re)create mundane existences but also to recognize, celebrate and display significant milestones along the family life course. The following section features a balanced analysis of the potential and actual ambivalent effects of adopting new ICTs as a tool for exchanging care in transnational families. Preceding the final section, I address the apparent moral panic concerning whether the Filipino family, as an institution, is in decline due to transnational migration. Overall, this chapter provides an account of how Filipino transnational families create and maintain a sense of oneness and continuous co-existence through the adoption and usage of various forms of technology.

RESEARCH METHODS

This chapter draws on data collected as part of a larger multi-sited transnational ethnography of Filipino migrants who live in central Japan (Chubu region) and their family members in the Philippines. This study was mostly conducted between 2016 and 2020 and combines ethnographic approaches online and offline. Data were collected via in-depth interviews coupled with participation in and observation of 43 families; some members are living in Japan while others live in the Philippines. Data collection took place in five prefectures in Japan (Nagano, Aichi, Shizuoka, Gifu, and Mie) and in the Philippines (several parts of Metro Manila, the province of Bulacan, and Cavite). Some interviews and conversations were conducted online through Zoom, Skype, FaceTime, and other video conferencing media. Also, I actively followed the online behavior and posts of some of the respondents who became my "friends" on social media. Since transnational family members often utilize online technology to connect for various purposes (as elaborated in the chapter), I adopted a semi-virtual methodology in order to experience and deeply understand the texture and contours of their online interactions. In addition, virtual methodologies have become an important means of conducting research that satisfies the need to transcend temporal and spatial limitations.

In keeping with the larger study from which the data were drawn, respondents were selected by snowball sampling. Interviews were largely conducted in English with some mixture of Japanese and Tagalog (with translation). Some interviews during the fieldwork were recorded and transcribed while others were recorded only by detailed written notes, depending on the comfort of the respondents.

Since I was mostly in the homes and private spaces of respondents, I showed utmost respect regarding their desires, particularly related to sound recordings and photography. The data collected were examined and analyzed by focusing on common themes and patterns that emerged. Some of the themes identified resembled findings from relevant literature that I had reviewed. However, there were also new and interesting themes that provided fresh insight and nuance. When anomalies were found, these were isolated for deeper interrogation and clarification via electronic media after I had returned from the field.

Although the larger study interrogated the lives of members of 43 Filipino transnational families, only the most relevant narratives are considered in this chapter. Each of the families involved has at least one family member who lives, works, and/or studies in the Chubu region of Japan. Some of the Japan-based participants are permanent residents or citizens while others are undocumented migrants. To my knowledge, none of the participants are refugees or asylum seekers. I have also included "temporary" contract-based workers or students who came to Japan on a scholarship and privately funded students. The sample of participants in this study is diverse in terms of age, gender, social class, educational achievement, marital status, sexual orientation, and immigration status. However, I must highlight that, although it was not an intended outcome, due to the snowball sampling technique used, most of the respondents appear to be comparatively better-off compared to other Filipinos living in Japan. Therefore, the findings of this study cannot be generalized as the reality of all Filipino transnational families in Japan. For anonymity, pseudonyms are used in the narratives.

TECHNOLOGICAL OMNIPRESENCE ACROSS BORDERS

A new social environment of ubiquitous connectivity has transformed the lived experiences of transnational families. The omnipresence of the internet and other forms of digital media have facilitated and mediated familial communication in unthinkable ways. The dawn of what Madianou and Miller (2012, p. 125) termed "polymedia" signifies a crucial shift in the dynamics of international migration and the way that connections are maintained in transnational families. Conventionally, "co-presence" was perceived as tantamount to face-to-face communication and was preferable compared to interactions that were mediated by communication technologies. Baym (2010) contented that written internet-mediated communications such as emails lacked the social cues necessary for conveying emotional content and meanings, which, he argued, is vital for effective personal communication. Even with significant evolutions in ICTs, there is still widespread concern about the efficacy of the internet for interpersonal relationships (Turkle, 2011).

Nevertheless, the development and expansion of ICTs present remarkable possibilities and solutions to earlier challenges associated with communicating from afar. Recent studies have demonstrated how migrants and their families utilize digital media in creative ways to "do family" (see Baldassar et al., 2016; Francisco-Menchavez, 2018; Nedelcu & Wyss, 2016; Uy-Tioco & Cabalquinto,

2020). Madianou and Miller (2012), in their study of communication practices among transnational families, developed a "theory of polymedia" that elucidate how the flux of various ICTs creates a media environment where users can selectively use the most appropriate media to manage their relationships and satisfy their communication demands. This theory is useful to the extent that it allows us to see how one communication medium is related to other media. Moreover, it highlights the agency of users in selecting the media that best suit their needs. For instance, in the past, the sending of letters and packages was frustrating because of frequent delays and physical damage. However, in a polymedia environment, there is a plethora of alternate options (social media, mobile phones, video calling, etc.) which migrants and their families exploit at will. Rather than focusing on the unique properties or features of specific technologies, the concept of polymedia points us to how users exercise agency in navigating media environments and choosing suitable platforms from a range of communicative opportunities.

ICTs are temporal means by which geographically dispersed families engage in routine synchronized transnational communication enabling them to preserve and nurture bonds across time and space (Baldassar, 2008; Baldassar et al., 2016; Cabalquinto, 2018; Horst, 2006; Wilding, 2006). Widespread access to affordable mobile communication devices and platforms and their ubiquitous use invoke an ambiance of perpetual interaction (Boyd, 2012; Katz, 2011). Madianou (2014) explained how the availability of polymedia creates an "always on" presence among migrants and their families. This is what she later called "ambient co-presence" (Madianou, 2016, p. 183) whereby people, through the receipt of incessant updates and notifications, become highly and discretely aware of the everyday lives and activities of their significant others. This is facilitated through the background presence of those who use mobile and social media platforms. Other researchers have elucidated notions of "connected presence" and "mobile lives" to highlight how people have harnessed their newly-acquired capacities to connect with others and manage their increased mobility without jeopardizing the bonds they share with dispersed significant others (Elliott & Urry, 2010, p. 1; Licoppe, 2004, p. 135). Indeed, in her discussion of transnational families, Nedelcu (2012, p. 1340) referred to the "new geographies of everyday life" within which these families conduct their daily existence. In these new geographies,

> the (physically) absent [family member] renders himself or herself present by multiplying mediated communication gestures up to the point where co-present interactions and mediated communication seem woven in a seamless web.

These conceptions help us to better comprehend the interesting ways in which ICTs are transforming social life and how distant ties and connections are sustained, even if lived across international boundaries.

NEGOTIATING VIRTUAL INTIMACIES

Regardless of extended separation due to various forms of international migration, Filipino transnational families with members in Japan often endeavor to preserve and nurture their collective commitment to the endurance of their sense of kinship and familyhood. As the following narratives demonstrate, the families I studied made great effort to (re)enact and (re)create a sense of one-ness and continuous co-existence through the adoption and use of varied forms of technology.

Mundane Connections

Migrants I interviewed told me that they stay tuned to the daily happenings back home and that their ability to do that was extremely significant, to the extent that whenever there is a technical disruption on the part of the inter-net service provider (ISP) or when the online activities of family members and friends were "not normal," it would immediately result in anxiety and a need to restore connectivity. For instance, Jasmine (aged 48) not only enjoys live-streaming her shopping experiences and video chatting with her sisters while she is buying the commodities she will send to the Philippines for them, but she also communicates with them several times throughout the day and especially at night when they have their after-dinner chats and gossip sessions. Among the families I studied, daily rituals of family life in the Philippines are maintained across borders via ICTs – parents help children with homework, siblings engage in banter and gossip, women provide cooking tips to men, and romantic pas-sions are stimulated and reinforced.

The ability to "see" and "be" with their family members back home via vide-oconferencing significantly affects how migrants navigate their separation and their lives away from loved ones. This is especially true in the early stages of migration regardless of the length of stay abroad. Karen (aged 31) came to Japan for graduate studies. Because of the restrictions of her scholarship, she was not able to visit the Philippines to see her young son and her husband, as well as her other family members. She told me that in the first few weeks, she was distressed and cried daily. During those moments, she was able to comfort herself by video chatting and texting with her husband, mother, and sisters. For her, it was also important that she did a video call every night before her baby goes to bed so that she could give him a "goodnight kiss." In addition, throughout the day, she would receive updates on the daily activities of her family members and, most importantly, her son. Jose (aged 42), another migrant, has been in Japan for more than five years, and although his emotional struggles were more acute in his first two years, he still laments his separation from his family. But he is thankful for the ability to stay in touch with them on social media and to have dinner together several times a week, even if it is virtual.

ICTs' ability to bring separated family members together in the same room brings a sense of being integrated. Migrants are able to join the quotidian rou-tines of loved ones by being "always on" and available, though active conversa-tions may not take place. As I found, just the background sounds that signifies activity or the app-based "online" status is enough to create a subliminal sense of comfort and co-presence. As Licoppe and Smoreda (2005, p. 331) intimated, it is like "filling in absence by a sort of incantation."

Marking and Displaying Key Milestones

The convenience of smartphones and the growing popularity of Facebook and other media platforms such as Instagram, Viber, LINE, WhatsApp, and Zoom have truly altered how members of Filipino transnational families relate to each, but also, how they visually display their individual lives and collective commitments. Sharing pictures and videos of places visited, meals eaten, and other routine experiences not only allows dispersed family members to participate in the daily lives of each other, but it also sets the stage for more significant exchanges. In my study, I have found that it is very common for family members to post pictures or videos of events such as weddings, graduations, Christmas dinners, birthday parties, baptisms, the christening ceremony of a baby, and other family celebrations. Posting or sending these pictures and videos is especially important for those family members who could not participate in the event in a corporeal sense, primarily international migrants. When Clara's (aged 38) younger sister got married a few years ago, she was unable to visit the Philippines to attend the wedding but she was integrally involved in the planning and financing of the wedding. In the months and days leading up to the wedding day, she spent many hours calling, texting, and sending voice notes to family members back home to ensure that everything was properly arranged for the big day. Moreover, on the day, her nephew live-streamed the ceremony and reception party and posted the pictures and videos on Facebook, tagging Clara in the posts. She told me that although she was not physically present, she felt as if she was there in a very real sense. As she showed me the pictures in which she was tagged, she beamed with pride and unbridled joy, pointing out that she was the one who picked out the dress.

Family rituals are typically performed, experienced, and symbolized through the physical congregation of family members. Indeed, it is during family gatherings that kinship bonds are solidified through the physical expression of affection, the sharing of meals, the exchanging of gifts, and personal anecdotes. Lopez (2006) highlighted that, in the context of the Philippines, family celebrations are key to the building of unity among families and the strengthening of affection. With increased migration from the Philippines, it might seem that family traditions and the resultant benefits are disrupted. However, I found that even if these traditions and rituals have been gradually reshaped, they remain as vital and relevant as they ever were and their continued performance is facilitated by the instantaneous nature of recent communication media. Moreover, while the ways of communication and the opportunities to connect have been radically transformed, the basic structures, practices, and principles of family relationships remain fundamentally inviolable. Events like births, weddings, and deaths that happen across the life course can amplify the need for corporeal presence; and sometimes demand family members to show their commitment to the family. As Finch (2007, p. 79) articulated, "there is a real sense in which relationships do not exist as family relationships unless they can be displayed successfully."

Given the existence and proliferation of a "polymedia environment," the families in this study are able to create a shared consciousness of their familyhood. Furthermore, they are able to display their continued ties and commitments as a well-functioning family by publicly recognizing and signifying key milestones and momentous events when typical families would celebrate together.

Baldassar et al. (2016, p. 136) claimed that the less synchronous nature of older forms of media, such as letters, provided opportunities for families to smooth over the narrative of their family histories and idealize their relationships, creating and projecting a favorable impression of their families. Further, they contended that "the recent emergence of ubiquitous connectivity brings the mundane into sharper focus, ensuring attention to the minute detail of daily life at the expense of a more imaginative narrative." However, I argue that a sharp focus on the mundane does not necessarily lead to a discounting of a larger consciousness of noble familyhood. Besides, even if recent media exposes the family to more public scrutiny, the very same media allows for immediate action to restore the family's reputation and mitigate further damage. For instance, I found that when some family members "misbehaved" on social media, other family members or kin would use the same media or another very similar platform to reprimand the errant kin or to contact other kin who would manage the situation. Sometimes, this is done publicly but, depending on the underlying relationship, it is often done privately. I will return to this element of surveillance later.

AMBIVALENT CONNECTIONS AND DISCONNECTED INTIMACIES

Online Cosmopolitans?

Some Filipino migrants who share pictures and/or videos of iconic places visited, shopping sprees, and new fashionable clothes, handbags, and shoes are marking important milestones in their migration trajectories, inviting family members, friends, and other fictive kin to "like" and "comment" on their fortunes, accomplishments, and experiences. Their posts convey messages of affluence and accomplishment, signifying the migrants' sophistication and upward mobility. These transnational signals are the results of migrants' attempt to (re)create a cosmopolitan image of their lives in Japan and to show that they have become more modern and empowered through migration. As McKay (2012, p. 141) wrote "Cosmopolitans think of themselves as sharing a distinct set of feelings and attitudes, priorities and judgements, and practices of self-shaping that constitute their global belonging." Moreover, they often consciously shift their concepts of self away from that of their families and communities back home, creating a personal imaginary whereby they are open to new and different cultural ideas/experiences that are not necessarily supported by those back home.

Bryan (aged 28) is one of the most prolific Instagrammer and Facebook user among my respondents. He came to Japan in 2016 to join his mother who lives in a rural city in Central Japan. He is a construction worker but whenever he gets days off or extended holidays, he travels to iconic places around Japan. During these trips, Bryan often takes beautiful photos and videos and uploads them to social media platforms, tagging his relatives and friends. In one of his favorite posts, he is pictured in Shibuya, a very busy and spectacular area in Tokyo, known for its huge electronic billboards and flashing lights – the Times Square of Tokyo. Bryan's post is captioned "Shibuya Crossing Intersection." Later, in a comment, he wrote "Busiest intersection in the world!" Needless to say, he is fashionably clothed and his Nike sneakers are prominently displayed. When I spoke to him and mentioned the quality and perfect angle of the picture, he told me that he has a keen interest in photography and usually pays close attention to photographic details. I believe him. In the picture, it seems that Bryan was careful to ensure that he snapped the picture at the opportune time while there were Japanese-looking people in the background, as if to prove the authenticity of his post.

Other migrants, such as Jenelyn (aged 36), also post photos and videos that are interpreted as evidence of a successful migration experience. Her son, Chris (aged 10) said:

> My mother and father are over there in Japan. I think they have a beautiful life because they can travel and live in a nice country like Japan. I would like to live there too one day. I think they will send for me soon.

Although Chris is only 10 years old, he already aspires to migrate one day, inspired by the seemingly lavish lifestyle of his parents. Other children of migrants whom I spoke to also seem to have their own imaginaries of a future migration trajectory that would bring them the same accomplishments that are perceived from the photos and videos of their migrant family members. Indeed, these photos and/or videos often serve as the bases of motivational discussions, which usually happen with left-behind children and their caregivers. Not only children are inspired; other family members and friends are also drawn into virtual realities of luxurious lives that are predicated on stories that are not completely true. I found that, quite often, the stories shared are creatively crafted and staged by the migrants, calling the veracity of the photos and/or videos into question. For instance, Matt (aged 23) often shares photos and videos of himself driving a Honda sports car and he delights in the number of "likes" and "comments" he receives. The car is owned by his close friend who often allows him to drive it so it would seem that the car is actually his. However, he makes no effort to clarify the ownership of the car whenever he talks to loved ones back home.

We see, here, that Matt virtually displays an image of himself that is less accessible in real life but which he perceives to be desirable and inspiring, especially for his family members and friends in the Philippines. In fact, like doting fans, they look forward to his posts and when they are not forthcoming, he is requested to give updates about his recent exploits. Interestingly, these photos and videos are often circulated within the family and the community as evidence of the success and upward mobility of the individual and, by extension, the family. The photos and/or videos that migrants share reveal their personal interests and exploits but they also expose and reinforce the shared consciousness of what family members should aim for, particularly the younger ones. Moreover, even if the posts are based on a virtually constructed reality, they are potent enough to serve as valuable documentations and/or appearances of the family's upward mobility and create a sense of shared familial success.

"CARING ABOUT" SURVEILLANCE

The growing use of ICTs has positively affected the ways in which families maintain their sense of belonging. Yet, it also has important implications for the surveillance of family members, which can result in increased conflicts and discontents. Migration projects, while often linked to the achievement of certain familial goals, are sometimes grounded in individual's desire for autonomy and self-actualization. This is particularly true for those migrants whose identities, in part or whole, are in violation of certain principles and morals of the home country contexts. In a country like the Philippines, where more than 80% of the population is Roman Catholic and a vigorous Muslim minority is active in the southern islands, religion is pervasive and often obstructive. For Filipinos who identify as LGBTQ, opportunities to congregate with other members of that community or to live the lifestyle they desire may be highly restricted. This is particularly true for those who are from close-knit rural communities or relatively poor urban enclaves.

Matt is a gay man from a rural community in Davao. He migrated to Japan in 2017 to join his aunt. While he was encouraged to move to Japan by his aunt and cousins for economic reasons, a key motivating factor for him was his perception of Japan as a progressive country with less religious dogma – a place where he could live freely without the watchful eyes of family members and neighbors. Indeed, McKay (2012, p. 142) mentioned that cosmopolitans, or those aspiring to live cosmopolitan lifestyles, often seek to subscribe to secular belief systems and liberal values. Moreover, she articulated a social struggle whereby becoming cosmopolitan draws migrants into a process of transformation that pits them against parochial nationalists and religious fundamentalists. These apparent "enemies" are often found within migrants' own families.

Nowadays, when Matt uploads pictures and videos, he is careful not to post those that include his gay friends or when he is having a good time at a nightclub or gay bar. According to him, based on previous posts, he had to lie to his family when he was questioned about his sexuality and the morality of his regular group of friends. Because most his family members are fervent Catholics, he was reprimanded and reminded not to lose his faith. Moreover, since that incident, his mother has asked his aunt to watch him more closely. During further conversation with Matt, he told me that his family is concerned that he may be bringing the family's reputation into disrepute. Matt's careful construction of posts, based on what family members and friends back home may perceive, implies that the "selfies" that he posts are of a self that is not fully cosmopolitan or autonomous but which is simultaneously linked to the home context and to immoral "others" who might tarnish the reputation of his family.

Characteristically different from the active intentional surveillance discussed so far is another form, which is less obvious and potentially more invasive. Based on various features and capabilities of new media, users' online presence is increasingly more visible to family members and close friends. Nowadays, even "friends of friends" can access one's online information and share it. Truly, much of the information gleaned from social media is somewhat unintentional and based on indirect interactions, not just among people but between users and smart technologies, which provide information such as online status, the time a user was last active, the location of users and posts and the reactions of others to the posts of loved ones. This facilitates an ambient awareness of family members and friends as well as the people they associate with. These features are welcomed by the transnational parents I spoke to who are keen on monitoring their children without having to deliberately search for information or hunt them virtually. By receiving automatic online notifications, they are able to watch over their children and keep them safe.

Simon (aged 14), the son of one respondent is having disciplinary problems at school including alleged drug use. Because his parents who are both abroad (his mother is in Japan and his father is in Abu Dhabi) are usually very busy working, they often rely on technology-generated notifications to prompt them to take further actions like calling his grandparents in the Philippines to check on him or take disciplinary action. Actually, it was based on these constant notifications that his mother finally decided to take an extended visit to the Philippines to deal with the matter. It is interesting to note that much of the information Simon's parents glean from social media are indirectly accessed through the posts and status updates of his "friends" and the posts he is tagged in. This is similar to what Madianou (2016, p. 139) found in her study and a form of what she called "information leakage." She pointed out that even though parents are not the intended audience of these posts, they serve as an invaluable source of information, particularly for transnational parents.

While the geolocative features of social media and mobile devices are sometimes embraced by migrants when their posts are attached to geographic locations, particularly those who want to display when they visit iconic locations or sightseeing spots, there are possible ambivalent effects when users' online activities are linked to specific locations and timelines. For instance, I found that for couples who had trust problems before or after migration, this kind of information leakage can aggravate existing problems when the information gathered from automated notifications contradicts other deliberately shared details. This was the case with Herbert (aged 39) and Lucinda (aged 40) who had marital problems before he migrated to Japan for work. There has always been rumors that he was promiscuous and that he has several extramarital relationships with other women. After he migrated, those rumors did not subside and even intensified. Because of the history of their relationship, Lucinda is more attentive to his posts and promptly checks whenever she gets notifications about his activities. If there are any discrepancies, she confronts him, citing the "evidence" she gathered from online platforms. As other scholars have found (see Cabalquinto 2018; Francisco-Menchavez, 2018; Madianou & Miller, 2012; Wilding, 2006), the pre-existing quality and historical context of relationships are key factors that structure how ICTs affect family relations.

KEEPING THE FAMILY TOGETHER IN THE AGE OF ICTs

The Philippines has a long history of international migration, which means that a solid culture of migration has been established in society and in the psyche of Filipinos. While there are some reservations attached to the steady increase in overseas migration, generally, it remains valuable and is accepted as a viable means to promote family well-being.

Over the last five decades, the Philippine state has been steadily deploying workers to the global labor market. Currently, approximately 10% of the Philippine population are living and/or working in different regions of the world, including Japan. Consequently, sustained state-sponsored human capital exports have cemented international migration in the culture of the Philippines. It is well documented that the Philippines is a country of migration, and many Filipinos are expected to migrate at least once in their lifetime (Asis, 2006). Moreover, young people who are more educated and cosmopolitan have a higher likelihood of emigrating. The unceasing migration of overseas Filipino workers and the resultant increase in financial remittances have long attracted the attention of Philippine policymakers who identified the migration sector as a key economic driver and a cornerstone of the national economy. Consequently, international labor migration is an essential economic strategy pursued by the Philippine government (Francisco-Menchavez, 2018; Rodriguez, 2010). To sustain this strategy, the state often deploys a discourse of heroism to laud the efforts of overseas-based migrant workers. Migrants are often framed as self-sacrificing national martyrs who faithfully send back remittances to the homeland to care for family members, primarily children. These remittances, no doubt, have the potential to help improve educational outcomes and boost familial well-being. However, in the Philippines, many are worried about the negative impacts of parental migration on left-behind children and family life.

Given the foregoing, it appears that there is a moral panic regarding the erosion of Filipino family values and a rapid unraveling of the social fabric of Philippine society. It becomes necessary to question whether and under what circumstances can we say that the Filipino family is collapsing. In an age of increased migration and the dependence on ICTs, are transnational families able to transform and adequately satisfy care obligations? Are families able to cultivate care strategies that accommodate protracted separation over long distances? Are new technologies enough to facilitate new types of familial adaptation and resilience?

Even though recent scholarship has increasingly recognized new forms of family arrangements such as foster families and extended-family households, family ties and the expression of intimacy are still predicated on physical proximity, ignoring valuable perspectives on how intimacy and familial care are circulated across borders through material, symbolic, and emotional exchanges. Undoubtedly, the challenges inherent in these exchanges have likewise been ignored (Baldassar & Merla, 2014; Madianou & Miller, 2012). Since the early 2000s, a substantive body of work on what has been referred to as the "global care chains" provides insight on how migrants, primarily low-skilled females, have been forced to move from the global south to the global north to perform care work (see Hochschild, 2000; Parreñas, 2001; Yeates, 2012). While they do this, they inadvertently create care deficits and care drain situations in their home countries. While not totally rejecting the propositions of those scholars, what this chapter demonstrates is that a broader understanding of care and care circulation is more appropriate. As I have done throughout my analysis, it is important to go beyond a dyadic view to consider the extensive network of family relationships which are involved in the provision and exchange of care. In addition to the various actors involved, it is equally important to consider the different ways and forms of care and how it flows around the family network and among extended kin.

The fragmented nature of Filipino transnational families, undoubtedly, supports the idea that these families are disconnected. In fact, lack of communication and loss of intimacy is often cited as inherent challenges of family life across borders (see Dreby, 2010; Parreñas, 2005). It is true that increased human mobility has transformed the realities of families and the way that we understand and "do family." Yet, in this chapter, I demonstrated the ways in which new forms of communication shape intimate interactions and reconstitute the temporal and spatial aspects of Filipino transnational family life. The discussion undertaken supports and builds on recent scholarship which conceptualizes family life as a verb (doing family) rather than as a noun or an entity that is co-domiciled and necessarily place-bound. This perspective also highlights current trends in how families are constituted through sets of actions and gestures that possess certain meanings in particular situations. For instance, as presented in this chapter, communication practices such as regular videoconference while having dinner, virtual good night kisses, live-streaming weddings, and the posting of mundane activities on social media become the "fragments of daily life" (Morgan, 1996, p. 190). It is from these "fragments" that Filipino transnational families are able to weave their collective consciousness of a vibrant and viable family. This is possible because these "fragments" of family life are situated in a broader system of cultural meanings and symbolic value. Besides, scholars and policymakers alike have confirmed that, in the context of the Philippines, remittances and packages sent home have been used productively. Migrants and their families have built or renovated houses, started businesses, invested in financial portfolios and increased spending on children's schooling (see Aguilar et al., 2009; McCallum, 2021a; Yang, 2008). The fulfillment of roles, duties, and expectations, which are central to the maintenance of sustainable families, is being pursued in new and interesting ways (see McCallum, 2021b; Uy-Tioco & Cabalquinto, 2020). It seems that the hysteria surrounding the perceived collapse of the Filipino family, as it were, is unwarranted; and it is safe to declare that the Filipino family is alive and well. Having made that assertion, we cannot ignore the challenges involved in preserving familial bonds and keeping these families together.

CONCLUSION

The narratives presented in this chapter reveal that contemporary communication technologies have increasingly enabled transnational families to modify the setting and dynamics of their family routines and bolster their sense of family-hood. Despite extended periods of living apart, Filipino transnational families in this study have been able to cultivate and maintain a deep sense of collective existence across space and time. Even as migration and increased physical mobility have scattered family members, the creative use of a range of communication technologies have mitigated the detrimental effects on familial bonding and have allowed dispersed families to (re)construct the ways in which they exchange intimacy and provide care. In this chapter, we have seen that family members' notions of belonging and togetherness remain resilient, aided by innovative communication and transport technologies. We have seen that the proliferation of various internet-based technologies has spawned changes not only in the methods of communication, but also in the substance and potency of the relationships that underpin these communications.

I have argued that new technology-mediated communication patterns and practices adopted by transnational families are not characteristically different from interactions that take place in a context of physical proximity. Indeed, mundane as well as more significant milestones and rituals are (re)enacted and celebrated virtually. Moreover, new media has allowed for the public display of shared upward social mobility and migration successes, which lay the foundation for crafting future migration trajectories, primarily for younger family members. My findings challenge the existing paranoia that increased migration of family members necessarily results in emotional disconnections and the undermining of familial solidarity. In fact, this chapter offers an alternative to the idea that strong family relationships are predicated on physical face-to-face interactions, although my argument does not discount the importance of such encounters.

Despite the significant benefits that derive from the use of new media, as we saw in this chapter, there are equally important problematic aspects which must be considered. The increased potential for surveillance, coupled with heightened economic and material demands, can result in contentious relations and emotional burden, even if some family members benefit from these asymmetrical power relations. Nevertheless, closer examination of these social exchanges reveals opportunities for agency and the adoption of creative strategies in the management of privacy and the navigation of new media environments within which family life is experienced.

REFERENCES

Aguilar, F. V., Peñalosa J. E., Liwanag, T. B., Cruz, R., & Melendrez, J. M. (2009). *Maalwang Buhay: Family, overseas migration, and cultures of relatedness in Barangay Paraiso.* Ateneo de Manila University Press. ISBN: 978-971-550-593-2

Asis, M. M. B. (2006, January 1). *The Philippines' culture of migration.* Migration Information Source. https://www.migrationpolicy.org/article/philippines-culture-migration.

Baldassar, L. (2008). Missing kin and longing to be together: Emotions and the construction of co-presence in transnational relationships. *Journal of Intercultural Studies, 29*(3), 247–266.

Baldassar, L., & Merla, L. (2014). *Transnational families, migration and the circulation of care: Understanding mobility and absence in family life.* In Routledge Research in Transnationalism. Routledge.

Baldassar, L., Nedelcu, M., Merla, L., & Wilding, R. (2016). ICT-based co-presence in transnational families and communities: Challenging the premise of face-to-face proximity in sustaining relationships. *Global Networks, 16*(2), 133–144.

Baym, N. (2010). *Personal connections in the digital age.* Polity.

Boyd, D. (2012). Participating in the always-on lifestyle. In M. Mandiberg (Ed.), *The social media reader* (pp. 71–76). New York University Press.

Cabalquinto, E. C. B. (2018). We're not only here but we're there in spirit: Asymmetrical mobile intimacy and the transnational Filipino family. *Mobile Media & Communication, 6*(1), 37–52.

Dreby, J. (2010). *Divided by borders: Mexican migrants and their children.* University of California Press.

Elliott, A., & Urry, J. (2010). *Mobile lives.* Taylor & Francis.

Finch, J. (2007). Displaying families. *Sociology, 41*(1), 65–81.

Francisco-Menchavez, V. (2018). *The labor of care: Filipina migrants and transnational families in the
digital age.* University of Illinois Press.

Hochschild, A. R. (2000). Global care chains and emotional surplus value. In A. Giddens & W. Hutton
(Eds.), *On the edge: Living with global capitalism* (pp. 130–146). Jonathan Cape.

Horst, H. A. (2006.) The blessings and burdens of communication: Cell phones in Jamaican transnational social fields. *Global Networks 6*, 143–159.

Katz, J. E. (2011). *Mobile communication: Dimensions of social policy.* Transaction.

Licoppe, C. (2004). "Connected" presence: The emergence of a new repertoire for managing social
relationships in a changing communication technoscape. *Environment and Planning D: Society
and Space, 22*(1), 135–156.

Licoppe, C. & Smoreda, Z. (2005). Are social networks technologically embedded? How networks are
changing today with changes in communication technology? *Social Networks, 27*, 317–335.

Locke, C., Tam, N. T., & Hoa, N. T. (2014). Mobile householding and marital dissolution in Vietnam:
An inevitable consequence? *Geoforum, 51*, 273–283.

Lopez, L. (2006). *A handbook of Philippine folklore.* University of the Philippines Press.

Madianou, M. (2012). Migration and the accentuated ambivalence of motherhood: The role of ICTs
in Filipino transnational families. *Global Networks, 12*(3), 277–295.

Madianou, M. (2014). Smartphones as polymedia. *Journal of Computer-mediated Communication,
19*(2), 1–14.

Madianou, M. (2016). Ambient co-presence: Transnational family practices in polymedia environments. *Global Networks, 16*(2), 183–201.

Madianou, M., & Miller, D. (2011). Mobile phone parenting: Reconfiguring relationships between
Filipina migrant mothers and their left-behind children. *New Media & Society, 13*(3), 457–470.

Madianou, M., & Miller, D. (2012). *Migration and new media: Transnational families and polymedia.*
Routledge.

McCallum, D. G. (2021a). Going home to learn: Educational journeys of children in Filipino transnational families in Japan. In F. Peddie & J. Liu (Eds.), *Education and Migration in an Asian
context* (pp. 93–113). Springer Nature. https://doi.org/10.1007/978-981-33-6288-8

McCallum, D. G. (2021b). Affectionate remittances: Materialism and care in Filipino transnational families in Japan. *Current Sociology, 70*(6), 843–859. https://doi.org/10.1177/00113921211034895

McKay, D. (2012). *Global Filipinos.* Indiana University Press.

Morgan, D. (1996). *Family connections: An introduction to family studies.* Polity Press.

Nedelcu, M. (2012). 'Migrants' new transnational habitus: Rethinking migration through a cosmopolitan lens in the digital age. *Journal of Ethnic and Migration Studies, 38*(9), 1339–1356.

Nedelcu, M., & Wyss, M. (2016). 'Doing family' through ICT-mediated ordinary co-presence:
Transnational communication practices of Romanian migrants in Switzerland. *Global
Networks, 16*(2), 202–218.

Parreñas, R. S. (2001). *Servants of globalization: Women, migration, and domestic work.* Stanford
University Press.

Parreñas, R. S. (2005). Long distance intimacy: Class, gender and intergenerational relations between
mothers and children in Filipino transnational families. *Global Networks, 5*(4), 317–336.

Parreñas, R. S. (2008). Transnational fathering: Gendered conflicts, distant disciplining and emotional
gaps. *Journal of Ethnic and Migration Studies, 34*(7), 1057–1072.

Parreñas, R. S. (2010). Transnational mothering: A source of gender conflicts in the family. *North
Carolina Law Review, 88*(5), 1825–1856.

Parreñas, R. S. (2012). The reproductive labour of migrant workers. *Global Networks, 12*(2), 269–275.

Rodriguez, R. M. (2010). *Migrants for export: How the Philippine state brokers labor to the world.*
University of Minnesota Press.

Robertson, S. (2014). The temporalities of international migration: Implications for ethnographic research. In S. Castles, D. Ozkul, & M. Cubas (Eds.), *Social transformation and migration: National and local experiences in South Korea, Turkey, Mexico and Australia* (pp. 45–60). Palgrave Macmillan.

Turkle, S. (2011). *Alone together*. Basic Book.

Uy-Tioco, C. S., & Cabalquinto, E. C. B. (2020). Transnational mobile carework: Filipino migrants, family intimacy, and mobile media. In J. Cabañes & C. Uy-Tioco (Eds.), *Mobile media and social intimacies in Asia. Mobile communication in Asia: Local insights, global implications* (pp. 153–170). Springer.

Wilding, R. (2006). '"Virtual" intimacies? Families communicating across transnational contexts'. *Global Networks, 6*(2), 125–142.

Yang, D. (2008). International migration, remittances and household investment: Evidence from Philippine migrants' exchange rate shocks. *The Economic Journal, 118*(528), 591–630.

Yeates, N. (2012). Global care chains: A state-of-the-art review and future directions in care transnationalization research. *Global Networks, 12*(2), 135–154.

CHAPTER 7

AN EXPOSITION OF THE MULTIDIMENSIONALITY OF THE TAGASALO PERSONALITY

Rizason L. Go Tian-Ng and Jofel D. Umandap

ABSTRACT

The tagasalo concept is a unique Filipino personality, indigenous to its culture and relevant within the family system. Carandang (1987) based this concept from her in-depth clinical practice and observation of Filipino family dynamics. The tagasalo is the family member who "catches" or "saves" the family and feels inordinately responsible for the care and welfare of other members of the family. Udarbe (2001) conducted further research and identified dynamics of the tagasalo personality. In the current study, the authors have extended the framework by exploring other dimensions aside from the compulsive and non-compulsive dimensions. The tagasalo also exhibits internalizing behaviors, an implicit tendency to be sensitive to other people, struggling with internal anxiety and stress; and externalizing behaviors by acting out explicitly to alleviate these anxieties. This chapter provides an in-depth theoretical-historical development of the tagasalo personality construct, locates it in broader psychological literature, and extends its potential by identifying multiple dimensions, supported with case illustrations and a composite case analysis.

Keywords: Tagasalo personality; family dynamics; internalizing behavior; externalizing behavior; Filipino families; Sikolohiyang Pilipino

Resilience and Familism: The Dynamic Nature of Families in the Philippines
Contemporary Perspectives in Family Research, Volume 23, 103–125
Copyright © 2023 by Emerald Publishing Limited
All rights of reproduction in any form reserved
ISSN: 1530-3535/doi:10.1108/S1530-353520230000023007

INTRODUCTION

The Filipino family is characterized with traditional values, culture, and religious heritage significantly contributing to its dynamics. Embedded in the core of the psyche include fulfilling familial duties, upholding family values and traditions, maintaining harmony, and developing a self-sacrificial attitude in honor of God and family. Viewed from a systemic lens, the family is an organized unit with interacting members fulfilling certain roles, adhering to implicit and explicit rules, striving to achieve homeostasis (Goldenberg & Goldenberg, 2012), such that these influence personality development. Within this context originates the development of the *tagasalo* personality.

SIKOLOHIYANG PILIPINO AND FILIPINO VALUES

Tagasalo research could be classified under Philippine indigenous psychology, a psychology that stems from the Filipino experience, mentality, and orientation (Enriquez, 1975, 1979), with culture and family as its repository of concepts significant to *Sikolohiyang Pilipino* research. Indigenous psychology considers the context of the people involved in the study of human behavior and psychology as culture-bound (Kim et al., 2006). Such research is a form of indigenization from within (Clemente, 2011).

Filipinos relate with one another beginning with their *loob*, their sense of self, emanating from a socialized and personal identity, and a social need to relate and connect with others through the relational value of *kapwa*. Fr. Jaime C. Bulatao (1964) used a metaphor in discussing individuation within the Filipino family. He likened family members to fried eggs in a pan, each with a distinct yolk, yet connected to one another with their white parts that it can be difficult to determine boundaries between eggs.

The tagasalo is anchored on a Filipino values system with *kapwa* at its core. To sustain the value of *kapwa*, one practices *pakikipagkapwa*, a deep connection of the *loob* (or self) of one with the *loob* of the other, which is a relational value. This *pakikipagkapwa* requires a constant sensing of the *loob* through *pakikiramdam*, attunement to the needs of the other. For many Filipinos who tend to avoid direct confrontation, the value of *pakikiramdam* is a powerful tool for communication.

This chapter examines the tagasalo as a fruition of Filipino values of *pakikipagkapwa* at its core, and *pakikiramdam* as a form of connection, care, and communication. The tagasalo's sense of *kapwa* and identity (*loob*) are directed toward the family's well-being. For such individuals, *pakikiramdam* is more heightened and enables them to deeply and actively sense the needs, thoughts, and feelings of members that manifests in behaviors that cultivate a tagasalo personality. The tagasalo uses *pakikipagkapwa* and *pakikiramdam* to maintain harmony within shifting family dynamics (Carandang, 1987). It becomes an astute and sensitive form of language expressed both explicitly in words and actions, as well as implicitly through their deep sense of responsibility. As such, it can be observed to be internalized and externalized behaviors and experiences.

With family-orientedness as another prominent value, *pakikiramdam* of the tagasalo toward the needs of others is developed within the early family system as its possible point of origin. While progressive ideas are gradually shaping contemporary family practices, parenting styles are still largely authoritarian, and reciprocity is still valued (Alampay & Jocson, 2011). Parents are expected to provide for their children; in turn, children are expected to set aside their individual interests in deference to parental authority or familial obligations. *Utang ng loob* becomes more deeply felt by the tagasalo who fulfills the debt of gratitude and sacrifices personal needs to rescue, protect, or distract the parents.

The tagasalo orients the self to and identifies with the family; hence, the personality is hinged on harmony within the family. Displaying respect for the elders, having strong family connections, and balancing close family relationships also manifest other Filipino values of *pagiging magalang* (being respectful) and *pagiging masunurin* (being obedient) as expressions of the tagasalo's filial piety. Thus, the responsibility of upholding family values and traditions to maintain harmonious relations is discerned and characterized by the tagasalo.

Despite parallelisms between the tagasalo personality and related concepts in other indigenous psychologies, it is considered indigenous to Filipino family dynamics. Within this motivational system, it has developed a tagasalo personality structure as distinct in its drive, needs, and actions when compared to counterparts in other cultures. With the increase of the diaspora phenomenon wherein Filipino parents opt to work abroad, children intuitively take on the role of tagasalo even in the presence of extended family stepping in to help care for children (Carandang et al., 2007). With this ongoing phenomenon affecting both micro- and macro-systems comes an increased need to learn more about tagasalo personality and its relevance in the Filipino family and society.

Dr Ma. Lourdes A. Carandang's (1987) clinical work with families for over 30 years resulted in her seminal book, *Filipino Children Under Stress*. She observed behavioral patterns that recur in typical family dynamics wherein some children absorbed the effects of family problems. In sensing underlying tensions, these children are overwhelmed, and develop anxious thoughts and feelings; thus, attempt coping behaviors that fulfill the role of the tagasalo or the savior in the family. These behaviors extend to caring for the needs of others even into their adult lives, relationships, career, family, and personal lives. Her work articulated the concept of tagasalo which brought it to the forefront of Sikolohiyang Pilipino.

THE DEVELOPMENT OF THE TAGASALO PERSONALITY

The tagasalo is identified as someone for others, giving more than receiving, and more self-sacrificial than self-serving. They feel the need to take care of and to help the family by making themselves more involved than other members.

The Vulnerable Child as the Tagasalo

Ramon is a five-year-old boy, the eldest among four children of a young couple. He was referred to therapy for extremely aggressive behavior: frequently screaming and crying at home, hurting his younger siblings, disobeying authorities in school, being very restless, and having a very short attention span. His parents, financially dependent on his paternal grandmother, quarreled frequently and constantly worried about their economic survival. Ramon was left feeling helpless thinking "if my parents are not ok, what would happen to my family?"

As a means to protect family equilibrium or lessen the tension, members in conflict use another member to triangulate (Kerr & Bowen, 1988). In cases of marital discord, the tagasalo as a child may be the triangulated member that a parent may focus attention on to lessen the need to relate with the other parent they are in conflict with. The young child may then feel the need to fulfill parental expectations in an effort to please one or both parents. Ramon, as a vulnerable child triangulated by his parents, absorbed the stress and acted as the family's "stress barometer." His symptomatic behaviors protected the equilibrium and responded to his family's crisis, making the family functional.

Carandang (1987) defined the word tagasalo from the root word *salo*, which means "to catch," and the prefix *taga,* meaning "the one who." Together, this means "the one who catches." A tagasalo is a member of the family who tends to catch other people's problems, attempts to make them their own, and endeavors to take care, rescue, and resolve conflicts themselves. Often, the most attuned, sensitive, and caring member absorbs the family's troubles and is most affected. They are described as the responsible member who listens and mediates, works toward harmony, and has a strong need for control and emotional distance (Udarbe, 2001).

The Family System of the Tagasalo

Ramon's case illustrates the patterns that recur typically among some Filipino families and how maintaining equilibrium with family dynamics can precipitate the development of a tagasalo personality. Evident in similar cases are family roles, identified by Carandang (1987) experienced by families in conflicts: the *powerful adult* may be a parent, grandparent, or even children who gain power through the possession of money or emotional control. The powerful adult, Ramon's affluent grandmother, exerted financial control over Ramon and his family. Conversely, the *oppressed adult,* left in a dependent or weak position, possessed little control over circumstances, just as Ramon's parents were financially dependent on the grandmother. Ramon was the *vulnerable child* and, as a tagasalo, absorbed the effects of the family's dependency on his authoritarian grandmother and acted out the stress experienced by his family. Compared to the vulnerable child, *sideline children* may not be as affected by the family problem or maybe not at all.

When generational boundary dissolution is experienced in the family system characterized by enmeshment, over-involvement, role-reversal, and even parentification, the child tends to adopt behaviors that maintain the equilibrium. Fullinwider-Bush and Jacobvitz (1993) found that when there was a boundary dissolution in the parent–child relationship, young adult daughters were less likely to practice exploration in their experiences of identity development outside of the family unit. In this sense, factors in the family system influence the personality development and identity of the daughter. This is related to Teng et al.'s (2021) qualitative study on parentified young adult daughters. Despite a sense of individual autonomy and sense of competence as contributors to the family, some lamented the lack of opportunity to socialize and participate in independent activities. For Bowen, triangulated daughters tend to feel enmeshed in the family system and unable to separate their own needs from their family's needs (Kerr & Bowen, 1988).

Tagasalo and Birth Order

The eldest child was theorized most likely to develop the tendency (Carandang, 1987) stemming from their closer proximity to parents which makes them more sensitive to the struggles and conflicts their parents encounter. The *youngest functioning-eldest* is one such exception when the youngest child takes on the role of a tagasalo (Carandang, 2007). Both eldest and youngest children have a special innate quality in their birth order, leaving the middle child in a naturally less differentiated position. Middle children who become tagasalo could be attributed to their drive to differentiate from their siblings as a result of trying to gain their parents' approval or trying to create a specialized position for themselves. In Udarbe's (2001) research, birth order was not the primary factor in the development of the tagasalo. External factors such as one's relationships with parents and siblings, and especially the family dynamic unique to each family, seemed to play a bigger role.

There may be one or more tagasalo or none at all (Carandang, 1987, 2007). Usually, to have more than one tagasalo is beneficial since two members would be able to support each other and prevent the other from being burnt out. Carandang (1987, 2007) also asserted that any family, rich or poor, may still experience their own kinds of conflict, such as financial or emotional, and a tagasalo is warranted for family balance and harmony.

THE TAGASALO AS A PERSONALITY

While earlier studies tended to focus on roles or values, the tagasalo is more encompassing, beginning from childhood, encouraged in the family system, and finds its place in an individual's personality development. Although this personality may have clinical manifestations present in therapeutic settings, the tagasalo as a personality tendency and as an identified role in families is one that Filipinos recognize (Perez, 2022).

Margaret Udarbe (2001) built on Carandang's work by highlighting positive roles and behaviors, emphasizing it to be a personality, not a complex nor a syndrome which is merely a number of behaviors grouped together to form a symptom of a disorder (Carandang, 1987; personal communication, April 17, 2017), that is developed over time and dictates the actions of an individual. She observed that many psychology students are drawn to the helping profession, and perhaps this motivation to help stems from the experience of being a tagasalo in their respective families. Of note is her understanding of the tagasalo in the family systems framework, acknowledging that a tagasalo personality tendency may further be reinforced by experiences, such as being triangulated to relieve stress when conflicts arise.

Both Carandang and Udarbe understood that tagasalo take on responsibilities as early as in their childhood. Within the family system, the vulnerable child exhibits a stronger sense of responsibility and is encouraged by the family system to take on the role of the helper, thereby enhancing their tagasalo identity (Go Tian-Ng, 2004; Udarbe, 2001). Over time, this is internalized such that it influences the development of their personality.

The tagasalo personality could be conceptualized as a personality structure that certain individuals develop over time due to their unique role that is integral to maintaining balance within the family unit. Yet, similar to personality disorders, if manifestations become rigid, pervade one's functioning, and negatively affect relationships, such tendencies could become problematic.

Basic Principles

Carandang (1987) developed some basic tenets in understanding the tagasalo. First, there is one tagasalo in every Filipino family and females are taught early in life to be a tagasalo. In the context of a Filipino society, females are expected to take charge of household chores early in life. Nurturance, flexibility, and responsibility are part of girls' training for their future roles of becoming homemakers; hence, their responsibility eventually develops into emotional care for family members. Carandang (2007) later noted that perhaps changing gender stereotypes and the evolving Filipino family structure may lessen the need for a tagasalo. Second, the tagasalo's self-worth stems from taking care of others, especially the parents whose approval they seek. Third, some tagasalo personalities have compulsive tendencies that can lead to emotional burnout. Fourth, the tagasalo are usually unconscious of their role, the reasons motivating them to absorb the family's problems, and the consequent guilt when failing to do so. Finally, the tagasalo tend to extend their duties of "catching" others' problems beyond the family, playing out their role even in personal and professional relationships.

Dynamics of the Tagasalo Personality

Udarbe's (2001) work resulted in identifying nine interacting dynamics that drive the needs and motivations of the tagasalo. As the tagasalo "catches" other family members, physically, mentally, or emotionally (Udarbe, 2001), they consider their *parents as central* to whom they need to please, to spare them from trouble, and to take care of them. They have a stronger *capacity to care* by being generous, approachable, and willing to self-sacrifice for the benefit of their family. They feel a stronger *sense of responsibility* inculcated earlier in life through household chores and taking care of parents and siblings. They have an *ability to listen* and an *ability to mediate* arising from a *need to maintain family harmony*.

While they *seek to be differentiated* particularly from a troubled sibling to balance the family systems, the tagasalo behavior may also be a projection of symptomatic needs by sending distress signals, such as acting out the tension, becoming a behavioral problem to distract from the conflict within the family system, or by absorbing the stress. The message of the overt behavior is to protect the equilibrium constricted around a conflictual situation that becomes functional for the family. Actively, some may *try to control* the situation of the family system by mediating and by resolving conflicts that threaten harmony. This need for control can either be the cause or the effect of their need to mediate, exert influence on the family, and their sense of responsibility to take action. Interestingly, in navigating these complex needs, there arises their own *need and capacity for emotional distance* as a form of compartmentalizing. Over time, this multilayered process perpetuates the tagasalo's personality development.

COMPARISONS WITH RELATED CONCEPTS

Notions related to the tagasalo personality resonate across many contexts and cultures, and have been widely studied in the literature. The concept of the tagasalo has been compared with other constructs (Gingrich, 2002; Udarbe, 2001): Adler's (1956) "redeemer complex," unconsciously takes an attitude of having to save or redeem another as a need to achieve a sense of superiority, Beattie's (1989) concept of "codependency," the experience of needing to be needed by others such that one's actions and behaviors center on sustaining this dynamic, and Miller's (1983) "enabler," the identified pleaser, family warrior, and caretaker, enabling others to rely on them, such that dysfunctional family patterns are sustained. A number of these concepts were developed in the context of alcoholism, a factor not considered in the conceptualization of the tagasalo personality.

Also in Western literature is the concept of parentification, where a child takes on adult or parent roles in the family (Jurkovic, 1998; Valleau et al., 1995). Children can be instrumentally parentified where they assume household responsibilities, or emotionally parentified where they take on parental roles. While not pathogenic in itself, when a child is overburdened with such responsibilities and experiences when it is not developmentally appropriate, they are adversely affected (Hooper et al., 2011).

Certain studies have linked parentification to being the tagasalo in the family (Teng et al., 2021). In Valleau et al. (1995), being parentified as a child has been linked with Peek and Trezona's "caretaker syndrome" in adulthood (1984, as cited in Valleau et al., 1995), a pattern of behavior wherein one is compelled to help others that they neglect their own needs. This concept comes close to the tagasalo personality, yet paints a more clinical picture; whereas, the tagasalo in the Filipino family systems need not always be problematic, as emphasized by Udarbe (2001).

Also related is familism, a Latino cultural value that emphasizes obligation, filial piety, family support, and obedience (Campos et al., 2014). While similar to Filipino family dynamics, it is more of a value, and not a personality nor a role. Familism may be more related to a strong sense of family, and this orientation may lead to tendencies of a tagasalo personality with studies indicating that familial obligations can affect developmental processes and outcomes particularly among children (Stein et al., 2014).

TAGASALO PERSONALITY SCALE: VALIDATION OF THE TAGASALO PERSONALITY

Garcia (1999) developed a preliminary tagasalo scale validated by Go Tian-Ng (2004) using the *Panunukat ng Pagkataong Pilipino* (PPP) (Carlota, 1985; Guanzon-Lapeña et al., 1998), a locally developed, valid, and reliable scale that measures 19 dimensions of personality. It correlated three factors linked to the tagasalo personality that support Carandang's and Udarbe's works: dependability and affiliation (DA), social anxiety in social situation (SASS), and responsibility to self and to others (RESP). A correlation between DA and RESP was observed and supported the observation that high DA tagasalo would have a strong need for parental recognition, considering their parents as central to their existence. They feel responsible for sparing them from family problems and avoid disappointing or hurting their parents' feelings as a form of respect or obedience. In the study, females scored highest across the three factors.

Dimensions of the Tagasalo Personality

Carandang (1987, 2007) differentiated compulsive and non-compulsive tagasalo. The compulsive tagasalo operate largely on unconscious needs and motivations and tend to be more maladaptive in nature. The non-compulsive are more aware of their motivations, tend to be more adaptive with more intentionality and deliberation in their actions and behaviors.

Compulsive Tagasalo

A compulsive tagasalo has an automatic and unconscious behavioral pattern to help others without much insight into their own needs. Usually lacking basic trust and security, such compulsion may be the manifestation of a lack of love and nurturance. The compulsive tagasalo anticipates other people's needs, inadvertently hoping that their own needs are provided for by others. Being compulsive becomes counter-intuitive as their seemingly independent and capable behavior tend to outwardly depict that they are self-sufficient and do not expect care nor nurturance (Carandang, 1987, 2007). Such compulsion is a reaction formation that stems from their own lack of unconditional positive regard and their repressed needs to receive emotional care. They hope to gain their affection and approval by compulsively behaving in such ways. They can be driven by a number of motives, such as a need for compassion, a need to find personal significance and external assurance, trying hard to be approved of, and recognized to the point of neglecting their own needs. As Carandang (1987) described compulsive behavior as unconscious, this research equates compulsion with level of awareness; hence, being a compulsive tagasalo demonstrates a low level of self-awareness.

Non-compulsive Tagasalo

The non-compulsive tagasalo is described as more adaptive, occupying their role naturally without being compulsively fixated on it. Perhaps in receiving unconditional love and respect from loved ones, they are not compelled to seek these unconsciously. They may also have acted more compulsively before but have gained enough self-awareness and self-understanding (Carandang, 1987; personal communication, April 17, 2017). Equally driven by compassion and care for their loved ones and a need for relational harmony, this healthier tagasalo is more emotionally secure, helps out of willingness, and sets reasonable boundaries and expectations from themselves and from others. For these reasons, this research supports non-compulsive tendencies as possessing a higher level of awareness of their behavior. Being a tagasalo can be healthy when non-compulsive but unhealthy when compulsive (Carandang, 1987).

METHODOLOGY

Qualitative methods were used to explore the multifaceted nature of the tagasalo personality and to understand their inner experiences and behavioral expressions. A thematic analysis of reflective essays written by self-identified tagasalo was first conducted, followed by the presentation of a composite case. Informed consent was obtained, participant confidentiality was maintained, and ethical considerations and protocols were followed.

Thematic Analysis of Reflective Essays

Aside from reviewing the original case studies from Carandang's book and from Udarbe's dissertation, the researchers analyzed the reflection papers of six undergraduate psychology students – 5 females and 1 male – who volunteered to write about their experiences after an orientation-lecture on the tagasalo Personality based on two (2) questions: *Why do you believe that you are a tagasalo? How does this manifest in your day-to-day life?* Students were reminded that submissions were purely voluntary and do not merit any extra points to their class standing. Additionally, their submissions were indicative of their willingness to submit their essays for research purposes while their identities were assured of confidentiality. The essays were subjected to thematic analysis wherein anecdotes were highlighted based on Udarbe's dynamics of a tagasalo, and distinguished based on the manner in which it was experienced.

Composite Case Study

The researchers compiled clinical case studies of clients spanning three years or longer in therapy who self-identify as tagasalo. A composite case material was developed following Duffy's (2010) six-step guidelines to analyze themes relevant to understanding the tagasalo personality, to protect the participants' confidentiality, and to better illustrate the phenomenon. First, the theoretical focus of the composite case was identified. As an exposition of the tagasalo personality, the chapter aimed to accurately depict its development and presentations in both clinical and non-clinical settings. Second, individual cases were shortlisted, and four client cases were identified as containing relevant material. These cases were written-up separately, then studied concurrently. Third, illustrative clinical material depicting the experiences of each identified tagasalo case was summarized. Fourth, a single composite case was constructed from these materials to develop a coherent narrative of a tagasalo as a single case. Fifth, demographic details from each of the cases were integrated, ensuring that the case remains cohesive without overusing elements from any single case source. Finally, the case is comprehensively presented as a composite material.

While complicated and lengthy, the use of these guidelines ensures that the resulting composite case material portrays a thicker and richer description of the tagasalo personality. An added advantage is that this process enables complete anonymity for the clients and prevents unintended breaches of confidentiality (Duffy, 2010). The use of composite cases in qualitative research has been useful in various applications and contexts, such as in presenting interview data from public figures (Willis, 2019), to develop instructional cases in educational and research settings (Ensminger et al., 2021), and in developing therapeutic approaches for specific populations (Golden & Oransky, 2019).

Integration of Thematic Analysis and Case Studies

Results from both methods were then analyzed, compared, and discussed iteratively. The researchers drew from their own work, validating results with their own personal and professional experiences, and resulted in the development of a new and enhanced framework to understand the tagasalo personality. To ensure validity of the results, certain procedures, such as triangulation with publicly available content and author reflexivity were used to assess for truthfulness and legitimacy of the derived framework (Creswell & Creswell, 2017). An external review was also conducted in the process of finalizing the manuscript.

RESULTS

Themes Supporting Behaviors Characterizing the Tagasalo Personality

Following are themes culled from the six essays that support the dynamics behind the personality as identified by Udarbe (2001).

Sense of Responsibility

All essay writers saw themselves as having sense of responsibility. They took initiative and exhibited the need to be depended on, which can be attributed to how their parents set expectations and assigned roles to them from a very young age. "I became a tagasalo because of the way I had to deal with my younger brothers growing up. I was told to take care of my brothers" and "It is tiring but I felt that if I didn't, who would?"

The Ability for Listening

Three of the essay writers were open to communicating and listening to others, and able to pick up implicit cues and understand other people's situations. This demonstrates keen observation and sensitivity to surroundings, a Filipino trait of *pakikiramdam*. "Even if they don't explicitly tell me, I could pick up that things were off. I'd notice my cousins' attempt to interact with their parents," "I became more aware and alert about their interactions, which later on led me to carry some of their conflict with me as well," and "As I reached the latter years of high school, my parents would open up more to me about their struggles with my siblings and with each other."

The Need to Mediate

Two essays depicted this need, driven by emotional motivations toward situations as seen in the quotes: "I was driven to letting family members talk it out because I felt that they wouldn't address their problems if I didn't mediate for them," "I felt obligated to mediate for my cousins and it hurt me that my younger cousins couldn't experience the same dynamic [in my family]," and "I act as the mediator when my parents have arguments."

The Need for Harmony

As with the need to mediate, this need may be due to the general emotion of anxiety they feel when they cannot solve problems, feeling fearful, guilty, and hurt. Hence, to counter the anxiety, all essays showed the tagasalo would strive for harmony. "I realize I take it to heart too much and actively try to patch things up myself" and "I felt the need to do something when my parents' siblings would talk to me about their problems."

The Need for Control

This need was also observed across all essays and overlaps with the needs to mediate and for harmony. The quotes highlight the tagasalo's concern with their influence and power as they exhibit feelings of guilt when they are unable to take charge of or control a situation. "I have to take my parents' role and take charge whenever they weren't around," "I've assumed the responsibility of keeping house in order, being the point person between the household help and my parents who are in the U.S. with my pregnant sister," and "If my mom doesn't tell me, I still do the ordering around."

The Parents as Central
This feature was evident in all essays. The tagasalo constantly consider their parents when contemplating on their actions which may translate to the *utang ng loob* they may feel toward their parents. "I do household chores just so my parents wouldn't be mad at me," "I volunteer to do errands for them, accompany them to appointments, drive for them, go to mass with them, treat them sometimes, among others, so that I can do my part in getting whatever stress they have off their shoulders," and "She was worrying and I could feel it. I 'caught' her through reassurance that, as a system, we were still functioning."

Capacity for Caring
Exhibited in five essays, the quotes related to this theme distinctly exhibit how the behaviors of a tagasalo may extend beyond their families, and how they tend to sacrifice their well-being for others. "I was acting as the caring figure and always giving way (paumaya, Visayan dialect) which became a force of habit than a responsibility I had to do," "I helped a very close friend and I wanted to leave because he tends to abuse me physically and mentally, but every time I just get pulled back by my guilt to help him," and "... think of others before myself, although sometimes it isn't healthy because it can reach a point where I blame myself and carry unnecessary burden."

The Tagasalo as Sibling (Need to be Different in the Eyes of the Parents)
This need to differentiate themselves by being more dependable and responsible was observed in four essays. "If my brothers want something the same I do, I must always 'be the better person' and let my brothers get it first," "Even if I'm the youngest in the family, I was raised to be more mature than my actual age," and "She's [roommate] been slacking off because I always do the grown-up things for us."
    A tagasalo may also differentiate themselves in negative, and not just positive ways. While these quotes did not include this converse tendency, the negative differentiation may also occur in the development of the tagasalo personality as seen in Ramon's case.

Capacity for Emotional Distance
This need was observed in three essays. While the tagasalo may experience negative emotions of the compulsive type, some may look past these to find fulfillment in their roles. "I realize I take it to heart too much and actively try to patch things up myself" and "It's a draining role but it also gives me fulfillment because for the times that I cannot deal with my own problems at least I can relieve someone else of their troubles."

New Dimensions: The Internalizing and Externalizing Behaviors of the Tagasalo
The research revealed more dimensions: externalized as when behaviors are expressed, verbalized, acted out and upon; and internalized when behaviors are

non-verbal, implicit, and felt. Both internalizing and externalizing behaviors were described by Achenbach (1966) in his study of adaptive and maladaptive functioning among children's behaviors. The analysis for each dimension integrated Carandang's clinical observations, Udarbe's research, and the reflective essays.

Internalizing Behaviors

These are characterized as one's difficulty in coping with negative feelings and directing feelings inward, thus, are not immediately observable. Achenbach (1966) described internalizing behaviors such as social withdrawal, depression, tension, fearfulness and anxiety, difficulty concentrating, engaging in negative self-talk, self-blame, and guilt. Carandang (1987) validated these tagasalo behaviors as internalizing emotional conflict among loved ones. They feel a deep awareness of emotional conflicts, taking to heart any issues occurring within their family and even from their surroundings. They are emotional receptacles who internalize the family's problems so the stress stays within them.

Internalizing behaviors may fall within the emotional parentification concept but constitute behavior that goes deeper than fulfilling the roles of a parent. An internalizing tagasalo can be described as sensitive, reactive, anxious, and prone to negative feelings. These tendencies can cause complications as they make the tagasalo more prone to being overburdened which could explain somatic symptoms and complaints.

A post hoc analysis of the cases identified the following internalizing behaviors: Lota was a 30-year-old nurse described in Carandang's book as the *total tagasalo*. She took care of others, being fully involved, and catered to her family's psychological and physical needs. Another is Danilo, an 8-year-old who refused to go to school due to being beset with many fears. He was inhibited, his mannerisms described as rigid and stiff, as if containing and protecting internal turmoil. Lastly, Tina, a 41-year-old lawyer who became ill and was confined in the hospital for high blood pressure, depression, panic attacks, headache, ulcer, backache, nausea, heart palpitation, and loss of appetite. During her consultation, she mentioned not wanting to burden God and regretted taking so much of Dr Carandang's time.

Analysis of Udarbe's study of family dynamics pointed to internalizing behaviors as being more emotional, fearful, nervous, quiet, and calm like a mother. They are often nicknamed "mama's junior," "mother's listener," "mother's tagasalo," "shock absorber," "source of strength," acting as *"padre de familia,"* or as "mediator to *tatay"* (father). They are most aware and most attuned to others' feelings: they could feel their mother's worries, feel upset for their parents who were disappointed with other family members, more concerned with and deeply attached to the family, and more worried about family matters. They avoid fights and confrontations, have high expectations, yet are emotionally burdened with guilt and fatigue.

There is the presence of strong emotions and sense of duty or guilt that indicate the tagasalo's sense of *pakikiramdam,* being sensitive to their surroundings. "Ever since I was younger, I've felt a certain pressure within the dynamics of both my immediate family and my extended family," "I felt responsible and blamed myself when my second sister got pregnant," "I knew, without my mom saying, that I had to [*sic.*] in the hospital 24/7 for the major operation," "I wanted my parents to be proud of me and notice that their work as parents is paying off, too," "... I need to help others because I understand what they're going through," "I feel guilty about keeping my earnings to myself, and not having to support me is enough for her (mother)," and "I'm really sensitive when people start to argue with each other."

Externalizing Behaviors

Externalizing tagasalo personalities have difficulty coping and tend to direct their thoughts and feelings overtly, or to manifest more observable behaviors. Achenbach (1966) identified externalizing behaviors in children as hyperactivity, antisocial and delinquent behavior, negative engagement with peers, hostility and aggressiveness, and other disruptive, extraverted, and acting out behaviors. The tagasalo act out these behaviors actively, excessively, and explicitly as coping behaviors to help the family.

Externalizing behaviors are likened to instrumental parentification but the tagasalo behavior goes beyond the mere fulfillment of chores and roles of "fixer" or "mediator" inculcated by parents. To illustrate, externalizing behaviors could manifest in the tagasalo pursuing scholastic or professional achievement to engender pride in the parents or managing responsibility in the family or household to compensate for any stresses in the family. Toward the other end of the spectrum, they may seem like the cause of the conflict itself by externalizing various maladaptive coping behaviors, such as hoarding, emotional eating, or a tendency to neglect the self.

Some examples of externalizing behaviors in Carandang's book include: Alma, a 10-year-old who screamed and acted violently and pushed her cousin into a swimming pool. Mario, a 7-year-old, was caught stealing and lying. An unnamed 8-year-old girl angrily confronted the mistress of her father. Renato, a 5-year-old, displayed violent, oppositional behavior, and attempted to steal money to alleviate his parents' sufferings. Fely was a 35-year-old married woman who finished her doctoral studies as a gift to her father. She was still taking care of her parents when her own son acted out in school, signaling his need for her to take care of her own family. An unnamed 33-year-old woman wanted her parents' approval through academic achievement and worked compulsively to achieve excellence, almost to perfection.

For Udarbe, externalizing tagasalo behavior includes taking in too many responsibilities, obligations, and activities to primarily help and care for their family. They constantly adjust to avoid conflict, such as choosing career paths to accommodate their parent's preferences or delaying career development to care for them. They live with their parents or nearby to constantly check-in on family and loved ones. They may become fully involved in catering to their family and take ownership of family problems. One particular tagasalo kept secrets regarding marital problems and family business issues so no one else would worry, and another applied for work leave to help the father's business. They sacrificed for others, being thrifty themselves. They were protective of siblings, cared for, and anticipated the family's needs. They bridged the gap between parents and siblings. One aimed to take up law to help indigenous people. Consequently, they may develop a more dominant or serious personality needed to handle responsibility and manage people's lives.

Externalizing behaviors are intended to actively take control as a manifestation of their sense of responsibility and their need to differentiate themselves from siblings. "I studied very hard for me to achieve the grades my brother used to get so that my parents would feel less bad about their efforts," "I would take it upon myself to make sure things at home were always fixed for my brothers," "I would be the type to volunteer to stay after school, have the initiative to ask teachers if they'd need any help, and even discipline my classmates," "I took it upon myself to take care of my younger cousins the way my parents took care of me," "I tried to bridge my tita [aunt] and her kids whenever I could," "I'd invite my cousin to participate and would even encourage my younger cousin to approach her instead of me," and "I was the one who took charge in ordering food and buying the groceries for us because he [older brother] was too lazy to do them."

Some may tend to exhibit negative externalizing behaviors in childhood that become more helpful as they mature. To illustrate, Diego is the younger brother of Anton by five years. As a toddler, Diego was known for his quick temper and was described as fussy and demanding. Growing up, he witnessed how Anton's more oppositional behavior and poor grades caused their parents' arguments. He also realized he was different from his older brother who made friends easily and was talented at sports, while he was more introverted. Thinking he was able to make his parents feel better when he behaved properly and earned high marks in school, he decided his goal was to be the "perfect son" to make them happy. As an adult, Diego took it upon himself to pacify his parents and reprimand Anton when he did something to upset their parents.

Integrating the Multidimensions of the Tagasalo Personality

Carandang (personal communication, April 17, 2017) supported that a tagasalo can live out the role internally and externally, and that a compulsive tagasalo may manifest the personality more strongly than a non-compulsive tagasalo. Further exploration led to a more nuanced understanding expanding from compulsive–non-compusive to also internalizing and externalizing behaviors which can also vary across contexts. Thus, the concept could be viewed as three dimensions, where the tagasalo personality could be high or low on awareness, and could similarly fall on high to low levels of both internalizing and externalizing behaviors. A visual representation may resemble a control panel where each dimension would have low or high levels.

As mentioned, non-compulsive behaviors that demonstrate high awareness are considered more adaptive while compulsive behaviors with low awareness are less adaptive. Levels of internalization depict a tagasalo personality's tendency to internalize responsibility, with high levels being more problematic as this could

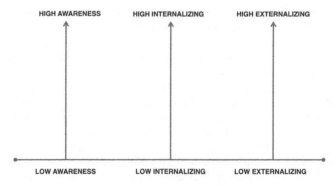

Fig. 7.1.   Profile Depicting Variations in a Tagasalo Personality Based on Level of
Awareness and Range of Internalizing and Externalizing Behaviors.

lead to resentment, and in clinical cases, symptoms of anxiety or depression.
Levels of externalization pertain to overt behaviors that act out the tagasalo's
sense of responsibility. Here, behaviors may be more adaptive, such as extending
support for members or maintaining family ties. Conversely, behaviors may be
more maladaptive, such as being more controlling or overinvolvement in family
matters. The proposed model illustrates possible profiles of a tagasalo personality
(Fig. 7.1).

Manifestations of the Tagasalo Personality
Fig. 7.2 exhibits possible profiles in levels of awareness, internalizing tendencies, and externalizing behaviors that characterize an individual with tagasalo
personality.

As Carandang (1987) asserted, profiles with low awareness tend to manifest
more dysfunctional behaviors. In this cluster, those with low internalizing and
high externalizing behaviors may rely heavily on a complex set of compulsive
externalizing behaviors, both adaptive and maladaptive. Profiles with high internalizing and low externalizing behaviors may experience high internal distress,

Level of Awareness			
Low		*High*	
Low Internalizing Low Externalizing *Not tagasalo*	Low Internalizing High Externalizing *Tagasalo*	Low Internalizing Low Externalizing *Not tagasalo*	Low Internalizing High Externalizing *Tagasalo*
High Internalizing Low Externalizing *Tagasalo*	High Internalizing High Externalizing *Tagasalo*	High Internalizing Low Externalizing *Tagasalo*	High Internalizing High Externalizing *Tagasalo*

Fig. 7.2.   Characterizations of the Tagasalo Personality in Individuals Based on
Manifestations on the Three Dimensions.

yet feel helpless as there is a lack of insight into what is causing the distress. A maladaptive profile has both high internalizing and high externalizing tendencies, with a combination of compulsiveness, high internal distress, and behaviors that tend to cause burnout in the individual. The low awareness contributes to the compulsions in their behaviors that heightens stress instead, and may even sustain dysfunctional behaviors in other family members.

With higher awareness of their motivations, those with low internalizing behaviors and high externalizing behaviors may be the most adaptive profile as one is more intentional and empowered in their actions, less internal distress is felt, and care for the family is genuinely manifested in their behaviors. Those with high internalizing behaviors and low externalizing behaviors may be internalizing the family's problems as emotional receptacles, yet unable to externalize the stress. As seen in Diego's case, such profiles may be more common in children who feel less empowered. It is possible that the distress felt at this stage influences the learned internalizing and externalizing behaviors that may later develop. Similar to low awareness, profiles that are both high internalizing behaviors and high externalizing behaviors may have an inability to cope with perceived expectations and tend to seek more unrealistic solutions. An individual with low internalizing and low externalizing behaviors, regardless of the level of awareness, is not considered a tagasalo.

Bella: A Composite Case Study

A more vivid portrayal illustrates the development of a tagasalo personality. Bella is the second eldest child in a family of seven children, with a significant age gap between her and her younger siblings. Her childhood narratives were filled with assuming responsibility toward their care as she felt no one else would or because she was expected to do so. Academically inclined and organized by nature, she felt compelled to tutor them until late at night, even if that necessitated staying up much later to finish her own school requirements. She recalled completing assignments for a sibling to acquiesce to her parent's requests. When their parents would fight, she would herd the younger ones to a separate part of the house in an effort to protect them from the conflict. Whenever a sibling would get in trouble in school, they would request that she keep an eye on this sibling. When they were teenagers, her older brother got into trouble with his friends and she felt pressured to cheer her parents up to distract them from the news. When he started going out more frequently, she opted to stay home most weekends to keep her siblings company.

She admitted to feeling so burdened that she insisted on staying in a dorm for college, citing a need to be independent and free then. She recalled experiencing a sense of detachment from her family, later realizing that it could have been her way of coping with the emotional fatigue and isolation inherent in her assumed role. After college, her eldest brother chose a career abroad and Bella felt obligated to return home. Now an accountant in her thirties, Bella is still called on to mediate, to guide her younger siblings in their studies and decisions, and to be their mother's confidante.

She tended to internalize the tension felt in the family, anticipating conflicts, feeling overwhelmed by family demands, and manifested symptoms of depression and anxiety. Her externalizing behaviors were a mix of adaptive and maladaptive ones, ranging from caring behaviors toward her siblings and constantly reassuring her mother while focusing on her career to the detriment of any romantic relationships, and escaping conflict by losing herself in books and movies. While her efforts to care for the family are done out of love, she admitted to giving in to their requests at the expense of her own needs, at times, feeling selfish when she would refuse. She carried this sense of responsibility even at work, where many colleagues relied on her. She was proud of her work ethic, but admitted to feeling burdened because of her workload and her sense of responsibility toward her department.

Bella's case aligned with the tagasalo personality (Go Tian-Ng, 2004) with her strong sense of responsibility toward her siblings, her need to be dependable and maintain strong ties with family members, and her tendency to feel apprehensive and inept in social situations. Fig. 7.3 illustrates a gauge of Bella's profile using the proposed framework, with a mid to high level of awareness, high internalizing, and high externalizing behaviors. While she gained much awareness in therapy, she still struggled to define boundaries and felt "stuck" most times. Sacrificing her own needs for familial obligations gave her a sense of fulfillment. While this may be tiring, she felt more confident and empowered knowing she did what she could do for them. This sense of agency is heightened, she reflected, when she was also able to acknowledge and meet her own needs.

DISCUSSION

Multidimensional Perspective of the Tagasalo Personality

A significant finding of this exposition is the addition of two dimensions, internalizing and externalizing behaviors, that can be helpful in understanding adaptive or maladaptive *tagasalo* behavior. For those who tend to internalize, finding

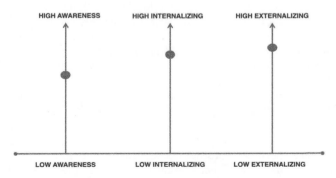

Fig. 7.3.   Bella's Profile Depicting Levels of Awareness, Internalizing Tendencies, and Externalizing Behaviors.

healthier ways to express their needs for harmony and care for family may be ideal areas for growth. For those who tend to externalize, they may focus on regulating their helping behaviors so they may also enhance their capacities for boundary setting. Such behaviors, as influenced by a sense of filial responsibility, may be related to a study by Toro et al. (2019) wherein young Latino adolescents experienced high levels of expressive filial responsibility, acting as mediators or intercessors for the emotional buffering of the family. Meanwhile, those who experienced instrumental filial responsibility were observed to maintain the physical needs of the household, such as buying groceries. This is similar to internalized tagasalo behavior of experiencing emotional anxiety and conflict and externalizing tagasalo behavior of fulfilling chores and acting out their roles.

This idea of internalizing and externalizing behaviors may be evident when one internalizes delayed filial responsibility. Funk (2012) noted that middle-aged participants seem more likely to externalize filial responsibility toward their aging parents with an internalized reciprocal framework, wherein one attributes their expression of filial responsibility as a balancing of accounts for their parent's care for them. They were more likely to internalize a need to "repay" the parents and externalize care with that mindset. This is similar to the Filipino value of reciprocity or *utang ng loob*. The internalizing and externalizing tendencies manifest in emotions felt as a sense of discomfort or anxiety when not addressed, as evident in a study on tagasalo (Go Tian-Ng, 2004), where *Responsibility*, and *Dependability and Affiliation* are possibly related to externalizing behaviors while *Anxiety in Social Situations* is also possibly linked to internalizing behaviors.

Another significant contribution is the integration of the internalizing and externalizing dimensions with Carandang's compulsive and non-compulsive dimensions, providing a more discriminating view. These can be intersected with Udarbe's description of their motivational needs. As the tagasalo navigates various life experiences, the interaction of needs, motivations, and contexts invariably change along with one's level of awareness and the manifestations of internalizing and externalizing behaviors. Variations and distinct differences in these combined factors can be difficult to deconstruct. Hence, this framework provides a lens to appreciate where the tagasalo is in their unique process, and can help identify important areas of growth and change. As Carandang (personal communication, April 17, 2017) advocated for a holistic understanding of the person, it becomes increasingly important to consider the inner world of the tagasalo, their unique perspectives, contexts, and developmental needs.

IMPLICATIONS OF THE STUDY

The proposed framework is novel in the study of Filipino personality and family dynamics and systems. It allows practitioners and researchers to acknowledge layers of *pakikipagkapwa* within interactions and *pakikiramdam* within relationships. Despite their seeming dysfunctionality in thinking and behavior, or an idealization of the tagasalo as a member of the family, this conceptual understanding validates their experience toward acceptance and understanding.

Therapeutic Work with the Tagasalo Personality

This framework helps shed light on their role and significance in the Filipino family system, and allows clinicians a useful assessment and reflective tool to develop insight, and from which to determine treatment goals. Understanding the tagasalo personality facilitates clinical work into adopting healthier and more helpful behavior. Part of the therapeutic work is enabling one to gain more perspective, reframe, and establish psychological distance so that they are able to learn more ways to understand and care for themselves and others. This can build agency and empower those who occupy this role and can engender positive, healthy, and beneficial shifts in family dynamics. Specifically, from a less stigmatized or romanticized perspective, clinicians can understand and allow clients to explore creative ways to be a tagasalo, instead of resorting to extreme measures toward self-preservation, such as detaching from the family system which may then adversely affect their relational needs.

In cases where the personality is compulsive and high in internalizing and externalizing behaviors, clinicians can utilize a therapeutic strategy to increase awareness and regulate emotions. The clinician could ask: *Are you aware of these behaviors [internalizing/externalizing]? Are these behaviors affecting you [positively/negatively]? What is motivating you to engage in these behaviors [internalizing/externalizing]? What needs are being met when you are a tagasalo? Are you able to connect your tagasalo behaviors, whether externalizing or internalizing, and your needs and motivations?* When informed of the magnitude and consequences of one's internalizing and externalizing behaviors, some compulsions are surfaced and other behavioral interventions might then prove effective.

Locally developed interventions with unique insight into the Filipino psyche, such as brief humanistic interventions can focus on building strengths and positive behaviors (Tanalega, 2004). Therapeutic work can consider balancing the tagasalo's individuation and connectedness needs as the *kapwa* can also uphold healthier boundaries between the tagasalo and other family members by attenuating the expression of internalizing and externalizing behaviors. For a tagasalo to achieve healthy functioning, one must individuate and differentiate themselves from one's family (Goldenberg & Goldenberg, 2012) so that their own well-being is not conflated with the family's well-being. In the Filipino family, the collectivist culture is tied to family-orientedness. Awareness of one's well-being as different from the family's well-being may be crucial, but it is also important that one acts to benefit not just oneself, but also the family (Alampay, 2014).

Limitations and Recommendations for Research

This exposition stems from much clinical, educational, and research work, drawing from various sources and cases, toward a more nuanced understanding of the role of the tagasalo in the family system. As expository work based on early literature, essays, and clinical work, there are still many limitations. While in the psyche of many Filipinos, there is a dearth of current literature on the tagasalo personality and this work hopes to instigate further research. Such may explore tagasalo, parentification, and familism together to nuance important differences and similarities in various cultures. Studies comparing tagasalo tendencies with more established personality tendencies, such as dependent or obsessive compulsive personality tendencies, may also surface similarities and distinctions.

More studies are needed on factors contributing to its development, in further examining the proposed profiles and dimensions, and in identifying more effective clinical interventions. With quantitative studies, psychometric tools using the dimensional characteristics of the framework can objectively examine the degree of these behaviors as a measure of tagasalo profiles. Research on the interaction effects of awareness and internalizing and externalizing tendencies may validate maladaptive and adaptive profiles. Other constructs and variables, such as level of agency, age, gender, and other contextual factors may also be considered. Qualitative studies may explore cases and narratives of those with tagasalo tendencies, or to explore Filipino families where a tagasalo steps back or leaves the family system. In such situations, how would the family system adjust to the resulting disequilibrium in the system?

CONCLUSION

This research discussed the historical-conceptual framework of the tagasalo personality, grounded on indigenous Philippine psychology, based on Carandang's dimension of compulsive and non-compulsive behavior, and Udarbe's dynamics of the tagasalo. It also integrated current literature on the tagasalo personality, juxtaposed with related concepts in wider literature, such as parentification and familism. Tagasalo is deeply attached to family and usually viewed as the emotional pillar and source of strength. When the family is in conflict, they may exhibit internalizing and externalizing behaviors to alleviate the stress and tension. Perceived expectations with regard to their role to mediate and repair are internalized and may become expressive forms of responsibility. Reflective essays depicted these dimensions with illustrative quotes and a composite case portrayed a rich description of a tagasalo. This chapter hoped to convey the distinct significance of this indigenous tagasalo personality in identity development within Filipino family systems. Such contributions can pave the way for clinical work and programs that seek to help Filipino individuals and families, and in furthering research in Philippine personality psychology.

ACKNOWLEDGMENTS

The authors would like to thank the following: Maureen Isabel Aguilar, Sofia Althea Calub, Mariel Santos, and students of Theories of Personality AY 2016–2017 (UP DIliman), Danielle Justine Gan for her edits, Gabrielle Therese Madrigal for assisting in the thematic analysis, and Karina Therese Fernandez for reviewing the manuscript and for encouraging this collaborative work to ensue.

REFERENCES

Achenbach, T. M. (1966). The classification of children's psychiatric symptoms: A factor analytic study. *Psychological Monographs, 80*, 1–37.

Adler, A. (1956). *The individual psychology of Alfred Adler: A systematic presentation in selections from his writings* (1st ed). Basic Books.

Alampay, L. P. (2014). Parenting in the Philippines. In H. Selin & P. Schvaneveldt (Eds.), *Parenting across cultures: Childrearing, motherhood and fatherhood in non-Western cultures* (pp. 105–121). Springer.

Alampay, L. P., & Jocson, M. R. M. (2011). Attributions and attitudes of mothers and fathers in the Philippines. *Parenting, 11*(2–3), 163–176. https://doi.org/10.1080/15295192.2011.585564

Beattie, M. (1989). *Beyond codependency and getting better all the time*. Harper/Hazelden.

Bulatao, J. C. (1964). Hiya. *Philippine Studies, 12*(3), 424–438.

Campos, B., Ullman, J. B., Aguilera, A., & Dunkel Schetter, C. (2014). Familism and psychological health: The intervening role of closeness and social support. *Cultural Diversity and Ethnic Minority Psychology, 20*(2), 191–201.

Carandang, M. L. A. (1987). *Filipino children under stress*. Ateneo de Manila University Press.

Carandang, M. L. A, Sison, B. A., & Carandang, C. (2007). *Nawala ang ilaw ng tahanan*. Anvil.

Carlota, A. J. (1985). The development of the Panukat ng Pagkataong Pilipino (PPP). *Philippine Journal of Educational Measurement, 4*, 55–68.

Clemente, J. A. (2011). An empirical analysis of research trends in the *Philippine Journal of Psychology*: Implications for Sikolohiyang Pilipino. *Philippine Social Sciences Review, 63*(1), 1–8.

Creswell, J. W., & Creswell, J. D. (2017). *Research design: Qualitative, quantitative, and mixed methods approaches*. Sage Publications.

Duffy, M. (2010). Writing about clients: Developing composite case material and its rationale. *Counseling and Values, 54*(2), 135–153.

Enriquez, V. G. (1975). Ang batayan ng Sikolohiyang Pilipino sa kultura at kasaysayan. *General Education Journal, 29*, 61–88.

Enriquez, V. G. (1979). Towards cross-cultural knowledge through cross-indigenous methods and perspective. *Philippine Journal of Psychology, 12*, 9–15.

Ensminger, D. C., Frazier, E. W., Montrosse-Moorhead, B., & Linfield, K. J. (2021). How do we deepen our story reservoir by designing, developing, and writing instructional cases for teaching evaluation? *New Directions for Evaluation, 1*(172), 85–102.

Fullinwider-Bush, N. E. L. L., & Jacobvitz, D. B. (1993). The transition to young adulthood: Generational boundary dissolution and female identity development. *Family Process, 32*(1), 87–103.

Funk, L. M. (2012). 'Returning the love', not 'balancing the books': Talk about delayed reciprocity in supporting ageing parents. *Ageing & Society, 32*(4), 634–654.

Garcia, W. C. (1999). *A measure of tagasalo*. Unpublished Paper.

Gingrich, F. C. (2002). Pastoral counseling in the Philippines: A perspective from the West. *American Journal of Pastoral Counseling, 5*(1–2), 5–55.

Go Tian-Ng, R. (2004). A construct validation of the tagasalo personality using the Panunukat ng Pagkataong Pilipino (PPP). *Philippine Journal of Psychology, 37*(2), 35–49.

Golden, R. L., & Oransky, M. (2019). An intersectional approach to therapy with transgender adolescents and their families. *Archives of Sexual Behavior, 48*(7), 2011–2025.

Goldenberg, H., & Goldenberg, I. (2012). *Family therapy* (8th ed.). Brooks/Cole, Cengage Learning.

Guanzon-Lapeña, M. A., Church, A. T., Carlota, A. J., & Katigbak, M. S. (1998). Indigenous personality measures: Philippine examples. *Journal of Cross-Cultural Psychology, 29*(1), 249–270.

Hooper, L. M., DeCoster, J., White, N., & Voltz, M. L. (2011). Characterizing the magnitude of the relation between self-reported childhood parentification and adult psychopathology: A meta-analysis. *Journal of Clinical Psychology, 67*(10), 1028–1043.

Jurkovic, G. J. (1998). Destructive parentification in families: Causes and consequences. In L. L'Abate (Ed.), *Family psychopathology: The relational roots of dysfunctional behavior* (pp. 237–255). Guilford Press.

Kerr, M. E., & Bowen, M. (1988). *Family evaluation: An approach based on Bowen theory*. W. W. Norton & Co.

Kim, U., Yang, K., & Hwang, K. (2006). Contributions to indigenous and cultural psychology: Understanding people in context. In U. Kim, K.-S. Yang, & K.-K. Hwang (Eds.), *Indigenous and cultural psychology: Understanding people in context* (pp. 3–25). Springer Science + Business Media. https://doi.org/10.1007/0-387-28662-4_110.1007/0-387-28662-4_1

Miller, P. H. (1983). *Theories of developmental psychology*. W.H. Freeman.

Perez, A. (2022). Exploring the tagasalo personality and its implication as a localized personality scale. *International Journal of Entrepreneurship, Business and Creative Economy, 2*(1), 48–66.

Stein, G. L., Cupito, A. M., Mendez, J. L., Prandoni, J., Huq, N., & Westerberg, D. (2014). Familism through a developmental lens. *Journal of Latinalo Psychology, 2*(4), 224.

Tanalega, N. E. (2004). *Counseling Filipinos—Briefly*. Ugnayan at Tulong para sa Maralitang Pamilya (UGAT) Foundation.

Teng, J. C. C., Hilario, A. D. F., Sauler, L. M. A., de los Reyes, M. C. M., & Arcinas, M. (2021). Parentification experiences of Filipino young professional daughters during the COVID-19 pandemic. *Journal of Humanities and Social Sciences Studies, 3*(4), 19–32.

Toro, R. I., Schofield, T. J., Calderon-Tena, C. O., & Farver, J. M. (2019). Filial responsibilities, familism, and depressive symptoms among Latino young adults. *Emerging Adulthood, 7*(5), 370–377.

Udarbe, M. H. (2001). The tagasalo personality. *Philippine Journal of Psychology, 34*(2), 45–65.

Valleau, M. P., Bergner, R. M., & Horton, C. B. (1995). Parentification and caretaker syndrome: An empirical investigation. *Family Therapy, 22*(3), 157–164.

Willis, R. (2019). The use of composite narratives to present interview findings. *Qualitative Research, 19*(4), 471–480.

CHAPTER 8

MAINTAINING PERSONHOOD AND IDENTITY IN DEMENTIA: FAMILIES AS PARTNERS IN CARE

Tricia Olea Santos, Hanna K. Ulatowska and Carla Krishan A. Cuadro

ABSTRACT

Dementia is characterized by the progressive decline in cognitive and daily functioning. Although the decline is often the defining characteristic of dementia in biomedical models, several scholars highlight the preserved skills of persons with dementia. Identity, or a sense of self, is among the areas relatively preserved in the later stages of dementia. It is the window through which caregivers understand the subjective experiences of persons with dementia.

This qualitative exploratory study highlights the value of social relationships, particularly the role of the Filipino family in recognizing personhood and maintaining identity in dementia care. Preserving identity entails understanding the person's unique characteristics that reflect one's sense of self. In a highly collectivistic culture, such as the Philippines, the family is crucial to preserving identity and overall well-being in dementia. This study explores the perspectives of 15 Filipino caregivers as regards caring for a family member with dementia. Participants discuss changes in family structure and the challenges in dementia care. More importantly, they delve into strategies used to preserve identity and encourage life participation in their loved one with dementia. Essential Filipino cultural values in dementia care, such as collectivism, religion, and the values of filial piety and utang na loob *(or debt of gratitude) are further discussed.*

Keywords: Dementia; family; Philippines; care; filial piety; cultural values

Resilience and Familism: The Dynamic Nature of Families in the Philippines
Contemporary Perspectives in Family Research, Volume 23, 127–144
Copyright © 2023 by Emerald Publishing Limited
All rights of reproduction in any form reserved
ISSN: 1530-3535/doi:10.1108/S1530-353520230000023008

INTRODUCTION

Dementia is a degenerative condition characterized by declines in cognition, behavior, and daily function. In the Philippines, dementia incidence is 16 per 1,000 person-years (Dominguez, Fowler, & de Guzman, 2020; Dominguez, Guzman, Reandelar et al., 2018). Based on this rate and the projected growth of Filipino senior citizens, it is estimated that there are around 149,606 new dementia cases in 2020, an additional 220,632 cases by 2030, around 295,066 more cases in 2040, and 378,461 additional new cases in 2050 (Dominguez, Jiloca, Fowler, et al., 2021; Dominguez et al., 2018).

There is a distinct stigma associated with dementia. Oftentimes it is referred to as the never-ending death (Cohen & Eisdorfer, 1986). Persons with dementia vividly depict their experience as losing themselves and being an empty shell (Snyder, 2006). Not surprisingly, dementia is also described as a social disability: it is commonplace to exclude persons with dementia from participating in conversation and expressing opinions. This social isolation often results in a diminished sense of self. Persons with dementia feel devalued by others and indicate vulnerability, frustration, and depression (Skaalvik et al., 2016; Sabat, Napolitano, & Fath, 2004).

IDENTITY AND PERSONHOOD: A BROADER SCOPE IN DEMENTIA CARE

These threats to personhood have prompted scholars and medical professionals to shift focus from the biomedical perspective to the intrinsic humanity of persons with dementia. They highlight preserved abilities as opposed to losses in dementia, insisting that memory impairment need not be equated to a person's loss of identity (Kitwood & Bredin, 1992). Additionally, they emphasize the need for person-centered dementia care, including both the biomedical aspects and psychosocial needs of these individuals.

Identity, or a sense of self, is the lens through which others understand how persons with dementia cope with their experiences, relate to others, and respond to intervention (Caddell & Clare, 2010). Identity is reflected in one's personal memories, social roles, and unique personal traits. Studies suggest how persons with dementia can express identity in socially supportive environments despite communication difficulties. Memories of personal events tend to be preserved in individuals with mild-to-moderate dementia via various communicative strategies to highlight significant life events (Ulatowska et al., 2020).

In the moderate-to-severe stages of dementia, identity may be expressed through emotions, relating one's mood or quality of life (Norberg, 2019). Identity may also be demonstrated through personal mannerisms, preferences, and one's role in the family (Cohen-Mansfield et al., 2000). Additionally, identity in dementia can be displayed via intact social abilities, such as initiating social contact, and being polite and helpful to others (Sabat & Collins, 1999). Preserving identity for as long as possible has a significant effect on the progression of dementia. It is central to dementia care as it enables persons to function optimally in their environment.

The social environment is crucial to preserving identity in dementia. The behavior of persons with dementia is not only influenced by neuropathology, but also by the behavior of others and how they relate to those with dementia. Whereas an unsupportive social environment stifles the well-being of persons with dementia, a highly positive one significantly improves their well-being (O'Connor et al., 2007).

The value of a supportive family environment cannot be overemphasized in dementia care. Family caregivers directly cater to the psychosocial needs of persons with dementia and are fundamental to preserving identity (Sabat & Harre, 1992). They are a source of information regarding the past and present identity of persons with dementia. They also provide relevant information as regards meaningful activities, and the best way to tap preserved strengths (Snyder, 1999).

FILIPINO CULTURE AND THE ROLE OF THE FILIPINO FAMILY IN DEMENTIA CARE

Culture is integral to dementia care. Knowledge of cultural factors enables one to better understand perceptions of the dementia experience and the factors involved in care. In the Philippines, much has yet to be studied regarding aging and dementia in Filipinos.

The Filipino culture has both Eastern and Western influences: pre-colonial traditions, Catholic concepts from the Spaniards, and Western medicine and education from the Americans (Enriquez, 1992). Filipino cultural identity is primarily characterized by collectivism in family and society and devotion to one's religion.

In the Philippines, declines in memory are often viewed as part of normal aging. Family members who are present with memory loss are typically excused as being preoccupied with something or exhibiting a side effect of medication (McBride et al., 2005). Families tend to be very protective of the family member with dementia and may delay early diagnosis (McBride, 2006). Medical decision-making is typically done in consultation with friends, family, or a church minister prior to consulting a specialist (McBride et al., 1996). In traditional families, the oldest child is often the primary decision-maker. Family members who are healthcare professionals are typically responsible for educating the family and advocating for the person's needs (McBride et al., 2006).

The Filipino family is a unique fundamental support system in maintaining identity in dementia. The steadfastness of the Filipino family in caring for aging parents is well-documented in literature (Jocano, 1998; McBride, 2006). According to the 1996 Philippine Elderly Survey and the 2007 Philippine Study on Aging, it is common for older Filipinos to co-reside with their children (Cruz et al., 2016). Given the high levels of mutual support, co-residence is beneficial to both parents and their children: children give economic support, whereas parents provide companionship and emotional support (Cruz et al., 2019). There is generally a high level of life satisfaction among older Filipinos brought about by multigenerational support.

In addition to collectivism, cultural values directly influence the Filipino family's approach to caregiving and preserving identity in dementia. The obligation of caring for aging parents is deeply rooted in Filipino families (Natividad & Cruz, 1997). This stems from inherent values of filial love and devotion to one's parents. This care is deepened by the value of *utang na loob* or *debt of gratitude* which is a moral obligation to care for parents in return for their sacrifices in raising the family (Hollnsteiner, 1964; Kaut, 1961). Caring for aging parents serves as a source of comfort and validates the family's cultural values: it is an honor to serve one's parents till the end of their days regardless of the strain it places on the Filipino caregiver (McBride, 2006). Religion is also another cultural factor that enhances one's outlook in life and helps families and older adults in overcoming hardship (Cruz et al., 2019).

Stigma is typically associated with institutionalizing aging parents: it is the family's responsibility to care for older adults. The care given to older adults is attributed to the Christian/Catholic religion; whereby these strongly held beliefs reinforce closely knit family relationships (Aligan, 2016). Most older Filipinos expect their children to take care of them in times of illness, with the daughter as the preferred and most likely caregiver in old age (Cruz et al., 2019). Unmarried children are also more likely to care for parents in their old age than married children.

At present, there are no social and health policies specific to dementia care nor is there a nationwide supportive healthcare system in the Philippines that caters to the needs of persons with dementia. The government's healthcare subsidy covers only a small percentage of the total costs of caring for a person with dementia at home, and most of the expenses are out of pocket. Family caregivers frequently resort to reducing work hours or resigning entirely to care for the person with dementia (Vega, Cordero, Palapar, et al., 2018). Financial difficulties, in addition to the work involved in caregiving, often place added strain on the Filipino caregiver. A recent initiative, the National Dementia Plan in the Philippines (Cruz & Dominguez, 2020), is underway, with studies conducted on the country's demographics and dementia care in the local setting. Long-term home-based care is being studied closely and is viewed as the more viable means of care as opposed to skilled nursing facilities.

To date, many studies focus on caregiver burden and stress in dementia. Very few studies have investigated the family structure and relationships in dementia care (La Fontaine & Oyebode, 2013). This study examines caregiver perspectives regarding dementia care in the Filipino context. It probes into the characteristics and structure of the Filipino family, and the challenges in caring for a loved one with dementia. It also analyzes cultural and relational factors that influence dementia care and the preservation of identity in dementia.

METHOD

This exploratory study primarily examined caregiving in the Filipino context, closely looking at the perspectives of adult children who care for a relative with dementia and the cultural factors that influence care. Additionally, this study analyzed the role of the Filipino family as a primary support system in preserving and maintaining identity in dementia.

Participants

Purposive sampling was used in this study. Fifteen informal caregivers of persons with dementia (12 females, 3 males) participated in the study. Most caregivers were adult children living with and caring for a relative with mild-to-moderate severity levels of dementia. The mean age of caregivers was around 51 years old. All participants finished a college degree (mean level of education: 18 years). Eight of the fifteen participants were healthcare professionals. This sample was relatively homogenous as regards educational level and socioeconomic status (i.e., ability to financially support medical needs and daily living expenses).

Data Collection

Detailed information on caregiver perspectives was drawn from qualitative surveys (Braun et al., 2020). Several simple, open-ended questions were asked concerning the participants' caregiving experiences. These focused on family structure, challenges and modifications to family life, and life participation activities engaged in by the relative with dementia. Participants were encouraged to give detailed responses to questions. Participants were provided with written information about the aims and procedures of the study. They gave written informed consent prior to taking part in the study.

Data Analyses

Data were analyzed following Braun and Clarke's (2006, 2020) reflexive thematic analysis framework. The authors familiarized themselves with the data and developed systematic codes of the collated data. Initial themes, or patterned responses sharing a central concept (Braun & Clarke, 2006, 2020), were derived from the coded data. Themes were later reviewed and refined by the authors, prior to writing the report.

RESULTS

Several main themes were expressed by the caregivers, namely: the reorganization of the family structure and collectivism in society, challenges and coping strategies in caregiving, and preservation of identity in dementia via life participation activities. Particular Filipino cultural values in caregiving and preserving identity in dementia were also conveyed. Results in each section were indicated below.

Family Structure and Collectivism

All participants were informal caregivers of their relative with dementia. Responsibilities generally included budgeting, maintaining the relative's personal hygiene, and arranging medical appointments and communicating with the doctors. Some caregivers hired additional help. The extended family was also involved in care. This organized system was described by one of the caregivers:

> Nanay [Mom] takes the brunt of taking care of Tatay [Dad], ensuring that he takes his medicines and bathes every day. I have two aunts living with us, and they're the ones who cook our food and keep an eye on Tatay when I or Nanay needed to attend to other matters. We all take turns keeping track of where he is and what he is doing. My sister also lives nearby, so she would often drop by to check on Tatay and keep him company or drop off fruits and groceries.

Health professionals in the family took a more active role in addressing medical needs. A caregiver who was a doctor spoke of close communication with a fellow colleague:

> I sought consult with a neurologist who happened to be my classmate in medical school. The neurologist saw her in (the) clinic, did a few office-based tests ... (MRI) Findings came back ... My classmate and I had a private conversation, and he advised me to prepare for the "journey" ahead.

Family members in neighboring towns or outside of the Philippines were also involved in care, sending care packages and being assigned dates to call in order to engage with the relative with dementia:

> Our eldest is a nurse in the US and he would video call, check on the medicines Tatay [Dad] is taking, send pasalubong boxes [care packages] on stuff that Tatay likes from the US. My other brother in Australia also often video calls and sends care packages.

Despite occasional exasperation expressed by the caregivers, most participants spoke of their family as a unit of support, conveying how helpful it was to share the load of caring for their relative with dementia.

> I also have bouts of depression ... Taking care of Tatay [Dad] could be exhausting, and it is easy for me to get exasperated when I have to repeat explanations or clean up after him. It helps that Nanay [Mom] is my partner in caring for Tatay ... It also helps that ... my two aunties... assist with household chores, especially in days when I feel overwhelmed.

In addition to the family, collectivism in society was seen in the help received from friends, neighbors, and the church community.

Challenges and Coping Strategies in Caregiving

All participants spoke of the sudden shift in family structure. One caregiver shared the sad realization of shifting roles for a parent who was a source of strength and stability:

> There was a huge shift in our family dynamics. I was thrust into the role of the caregiver when before, he was the one taking care of me. It was not an easy transition ... Tatay [Dad] had difficulty adjusting to that ... Tatay must have felt that the reins of power (were) no longer in his hands.

One caregiver occasionally second-guessed decisions she and her siblings made for their father:

> There's always the struggle about – are we making the right decisions for his/their health? None of us have been in this position before so my parents' growing old let alone getting

sick, and being totally dependent is very new for us. And it seems to have come so fast and is progressing quickly. We just rely on each other, our friends' experiences taking care of their elderly parents ....

Another caregiver described her father's hesitation in asking for help from his children:

I often feel his hesitation, his feeling of embarrassment that it is now him needing assistance. There were times when I could hear his steps outside my bedroom door, and it would take a while before he would knock – like he was still gathering his thoughts, or debating whether he should bother me. I couldn't blame him for feeling that way.

Life modifications were also made to the caregiver's career choices. Family members often declined jobs that were no longer compatible with caring for the relative with dementia:

When an offer was made for me ..., I respectfully declined as I anticipated heavier caregiver responsibilities in the years ahead as my Mom's and Dad's health will be declining. I went back home and turned down an international career, holding onto faith that that is the right decision to make. Family first, career to follow.

Several primary caregivers chose to stay home full-time to care for their relative with dementia.

Sometimes in the middle of the night ... He wanted to go out of the house; he said he wanted to go home because his wife and children were waiting. He (would not) sleep. We (had) to watch him the whole night because he might do something that will harm himself. He became like a little child who should not be out of sight. So we decided that I should stop my secular work to care for him.

In carrying about activities of daily living, caregivers reported the need for a daily schedule for meals and activities. Others indicated the importance of devices to maintain their relative's orientation:

I made them follow a schedule ... The calendar and wall clock (were) always visible to him to easily orient him ... And to lessen my dad's frustration at home, I asked them to stop rearranging (furniture) at home ... kasi mandalas siyang madisorient [because he frequently gets disoriented] with his surroundings.

One caregiver spoke of the importance of family albums and frequent video phone calls:

The photo album became an important tool for the caregiver to create conversation ... The caregiver usually video calls the family members when she is feeling sad so video calls help ... (family) keeps in touch with her even if she really doesn't know who we are anymore.

Among the different challenges, safety was a main concern for most caregivers. Keeping track of their relative with dementia prompted the need for family members to schedule times when they kept an eye on their relative:

One time, we just saw him starting to walk on a loose plank which he put on the edge of the third floor of the house connecting it to the branches of the mango tree. He couldn't understand the danger of walking on an unstable surface from that high as if he were in a tightrope ... To mitigate instances such as these, we have schedules on family members who should be with him most of the time.

Neighbors occasionally assisted in watching over the relative with dementia:

> One of our biggest (challenges) is when she sneaks out of her house and can't find her way back home. We first tried to lock her door ... but she still managed to get out through the windows which we never expected 'cause it is high ... she used a chair to climb to the window. She had bruises in her face and arms, and sprain in her legs because of that incident. We decided to hire someone to look after her in the daytime and our neighbor volunteered to keep an eye on her for free.

Communication was another challenge expressed by caregivers. One caregiver who was a physician spoke of the frustration which resulted from being unable to comfort a parent:

> She complained of a lot, "Nahihirapan ako." ["I am having a hard time'] For a caregiver, since we don't know where her pain is coming from, it became exhausting. I (started) to feel useless in the situation since I could not provide comfort to her.

Another caregiver spoke of frustration expressed by her Mom over her condition:

> Mom loses her temper especially when she feels helpless, dependent and misunderstood ... We just patiently teach her as if we are teaching a child. Sometimes she would cry because she feels that she is a burden, but we just continuously show her and assure her that she is well loved by us.

Challenges also arose from competing demands in managing their parent's business in addition to their own. Responsibilities were also divided between caring for the older relative and raising a family:

> Before, our focus was raising our children, now the focus is taking care of (parents) ... We were not prepared for this change since we have just started our family.

Challenges in addressing the health needs of the relative with dementia were also expressed. One caregiver described a set family schedule to ensure appropriate medication intake:

> He forgets to take his medicines, or sometimes double doses because he couldn't remember that he already took them. Nanay [Mom] times it so that they both take their medicines together, and there are pill organizers so that we could track if he has taken them already.

During the time of the COVID-19 pandemic, families constantly used various strategies to ensure the safety of their loved one:

> To help him remember, I posted signs like "Please mask up" and accentuated the message by attaching a real mask to the sign. In the kitchen, I also posted "Please wash hands frequently" as reminders ... (these) cut down the number of times I had to explain concepts to him ....

Another challenge was keeping the relative with dementia in isolation during the pandemic. This required constantly reiterating reminders, using visual signs, and even watching church videos explaining the importance of masking and vaccinations:

> (Our) religious organization...released a series of videos and materials that addressed these issues. The materials explained the importance of vaccines and following health protocols. These were anchored on Bible-based principles of loving one's neighbor and the value of life. Tatay [Dad] was much more ready to be vaccinated and more willing to just stay at home after viewing the videos.

Sundowning was another challenge expressed by caregivers with dementia. Several caregivers mentioned music or taking walks around the neighborhood as a means of coping with this:

> Music is also a powerful tool to counteract sundowning. We would play the songs of praise that he is familiar with. Listening to them calms him down and uplifts his mood, especially at the end of the day.

Humor was another strategy used by several caregivers to address difficulties in caregiving. One caregiver recounted how her husband often teased and tried to make the parent laugh. Another spoke of making light of difficult situations:

> Humor also helps ... Sometimes, when there is a mishap, we try to make it feel like it's an adventure and we turn it into a funny incident.

Another person used humor with her mother in the later stages of dementia:

> She could not carry (out) a conversation anymore ... Still, I engaged her in conversations hoping to enhance what little mental or social skills left of her. I didn't care if our conversations didn't make sense. Just the sound of her voice was enough for me. Most of the time, we ended up laughing at our own senselessness.

One caregiver who was familiar with dementia spoke of the importance in educating the rest of the family to better understand what their loved one was experiencing:

> When my family realized he had this illness, I gave them all a book on Alzheimer's so that they can understand what is going on with him and learn how to deal with him, asking him the right questions ... I (also) shared ... another book that had real stories from people who had a loved one with this illness. We also had a "blog" so each one could be in the "same page" or "in the loop" as (to) what is going on with him in real time ... his physical & mental health & condition; when is the good time to come and see him, when is the bad time.

Life Participation

Despite shifts in roles of the relative with dementia from caregiver to care recipient, family members continued to allow their relative with dementia to engage in simple day-to-day tasks or make minor choices in activities of daily living:

> At home, he would cook and prepare a meal for himself whenever he was alone. He read a lot every single day. He could even mend his socks, replace the button of his shirts, shine his shoes ... He would plant different fruit-bearing trees around our house and clean the yard. He also had pets like dogs and cats. Papa was an animal lover.

Reminiscing about past events was a favorite activity of many relatives with dementia. This was recounted by one of the caregivers:

> I would take out our family albums and we would browse ... old photos. She would talk about my grandparents who were long gone. I would ask her the names of her late parents and her siblings. She loved to tell stories that happened 40 years ago and she acted like (they exist) today.

Discussions typically centered on the interests of the relative with dementia. A person who enjoyed traveling reminisced about past vacations with his wife. Another person who enjoyed shopping showed excitement in discussing fashion and clothes. One daughter asked her father to teach her his first language. A person who used to be active in social media would continue to do so with the help of his daughter. One caregiver spoke of significant life experiences:

> We talk about past experiences like ano yung childhood experience niya [like ... his childhood experience] with World War II, his life in the province ... Our experiences as family when we were small. Those are the things he remembered well.

Another caregiver shared discussions regarding present events and family news:

> We try to engage her in conversation about what is happening in the movies/television series she is currently watching. When there is significant positive news from family or friends, we would also update her. The negative news, we would soften or delay a bit, but still let her know. I would shield her ... from finding out about the daily problems of bringing food to the table and running a household, as in my opinion she should no longer be burdened by those worries.

Caregivers also provided opportunities to visit familiar places:

> We...try to surround her with familiar things that may spark a memory for her...We just take her out for a ride in the car and take her to familiar places like the church she used to go to, the school where she taught for so many years, or show her some family albums and pics.

Several caregivers recognized the importance of spiritually nurturing their loved ones with dementia:

> We still try ... to continue caring for not just Mom's physical and emotional well-being but also her spiritual nourishment because, prior to her dementia she ...used to be active in church, ... that is why we continue to engage her in online masses, rosaries, ... and spiritual talks. A lay minister also comes to her house on Sundays to give her holy communion ... She also has a grotto in the garden so we encourage her to offer some flowers and help her pray because sometimes she already forgets the lines to the prayers.

Persons with a strong religious identity were allowed to lead a prayer or participate in prayer groups. The church also supported opportunities for the person with dementia to be involved and to encourage younger members of the church.

> We always included Papa in our family worship/Bible study, even if it seemed that he was not into it anymore but sleeping. Before, he used to give brief comments in our discussions and we also let him lead the prayer during meals. He loves doing it! In the end, we just wanted him to be there.

Other caregivers entertained their loved one by playing cards and board games, accompanying them shopping, or watching a favorite show together. One person with dementia really enjoyed singing and playing the piano:

> He played "by ear" so ... I encouraged him to play the piano ... and (sing) along. He ... knew how to sing and had a good voice. He loved Frank Sinatra, Andy Williams ... He even (encouraged) our granddaughter to play his guitar and she learned it too.

Several caregivers spoke of gardening as a particular life participation activity enjoyed by their relative with dementia:

> He also enjoys gardening and it gives him a sense of pride when we harvest the fruits and vegetables that he planted. When there are people who buy his ornamental plants, he would often smile when he counts how much he earned. I think it is a validation on his part that he could still support his family despite his condition.

Another caregiver allowed her mother to watch her garden:

> Once in a while, I would ask the caregivers to sit her outside with me as I do gardening – something which she loved to do in earlier years ... She would sit outside with me ... pointing out which plants to repot and where to place them. The dirty work ... would of course be mine.

Music was another important means of life participation mentioned by several caregivers:

> She would also sing karaoke with the caregivers and ... with me. I was once surprised ... when she sat down before our digital piano, she began playing. Slowly and in incomplete measures, but still in segments/phrases of music that could be recognized and ... clearly purposeful/not random.

Caregivers also mentioned how relatives were more enthusiastic when talking about cooking and baking. One participant whose father used to enjoy cooking allowed him to participate on a smaller scale:

> He would attempt to cook pero more of giving instructions na lang [but more of giving instructions only]. He had difficulty preparing the ingredients already and selected dishes na lang ang naaalala niya [he could only remember select dishes].

Another caregiver spoke of providing art materials for her mother who was a former teacher:

> My sister bought her coloring books for adults and a box of big crayons. Mama was so thrilled. Her eyes (lit) up when she saw the big crayons. She could hardly wait to get started. We had so much fun choosing the right color and doing it together.

Cultural Values in Caregiving

Despite the challenges in caregiving, family members discussed inherent cultural Filipino values which facilitated personalized care. Respect for one's parents in old age was heavily stressed, with several caregivers quoting the Bible to reinforce their obligation to care for aging parents:

> For me, true Christians should heed the Bible's command to "Honor your father and your mother." Whatever our attainments in life, this obligation does not cease when our parents become old. Aged parents are among those we should have to provide for, even if this involves considerable sacrifices, emotionally and financially ... Family members must have constant contact with them, talk to them as often as they want, and let them feel love and loving concern.

Regardless of the emotional and physical challenges in caregiving, religion was cited as a source of support for most caregivers:

> Having Papa at home permanently presented many challenges, especially when his dementia worsened. But we took it one day at a time. The Bible helped us immensely apply its principles of honoring older ones, especially our parents. When everything got tough, we strove to practice godly devotion and prayer at home.

Several caregivers spoke of intergenerational support, including grandchildren providing direct care for a grandparent with dementia. Caring for aging relatives was generally accepted by members of the family:

We happily accepted our responsibilities in caring for our grandma and made her part or our daily life. I (was) assigned by my mom to give food to my grandma, and sometimes to feed her if she's weak or not feeling well. During weekends I regularly clean her room ... My mom (made) sure she's in good health and (has) her checked by a neighbor doctor every 2 months.

Despite the availability of hired help, caring for a person's bathing and toileting needs was a very private matter in families. These needs were primarily attended to by the family:

Mom was more noticeably dependent already on Dad. Dad, though nine years her senior, would still be the one to give her seated showers at my sister's house... – notwithstanding the availability of a caregiver there, hired by my sister. Dad said he and Mom found it awkward to have a stranger give her baths.

The concept of bathing was elaborated on by one of the caregivers:

When I (had) to bathe mama, ... she became combative. I tried to understand her, be patient with her and gently explain to her why I needed to shampoo her, why I needed to soap her ... It took me some time to realize that mama is the conservative type and very modest. It was humiliating for her that someone was bathing her. This was something she could not express.

As the needs of the relative with dementia increased, several caregivers expressed how institutionalization was not an option for the family member:

As a (medical) practitioner, I have nothing against other people choosing that latter option (institutionalization); But as a Filipino and drawing upon our culture, it is unthinkable and outright unacceptable for me to do that.

Utang na loob or *debt of gratitude* was often expressed indirectly, with more emphasis placed on the implied social obligation of caring for the loved one despite the difficulties involved in dementia care. One caregiver shared gratitude for being part of her mother's journey, discussing her emotional attachment to her mother and the contentment experienced in providing this care:

There were years of anxiety, uncertainty and depression. But it was worth it. It gave me the opportunity to spend quality time with my mother in the twilight of her life. It gave me the chance to show how much I love her. My mother's condition transformed me into a physical person constantly hugging her and telling her I love her so much ... Caring for my mother was the most challenging, exhausting yet most fulfilling task I ever did.

The value of life participation and preserving and maintaining identity for as long as possible was summarized by a caregiver:

I would often pity the patient (with dementia) because it seemed to me that dementia ... is the first tolling of a death knell. Taking care of Tatay [Dad] made me realize that dementia is not a death sentence. It reinforced my belief that caring for loved ones in their old age, with the challenges of failing memory due to dementia, is a privilege. It is a privilege that our family continues to give Tatay a sense of community as we take care of him, surrounded by people he loves and in a place he calls home. Even as dementia continues to whittle away the past, Tatay is very much in the present. He is not less of a person because of dementia. He has not lost his identity nor worth. That even if the progression of the disease is inevitable, there are moments of grace when Tatay is Tatay.

DISCUSSION

This study has examined perspectives of informal caregivers on dementia care, highlighting the fundamental role Filipino families play in preserving and maintaining identity in dementia. Individuals with dementia yearn for meaningful relationships and have an inherent need to bond with family members (Sabat, 1998). The caregivers in this study recognize this distinct need and emphasize the importance of fostering positive relationships with their relative, even in the later stages of dementia. Strong family relationships give much happiness and pride to persons with dementia (Batra et al., 2016). Additionally, they bring about a sense of confidence and empowerment (Kitwood, 1993).

Given the heterogeneity in experiences of dementia, optimal care is shaped via meaningful activities unique to each person (Norberg, 2019). Families are in a special position to create opportunities to maintain meaningful relationships that recognize the preserved identity of individuals with dementia. In this study, caregivers have utilized highly meaningful activities (i.e., listening to preferred music, or engaging in premorbid multisensory activities) to preserve the identity of their loved one. These promote some form of independence and social connections necessary in maintaining identity in dementia.

Additionally, the caregivers in this study created opportunities for their loved ones to exercise autonomy in daily living (i.e., allowing them to choose meals/clothing or lead the family prayer). Autonomy in these tasks could further support identity and improve the quality of life in persons with dementia by enabling them to feel helpful and socially connected to significant others (Clare, 2017).

In addition to meaningful activities, caregivers have also nurtured communicative relationships to shape their relative's experience of dementia. According to Kitwood and Bredin (1992), elements of well-being in dementia are demonstrated in the person's ability to initiate contact, express emotions and desires, and show pleasure in activities. Persons with dementia long for opportunities to share past life experiences with others (Clare et al., 2003). Communicative interactions allow caregivers to understand one's subjective experiences via personal stories, feelings, and opinions.

The caregivers in this study reminisced with their relative about past meaningful experiences pertaining to the family or prior careers. Studies (Hamilton, 2019; Sabat & Harré, 1994; Ulatowska et al., 2020) suggest how personally relevant stories are central to accessing and maintaining identity in dementia. Despite difficulties with recounting recent activities, memory of events in late adolescence and early adulthood – particularly emotional events – is relatively preserved in dementia. In the mild-to-moderate stages, persons with dementia demonstrate an ability to select self-defining personal memories which closely highlight their values, life goals, and who they are (Rathbone et al., 2019; Ulatowska et al., 2020).

Personal stories benefit both the individuals with dementia and their caregivers: sharing meaningful stories provides individuals an opportunity to connect with others and affirm their identity, while expressing dignity in a life well-lived (Sabat & Collins, 1999). Stories as a family member or a retired professional provide a sense of continuity of one's role in society and acknowledge the person's life accomplishments (Clare et al., 2008). Additionally, caregivers are afforded a window into the person's dementia experience, values, and emotions and foster respect for and acceptance of the person with dementia (Mills, 1997).

Of particular interest are the cultural factors which contribute to preserving identity in dementia, such as family relationships and values in caregiving. All caregivers in this study indicated how the Filipino family exercises a major role in the care of its older members. This is heightened by the lack of significant government support to address needs of its older citizens' population (Cruz et al., 2019).

Given the highly collectivistic nature of Filipino families, there are inherent personal relationships developed within the family. One of the strongest relationships between a parent and child is that of *utang na loob* or *debt of gratitude* which is crystallized in the sense of obligation children have for their parents (Kaut, 1961). According to Rungduin et al. (2016) *utang na loob* is described in the context of acknowledging kindness received, implicit reciprocity, and social responsibility and obligation. In caring for a family member, the sense of obligation may be manifested in the extra effort to show kindness and respect while tending to the physical and psychological needs of another (Rungduin et al., 2016). There is a strong cultural component to *utang na loob* in that the "social demand of returning the good deed becomes salient" (Rungduin et al., 2016, p. 22). Hence, the cultural value in caring for older members of the family is both deeply rooted in families and indispensable in dementia care. The gift of life given by parents is a unilateral debt which cannot be repaid by children; thus, children have a sense of obligation to care for their parents in old age (Kaut, 1961).

Familism is common, whereby Filipino families place the family's welfare before oneself (Medina, 1991). Filipinos tend to value smooth interpersonal relations rather than engage in conflict when providing care for family members with dementia.

Relatives tend to be informal caregivers who have not received special training in dementia care. Similar to findings by Cruz et al. (2019), changes in the family dynamic may require altering family priorities (i.e., working fewer hours or quitting one's job) when a person becomes the primary caregiver. *Utang na loob* (or *debt of gratitude*) accounts for the personalized care of the family member with dementia and fuels the need for maintaining the identity of and social connectedness to the loved one with dementia.

Despite challenges in caregiving, participants in this study have shared various means of coping with caregiver burden. Similar to the study by Varona et al. (2007) on family caregivers in the Philippines, memory and behavioral issues in persons with dementia tend to be strong predictors of increased caregiver burden. As a highly collectivistic culture, Filipinos utilize intergenerational care, friends, and even the church among their support systems (Parveen & Morrison, 2009; Santos & Ulatowska, 2018).

As with this study, Filipino caregivers emphasized the positive aspects of caregiving, highlighting the cultural trait of resilience and strength in successfully adapting to challenges of caregiving (Cruz & Dominguez, 2020). Oftentimes, gratitude would be expressed via contentment or happiness for caring for another despite difficulties (Rungduin et al., 2016). Similar to other studies (Ivey, Ladtika, Price, Tseng, Beard, Liu, Fetterman, Wu, & Logsdon, 2013), participants in this study indicated how caregiving was not perceived as a burden but rather as a means of giving back. When presented with challenges, Filipino caregivers demonstrated similar coping mechanisms of reliance on one's family and faith for emotional, moral, and spiritual help (McBride, 2006). Positive coping to challenges in caregiving was often attributed to traditional family values and one's Catholic/Christian faith (Ivey et al., 2013).

CONCLUSION

Recognizing personhood and identity is fundamental to dementia care. Despite cognitive–linguistic declines, growing evidence reveals preserved identity even in the later stages of dementia. This chapter brings to light the intrinsic humanity of dementia and the crucial role families play in maintaining identity for as long as possible. In supporting personhood and identity in dementia, the quality of life and well-being of these individuals are dramatically improved and negative experiences are alleviated.

Person-centered dementia care emphasizes individualized treatment: studying one's past and present identity and current needs. There is value in providing opportunities to share personal stories and engage in meaningful activities. These promote social connectedness and allow caregivers to witness personal expressions of identity. Caregivers have an opportunity to understand the person's lived experience, promote respect and acceptance for these individuals, and provide care tailored to the unique needs of the person.

The family has a valuable role in enabling persons with dementia to live full lives. It is an indispensable support system that reinforces personhood and identity, by recognizing the preferences and needs of individuals with dementia. The family facilitates personal connections to others and helps focus on preserved skills as opposed to losses.

Dementia care is also strongly defined by cultural factors. Given the strength of the bond and the cultural values imbided in Filipino families, home-based dementia care is viewed as the more viable option as opposed to skilled nursing care. Considering the cultural norm of caring for older members of the family and the high level of intergenerational and community support, the Filipino family is an ideal support system that allows persons with dementia to live meaningful lives. Additionally, religion is another factor valued by Filipinos which facilitates coping with challenges in dementia care and recognizing personhood in dementia.

In addressing the challenges of caring for a relative with dementia, there is a recognized need to support Filipino families. It is important to emphasize the positive aspects of caregiving: encouraging and providing them with the necessary support, and educating them on approaches to dementia care and caregiver coping strategies. There is also a need to develop healthcare policies to further support aging Filipinos, particularly those with dementia.

ACKNOWLEDGMENTS

The authors are grateful to the participants for their wisdom and insights regarding caring for their loved one with dementia. Gratitude is also expressed to Cheryl Encarnacion, Teresa Olea, and McDonald and Catherine Pastor for their assistance in this study.

REFERENCES

Aligan, R. (2016). God and the concept of death and suffering in the Philippine context. *Theology and Thought, 77*, 66–98. https://doi.org/10.21731/ctat.2016.77.662564

Batra, S., Sullivan, J., Williams, B. R., & Geldmacher, D. S. (2016). Qualitative assessment of self-identity in advanced dementia. *Dementia, 15*(5), 1260–1278.

Braun, V., & Clarke, V. (2006). Using thematic analysis in psychology. *Qualitative Research in Psychology, 3*(2), 77–101. https://doi.org/10.1191/1478088706qp063oa

Braun, V., & Clarke, V. (2020). One size fits all? What counts as quality practice in (reflexive) thematic analysis? *Qualitative Research in Psychology, 18*(3), 328–352. https://doi.org/10.1080/14780887.2020.1769238

Braun, V., Clarke, V., Boulton, E., Davey, L., & McEvoy, C. (2020). The online survey as a qualitative research tool. *International Journal of Social Research Methodology, 24*, 1–14. https://doi.org/10.1080/13645579.2020.1805550

Caddell, L. S., & Clare, L. (2010). The impact of dementia on self and identity: A systematic review. *Clinical Psychology Review, 30*(1), 113–126. https://doi.org/10.1016/j.cpr.2009.10.003

Clare, L. (2017). Rehabilitation for people living with dementia: A practical framework of positive support. *PLoS Medicine, 14*(3), e1002245. https://doi.org/10.1371/journal.pmed.1002245

Clare, L., Rowlands, J., Bruce, E., Surr, C., & Downs, M. (2008). The experience of living with dementia in residential care: An interpretative phenomenological analysis. *The Gerontologist, 48*(6), 711–720.

Clare, L., Woods, R., Moniz Cook, E., Orrell, M., & Spector, A. (2003). Cognitive rehabilitation and cognitive training for early-stage Alzheimer's disease and vascular dementia. *Cochrane Database Systematic Review, 4*, CD003260.

Cohen, D., & Eisdorfer, C. (1986). *The loss of self: A family resource for the care of Alzheimer's disease and related disorders.* W.W. Norton.

Cohen-Mansfield, J., Golander, H., & Arnheim, G. (2000). Self-identity in older persons suffering from dementia: Preliminary results. *Social Science & Medicine, 51*(3), 381–394.

Cruz, G. T., Cruz, C. J. P., & Saito, Y. (Eds.). (2019). *Ageing and health in the Philippines.* Economic Research Institute for ASEAN and East Asia (ERIA).

Cruz, G. T., Natividad, J., Gonzales, M., & Saito, Y. (2016). *Aging in the Philippines: Findings from the 2007 Philippine study on aging.* University of the Philippines Population Institute and Demographic Research and Development Foundation.

Cruz, P. S., & Dominguez, J. C. (2020). Challenges and coping strategies in family-based dementia care in the Philippines: Supportive and therapeutic environments. *Alzheimer's & Dementia, 16*(Suppl 8), e042813.

Dominguez, J., de Guzman, F., Reandelar, M., Jr, & Thi Phung, T. K. (2018). Prevalence of dementia and associated risk factors: A population-based study in the Philippines. *Journal of Alzheimer's Disease, 63*(3), 1065–1073.

Dominguez, J., Fowler, K. C., & De Guzman, M. F. P. (2020). In support of a national dementia plan: A follow-up study for dementia incidence and risk profiling in Filipino homes: Epidemiology/prevalence, incidence, and outcomes of MCI and dementia. *Alzheimer's & Dementia, 16*, e043294.

Dominguez, J., Jiloca, L., Fowler, K. C., De Guzman, M. F., Dominguez-Awao, J. K., Natividad, B., Domingo, J., Dominguez, J. D., Reandelar, M., Jr, Ligsay, A., Yu, J. R., Aichele, S., & Phung, T. (2021). Dementia incidence, burden and cost of care: A Filipino community-based study. *Frontiers in Public Health, 9*, 628700. https://doi.org/10.3389/fpubh.2021.628700

Enriquez, V. G. (1992). *From colonial to liberation psychology.* University of the Philippines Press.

Hamilton, H. (2019). *Language, dementia, and meaning making*. Palgrave Macmillan.

Hollnsteiner, M. R. (1964). Reciprocity in the lowland Philippines. In F. Lynch (Ed.), *Four readings on Philippine values* (pp. 22–49). Ateneo de Manila Press.

Ivey, S. L., Laditka, S. B., Price, A. E., Tseng, W., Beard, R. L., Liu, R., Fetterman, D., Bei Wu, B., & Logsdon, R. G. (2013). Experiences and concerns of family caregivers providing support to people with dementia: A cross-cultural perspective. *Dementia, 12*(6), 806–820.

Jocano, F. (1998). *Filipino social organization: Traditional kinship and family organization*. Manila: Punlad Research House.

Kaut, C. (1961). Utang Na Loob: A system of contractual obligation among tagalogs. *Southwestern Journal of Anthropology, 17*(3), 256–272. https://doi.org/10.1086/soutjanth.17.3.3629045

Kitwood, T. (1993). Towards a theory of dementia care: The interpersonal process. *Ageing & Society, 13*(1), 51–67.

Kitwood, T., & Bredin, K. (1992). Towards a theory of dementia care: Personhood and well-being. *Ageing & Society, 12*(3), 269–287.

La Fontaine, J., & Oyebode, J. R. (2013). Family relationships and dementia: A synthesis of qualitative research including the person with dementia. *Ageing and Society, 34*(7), 1243–1272. https://doi.org/10.1017/S0144686X13000056

McBride, M. (2006). Working with Filipino American families. In G. Yeo & D. Gallagher-Thompson (Eds.), *Ethnicity and the dementias* (2nd ed., pp. 189–207). Taylor & Francis.

McBride, M., Fee, C., & Yeo, G. (2005). Filipino American elders. In G. Yeo (Ed.), *Mental health aspects of diabetes in elders from diverse populations* (pp. 584–596). Stanford Geriatric Education Center, Stanford University.

McBride, M., Morioka-Douglas, N., & Yeo, G. (1996). *Aging and health: Asian/Pacific island American elders* (2nd ed.) Stanford GEC.

McBride, M., Nora, R., & Periyakoil, V. J. (2006). Filipino Americans. In R. Adler & H. Kamel (Eds.), *Doorway thoughts: cross-cultural health care for older adults* (Vol. 2, pp. 37–57). Jones and Bartlett Publishers.

Medina, B. T. G. (1991). *The Filipino family: A text with selected readings*. University of the Philippines Press.

Mills, M. A. (1997). Narrative identity and dementia: A study of emotion and narrative in older people with dementia. *Ageing & Society, 17*(6), 673–698.

Natividad, J. N., & Cruz, G. T. (1997). Patterns in living arrangements and familial support for the elderly in the Philippines. *Asia-Pacific Population Journal, 12*(4), 1–10.

Norberg, A. (2019). *Sense of self among persons with advanced dementia* (pp. 205–221). Exon Publications.

O'Connor, D., Phinney, A., Smith, A., Small, J., Purves, B., Perry, J. Drance, E., Donnelly, M., Chaudhury, H., & Beattie, L. (2007). Personhood in dementia care: Developing a research agenda for broadening the vision. *Dementia, 6*(1), 121–142.

Parveen, S., & Morrison, V. (2009). Predictors of familism in the caregiver role. *Journal of Health Psychology, 14*(8), 1135–1143.

Rathbone, C. J., Ellis, J. A., Ahmed, S., Moulin, C. J., Ernst, A., & Butler, C. R. (2019). Using memories to support the self in Alzheimer's disease. *Cortex, 121*, 332–346.

Rungduin, T., Rungduin, D. C., Aninacion, J. G., Catindig, R. B., & Gallogo, L. S. (2016). The Filipino character strength of Utang na Loob: Exploring contextual associations with gratitude. *International Journal of Research Studies in Psychology, 5*(1), 13–23.

Sabat, S. R. (1998). Voices of Alzheimer's disease sufferers: A call for treatment based on personhood. *Journal of Clinical Ethics, 9*, 35–48.

Sabat, S. R., & Collins, M. (1999). Intact social, cognitive ability, and selfhood: A case study of Alzheimer's disease. *American Journal of Alzheimer's Disease and Other Dementias, 14*(1), 5–64.

Sabat, S. R., & Harre, R. (1992). The construction and deconstruction of self in Alzheimer's disease. *Ageing and Society, 12*, 443–461.

Sabat, S. R., & Harré, R. (1994). The Alzheimer's disease sufferer as a semiotic subject. *Philosophy, Psychiatry, and Psychology, 1*(1), 145–60.

Sabat, S. R., Napolitano, L., & Fath, H. (2004). Barriers to the construction of a valued social identity: A case study of Alzheimer's disease. *American Journal of Alzheimers Disease, 19*(3), 177–185. http://dx.doi.org/10.1177/153331750401900311

Santos, T. O., & Ulatowska, H. K. (2018). Comprehension of medical information in elderly migrant Filipino Americans: Does culture matter? *Journal of Aging and Social Change, 8*(1), 79–90.

Skaalvik, M. W., Norberg, A., Normann, K., Fjelltun, A. M., & Asplund, K. (2016). The experience of self and threats to sense of self among relatives caring for people with Alzheimer's disease. *Dementia, 15*(4), 467–480.

Snyder, L. (1999). *Speaking our minds: Personal reflections from individuals with Alzheimer's*. Freeman.

Snyder, L. (2006). Personhood and interpersonal communication in dementia. In J. Hughes, S. Louw, & S. Sabat (Eds.), *Dementia: Mind, meaning, and the person* (pp. 259–276). Oxford University Press.

Ulatowska, H. K., Santos, T. O., Walsh, D. G., Patterson, R., Aguilar, S., & Lagus, J. (2020). The journey of identity of World War II veterans with and without dementia. *The Journal of Aging and Social Change, 10*(4), 1–17.

Varona, R., Saito, T., Takahashi, M., & Kai, I. (2007). Caregiving in the Philippines: A quantitative survey on adult–child caregivers' perceptions of burden, stressors, and social support. *Archives of Gerontology and Geriatrics, 45*(1), 27–41.

Vega, S. F. D., Cordero, C. P., Palapar, L. A., Garcia, A. P., & Agapito, J. D. (2018). Mixed-methods research revealed the need for dementia services and human resource master plan in an aging Philippines. *Journal of Clinical Epidemiology, 102*, 115–122.

CHAPTER 9

SEXUAL IDENTITY VISIBILITY AND COMPOUNDING STIGMA IN THE FAMILIAL CONTEXT: LIFE HISTORIES AMONG FILIPINO MSMs LIVING WITH HIV

Jerome V. Cleofas and Dennis Erasga

ABSTRACT

Stigma remains to be a major barrier to addressing the sustained rise of human immunodeficiency virus (HIV) infections in the Philippines. Gay, bisexual, and other men who have sex with other men (MSMs) (G/B/MSM) living with HIV experience compounded stigma due to their sexual identity and HIV seropositive status. The family has been identified as one of the main sources of homonegativity and HIV-related discrimination. Drawing from the family life histories of 31 Filipino MSMs living with HIV, the authors demonstrate the concept of compounding stigma, *which posits that the extent and nature of gender- and sexuality-based stigma experienced in early life may potentiate or mitigate the experience of HIV stigma in later life in the context of the family. Narrative analysis of the family life histories reveals a central factor that shaped the sexual development and stigma experiences of MSMs living with HIV:* sexual identity visibility in the family (SIVF) *– the family's extent of knowledge and/or acceptance of their sexuality. Three core narratives emerged from the data that categorize informants based on the type of SIVF present in their family life viz.* full, partial, *and* invisible. *Results also trace the resultant*

Resilience and Familism: The Dynamic Nature of Families in the Philippines
Contemporary Perspectives in Family Research, Volume 23, 145–161
Copyright © 2023 by Emerald Publishing Limited
All rights of reproduction in any form reserved
ISSN: 1530-3535/doi:10.1108/S1530-353520230000023009

life trajectories for each core narrative and reveal three forms of compounding stigma: low compounding stigma *or* compounding acceptance, compounding enacted stigma, *and* compounding internalized stigma.

Keywords: Family; HIV/AIDS; MSM; sexual identity; stigma; LGBT

INTRODUCTION

Stigma remains to be a major barrier to preventing and addressing HIV infections and acquired immunodeficiency syndrome (AIDS). Evidence suggests that HIV-related stigma negatively affects the delivery of sexual health promotion services, adoption of HIV protective behaviors (Thapa et al., 2018), access to HIV healthcare services (Adia et al., 2018; De Los Santos et al., 2020), and the psychological and social well-being of persons living with HIV (PLHIVs) (Chambers et al., 2015; Rueda et al., 2016). In the Philippines, a country with one of the most rapidly growing HIV epidemics in the world (Restar et al., 2018), PLHIVs and individuals at risk for HIV continue to experience HIV-stigma-induced challenges despite the increasing awareness regarding the disease and the recent amendment of the country's HIV Law (RA 11166) in 2018 (Adia et al., 2018; Calaguas, 2020).

Goffman (1963), the sociologist who pioneered the concept of stigma, posited that stigma occurs when negative meanings and attitudes are attached to one or more discrediting characteristics, such as homosexuality, resulting in avoidance, lack of acceptance, unfair treatment, and other forms of discrimination against individuals who have said stigmatizing characteristic/s. Following Goffman's lead, Florom-Smith and De Santis (2012) forwarded HIV stigma as a construct that can be categorized into two types: *felt/internalized stigma*, which refers to the fear of being discriminated against, and *enacted stigma*, which refers to being discriminated against, because of their seropositive HIV status.

PLHIVs may possess discrediting and stigmatic traits other than their HIV serostatus that can further fuel discrimination, such as being a sexual or racial minority. This is often referred to as compounded or layered stigma, which is a commonly examined phenomenon among PLHIVs who are G/B/MSM. Studies in the Philippines (Adia et al., 2018; Canoy & Ofreneo, 2012, 2017) and elsewhere (Chambers et al., 2015; Rueda et al., 2016) demonstrated how the well-being of MSMs living with HIV had been negatively impacted by their experiences of homonegativity and HIV stigma. At times, MSMs living with HIV had to conceal their sexual identity, HIV status, or both, to avoid being discriminated against and losing opportunities in life (Adia et al., 2018; Calaguas, 2020; Canoy & Ofreneo, 2017; Tuppal et al., 2019).

We propose to expand the concept of "compounded stigma," and instead use "compounding stigma." Adding the suffix *-ing* signifies that the G/B/MSM sexual identity and HIV status are stigmatic traits that are dynamically interacting with each other and may demonstrate changes in terms of development over the lifespan of the individual. Evidence suggests that felt and experienced stigma due to being G/B/MSM and HIV positive are linked (Berg & Ross, 2014;

Tsang et al., 2019). However, the methods in these studies merely offer cross-sectional (or situational) snapshots of the interactions between these two stigmatic conditions. Chronologically, being G/B/MSM usually occurs first in the life course prior to becoming HIV positive. There is reason to suspect that the extent of stigma they received due to their sexual identity during their earlier life may have contributed to their sexual development and behaviors, their becoming and being HIV positive, and their felt/experienced stigma related to their HIV status. Prior research has linked early sexuality experiences to being HIV-positive and becoming seropositive (Adam et al., 2017; Halkitis et al., 2008; Logie et al., 2019). However, these studies mainly considered adverse life events and did not interrogate how the extent or absence of G/B/MSM-related stigma potentiated or weakened HIV stigma. In this study, we explored this phenomenon of compounding G/B/MSM- and HIV-related stigma among Filipino MSMs living with HIV within the context of the family.

The family is one of the primary social institutions that influence the sexual development and health outcomes of individuals (Samaco-Zamora & Fernandez, 2016). One of the major cultural values of the Philippines is family-orientedness (Medina-Belen, 2015). However, the family can also perpetuate enacted G/B/MSM and HIV-related stigma against affected members. Prior studies have demonstrated how MSM PLHIVs experience discriminatory treatment from other family members (Chavez et al., 2016; Ofreneo & Canoy, 2017; Ruga, 2020).

We argue that the nature of stigma is shaped by its situatedness in a specific location of the social life of the stigmatized other, and their relational proximity to the actual and potential perpetrators of discrimination. Since the family is a stable and proximate social group in the life of Filipinos across their lifetime (Medina-Belen, 2015), the familial context is an ideal social location to examine how earlier G/B/MSM stigma compounds with HIV stigma in later life. More than a semantic change, *compounding* as a characteristic of stigma connotes a modality of complexity, which is defined by the mutual impacts of situatedness, co-presence, and relational proximity. To our knowledge, this specific phenomenon of compounding stigma in the familial context has not yet been fully explored in the literature; hence, this present study.

LOCAL CONCEPTUALIZATION OF STIGMA

Stigma does not have an exact or definitive equivalent in the Tagalog vernacular (Filipino). Interestingly, a bevy of autochthonous terms may proxy what it connotes within the Filipino cultural context. For the sake of simplification, we grouped homegrown words into two broad types. The first type includes the following Tagalog words: *dungis* (*stain/blemish*) as in *a stain in one's name or a blemish in his family's reputation*; *mantsa* (*smudge*) as in *a smudge on his image*, and *dusta* (*dishonor*) as in the phrase: *you dishonored your father's name*. The second type resembles the original English usage of the concept as the stigma's base referent is a *brand* of a (set) of traits or a *label* attached to a person. Two local terms are instructive: *bansag* (*a moniker*) and *alyas* (*alias*). Unlike the first type, stigma cast in such terms is not necessarily derogatory, devaluing, or compromising. Instead, they may function and be taken as sort of *tags* – either *positive* or *negative* amplifying certain personal features, experiences, or skills. Examples of such popular monikers include "si Pedrong *kabayo* (Peter, the horse)," or "si Rizal ang *bayani* (Rizal, the hero)." Each case highlights the idiosyncratic brand associated with the *circumstances about* a person. The stigma in such cases is not a metaphorized characterization, but rather, a unit of social distinction such as that of stereotypes as seen in previous stigma research in the Philippines (e.g., Tanaka et al., 2018). In sociological parlance, the first type of stigma may be seen as purely symbolic in nature yet deeply *personal* in implications. Thus, stigma is metaphorized as a literal stain that can be seen or can be attached to a person. The second type, however, tends to be analogical in nature and is *associational* in spin-offs.

In the Philippines, the stigma of being G/B/MSM and HIV positive both fall under these two local types of stigma. There are local labels for sexual minority identities, as documented in a country report on LGBT rights (USAID, United Nations Development Programme (UNDP), 2014). Some of these include *bakla* for gay males, *silahista* or *AC/DC* for bisexual, and *tripper* for straight-identifying men who have sex with other men. However, *bakla* usually suffices as a general term to describe most types of men desiring other men. Monikers for positive HIV status are also being used for PLHIVs, such as *posit* (clipped from the word "positive"). Among friends with shared sexual identities and other allies, these labels may be harmless and even sometimes used candidly. However, for other social groups, such as those in school and church, these can be derogatory. Sexual socialization in the family is still rooted in Catholic dogma and heteronormative practices. Hence, there is a common notion that being G/B/MSM and/or PLHIV is a *kahihiyan sa pamilya* (shame/dishonor to the family). There are colloquial labels that are applicable to both sexual minorities and PLHIVs, such as *malandi* (slutty) or *maduming dugo* (dirty/spoiled blood), which can be used by family members and other social groups to stigmatize them. These convergences in the local language of stigma as applied to G/B/MSMs and PLHIVs provide another justification to examine compounding stigma in the Filipino familial context.

METHODS

Study Design

The data used for this chapter come from a larger qualitative dissertation project that examined various perspectives of sexual and HIV stigma among Filipino MSMs living with HIV (Cleofas, 2016). Specifically, the design used for this study is narrative analysis. This qualitative design appeals to the theory of narrative constructionism, which posits that human beings are meaning-makers, who use narratives "to interpret, direct and communicate life and to configure and constitute their experience and their sense of who they are" and represent the sociocultural contexts wherein their lives are embedded in (Smith & Monforte, 2020). For this study, narrative analysis was applied to the life histories of the MSMs living with HIV, with a focus on their familial context, sexual development, and being HIV positive.

Key Informants

A total of 31 key informants were interviewed for this study. The eligibility criteria for purposive selection are (1) male gender; (2) aged between 18 and 59 years; (3) referred by the partner community-based HIV organization as HIV seropositive; (4) has contracted HIV through sex with other males; and (5) without debilitating physical or mental conditions. Table 9.1 shows the background profile of the informants of the study.

Data Gathering Procedure

We partnered with The Project Red Ribbon (TRR), a community-based HIV organization, for the recruitment of participants. The TRR staff invited potential participants for the study and also offered a private office space for interviews. All in all, seven Saturdays and four Sundays were spent on data collection. Two to five interviews were conducted every visit.

Table 9.1. Background Characteristics of Key Informants ($N=31$).

Characteristics	n	Percent
Sociodemographic Characteristics		
Age		
Below 20 years	3	10
20–24 years	8	26
25–29 years	11	35
30–34 years	7	23
35 years and above	2	6
Educational attainment		
College graduate	17	54
College undergraduate	7	23
High school graduate	7	23
Employment status		
Employed	16	52
Unemployed	12	38
Student	3	10
Family Characteristics		
Family structure (before age of majority)		
Nuclear	18	58
Extended	13	42
Self-reported household income status		
High income	2	
Middle income	16	52
Low income	13	42
Current living arrangement		
Living with immediate family members	15	58
Living with extended family members only	5	16
Living with non-relatives	5	16
Living alone	3	10
Time Period Since HIV Diagnosis		
Less than six months prior to the interview	4	13
Six months to one year prior to the interview	13	42
One year and one day to two years prior to the interview	11	35
More than two years prior to the interview	3	10

The interviews were all conducted by the main dissertation proponent. Prior to each interview, the first author (J.V.C.) secured formal informed consent. J.V.C. used semi-structured, open-ended questions, designed to make the interview interactional, conversational, informal, fluid, researcher-facilitated, and participant-driven (Marvasti, 2004). The participants were encouraged to state thoughts, feelings, and reflections that coincide with the circumstances that they are sharing. Follow-up questions were asked as needed. All interviews were audio-recorded. Since the study was done in the National Capital Region (NCR), Philippines, the interview was conducted in Tagalog and/or English, the prevailing languages in the region. J.V.C. also made observational and reflective notes during and after interviews.

Ethical Considerations

The protocol of this study was granted ethical clearance by St. Paul University Manila Institutional Ethics Review Committee and adhered to the principles of research ethics of the Declaration of Helsinki. Free, prior informed consent was secured from participants. To observe privacy and confidentiality, we concealed their identities by assigning pseudonyms and kept all data in encrypted digital storage devices. J.V.C., a registered nurse, offered himself for debriefing sessions after each interview. Each interviewee was provided with meals during a meager stipend of PhP 500.00.

Narrative Analysis Procedure

J.V.C. transcribed all the interviews verbatim and noted non-verbal cues and psycho-emotional markers. While listening to the audio-recorded interview, J.V.C. created reflective notes to aid in the analysis (Halcomb & Davidson, 2006). The transcripts were then read and reread to gain familiarization. This study utilized the narrative analysis method by Bamberg (2012) to make sense of interview data. Narrative analysis attends to themes, plots, and structures. Through this analytic strategy, central plots and common events emerging across groups of participants emerged. Central plots are larger scripts of motivations that define the characters, events, crises, and resolutions in the life histories. During analysis, we identified narrative themes and thematic relationships and identified the structure of the emerging central story (Smith & Monforte, 2020).

Ensuring Trustworthiness

We employed strategies to ensure the trustworthiness of the findings (Lincoln & Guba, 1985). For credibility, J.V.C. personally conducted the interviews and transcribed them to ensure prolonged engagement with the narratives. The second author (D.E.) helped in tempering the analysis through peer reviewing the initial qualitative coding. Also, ours was a relatively large sample size for a qualitative study; hence, data saturation is assured. For transferability, dependability, and confirmability, we organized an audit trail of all the raw analytic products of our processes.

RESULTS

From the narrative analysis of the interviews emerged a central factor that influenced the family context of the lives of the informants as MSMs and their becoming and being HIV positive: *SIVF*. We define SIVF as the nature of the family's consciousness and acceptance of the informants' sexual identity/ies (i.e., being G/B/MSM and PLHIV). SIVF is also characterized by the extent to which the informants can express their sexual identities to their families. We argue that SIVF is both a manifestation of and a salient factor that shapes the compounding stigma among MSMs living with HIV. Moreover, we posit that SIVF shapes an individual's sexual health across the lifespan. We chose the term "visibility" for this phenomenon to signify how the family members "see" their MSM members, how MSM members "see" themselves in the context of their G/B/MSM sexual identity, and how these perspectives shape each other in facilitating or diminishing the compounding sexual stigma, and the sexual development outcomes of the MSM members. This notion of sexual identity visibility in the context of the family also borrows and innovates Goffman's conceptualization of the visibility of stigma. Goffman (1963) suggests that the way individuals and groups interact with the stigmatized is the "known-about-ness" of the condition that draws in stigma and discrimination.

Three core narratives emerged from the life histories of the informants in the context of their families, which depict the trajectories of sexual development, becoming and being HIV positive, and the compounding sexual stigma experienced by the MSMs living with HIV. These three core narratives describe the life events of the informants as influenced by their SIVF. The core narratives are labeled based on the nature of the informants' SIVF: (1) *full SIVF (F-SIVF)*; (2) *partial SIVF (P-SIVF)*; and (3) *invisible SIVF (I-SIVF)*.

Moreover, evinced by the data, common life segments represented by sexual development milestones appear to run across the three core narratives. However, the way these life segments are experienced is based on their SIVF; each life segment plays out differently in every core narrative. These life segments are (a) self-identification and acceptance of sexual identity; (b) family consciousness of sexual identity; (c) expression and exploration of sexuality; (d) risky sexual behaviors; (e) personal coping with HIV; and (f) family coping for PLHIV member.

Full Sexual Identity Visibility in the Family

Self and family acceptance is the main theme of the F-SIVF narrative. We categorize seven informants whose sexual lives transpired according to this narrative (Apple, Kristof, Dennis, Ranger, Berns, Vlad, & Tony). As young boys, they were able to identify early on that they felt attraction toward other males and did not engage in traditionally masculine activities. F-SIVF informants reported that they accepted their homosexual desires early and without much internal struggle. Ranger (51 years) shares,

> Actually, there was no period in my life that I had to discern if I was gay. Because from the very start, I instinctively knew that I am gay. And that I am not like other normal boys ....

What facilitated this self-acceptance is the openness and tolerance of the family members toward their sexuality and gender expression. Berns (23 years) mentions how the old matriarch of their family felt about him being gay: "[my grandmother] doesn't question about me because she accepts it. She knew me from the start… She knows about my sexuality. She really accepts me." When the SIVF is full during child, the faster and easier the self-acceptance of the informants' sexual identity.

Due to the acceptance of the family members of their sexual identity, their sexual self-expression also became unrestrained. The informants frequently correlate femininity and flamboyance with gayness, and report that their relatives tolerate and even encourage their engagement in gay-related activities, Berns adds, "…dance troupes would get me. Every time I wanted something, 'Nanay, we have a costume. We need it …' Then my grandmother would get money for me." Moreover, family members of informants with F-SIVF also allow them to pursue romantic and sexual relationships with other males. Informants report that they can present their boyfriends to their relatives without being shunned, like Tony (26 years) who narrates, "… my family knows my boyfriend. They know that I live with him. And then when there's an occasion like Christmas, our families are together."

In terms of risky sexual behaviors, F-SIVF informants demonstrated knowledge of HIV and sexually transmitted infections (STIs) early on. Some of them even reported that they openly talked about safe sex practices in the family, as their relatives knew that they were sexually active. Unlike those from other core narratives, their engagement in unsafe sex was due to personal volitions, rather than influenced by their experiences in the family. When F-SIVF informants got tested and learned about their positive HIV status, it was relatively easier for them to accept their condition. Apple's reaction when he received his diagnosis was rather light; he narrates, "…when the HIV counselor told me, 'you are positive for HIV…,'" I didn't feel much. My only response was, 'okay, okay.'" Furthermore, the F-SIVF MSMs living with HIV are actively engaged in HIV advocacy after the discovery of their status and recovery from the initial symptomatic phase they experienced. Kristof (23 years) describes his advocacy work, "… I am vocal about my campaign and my advocacy … I post about events. I look for participants. I give condoms to whoever."

Finally, in this core narrative, informants were less worried about disclosing their HIV status to their family members. They claimed that their relatives' earlier acceptance of their same-sex desire made it easier for them to come out as HIV positive. Vlad (26 years) explains how he broke the news to his mother, "'Mommy, there are medications for HIV… like maintenance drugs … I will not die immediately…' Then, everything was okay with her. I was also able to tell my siblings." Families, where the sexual identity of the infected member is fully visible, are likewise able to openly talk about their HIV status and are actively engaged with the HIV-positive members' care. It can be gleaned from the life trajectories among F-SIVF informants that families who demonstrate better and more immediate acceptance of the G/B/MSM identity would most likely also exhibit better acceptance of the HIV status of the affected member. F-SIVF promotes *low compounding stigma* or *compounding acceptance:* wherein minimal G/B/MSM-related stigma in the family leads to minimal HIV-related stigma in later life (see Table 9.2).

Partial Sexual Identity Visibility in the Family

In the P-SIVF core narrative, the family is conscious of the sexual identities of the MSM member living with HIV. However, compared to F-SIVF, the family members are less accepting of these identities, thus, the term, "partial." We categorize 12 informants whose lives closely followed this narrative (Harry, Chan, James, Samuel, Arvin, Jerry, Ronald, Rene, Pat, Chase, Pierce, and Kevin). They, too, had identified their homosexual tendencies early during their childhood. However, because their social environment does not tolerate being gay, they initially fought their emerging desires. Ronald (30 years), for instance. shares that he even tried to have a relationship with a girl, "before I went to high school, I tried having a girlfriend." They would eventually accept and deal with their same-sex desires. Moreover, unlike those from F-SIVF who felt that they did not have to formally come out in the family, P-SIVF informants had to intentionally come out to their family members.

A salient reason why P-SIVF informants fought against their emerging desires and delayed their acceptance was that their family made them feel that being gay was not acceptable at home. These could be through explicit negations against having same-sex desires through calling out, expression of disapproval, physical abuse, and differential treatment. An extreme example was the experience of Kevin (19 years) who mentions,

> [...] [my father] always spanks me ... my god, I experienced being hit by a wire, a pipe, a hose. I also experienced getting hit by a smoldering stick ... just because my fingers were "too soft."

Homonegativity was also expressed implicitly by the family by establishing heteronormative rules and routines in the home, and exposing members to conservative beliefs such as Christianity. James (23 years) narrates how anti-gay messages

Table 9.2. The Life History in the Family Context Among F-SIVF Participants.

Core Narrative	Life Segments of Sexual Development and Being HIV Positive					
	Self-Identification, and Acceptance of Sexual Identity	*Family Consciousness of Sexual Identity*	*Expression and Exploration of Sexuality*	*Risky Sexual Behaviors*	*Personal Coping with HIV*	*Family Coping for PLHIV Member*
F-SIVF	Early identification and complete self-acceptance	Tolerance and acceptance of family members	Unrestrained expression of sexual identity	Awareness of safe sex practices	Early acceptance and positive coping with HIV	Family support and involvement in HIV care

Low compounding stigma/compounding acceptance: Family acceptance of sexual identity spills over from members' G/B/MSM identity to their being HIV positive from the Church affected him: "... the Church always says, 'it's bad to be gay... I was reading the bible to sort of cure myself ... because my family says that it's the cure for homosexuality."

Since their sexual identity is not tolerated at home, the MSM members restrain their own sexual expressions and modify their behaviors when they are with the family. They would resort to covert dating and mating to satisfy their sexual desires, find suitable mates in queer spaces that are also inaccessible to their relatives, meet people on online gay dating sites, and join gay and bisexual "clans." Some would frequent gay bars, gay bathhouses, and old movie houses where they can perform their sexual acts. Pierce (28 years) narrated his first experience at a gay bar:

> [...] I got to know [name of the bar]. I was surprised about the live act. Men kissing each other. I was like, "what is this?" I cannot see myself being like that at first then they encouraged me ....

The P-SIVF informants admitted that the uninhibited nature of these spaces placed them at risk of engaging in unsafe sex. Aside from the risks that came with doing sex acts in these places, they also mentioned that their lack of restraint in sex was them compensating for the lack of sexual freedom they had back home. Some of the P-SIVF informants like Chan (23 years), Kevin, and Ronald (27 years) had to also engage in transactional sex because they had to survive after being abandoned by their families. This increased their exposure to HIV and STIs risk.

The discovery of their reactive HIV antibody test induced negative thoughts and emotions from the MSMs with P-SIVF. One of the major reasons why P-SIVF informants have felt dejection, anxiety, and a sense of doom due to how their families would react to their status. Pat (28 years), who had only incompletely disclosed his status to family members, admits,

> [my father] does not even know my situation yet. So it's difficult to open up to him. Because I am scared to open up to him because he might send me away. He might curse me.

When the family learns about their condition, the infected members would receive "discriminatory" treatment from other members, especially those who disproved their same-sex desires in the beginning. They would be frequently reminded that their being HIV-positive is a consequence of choosing to be gay. P-SIVF MSMs living with HIV would experience being devalued, blamed, and isolated by their family members. Kevin tearfully narrates,

> [...] it's as if they don't see me as a human being. Even my food and utensils are separated. I have a separate sleeping area... I told them, "don't be disgusted by me. Because I'm not dead yet. I'm still a person."

As seen in Kevin's story, the extent of abuse and neglect he received due to his being gay in his early life was also applied to him when he came out as HIV positive. Ironically, the visibility of the HIV status renders P-SIVF informants "invisible" (i.e., being neglected, shunned, and isolated).

From the life trajectories of P-SIVF informants, we can glean that families who exhibited discrimination against the same-sex desires of a particular member during their early life would most likely demonstrate discrimination against the infected member due to HIV status. P-SIVF facilitates *compounding enacted stigma*: wherein enacted G/B/MSM stigma in the family spills over and potentiates enacted HIV stigma in later life. Goffman (1963) explained that individuals and groups who are in constant proximity to the stigmatized may also sustain their prejudices against the latter. The P-SIVF informants managed their stigmatized sexual identities by concealment (i.e., acting more masculine and denial of having homosexual desires) and practicing their sexual affairs in secret to hide their stigmatized sexuality from their families (see Table 9.3).

Invisible Sexual Identity in the Family

As implied by the term "invisible," the I-SIVF narrative is characterized by families who, in most part of the lives of the informants, were not aware of the same-sex desires and activities of the infected member. We categorize 12 informants whose life histories demonstrated the features of this core narrative (Korin, Juan, Topher, Lennon, TeeJay, Edward, Ronnie, Vohn, Emjay, Jerald, Nash, and Eljay). During their early lives, the majority of the I-SIVF informants identified as straight and lived heterosexual lives. For instance, Jerald (30 years) shared, "… my school knew me as a womanizing playboy." Many of them dreamed of marrying a woman and establishing a heterosexual-headed family in the future. A few I-SIVF informants admitted that during their youth, they felt some attraction to other males; however, because of their engagement in intimate heterosexual relationships, no one in the family knew or even suspected it.

Unlike those categorized in other core narratives, I-SIVF informants did not receive homophobic treatments in their family prior to getting infected with HIV, because they identified as or presented themselves as heterosexual. Even those who admitted that they had latent attraction were not known by their family members because they acted straight and masculine until they were emancipated from home. Korin (33 years) explains that despite his sexual confusion, he maintained a macho persona because he did not want to be ridiculed.

Table 9.3. The Life History in the Family Context Among P-SIVF Participants.

Core Narrative	Life Segments of Sexual Development and Being HIV Positive					
	Self-identi- fication, and Acceptance of Sexual Identity	*Family Consciousness of Sexual Identity*	*Expression and Exploration of Sexuality*	*Risky Sexual Behaviors*	*Personal Coping with HIV*	*Family Coping for PLHIV Member*
P-SIVF	Struggling self- acceptance	Homonegativity among family members	Restrained, policed, and covert sexual expression	Socio-emotional compensation as precursors of risky sex	Struggling with self- acceptance and negative coping with HIV	Stigmatic and restrained care of the family

Compounding enacted stigma: Enacted G/B/MSM stigma in the family spills over to enacted HIV-related stigma.

[...] If I want to be respected, you have to appear respectable to other people. Because if I grew my hair and wore a skirt – I can see how they are discriminated against, and I don't want to experience that.

Most of them also had homophobic tendencies and had internalized the belief that being gay is an undesirable trait in society.

Relative to informants from the other core narratives, the homosexual awakening of I-SIVF informants transpired later in life, specifically during their late teenage years to their twenties, when they were spending less time at home. Some of them tried to address their confusion by discreetly looking for mates, usually, those who were straight-passing like them, so their heterosexual persona would be maintained. Others reported that they did not realize they would enjoy laying with another of the same sex until they were seduced by a friend, coworker, or stranger, which eventually led them to like engaging in homosexual intercourse. Lennon (28 years), who was already married to his own wife during this time, learned about sex with another man through an orgy with a male colleague, the colleague's wife, and other friends. He shares, "At first, we would penetrate his wife. When his wife got exhausted, we would penetrate him."

As they sexually experimented relatively later than informants from other core narratives and were very discreet in mating with other men, I-SIVF informants claimed that they were unaware of safe sex behaviors and did not receive the sex educational campaigns that usually targeted younger MSMs. They also engaged in relatively riskier sexual behaviors: unprotected sex with multiple partners, orgies, and sex in public places. Eljay (28 years) admits that he did not know the function of condoms before. "Condoms meant nothing to me before. Because I did not know. Maybe it was simply for safety. And so that I won't get dirty." However, they admit that even when they were already actively practicing homosexual intercourse, they maintained their homonegativity and would sometimes feel guilt after performing these acts.

I-SIVF informants had the most dramatic stories of being diagnosed with HIV infection. First, due to their lack of knowledge about the need for regular testing, many of them discovered being HIV positive when they were already suffering opportunistic infections. For instance, Edward (24 years) recollects his ordeal: "It came to the point when I got paralyzed due to crypto meningitis .... Then my appearance got worse. I couldn't recognize myself." Second, they expressed deep remorse after knowing their status. They consider their HIV infection as a grave mistake that burdens them with guilt. Since they were "originally" heterosexual, they feel regretful for transitioning to being MSMs. They felt it was the reason why they were cursed to have the disease in the first place.

As regards their family's role in their HIV experiences, there were two outcomes that were gleaned from this narrative. First, there were those who, because of the advanced nature of their infection, had to seek help from their relatives, they had to come out as HIV positive. Their family members were very shocked and disappointed because they had no prior knowledge of the informants' tendencies to have sexual relations with other men. However, after the disclosures, the family became more involved in their care. Emjay (29 years) shares how his mother supported him: "She cried when I told her about it. But what came out

of my mother's mouth was, 'your fight is my fight. Your fight is our fight ....'"
Nevertheless, despite the understanding of their family members among those
who chose to disclose their status, they continue to feel lingering regrets about
their sexual life choices. In this circumstance, it can be gleaned that for I-SIVF
informants who did not receive G/B/MSM stigma because of "passing" as straight
(Goffman, 1963), family members were more likely to become allies when they
disclosed their condition (compared to P-SIVF informants), arguably due to the
heteronormative practices that MSMs embodied in their early life.

Second, there were I-SIVF MSMs living with HIV, who were able to conceal
the fact that they are infected by the virus because they were asymptomatic. Until
the time of the interview, their families were not aware of their sexual identity
and HIV status. These informants shared that because of their non-disclosure,
they could not seek assistance from family members, and had to deal with their
health needs on their own. Ronnie (30 years) shares, "I cannot even tell them I'm
gay right? What more if they find out about my HIV?" From the life trajectories
of I-SIVF informants, it can be observed that the informants had self- and other-
directed homonegativity, and these negative attitudes toward same-sex desires
intensified their felt stigma when they contracted HIV. I-SIVF facilitates *compounding internalized stigma*: wherein internalized homonegativity spills over and
potentiates internalized HIV-related stigma (see Table 9.4).

DISCUSSION

In this study, we proposed the concept of *compounding stigma*, arguing that
earlier G/B/MSM stigma experiences can influence how HIV stigma is experienced later in life. We unpacked this phenomenon in the family, through the life
histories of MSMs living with HIV. We differentiate from the current scholarship of compounded or multilayered stigma by departing from cross-sectional

Table 9.4. The Life History in the Family Context Among I-SIVF Participants.

Core Narrative	Life Segments of Sexual Development and Being HIV Positive					
	Self-identification, and Acceptance of Sexual Identity	*Family Consciousness of Sexual Identity*	*Expression and Exploration of Sexuality*	*Risky Sexual Behaviors*	*Personal Coping with HIV*	*Family Coping for PLHIV Member*
I-SIVF	Late identification and/or extended repression of same-sex desire	Unawareness of family members	Masculine and heterosexual expression in early life; late exploration of same-sex desire	Lack of safe sex awareness; engagement in risky sex	Remorseful coping	Family involvement in care; OR, HIV status is undisclosed to family members

Compounding internalized stigma: Internalized G/B/MSM stigma in the family spills over to internalized HIV stigma.

and intersectional perspectives and drawing focus specifically on how these two stigmatic characteristics interacted with each other across the lifespan in the context of the family and shaped the sexual development and HIV outcomes of the informants through a narrative, life history approach. Our study emphasizes chronological-interactional co-presence of the two stigmatized traits, its situatedness (i.e., family), and relational proximity across the lifespan. While we acknowledge our study's limitation that certain social backgrounds were underrepresented in our pool of informants (e.g., non-NCR PLHIVs), we hope that the present research contributes to the continuing understanding of HIV stigma in Southeast Asian populations.

Furthermore, our study provides narrative empirical evidence on local conceptualizations of stigma in the Philippines. In our assertions in the introduction, we forwarded two intertwined types of stigma in the country's context: *dungis/mantsa/dusta* and *bansag/alyas*. From the insights drawn from the life histories of the informants, the extent to which being *bakla* and *posit* moves from being a harmless *bansag/alyas* to a discriminatory *dungis/mantsa/dusta*, is influenced by the extent to which these labels are known and accepted by the family.

Our findings forward the central role of SIVF (i.e., consciousness and/or acceptance) in shaping sexual development, becoming HIV positive, and the way early G/B/MSM stigma compounds HIV stigma in later life. Informants who experienced being discriminated against by their family members for having same-sex desires and non-heterosexual tendencies struggled to accept their sexuality during their early years (P-SIVF). Apparent in the stories of partially visible MSMs living with HIV is compounding enacted stigma: the spillover of the family's enacted homonegativity on their enacted HIV stigma, which negatively impacts the coping, self-acceptance, and overall health of the MSM member living with HIV. This finding confirms earlier research in the Philippines (Ruga, 2020) and elsewhere (Adam et al., 2017; Logie et al., 2019) that suggests the possible links between family gender-based abuse and violence in early life with HIV-related discrimination among PLHIVs.

Moreover, the narratives of sexual invisibility in the family also emerged from the collection of stories (I-SIVF). Internalized homonegativity during the early years and emerging adulthood of the informants may contribute to the felt HIV stigma. Compounding internalized stigma has been observed among those who concealed their same-sex desires and/or activities from their family, including those who discovered their homosexual tendencies later in life. Their compounded internalized HIV stigma may hinder their self-acceptance despite the care provided by the family or may lead to them not disclosing to or seeking help from their family because of fear. This confirms prior evidence demonstrating the association between non-disclosure of sexual identity and HIV status to the family due to fear of stigma (Berg & Ross, 2014; Chavez et al., 2016; Florom-Smith & De Santis, 2012; Smith et al., 2008).

On the other hand, the results of the narrative analysis also offer a more positive life trajectory. MSMs living with HIV whose sexual identity has been fully visible to their family from the start indicate that the family acceptance of members' sexuality bolsters their self-acceptance (F-SIVF). Moreover, when MSMs living with HIV had experienced less discrimination and more tolerance at home for their same-sex desires during their childhood, they tend to demonstrate less internalized HIV stigma, more readiness to disclose their status in the family, and better physical and psychological coping with the disease. Their life histories depict a counterfactual scenario; G/B/MSM members of an inclusive and non-discriminating family would experience low compounding stigma if they contract HIV; the family's acceptance of sexual identity can spill over to acceptance of HIV status. This result corroborates the findings of earlier research that emphasized how acceptance and support from family members are linked to better health and well-being outcomes for PLHIVs (Adia et al., 2018).

The life stories of the MSMs living with HIV extend Goffman's (1963) theorization of stigmatization in society by demonstrating how different stigma symbols or traits can compound on each other and create different life outcomes based on the extent that the "normals" and the "wise" around the informants view their sexual and HIV identity. The concept of SIVF potentiates Goffman's idea of stigma visibility and entangles it to the extent to which these traits of being G/B/MSM and HIV-positive are obtrusive and perceived by the family. This visibility influences how these traits can accentuate or soften each other throughout the lives of the informants. Also, the experiences reveal how the act of concealment as a form of stigma management is influenced by visibility and compounding stigma in the familial context. Moreover, other concepts and assertions of Goffman were demonstrated in the life histories of the informants: the concept of "passing" through performing heterosexuality and good health; and the negative social-psychological effects of being stigmatized, both other- and self-directed.

CONCLUSIONS

This study contributes to HIV and family literature by conceptualizing the novel construct of *compounding stigma* that offers a more expansive understanding of the co-presence of and life-course-based relationship between G/B/MSM and HIV stigma as demonstrated by PLHIVs' family life histories. Our findings enrich the current understanding of HIV stigma by featuring the nuances in the nexus of common forms of stigma (i.e., enacted stigma, internalized/felt stigma) across differing discrediting traits present among individuals (i.e., being G/B/MSM and HIV positive). Moreover, our present research highlights the role of the family in mitigating or compounding the stigma experienced by MSMs living with HIV in terms of their sexual minority and HIV status. Our findings contextualize Goffman's seminal work on stigma by portraying how the modality of co-presence of these two stigmatic traits of being *bakla* or *posit* is nuanced, and are influenced by the PLHIVs situatedness and relational proximity with the family throughout the lifespan.

Our findings indicate that the extent and nature of HIV-related stigma are linked to factors that are present in the lives of PLHIVs even prior to their infection. Hence, our study amplifies the importance of advocating for policies and initiatives that promote gender- and sexuality-inclusive spaces as early as childhood, especially at home. Future research can explore the concept of compounding stigma in other social spheres of PLHIVs, such as community, peer network, school, and work. PLHIVs with other discrediting traits other than being HIV positive (e.g., engagement in sex work and being a drug user) can also be another focal point of future compounding stigma studies.

REFERENCES

Adam, B. D., Hart, T. A., Mohr, J., Coleman, T., & Vernon, J. (2017). HIV-related syndemic pathways and risk subjectivities among gay and bisexual men: A qualitative investigation. *Culture, Health & Sexuality, 19*(11), 1254–1267. https://doi.org/10.1080/13691058.2017.1309461

Adia, A. C., Bermudez, A. N. C., Callahan, M. W., Hernandez, L. I., Imperial, R. H., & Operario, D. (2018). "An evil lurking behind you": Drivers, experiences, and consequences of HIV-related stigma among men who have sex with men with HIV in Manila, Philippines. *AIDS Education and Prevention, 30*(4), 322–334. https://doi.org/10.1521/aeap.2018.30.4.322

Bamberg, M. (2012). Narrative analysis. In H. Cooper, P. M. Camic, D. L. Long, A. T. Panter, D. Rindskopf, & K. J. Sher (Eds.), *APA handbook of research methods in psychology, Vol. 2. Research designs: Quantitative, qualitative, neuropsychological, and biological* (pp. 85–102). American Psychological Association. https://doi.org/10.1037/13620-006

Berg, R. C., & Ross, M. W. (2014). The second closet: A qualitative study of HIV stigma among sero-positive gay men in a southern US city. *International Journal of Sexual Health, 26*(3), 186–199. https://doi.org/10.1080/19317611.2013.853720

Calaguas, N. P. (2020). Factors affecting the intent to use HIV testing services of Filipino men who have sex with men: A structural equation model. *Journal of the Association of Nurses in AIDS Care, 31*(6), 621–631. http://doi.org/10.1097/JNC.0000000000000179

Canoy, N. A., & Ofreneo, M. A. P. (2012). Becoming and being HIV-positive: The subjective experience of young Filipino gay men living with HIV. *Philippine Journal of Psychology, 45*(2), http://www.ejournals.ph/form/cite.php?id=1197

Canoy, N. A., & Ofreneo, M. A. P. (2017). Struggling to care: A discursive-material analysis of negotiating agency among HIV-positive MSM. *Health, 21*(6), 575–594. https://doi.org/10.1177/1363459315628040

Chambers, L. A., Rueda, S., Baker, D. N., Wilson, M. G., Deutsch, R., Raeifar, E., Rourke, S. B., & Team, T. S. (2015). Stigma, HIV and health: A qualitative synthesis. *BMC Public Health, 15*(1), 848. https://doi.org/10.1186/s12889-015-2197-0

Chavez, M. F. C., Maloles, M. V., & Manzano, M. P. L. (2016). The phenomenology of patients living with HIV: Its implications on their coping mechanism. *LPU - Laguna Journal of Arts and Sciences, 2*(3). 85–95.

Cleofas, J. V. (2016). *Queering the family stigma experiences of Filipino MSMs living with HIV* [Doctoral dissertation]. Manila, Philippines: De La Salle University. https://animorepository.dlsu.edu.ph/etd_doctoral/1364/

De Los Santos, J. A. A., Tuppal, C. P., & Milla, N. E. (2020). The correlates of health facility-related stigma and health-seeking behaviors of people living with HIV. *Acta Medica Philippina* (pp. 1–8). https://doi.org/10.47895/amp.vi0.4447

Florom-Smith, A. L., & De Santis, J. P. (2012). Exploring the concept of HIV-related stigma. *Nursing Forum, 47*(3), 153–165. https://doi.org/10.1111/j.1744-6198.2011.00235.x

Gerhardt, U. (1994). The use of Weberian ideal-type methodology in qualitative data interpretation: An outline for ideal-type analysis. *BMS: Bulletin of Sociological Methodology/Bulletin de Méthodologie Sociologique, 45*, 74–126. http://www.jstor.org/stable/24311610

Goffman, E. (1963). *Stigma; Notes on the management of spoiled identity*. Prentice-Hall.

Halcomb, E. J., & Davidson, P. M. (2006). Is verbatim transcription of interview data always necessary? *Applied Nursing Research, 19*(1), 38–42. https://doi.org/10.116/j.apnr.2005.06.001

Halkitis, P. N., Siconolfi, D., Fumerton, M., & Barlup, K. A. (2008). Risk bases in childhood and adolescence among HIV-negative young adult gay and bisexual male barebackers. *Journal of Gay & Lesbian Social Services, 20*(4), 288–314. http://doi.org/10.1080/10538720802310709

Lincoln, Y. S., & Guba, E. G. (1985). *Naturalistic inquiry*. Sage Publications.

Logie, C. H., Wang, Y., Marcus, N., Levermore, K., Jones, N., Ellis, T., & Bryan, N. (2019). Syndemic experiences, protective factors, and HIV vulnerabilities among lesbian, gay, bisexual, and transgender persons in Jamaica. *AIDS and Behavior, 23*(6), 1530–1540.

Ofreneo, M. A., & Canoy, N. (2017). Falling into poverty: the intersectionality of meanings of HIV among overseas Filipino workers and their families. *Culture, Health & Sexuality, 19*(10), 1122–1135. https://doi.org/10.1080/13691058.2017.1294261

Marvasti, A. B. (2004). *Qualitative research in sociology*. Thousand Oaks.

Medina-Belen, T. G. (2015). *The Filipino family*. University of Philippines Press.

Restar, A., Nguyen, M., Nguyen, K., Adia, A., Nazareno, J., Yoshioka, E., Hernandez, L., & Operario, D. (2018). Trends and emerging directions in HIV risk and prevention research in the Philippines: A systematic review of the literature. *PLOS ONE, 13*(12), e0207663. https://doi.org/10.1371/journal.pone.0207663

Rueda, S., Mitra, S., Chen, S., Gogolishvili, D., Globerman, J., Chambers, L., Wilson, M., Logie, C. H., Shi, Q., Morassaei, S., & Rourke, S. B. (2016). Examining the associations between HIV-related stigma and health outcomes in people living with HIV/AIDS: A series of meta-analyses. *BMJ Open, 6*(7), e011453. https://doi.org/10.1136/bmjopen-2016-011453

Ruga, E. C. (2020). Exploring the experiences of gender-based violence and the associated psychosocial and mental health issue of Filipinos living with HIV. *Academia Lasalliana Journal of Education and Humanities, 2*(1), 1–13.

Samaco-Zamora, M. C. F., & Fernandez, K. T. G. (2016). A grounded theory of Filipino wellness (Kaginhawaan). *Psychological Studies, 61*(4), 279–287. https://doi.org/10.1007/s12646-016-0373-7

Smith, B., & Monforte, J. (2020). Stories, new materialism, and pluralism: Understanding, practising and pushing the boundaries of narrative analysis. *Methods in Psychology, 2*, 100016. https://doi.org/10.1016/j.metip.2020.100016

Smith, R., Rossetto, K., & Peterson, B. L. (2008). A meta-analysis of disclosure of one's HIV-positive status, stigma, and social support. *AIDS Care, 20*(10), 1266–1275. https://doi.org/10.1080/09540120801926977

Tanaka, C., Tuliao, M. T. R., Tanaka, E., Yamashita, T., & Matsuo, H. (2018). A qualitative study on the stigma experienced by people with mental health problems and epilepsy in the Philippines. *BMC Psychiatry, 18*(1), 325. https://doi.org/10.1186/s12888-018-1902-9

Thapa, S., Hannes, K., Cargo, M., Buve, A., Peters, S., Dauphin, S., & Mathei, C. (2018). Stigma reduction in relation to HIV test uptake in low-and middle-income countries: A realist review. *BMC Public Health, 18*, 1277. https://doi.org/10.1186/s12889-018-6156-4

Tsang, E. Y.-ha, Qiao, S., Wilkinson, J. S., Fung, A. L.-chu, Lipeleke, F., & Li, X. (2019). Multilayered stigma and vulnerabilities for HIV infection and transmission: A qualitative study on male sex workers in Zimbabwe. *American Journal of Men's Health, 13*(1), 155798831882388. 1–11. https://doi.org/10.1177/1557988318823883

Tuppal, C. P., Ninobla, M. M. G., Reñosa, M. D. C., Ruiz, M. G. D., Loresco, R. C., Tuppal, S. M. P., & Panes, I. I. (2019). Living with HIV/AIDS among men having sex with men (MSM) in the Philippines: Internet ethnography of HIV life stages. *Journal of Global Health Reports, 3*, e2019090. https://doi.org/10.29392/joghr.3.e2019090

USAID, United Nations Development Programme. (2014). *Being LGBT in Asia: The Philippines country report*. United Nations Development Programme. https://pdf.usaid.gov/pdf_docs/PBAAA888.pdf

CHAPTER 10

FAMILY RELATIONSHIP, MENTAL WELL-BEING, AND LIFE SATISFACTION DURING THE COVID-19 PANDEMIC: A MEDIATION STUDY AMONG FILIPINO GRADUATE STUDENTS

Jerome V. Cleofas and Ryan Michael F. Oducado

ABSTRACT

The 2019 coronavirus disease (COVID-19) pandemic has profoundly affected family and school life. Evidence demonstrates how pandemic-induced online learning and home confinement can influence family dynamics and, consequently, students' mental health and quality of life. This chapter extends the literature by building upon the perspective of family systems theory and focusing the analysis on graduate students who are underrepresented in COVID-19 research. Drawing from an online survey among 337 graduate students enrolled in a state university in the Philippines during the second year of the pandemic, this study examines the three family relationship domains (cohesion, expressiveness, and conflict), their predictive relationships with life satisfaction, and the mediating role of mental well-being on these relationships. Findings indicate favorable levels of cohesion, expressiveness, and conflict in the family. Respondents' age, sex assigned at birth, and marital status were significantly correlated with at least one domain of family relationship. Cohesion

Resilience and Familism: The Dynamic Nature of Families in the Philippines
Contemporary Perspectives in Family Research, Volume 23, 163–182
Copyright © 2023 by Emerald Publishing Limited
All rights of reproduction in any form reserved
ISSN: 1530-3535/doi:10.1108/S1530-353520230000023010

and expressiveness yielded significant positive predictive relationships on mental well-being and life satisfaction. Furthermore, findings indicate the partial mediation of mental well-being on the relationship between cohesion and life satisfaction and full mediation on expressiveness and life satisfaction.

Keywords: COVID-19; family relationship; graduate students; life satisfaction; mental health; Philippines

INTRODUCTION

The COVID-19 pandemic has profoundly affected family, school, and work life. As of March 20, 2022, 468 million cases and over 6 million deaths due to COVID-19 have been registered globally since the SARS-CoV-2 virus was first discovered in early 2020 (World Health Organization (WHO), 2022a). To prevent the spread of the disease, governments have implemented policies to mandate health protective behaviors (i.e., masking, sanitation, and physical distancing) and regulate the mobility of individuals (Rabacal et al., 2022). Many aspects of life, such as work, commerce, and school, have transitioned online and have invaded the home, resulting in changes in family routines (Prime et al., 2020). With adults engaging in work-from-home (WFH) set-up and younger members doing online and/or distance learning, family members get to spend more time together during the COVID-19 crisis. The quality of their family relationship has become a more salient factor in their well-being. Evidence suggests that families with better resilience foster better mental health and adaptive coping and decreased stress among their members, especially the younger ones, during the pandemic (Gayatri & Irawaty, 2021). On the other hand, COVID-19 research also indicates the association between disruption and instabilities within the family and adverse psychological outcomes, such as depression and anxiety (Guo et al., 2021; López-Núñez et al., 2021).

The Philippines is among the countries that struggled to curb the coronavirus outbreak. More than 3.6 million cases and 59,000 deaths due to COVID-19 have been registered since the beginning of the global epidemic. As of March 16, 2022, only 65 million Filipinos had been vaccinated, which is still far from the 70% target immunization (World Health Organization (WHO), 2022b). The country has been placed in one of the longest lockdowns in the world (from March 2020 to March 2022) (Gutierrez, 2022). Moreover, the Philippines has sustained its ranking within the bottom five countries in terms of COVID resilience since mid-2021 (Lew et al., 2022). This long-standing exposure to COVID-19-related adversities has impacted Filipinos and their families. In a survey conducted among Filipinos during the first year of the pandemic, 66% of the respondents reported feeling fearful and anxious during the coronavirus outbreak, primarily due to the impacts of COVID-19 on family life, day-to-day lifestyle, travel plans, and work/school arrangements (Blackbox Research Team, 2020). Critical problems during the pandemic among Filipino households are disruptions in livelihood, food security, educational opportunities, and access to health care (World Vision,

2020). Moreover, prolonged stay-at-home, concern for family members, and family's financial difficulties were significantly linked to pandemic-related distress, anxiety, and depression among Filipino adults (Aruta, 2021; Tee et al., 2020).

COVID-19 research in the field of education not only highlighted the challenges and opportunities that arose in the abrupt transition from traditional classroom to pure online/distance education, but also provided glimpses into the state of the family during the pandemic. Evidence from the Philippines (Baticulon et al., 2021; Cleofas, 2021; Tus, 2021) and elsewhere (Carrión-Martínez et al., 2021; Sharin, 2021) suggest that the conditions and dynamics of the family were linked to students' educational outcomes (i.e., academic performance and online student engagement), mental health, and well-being. Filipino families with students had to reimagine their routines to accommodate remote education at home (Agaton & Cueto, 2021; Andrada-Poa et al., 2021; Cleofas et al., 2021). This study focuses on the family relationships, mental health, and well-being of students at the graduate school level who are underrepresented in COVID-19 research in the Philippines.

Unlike students from basic and college education levels, graduate students are more diverse in terms of demographic and socioeconomic background (Ericta, 2013; Japan International Cooperation Agency (JICA), 2015). Graduate students also experience unique challenges related to the advanced education that they are receiving (Oducado et al., 2021). Moreover, the positions that graduate students have in their families may also vary (Bilodeau et al., 2021), which can affect the quality of family, work, and university life of graduate students. For instance, single children members of the family who pursue graduate school may experience more work–life balance compared to their married parent counterparts (Rungduin & Miranda, 2018). On the other hand, Springer et al. (2009) have demonstrated the challenges of juggling studying and parenting among graduate students who are mothers.

In the Philippines, most graduate students are also engaged in full-time work while pursuing their advanced degrees (Rungduin & Miranda, 2018). Even before the pandemic, the balancing act that students perform to cope with the overlapping roles at work, school, and in the family has been a common theme in graduate education research in the Philippines (e.g., Cleofas & Mijares, 2022; Rungduin & Miranda, 2018) and elsewhere (e.g., McCutcheon & Morrison, 2018; Pitt et al., 2021). There is reason to suspect that due to pandemic-induced home confinement, WFH set-up, and online learning, the influence of the family on the overall quality of life of graduate students has become more pronounced during the pandemic.

THEORETICAL FRAMEWORK AND HYPOTHESIS BUILDING

We used the perspective of family systems theory to understand how graduate students' family influences their mental health and life satisfaction during the COVID-19 pandemic. Family systems theory examines behavioral and health outcomes of members at the level of the family instead of the individual. Family systems scholars have considered various family-related variables as their focus of inquiry, such as communication, connectedness, subsystems, dyads, values, resilience, and coping (Fingerman & Berman, 2000). Anchored on this perspective, this study's main predictor and family-level variable is *family relationship*. We operationally define family relationship as a construct comprised of three domains based on Moos (1994) and Fok et al. (2014). First is *cohesion*, which refers to the extent to which family members support and get along well and feel a sense of togetherness. Second is *expressiveness*, which refers to the extent to which members can talk openly and easily initiate discussions, including personal problems. Third is *conflict*, which refers to the extent to which family members argue, get mad and violent toward each other (Fok et al., 2014). The perspective of family systems theory also suggests that the characteristics of individual members and the social position of the family also influence the extent to which they perceive the quality of the relationship functioning of the family (Fingerman & Berman, 2000). Evidence suggests that the individual's age, gender, and family position and the household's economic status are gradients associated with perceived family relationship (Okechukwu et al., 2021). Hence, we hypothesize that:

H_1. Sociodemographic characteristics are correlated with cohesion, expressiveness, and conflict.

Family Relationship and Mental Health

Mental health is a concept commonly examined through the lens of family systems theory. Theorists and practitioners posit that family functioning is linked to the psychological outcomes of its members (Fingerman & Berman, 2000). Pre-pandemic research has linked positive family relationship with optimal mental health outcomes among its members, such as improved individual resilience (Huang et al., 2018), psychological adaptation (Lee et al., 2019), flourishing (Keliat et al., 2019), and emotional intelligence (Foster, 2020). Cohesion and expressiveness have been indicated as protective factors against suicidality and substance abuse (Allen et al., 2014), behavioral addiction (Hwang et al., 2014), and depression and anxiety symptoms (Lee et al., 2019). On the other hand, conflicts in the family have been associated with higher risks for depression (Carona et al., 2021), aggressive behaviors (Estévez López et al., 2018), and substance abuse (Antunes et al., 2018). The correlation between quality of family relationship and mental health outcomes have also been indicated by research conducted during the COVID-19 outbreak (Guo et al., 2021; Karmacharya et al., 2020; López-Núñez et al., 2021; Martin-Storey et al., 2021). A study among Filipino Americans revealed that their family environment influenced the behavioral health of adolescent members (Javier et al., 2018). For this study, the mental health outcome of interest is mental well-being, measured using the short Warwick–Edinburgh mental wellbeing scale (SWEMWBS). This construct refers to the extent to which individuals demonstrate various positive psychological indicators, including optimism about the future, feeling useful, being relaxed, ability to deal with problems, demonstrating clear thinking, social interaction and support, and ease in making decisions (Tennant et al., 2007). Previous research that has used this scale has noted moderate levels of mental well-being among Filipino adults (Cleofas & Oducado, 2021; Cleofas et al., 2022). In relating family relationships with mental well-being, we hypothesize the following:

H_2. Cohesion positively predicts mental well-being.

H_3. Expressiveness positively predicts mental well-being.

H_4. Conflict negatively predicts mental well-being.

Family Relationship and Life Satisfaction

Life satisfaction is a cognitive-judgmental construct that describes one's present status and prospects in life and is a good indicator of one's overall well-being and quality of life (Anand, 2016; Diener et al., 1985). Family systems theory has helped establish how the quality of relationships among family members within and across generations contributes to life satisfaction (Kim-Appel & Appel, 2015). This is corroborated by a grounded theory that suggests that the central tenet of wellness or "kaginhawaan" among Filipinos is the family (Samaco-Zamora & Fernandez, 2016). External family locus-of-hope has been known to buffer stress's effect on Filipino students' life satisfaction (Bernardo & Resurreccion, 2018). On the other hand, local literature has also indicated that the nature of family relationships can also be a source of poor life outcomes such as distress and loneliness among Filipinos (Aruta, 2021; Ortega et al., 2010). During COVID-19, family concerns have been linked to poor life and educational outcomes among Filipino medicine students (Baticulon et al., 2021). The strong influence of the family in shaping its members' life trajectories is a common feature in the cultural landscape of the Philippines (Medina-Belen, 2015). Meanwhile, studies elsewhere have indicated how cohesion, expressiveness, and conflict in the family are linked to life satisfaction before (Chin et al., 2019; Cho et al., 2021; Fastame, 2021; Hayles et al., 2018; Kim & Nho, 2020; Lu et al., 2021; Μπακύρτσης, 2021) and during the COVID-19 pandemic (López-Núñez et al., 2021). Hence, we hypothesize the following:

H_5. Cohesion positively predicts life satisfaction.

H_6. Expressiveness positively predicts life satisfaction.

H_7. Conflict negatively predicts life satisfaction.

Furthermore, COVID-19 studies conducted in the Philippines (Dela Rosa et al., 2022; Egcas et al., 2021; Guillasper et al., 2021) and other countries (Al Dhaheri et al., 2021; Rogowska et al., 2020) have demonstrated the link between positive mental health outcomes with higher life satisfaction among university students. There is reason to suspect that a possible pathway to which family

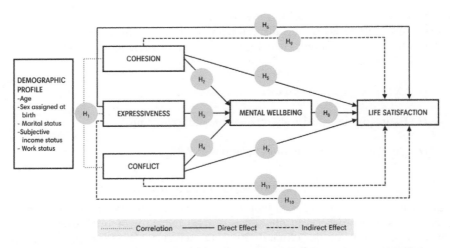

Fig. 10.1. The Hypothesized Model Indicating Mental Well-being as a Mediator Between Family Relationship Domains and Life Satisfaction.

relationship domains can influence life satisfaction among graduate students is through mental well-being, especially since previous empirical evidence has indicated similar directions of the relationships among these three constructs (Allen et al., 2014; Lee et al., 2019; López-Núñez et al., 2021). A previous study in Taiwan had empirically validated a mediated model among family relationship, psychological health, and life satisfaction (Lin & Yi, 2019), but this was conducted prior to the COVID-19 outbreak. Thus, we hypothesize the following:

H_8. Mental well-being positively predicts life satisfaction.

H_9. Cohesion has a positive indirect effect on life satisfaction through mental well-being.

H_{10}. Expressiveness has a positive indirect effect on life satisfaction through mental well-being.

H_{11}. Conflict has a negative indirect effect on life satisfaction through mental well-being.

Fig. 10.1 presents a visual diagram of the hypothesized model of the study.

METHODS

Study Design and Participants

This research is a component of a larger investigative online survey project that examined various social and psychological determinants of health behaviors related to the COVID-19 pandemic in a selected public tertiary educational institution in Western Visayas, Philippines. This present study utilizes a quantitative, cross-sectional, explanatory design, specifically mediation analysis. The minimum sample size required to conduct this mediation analysis based on $G*$power analysis is 222 (effect size=0.15, α error probability=0.05, power=0.95). The eligibility criteria for the target population in this study were as follows: (1) should be a graduate student enrolled in any master's or doctoral program offered by the selected university; and (2) should be living with family members during the period of COVID-19. From our pool of conveniently sampled student respondents from the institution, a total of 337 graduate students met the criteria and were included in the analysis.

Instrumentation

Demographic Profile Questionnaire

To measure the demographic characteristics of the participating graduate students, the following variables were asked: age, sex assigned at birth (male=1, female=0), marital status (single=0, married=1), self-reported/subjective income status (low income=0, middle to high income=1), and work status (working=1, not working=0).

Brief Family Relationship Scale (BFRS)

The main predictors of this study were assessed using the brief family relationship scale (BFRS; α=0.88) developed by Fok et al. (2014). BRFS measures the quality of the relational aspect of family functioning through three domains: cohesion, expressiveness, and conflict. Each of the 16 items is answered through a 5-point Likert scale (1=strongly disagree, 5=strongly agree). The BFRS is suitable for use to measure family relationships of populations from non-Western, collectivist cultures (Fok et al., 2014). A sample statement is, "My family members really support each other."

Short Warwick-Edinburgh Mental Wellbeing Scale

The mediator of this study is mental well-being, which was assessed using the SWEMWBS. SWEMWBS is a 7-item scale that measures the positive aspects of mental health of individuals (Tennant et al., 2007). Each item of the SWEMWBS is answered using a 5-point Likert scale (1=strongly disagree, 5=strongly agree). SWEMWBS can also indicate the presence of probable psychopathology, specifically depression risk. A sample item is, "I've been dealing with problems well." A previous study has noted its acceptable reliability in the Filipino population (α=0.87; Cleofas & Oducado, 2021).

Satisfaction with Life Scale

To measure the outcome variable of the study (life satisfaction), we used the satisfaction with life scale (SWLS) developed by Diener et al. (1985). SWLS is a

5-item, 7-point Likert scale (1=strongly disagree, 7=strongly agree) that assesses the overall subjective well-being of individuals using a cognitive-judgmental process. A sample statement is, "So far, I have gotten the important things I want in life." SWLS has demonstrated good reliability in a Filipino sample (α=0.87; Cleofas & Oducado, 2021).

Data Gathering Procedure and Ethical Considerations

The protocol of the research project was granted administrative clearance from the university's management for the ethical conduct of research. Google Forms was used to facilitate online data collection. The link to the online survey was sent to the emails of the students of the university. Informed consent was secured digitally. The first page of the form included the research objectives and procedures and the rights of the respondents. Their voluntary participation was signified by clicking yes, leading them to the survey proper. No private and sensitive information was collected from the respondents. All data were kept confidential within a two-factor authenticated encrypted cloud.

Data Analysis Procedure

JAMOVI 2.0.0.0 and JASP 0.16 software applications for Macintosh were used for statistical tests. To describe the key variables, we used frequency and percentage for categorical variables, and mean and standard deviation for continuous variables. To establish correlations between demographic characteristics with family relationship domains (H_1), we used independent t-test for dichotomous demographic variables, and Pearson R correlation test for continuous. To test for the mediated model of the relationships among BFRS, SWEMWBS, and SWLS (H_2-H_{11}), we applied Pearson R and Cronbach alpha to ascertain unadjusted correlations among the variables and internal consistency of the measurements of the constructs, which were pre-requisites for mediation analysis. Afterward, the general linear modeling mediation analysis module of JAMOVI was used to run the mediation analysis. Bias correction for the confidence interval was done via bootstrapping using 5,000 replicates. The R^2 values for the SWEMWBS (mediator) and SWLS (outcome) were computed using JASP. The key variables demonstrated normality based on non-significant Kolmogorov–Smirnov values.

RESULTS

Descriptive Statistics

Table 10.1 shows the descriptive statistics of the key variables in the study. In terms of demographic profile, the majority of the respondents were middle aged (mean=33.56±8.45), females (77%), married (54.30%), within middle to high subjective income status (75.67%), and are not working (68.25%). As regards family relationship domains, the average scores of respondents indicate a high level of cohesion (mean=27.47±3.77) and expressiveness (mean=17.55±2.89),

Table 10.1. Descriptive Statistics of Key Variables ($N=337$).

Variables	n (Mean)	% (SD)
Age[a]	33.56	8.45
Sex assigned at birth		
Male	77	22.85
Female	260	77.15
Marital status		
Single	154	45.70
Married	183	54.30
Subjective income status		
Low income	82	24.33
Middle to high income	255	75.67
Work status		
Working	107	31.75
Not working	230	68.25
Family relationship[a]		
Cohesion[b]	27.47	3.77
Expressiveness[c]	17.55	2.89
Conflict[d]	12.10	5.73
Mental well-being (SWEMWBS)[a,e]	28.63	4.88
Life satisfaction (SWLS)[a,f]	5.45	1.05

[a]Mean and standard deviation for continuous variables.
[b]Verbal interpretation for cohesion scores: low=6–14, moderate=15–22, and high=23–30.
[c]Verbal interpretation for expressiveness scores: low=4–9, moderate=10–15, and high=16–20.
[d]Verbal interpretation for conflict scores: low=6–14, moderate=15–22, and high=23–30.
[e]Verbal interpretation for SWEMWBS scores: low=7–18, moderate=19–27, and high=28–35.
[f]Verbal interpretation for SWLS scores: low=1–3, moderate=4–5, and high=6–7.

and a low level of conflict (mean=12.10±5.73). Furthermore, the sample demonstrates high mental well-being (mean=28.63±4.88) and moderate life satisfaction (5.45±1.05).

Correlation of Demographic Characteristics and Family Relationship Domains (H_1)

Table 10.2 presents the results of the bivariate statistics that test for the relationship between demographic variables and the three domains of family relationship. Findings suggest that cohesion levels are significantly higher among male ($t=3.028$, $p=0.003$) and married ($t=-2.063$, $p=0.04$) respondents. Moreover, results indicate that older ($r=0.124$, $p=0.023$) and married ($t=-2.67$, $p=0.008$) respondents reported significantly higher expressiveness scores. Lastly, age demonstrated a significantly negative relationship with family conflict, such that older respondents reported higher scores ($r=-0.148$, $p=0.007$).

Mediation Analysis of BFRS, SWEMWBS, and SWLS (H_2–H_{11})

Table 10.3 shows the results of the Pearson R tests among the family relationship domains, mental well-being, life satisfaction, and the reliability tests for the subscale. Cohesion and expressiveness demonstrated significant positive correlations with SWEMWBS ($r=0.403$, $p<0.001$) and SWLS ($r=0.502$, $p<0.001$).

Table 10.2. Correlation of Demographic Profile and Family Relationship Domains.

Demographic Profile	Cohesion			Expressiveness			Conflict		
	Mean ± SD	Statistic[a]	p-Value	Mean ± SD	Statistic[a]	p-Value	Mean ± SD	Statistic[a]	p-Value
Age	–	0.106	0.053	–	0.124*	0.023	–	–0.148**	0.007
Sex assigned at birth									
Male	27.80 ± 3.49	3.028**	0.003	17.69 ± 2.73	1.644	0.101	11.79 ± 5.59	–1.833	0.068
Female	26.34 ± 4.43			17.08 ± 3.34			13.14 ± 6.11		
Marital status									
Single	27.01 ± 4.09	–2.063*	0.040	17.10 ± 3.18	–2.67**	0.008	12.35 ± 5.89	0.751	0.453
Married	27.85 ± 3.44			17.93 ± 2.57			11.88 ± 5.61		
Subjective income status									
Low income	27.69 ± 3.46	0.711	0.478	17.74 ± 2.71	0.743	0.458	12.29 ± 5.97	0.391	0.696
Middle to high income	27.37 ± 3.89			17.48 ± 2.96			12.02 ± 5.64		
Work status									
Working	27.50 ± 3.87	0.274	0.784	17.56 ± 3.02	0.043	0.966	11.84 ± 5.87	–1.202	0.230
Not working	27.38 ± 3.56			17.54 ± 2.59			12.65 ± 5.37		

[a]Pearson R correlation (r-value) for continuous IV; independent t-test (t-value) for dichotomous IV.
*p<0.05, **p<0.01

Table 10.3. Cronbach Alpha Scores and Pearson R Correlation Test Results Among Family Relationship Domains, Mental Well-Being (SWEMWBS), and Life Satisfaction (SWLS).

Variables	α	(1)	(2)	(3)	(4)
(1) Cohesion	0.951				
(2) Expressiveness	0.890	0.830***			
(3) Conflict	0.925	−0.376***	0.340***		
(4) SWEMWBS	0.881	0.403***	0.393***	−0.073	
(5) SWLS	0.846	0.502***	0.470***	−0.142**	0.668***

*$p<0.05$, **$p<0.01$, and ***$p<0.001$.

Conflict was significantly negatively correlated with SWLS ($r=-0.142$, $p=0.009$). SWEMWBS significantly positively correlated with SWLS ($r=0.668$, $p<0.001$). All scales demonstrated acceptable Cronbach alpha scores ($\alpha=0.846$–0.951), indicating high internal consistency of the measures within the sample. Since the intended antecedents of SWLS (BFRS and SWEMWBS) yielded significant results, testing for the full mediation model was pursued.

Table 10.4 presents the estimates generated by JAMOVI general linear model mediation test for each path to address H_2–H_{11}. Family cohesion, expressiveness, and conflict were used as predictors, SWEMWBS as the mediator, and life satisfaction as the outcome variable. Among the domains of BFRS, cohesion (H_2: $B=0.357$, $p<0.001$, 95%CI$=0.085$–0.611) and expressiveness (H_3: $B=0.333$, $p=0.044$, 95%CI$=0.0004$–0.664) yielded positive, significant predictive relationships with SWEMWBS.

In terms of the influence of family relationship on life satisfaction, total effects scores indicate that the BFRS domains that significantly positively predicted SWLS are cohesion (H_5: $B=0.105$, $p<0.001$, 95%CI$=0.059$–0.152) and expressiveness (H_6: $B=0.064$, $p=0.036$, 95%CI$=0.004$–0.124).

Results also indicate that SWEMWBS significantly positively predicts SWLS (H_8: $B=0.119$, $p<0.001$, 95%CI$=0.097$–0.141). Furthermore, SWEMWBS had a significant indirect effect on the role of cohesion and expressiveness on SWLS. Specifically, SWEMWBS partially mediated the relationship between family cohesion and SWLS (H_9) as evidenced by significant results on both indirect effect ($B=0.034$, $p=0.011$, 95%CI$=0.010$–0.074) and direct effect ($B=0.063$, $p=0.001$, 95%CI$=0.025$–0.0991). On the other hand, SWEMWBS fully mediated the influence of expressiveness of family expressiveness and SWLS (H_{10}), as evidenced by a significant result on indirect effect ($B=0.039$, $p=0.044$, 95%CI$=0.0004$–0.079) and non-significant result on direct effect ($B=0.024$, $p=0.325$, 95%CI$=-0.022$–0.076). H_4, H_8, and H_{11} were not supported by the data. The overall model explains 47% of the variance of SWEMWBS and 76% for SWLS.

Table 10.4.   Direct Effect and Indirect Effect in the Proposed Research Model.

No.	Hypothesis	Direct Effects		Indirect Effects		Total Effects	
		Estimate	95%CI[a]	Estimate	95%CI[a]	Estimate	95%CI[a]
H_2	COH →SWEMWBS	0.357**	0.085–0.6112				
H_3	EXP →SWEMWBS	0.333*	0.0004–0.664				
H_4	CON →SWEMWBS	0.083	–0.007–0.160				
H_5	COH →SWLS	0.063**	0.025–0.0991			0.105***	0.059–0.152
H_6	EXP →SWLS	0.024	–0.022–0.076			0.064*	0.004–0.124
H_7	CON →SWLS	0.001	–0.014–0.015			0.011	–0.007–0.029
H_8	SWEMWBS →SWLS	0.119***	0.098–0.141				
H_9	COH →SWEMWBS →SWLS			0.042*	0.010–0.074		
H_{10}	EXP →SWEMWBS →SWLS			0.039*	0.0004–0.079		
H_{11}	CON →SWEMWBS →SWLS			0.010	–0.0006–0.019		

[a]95% confidence interval based on bias corrected bootstrap (N=5,000). *Note*: SWEMWBS-R^2 =0.470; SWLS-R^2 =0.757.
$*p < 0.05$, $**p < 0.01$, and $***p < 0.001$.

DISCUSSION

The goal of this present study is to examine the relationships among demographic profiles, family relationship, mental well-being, and life satisfaction. This study extends the family systems theory literature by using its perspective to provide a snapshot of the family life, mental health, and overall well-being of Filipino graduate students who are underrepresented in COVID-19 family research. Only four pandemic-related studies that exclusively featured graduate students in the Philippines are currently available in the literature and are focused more on online learning experiences than students' family lives (Núñez, 2022; Oducado et al., 2021; Osea, 2022; Panoy et al., 2022).

Contrary to early family research during the first year of the pandemic that highlighted the difficulties experienced by households due to the pandemic (e.g., Browne et al., 2021), the findings of our study suggests that graduate students report high levels of cohesion, expressiveness, and low levels of conflict in the family. It must be noted that the data were collected during the second year of the pandemic. Thus, the family might have gained a sense of mastery over the long-standing restrictions that come with pandemic-induced home confinement, as seen in previous research among Filipino single mothers (Andrada-Poa et al., 2021). Moreover, descriptive results also indicate high mental well-being and moderate life satisfaction among graduate students, which is a significant improvement from the high prevalence rates of mental health problems and life dissatisfaction during the early phase of the pandemic in the country (Tee et al., 2020).

Our first hypothesis is partially confirmed. Being male was linked to higher cohesion, as perceived by the respondents. Pre-pandemic, male family members spend more time outside the house (for work or leisure) compared to their female counterparts (Mopuri et al., 2019). This is similarly true in traditional Filipino culture; wherein outdoor affairs are usually assigned to male family members (Hays, 2019). We suspect that the mandated home confinement due to the coronavirus outbreak may have afforded them more periods of interactions with family than they used to, thus increasing their sense of togetherness with the family.

On the other hand, our results indicate that being married is linked to a better sense of cohesion and expressiveness in the family, which corroborates with previous evidence which demonstrated how married couples took advantage of home confinement to improve their relationships with their partners (Epifani et al., 2021) and children (Cleofas et al., 2021). A local case study in the Philippines demonstrated how even with physical distancing during the pandemic, parents were able to continue their intimacy with their spouses and routines of care for their children (Cleofas et al., 2021). Furthermore, younger respondents report lower expressiveness and higher conflict in the family. Previous research has demonstrated how, in the Philippines, young members usually have lesser voice and agency in the household, and talking back to adult members is considered disrespectful (Cruz et al., 2001).

Consistent with previous evidence, our findings for H_2, H_3, H_5, and H_6 suggest that cohesion and expressiveness are significant positive predictors of mental well-being (Guo et al., 2021; Karmacharya et al., 2020; López-Núñez et al., 2021; Martin-Storey, 2021) and life satisfaction (Chin et al., 2019; Cho et al., 2021; Fastame, 2021; Hayles et al., 2018; Kim & Nho, 2020; Lu et al., 2021; Μπακύρτσης, 2021). These findings are unsurprising since previous evidence has established the salient role of the family in Filipino culture for the improvement of the health and life outcomes of its members (Medina-Belen, 2015; Samaco-Zamora & Fernandez, 2016). As regards H_8, results of the present study indicate that mental well-being is a significant positive predictor of life satisfaction; this is consistent with COVID-19 research that have demonstrated the beneficial role of good mental health on the overall life quality among students in higher education in the Philippines (Dela Rosa et al., 2022; Egcas et al., 2021).

Contrary to previous studies (Antunes et al., 2018; Carona et al., 2021; Estévez López et al., 2018), our findings from the adjusted model did not confirm the significance of the relationship of conflict with both mental well-being and life satisfaction (H_4, H_7, and H_{11}). A possible reason for this is the average low level of conflict in the family reported by the respondents. We also suspect that beneficial effects of more positive domains of family relationship (i.e., cohesion, expressiveness) may overshadow the possible detrimental effects of family conflict if any.

Among the hypotheses tested in this study, our findings on the mediation analysis are our unique contribution to the literature. First, our results suggest that mental well-being significantly partially mediates the relationship between cohesion and life satisfaction (H_9); cohesion in the family improves mental well-being, which in turn facilitates higher life satisfaction. This is consistent with previous studies which demonstrate how the sense of togetherness and conformity among family members enhance their psychological resources, such as resilience and self-esteem, and overall life quality (Allen et al., 2014; Lee et al., 2019; Lin & Yi, 2019; López-Núñez et al., 2021).

Finally, the relationship between expressiveness and life satisfaction was fully mediated by mental well-being (H_{10}). This is a new finding which places importance on expressiveness in the family in maximizing the benefits of optimal mental health on quality of life. This confirms an important principle of family systems theory that places primacy on being able to communicate openly in the family to improve its members' emotional well-being and overall mental health (Fingerman & Berman, 2000). This finding is consistent with previous research that links family expressiveness with positive psychological outcomes and life satisfaction (Lee et al., 2019).

These mediation findings quantitatively confirm the qualitative model of *kaginhawaan* by Samaco-Zamora and Fernandez (2016), which posits that the core category of the construct of well-being among Filipinos is having good relations in the family. This Philippine-based grounded theory also indicates psycho-emotional well-being as a subordinate category as a requisite of overall well-being that is intensified by family togetherness. In addition, the findings on the complete mediation of mental health on family expressiveness and life satisfaction challenge the prevailing stigma on mental illness in the country. Filipinos have been known to be reluctant to share their experiences of psychological distress and mental health problems with their family members to maintain a positive environment and sense of resilience in the home (Tanaka et al., 2018). The present study provides empirical evidence that supports the normalization of open communication among family members regarding their stressors, negative feelings, and other psychological concerns, as these could foster positive mental health outcomes and life satisfaction.

Strengths and Limitations of the Study

To our knowledge, this is the first study in the Philippines that attempted to perform a mediation analysis on the constructs we used. Moreover, the relatively high effect sizes that were yielded indicate the model's good explanatory power. However, we present the following limitations. First, our study is limited to only one site and is cross-sectional in nature. Sampling was not randomized and focused exclusively on graduate students. These factors limit the generalizability of the results to other subpopulations in the Philippines. Second, there are salient constructs that can influence the life satisfaction of the graduate students that we were not able to measure and include in the model, such as family roles (i.e., parent and child), family type (e.g., nuclear versus extended and family of orientation versus family of procreation), and educational and work-related variables; hence, the confounding effects of these constructs were not explored. We recommend that these variables be included in future studies. Third, our research appealed to family systems theory as a general perspective for our inquiry and was unable to include Bowenian constructs (e.g., differentiation of self, emotional cut-off, etc.) (Bowen, 1978). Finally, the generalized linear modeling of JAMOVI, which we used to test for the mediated model, is a regression-based strategy. Future researchers can consider a more sophisticated modeling technique such as structural equations modeling.

CONCLUSION

The findings of this study highlight the significant role of family relationships, specifically in terms of cohesion and expressiveness, mental well-being, and life satisfaction during times of crisis, such as the COVID-19 pandemic. Through this case of graduate students, this present research contributes new empirical evidence that signifies the salience of family in the health and lives of Filipinos and demonstrates the possible pathways of how positive family relationships can translate to better lives of individual members through improved mental health. Moreover, results demonstrate how social position (i.e., age, gender, and civil status) influences an individual's perception of quality family relationships.

Recommendations

School administrators, health practitioners, and guidance counselors may consider including family members of graduate students in activities that promote mental health and address their psychological issues. Mental status of students must be periodically monitored. In online learning, school-initiated programs such as "family day" among graduate students may help engage the family members, hopefully increasing their cohesion and expressiveness.

Helping professions working with families with adult members experiencing mental health issues can consider intervening through a family systems approach, specifically improving cohesion (e.g., recommending shared activities at home and fostering readiness to support members who are schooling or working) and expressiveness (e.g., establishing routines for communication and improving capacities for open listening).

As we enter a post-pandemic world, future researchers are enjoined to conduct studies that examine how family relationships transitioned from extended confinement to post-lockdown and how this transition can affect the mental health and quality of life of its members. Moreover, researchers can consider conducting studies on a similar topic that utilize longitudinal designs, involve randomized samples from multiple sites, and collect other relevant variables, such as student engagement and well-being at work to improve the robustness of the analysis further and expand the explanatory power of the model.

ACKNOWLEDGMENT

We would like to thank the administrators of the university who supported this research project and all the graduate students who participated in our online survey.

DECLARATIONS

We have no conflicts of interest to declare. No funding was received for this study.

REFERENCES

Agaton, C. B., & Cueto, L. J. (2021). Learning at home: Parents' lived experiences on distance learning during COVID-19 pandemic in the Philippines. *International Journal of Evaluation and Research in Education, 10*(3), 901–911. http://doi.org/10.11591/ijere.v10i3.21136

Al Dhaheri, A. S., Bataineh, M. F., Mohamad, M. N., Ajab, A., Al Marzouqi, A., Jarrar, A. H., Habib-Mourad, C., Abu Jamous, D. O., Ali, H. I., Al Sabbah, H., Hasan, H., Stojanovska, L., Hashim, M., Abd Elhameed, O. A., Shaker Obaid, R. R., ElFeky, S., Saleh, S. T., Osaili, T. M., & Cheikh Ismail, L. (2021). Impact of covid-19 on mental health and quality of life: Is there any effect? A cross-sectional study of the MENA region. *PLOS ONE, 16*(3), 1–17. https://doi.org/10.1371/journal.pone.0249107

Allen, J., Mohatt, G. V., Fok, C. C. T., Henry, D., & Burkett, R. (2014). A protective factors model for alcohol abuse and suicide prevention among Alaska Native youth. *American journal of community psychology, 54*(1), 125–139. https://doi.org/10.1007/s10464-014-9661-3

Anand, P. (2016). *Happiness, well-being and human development: The case for subjective measures.* Human Development Report background paper, 2016. United Nations Development Programme. https://core.ac.uk/download/pdf/84310326.pdf

Andrada-Poa, M. R. J., Jabal, R. F., & Cleofas, J. V. (2021). Single mothering during the COVID-19 pandemic: A remote photovoice project among Filipino single mothers working from home. *Community, Work & Family, 25*(2), 260–278. https://doi.org/10.1080/13668803.2021.2006608

Antunes, H. D. A., Guerrero, M. R., De Goulart, B. N. G., & Oenning, N. S. X. (2018). Family relationship and use of illicit drugs among adolescents: The Brazilian students' health survey, 2015. *Revue d'Épidémiologie et de Santé Publique, 66*(suppl. 5), S282. https://doi.org/10.1016/j.respe.2018.05.121

Aruta, J. J. B. R. (2021). Socio-ecological determinants of distress in Filipino adults during COVID-19 crisis. *Current Psychology, 41*(11), 7482–7492. https://doi.org/10.1007/s12144-020-01322-x

Baticulon, R. E., Sy, J. J., Alberto, N. R., Baron, M. B., Mabulay, R. E., Rizada, L. G., Tiu, C. J., Clarion, C. A., & Reyes, J. C. (2021). Barriers to online learning in the time of COVID-19: A national survey of medical students in the Philippines. *Medical Science Educator, 31*(2), 615–626. https://doi.org/10.1007/s40670-021-01231-z

Bernardo, A. B., & Resurreccion, K. F. (2018). Financial stress and well-being of Filipino students: The moderating role of external locus-of-hope. *Philippine Journal of Psychology, 51*(1), 33–61. https://www.pap.ph/file/pjp/PJP-062018-3-Bernardo-&-Resurreccion.pdf

Bilodeau, J., Quesnel-Vallée, A., Beauregard, N., & Brault, M. C. (2021). Gender, work–family conflict and depressive symptoms during the COVID-19 pandemic among Quebec graduate students. *Preventive Medicine Reports, 24*, 101568. https://doi.org/10.1016/j.pmedr.2021.101568

Blackbox Research Team. (2020, December 14). *Coronavirus: Asia on edge.* Blackbox Corp. https://blackbox.com.sg/everyone/coronavirus-asia-on-edge

Bowen, M. (1978). *Family therapy in clinical practice.* Aronson.

Browne, D. T., Wade, M., May, S. S., Jenkins, J. M., & Prime, H. (2021). COVID-19 disruption gets inside the family: A two-month multilevel study of family stress during the pandemic. *Developmental Psychology, 57*(10), 1681–1692. https://doi.org/10.1037/dev0001237

Carona, C., Moreira, H., & Fonseca, A. (2021). Maternal depression and anxiety in an interpersonal context: The effects of positive–negative self-expressiveness within the family. *Current Psychology*, Ahead of print. https://doi.org/10.1007/s12144-021-02302-5

Carrión-Martínez, J. J., Pinel-Martínez, C., Pérez-Esteban, M. D., & Román-Sánchez, I. M. (2021). Family and school relationship during COVID-19 pandemic: A systematic review. *International Journal of Environmental Research and Public Health, 18*(21), 11710. https://doi.org/10.3390/ijerph182111710

Chin, Y. Y., Lim, F. Y., & Tan, K. M. (2019). *Social support, sense of belong, family functioning and life satisfaction* [Doctoral dissertation]. UTAR. http://eprints.utar.edu.my/id/eprint/3550

Cho, S., Park, S. S., & Hwang, K. R. (2021). The effects of family relationship difficulties on life satisfaction among the middle-aged in Gyeonggi-do: Moderating effects of family support services. *Korean Family Resource Management Association, 25*(4), 31–41. https://doi.org/10.22626/jkfrma.2021.25.4.003

Cleofas, J. V. (2021). Life interruptions, learnings and hopes among Filipino college students during COVID-19 pandemic. *Journal of Loss and Trauma, 26*(6), 552–560. https://doi.org/10.1080/15325024.2020.1846443

Cleofas, J. V., & Mijares, M. F. (2022). The role of professional self-care practices in lowering anxiety among Filipino teachers enrolled in graduate studies. *Teacher Development, 26*(2), 206–220. https://doi.org/10.1080/13664530.2022.2043422

Cleofas, J. V., & Oducado, R. M. F. (2021). COVID-19 death occurrences, pandemic fatigue, and well-being. *Journal of Loss and Trauma, 27*(7), 679–682. https://doi.org/10.1080/15325024.2021.1971423

Cleofas, J. V., Dayrit, J. C. S., & Albao, B. T. (2022). Problematic versus reflective use: Types of social media use as determinants of mental health among young Filipino undergraduates. *Health Promotion Perspectives, 12*(1), 85–91. https://doi.org/10.34172/hpp.2022.11

Cleofas, J. V., Eusebio, M. C. S., & Pacudan, E. J. P. (2021). Anxious, apart, and attentive: A qualitative case study of overseas Filipino workers' families in the time of COVID-19. *The Family Journal*, ahead of Print. https://doi.org/10.1177/10664807211006339

Cruz, G. T., Laguna, E. P., & Raymundo, C. M. (2001). *Family influences on the lifestyle of Filipino youth.* East-West Center.

Dela Rosa, R. D., Cleofas, J. V., & Oducado, R. M. F. (2022). X's and Y's in the midst of the pandemic: Generational identity, mental well-being and life satisfaction among Filipino adult learners. *European Journal of Educational Research, 11*(2), 1209–1218. https://doi.org/10.12973/eu-jer.11.2.1209

Diener, E., Emmons, R. A., Larsen, R. J., & Griffin, S. (1985). The satisfaction with life scale. *Journal of Personality Assessment, 49*(1), 71–75. https://doi.org/10.1207/s15327752jpa4901_13

Egcas, R. A., Oducado, R. M. F., Cleofas, J. V., Rabacal, J. S., & Lausa, S. M. (2021). After over a year of pandemic: Mental well-being and life satisfaction of Filipino college students. *Pertanika Journal of Social Sciences & Humanities, 29*(4), 2401–2416. https://doi.org/10.47836/pjssh.29.4.17

Epifani, I., Wisyaningrum, S., & Ediati, A. (2021, April). Marital distress and satisfaction during the COVID-19 pandemic: A systematic review. In I. F. Kristiana et al. (Eds.), *International conference on psychological studies (ICPSYCHE 2020)* (pp. 109–115). Atlantis Press.

Ericta, C. N. (2013, January 10). *The educational attainment of the household population (Results from the 2010 Census)*. Philippine Statistics Authority. https://psa.gov.ph/content/educational-attainment-household-population-results-2010-census

Estévez López, E., Jiménez Gutiérrez, T. I., & Moreno Ruiz, D. (2018). Aggressive behavior in adolescence as a predictor of personal, family, and school adjustment problems. *Psicothema, 30*(1). 66–73. http://doi.org/10.7334/psicothema2016.294

Fastame, M. C. (2021). Life satisfaction in late adult span: The contribution of family relationships, health self-perception and physical activity. *Aging Clinical and Experimental Research, 33*(6), 1693–1698. https://doi.org/10.1007/s40520-020-01658-1

Fingerman, K. L., & Bermann, E. (2000). Applications of family systems theory to the study of adulthood. *International Journal of Aging & Human Development, 51*(1), 5–29. https://doi.org/10.2190/7TF8-WB3F-TMWG-TT3K

Fok, C. C. T., Allen, J., Henry, D., & Team, P. A. (2014). The brief family relationship scale: A brief measure of the relationship dimension in family functioning. *Assessment, 21*(1), 67–72. https://doi.org/10.1177/1073191111425856

Foster, M. (2020). *The role of depressed mood and family expressiveness in young adults' ability to recognize facial expressions of emotions* (Honor's Program Thesis). Assumption College

Gayatri, M., & Irawaty, D. K. (2021). Family resilience during COVID-19 pandemic: A literature review. *The Family Journal, 30*(2), 132–138. https://doi.org/10.1177/10664807211023875

Guillasper, J. N., Oducado, R. M. F., & Soriano, G. P. (2021). Protective role of resilience on COVID-19 impact on the quality of life of nursing students in the Philippines. *Belitung Nursing Journal, 7*(1), 43–49. http://dx.doi.org/10.33546/bnj.1297

Guo, P., Yu, H., & Gao, J. (2021). Family relationship and psychological stress response of college students in Shanghai under the COVID-19 epidemic. *Chinese Journal of School Health, 42*(3), 412–416. https://doi.org/10.16835/j.cnki.1000-9817.2021.03.023

Gutierrez, J. (2022, January 4). The Philippines orders another wave of lockdowns amid a surge in cases. *The New York Times*. https://www.nytimes.com/2022/01/04/world/asia/philippines-manila-covid-lockdown.html

Hayles, O., Xu, L., & Edwards, O. W. (2018). Family structures, family relationship, and children's perceptions of life satisfaction. *School Psychology Forum: Research in Practice, 12*(3), 91–104.

Hays, J. (2019). Men in the Philippines. *Facts and details*. https://factsanddetails.com/southeast-asia/Philippines/sub5_6c/entry-3875.html

Huang, J., Zhang, J., & Yu, N. X. (2018). Close relationships, individual resilience resources, and well-being among people living with HIV/AIDS in rural China. *AIDS Care, 30*(suppl. 5), S49–S57. https://doi.org/10.1080/09540121.2018.1496222

Hwang, J. Y., Choi, J.-S., Gwak, A. R., Jung, D., Choi, S.-W., Lee, J., Lee, J.-Y., Jung, H. Y., & Kim, D. J. (2014). Shared psychological characteristics that are linked to aggression between patients with Internet addiction and those with alcohol dependence. *Annals of General Psychiatry, 13*(1), 6. https://doi.org/10.1186/1744-859X-13-6

Japan International Cooperation Agency. (2015). ASEAN University Network/Southeast Asia Engineering Education Development Network (Phase I & Phase II). https://www2.jica.go.jp/en/evaluation/pdf/2015_0704381_4_f.pdf

Javier, J. R., Galura, K., Aliganga, F. A. P., Supan, J., & Palinkas, L. A. (2018). Voices of the Filipino community describing the importance of family in understanding adolescent behavioral health needs. *Family & Community Health, 41*(1), 64–71. https://doi.org/10.1097/FCH.0000000000000173

Karmacharya, I., Shrestha, S., Paudel, S., Adhikari, L., Bhujel, K., & Shakya, K. L. (2020). Mental health status of Nepalese students during novel coronavirus disease (nCOVID-19) pandemic. *Europasian Journal of Medical Sciences, 2*(2), 13–21. https://www.nepjol.info/index.php/ejms/article/view/35633

Keliat, B. A., Triana, R., & Sulistiowati, N. M. D. (2019). The relationship between self-esteem, family relationships and social support as the protective factors and adolescent mental health. *Humanities and Social Sciences Reviews, 7*(1), 41–47. https://doi.org/10.18510/hssr.2019.715

Kim-Appel, D., & Appel, J. K. (2015). Bowenian family systems theory: Approaches and applications. In D. Capuzzi & M. D. Stauffer (Eds.), *Foundations of couples, marriage, and family counseling* (pp. 185–213). John Wiley & Sons, Inc.

Kim, E. H., & Nho, C. R. (2020). Longitudinal reciprocal relationships between self-esteem, family support, and life satisfaction in Korean multicultural adolescents. *Asian Social Work and Policy Review, 14*(3), 184–196. https://doi.org/10.1111/aswp.12208

Lee, Y., Lee, M., & Park, S. (2019). The mental health of ethnic minority youths in South Korea and its related environmental factors: A literature review. *Journal of the Korean Academy of Child and Adolescent Psychiatry, 30*(3), 88. https://doi.org/10.5765/jkacap.190019

Lew, L., Tan, A., Gitau, M., & Munoz, M. (2022, March 30). *The Covid resilience ranking: The best and worst places to be as Covid travel curbs fall away.* Bloomberg.com. Retrieved April 1, 2022, from https://www.bloomberg.com/graphics/covid-resilience-ranking/

Lin, W. H., & Yi, C. C. (2019). The effect of family cohesion and life satisfaction during adolescence on later adolescent outcomes: A prospective study. *Youth & Society, 51*(5), 680–706. https://doi.org/10.1177/0044118X17704865

López-Núñez, M. I., Díaz-Morales, J. F., & Aparicio-García, M. E. (2021). Individual differences, personality, social, family and work variables on mental health during COVID-19 outbreak in Spain. *Personality and Individual Differences, 172*, 110562. https://doi.org/10.1016/j.paid.2020.110562

Lu, N., Spencer, M., Sun, Q., & Lou, V. W. (2021). Family social capital and life satisfaction among older adults living alone in urban China: The moderating role of functional health. *Aging & Mental Health, 25*(4), 695–702. https://doi.org/10.1080/13607863.2019.1709155

Martin-Storey, A., Dirks, M., Holfeld, B., Dryburgh, N. S., & Craig, W. (2021). Family relationship quality during the COVID-19 pandemic: The value of adolescent perceptions of change. *Journal of Adolescence, 93*, 190–201. https://doi.org/10.1016/j.adolescence.2021.11.005

Medina-Belen, T. G. (2015). *The Filipino family.* University of Philippines Press.

McCutcheon, J. M., & Morrison, M. A. (2018). It's "like walking on broken glass": Pan-Canadian reflections on work–family conflict from psychology women faculty and graduate students. *Feminism & Psychology, 28*(2), 231–252. https://doi.org/10.1177/0959353517739641

Moos, R. H. (1994). *Family environment scale manual: Development, applications, research.* Consulting Psychologists Press.

Mopuri, R., Mutheneni, S. R., Kumaraswamy, S., Kadiri, M. R., Upadhyayula, S. M., & Naish, S. (2019). An epidemiological and spatiotemporal analysis to identify high risk areas of malaria in Visakhapatnam district of Andhra Pradesh, India, 1999–2015. *Spatial Information Research, 27*(6), 659–672. https://doi.org/10.1007/s41324-019-00267-z

Μπακούρτσης, X. (2021). The influence of work–family interface in function of work and life satisfaction. The teachers' case. *Psychology: the Journal of the Hellenic Psychological Society, 26*(3), 228–251. https://doi.org/10.12681/psy_hps.29154

Núñez, J. L. (2022). Lived experience of overcoming the feeling of isolation in distance learning in the Philippines: A phenomenological inquiry. *Pakistan Journal of Distance and Online Learning, 7*(2), 55–68. http://journal.aiou.edu.pk/journal1/index.php/PJDOL/article/viewFile/1330/172

Oducado, R. M. F., Parreño-Lachica, G., & Rabacal, J. (2021). Personal resilience and its influence on COVID-19 stress, anxiety and fear among graduate students in the Philippines. *International Journal of Educational Research and Innovation, 15*, 431–443. https://doi.org/10.46661/ijeri.5484

Okechukwu, F. O., Nnodim, E. J., Nnubia, U. I., Ezeonyeche, C. L., & Owoh, N. (2021). Issues relating to adolescents' perception of family relationship in Nsukka Urban, Enugu State. *Journal of Home Economics Research (JHER), 28*(2), 142–154. https://heran.org/wp-content/uploads/simple-file-list/JHER-Vol_28-No_-2-Dec_2021.pdf#page=142

Ortega, R. A., Hechanova, M., & Regina, M. (2010). Work-family conflict, stress and satisfactions among dual-earning couples. *Philippine Journal of Psychology*, *43*(1), 27–44.

Osea, E. A. (2022). Graduate studies schooling during COVID-19 pandemic: Doctorate and master's students experience in a private higher education institution in the Philippines. *International Journal of Business, Law, and Education*, *3*(2), 82–87. https://doi.org/10.56442/ijble.v3i2.55

Panoy, J. F., Andrade, R., Febrer, L., & Ching, D. (2022). Perceived proficiency with technology and online learning expectations of students in the graduate program of one state university in the Philippines. *International Journal of Information and Education Technology*, *12*(7), 615–624. http://doi.org/10.18178/ijiet.2022.12.7.1661

Pitt, R. N., Alp, Y. T., & Shell, I. A. (2021). The mental health consequences of work–life and life–work conflicts for STEM postdoctoral trainees. *Frontiers in Psychology*, *12*, 750490. https://doi.org/10.3389/fpsyg.2021.750490

Prime, H., Wade, M., & Browne, D. T. (2020). Risk and resilience in family well-being during the COVID-19 pandemic. *American Psychologist*, *75*(5), 631–643. https://doi.org/10.1037/amp0000660

Rabacal, J.S., Lausa, S. M., Egcas, R. A., Oducado, R. M. F., Cleofas, J. V., Tamdang, K. A. (2022). More than a year into the pandemic: Do higher education students still practice protective behaviors against COVID-19? *Journal of Education and Health Promotion*, *11*, 155. https://doi.org/10.4103/jehp.jehp_1235_21

Rogowska, A. M., Kuśnierz, C., & Bokszczanin, A. (2020). Examining anxiety, life satisfaction, general health, stress and coping styles during COVID-19 pandemic in Polish sample of university students. *Psychology Research and Behavior Management*, *13*, 797–811. https://doi.org/10.2147/PRBM.S266511

Rungduin, T. T., & Miranda, P. A. (2018). An exploration of the factors affecting graduate degree completion in a teacher education institution (TEI): Inputs for graduate program management and pedagogy. *AsTEN Journal of Teacher Education*, *3*(1), 41–54. https://po.pnuresearchportal.org/ejournal/index.php/asten/article/view/835

Samaco-Zamora, M. C. F., & Fernandez, K. T. G. (2016). A grounded theory of Filipino wellness (Kaginhawaan). *Psychological Studies*, *61*(4), 279–287. https://doi.org/10.1007/s12646-016-0373-7

Sharin, A. N. (2021). E-learning during Covid-19: A review of literature. *Journal Pengajian Media Malaysia (Malaysian Journal of Media Studies)*, *23*(1), 15–28. https://doi.org/10.22452/jpmm.vol23no1.2

Springer, K. W., Parker, B. K., & Leviten-Reid, C. (2009). Making space for graduate student parents: Practice and politics. *Journal of Family Issues*, *30*(4), 435–457. https://doi.org/10.1177/0192513X08329293

Tanaka, C., Tuliao, M. T. R., Tanaka, E., Yamashita, T., & Matsuo, H. (2018). A qualitative study on the stigma experienced by people with mental health problems and epilepsy in the Philippines. *BMC Psychiatry*, *18*(1), 1–13. https://doi.org/10.1186/s12888-018-1902-9

Tennant, R., Hiller, L., Fishwick, R., Platt, S., Joseph, S., Weich, S., Parkinson, J., Secker, J., & Stewart-Brown, S. (2007). The Warwick–Edinburgh mental well-being scale (WEMWBS): Development and UK validation. *Health and Quality of Life Outcomes*, *5*(1), 63. https://doi.org/10.1186/1477-7525-5-63

Tee, M. L., Tee, C. A., Anlacan, J. P., Aligam, K. J. G., Reyes, P. W. C., Kuruchittham, V., & Ho, R. C. (2020). Psychological impact of COVID-19 pandemic in the Philippines. *Journal of Affective Disorders*, *277*, 379–391. https://doi.org/10.1016/j.jad.2020.08.043

Tus, J. (2021). Amidst the online learning in the Philippines: The parental involvement and its relationship to the student's academic performance. *International Engineering Journal for Research & Development*, *6*(3), 1–15. https://doi.org/10.17605/OSF.IO/FHQX3

World Health Organization. (2022a, March 22). *Weekly epidemiological update on COVID-19 – 22 March 2022*. World Health Organization. https://www.who.int/publications/m/item/weekly-epidemiological-update-on-covid-19-22-march-2022

World Health Organization. (2022b, March 16). *Philippines situation*. World Health Organization. Retrieved March 31, 2022, from https://covid19.who.int/region/wpro/country/ph

World Vision. (2020, July 3). *Impact of Covid-19 to children and their families: A rapid assessment in the Philippines – Philippines*. ReliefWeb. https://reliefweb.int/report/philippines/impact-covid-19-children-and-their-families-rapid-assessment-philippines

FAMILIES OF OFWs, FARMERS, AND FISHERFOLKS

CHAPTER 11

RESPONSE AND COPING MECHANISMS OF OVERSEAS FILIPINO WORKERS (OFW) CHILDREN TO PARENTS' SEPARATION

Sunshine Therese S. Alcantara

ABSTRACT

Labor migration poses a risk to the family as a social institution. Dissolution of marriages among couples caused by infidelity and labor migration is considered to be one of the social costs of migration, where children of migrants are greatly affected. This study examines the response of children when they found out about their parent's infidelity and the ways of coping employed in dealing with the changed family situation. Nine participants aged 16–25 who are children of overseas Filipino workers (OFW) were interviewed. Thematic analysis was used to draw out recurring themes to answer the research questions. The results showed that there are negative feelings felt upon knowing the infidelity of their parent, either by their parent-left or the parent abroad. The relationship between the child and the parent who committed infidelity has been significantly interrupted. Additionally, friends were considered to be an essential source of support. The study contributed to the understanding that labor migration is one of the factors that contributed to strained relationships between husband and wife, and the children were the most affected.

Keywords: OFW children; parental infidelity; family; migration; marital issues; Philippines

Resilience and Familism: The Dynamic Nature of Families in the Philippines
Contemporary Perspectives in Family Research, Volume 23, 185–203
Copyright © 2023 by Emerald Publishing Limited
All rights of reproduction in any form reserved
ISSN: 1530-3535/doi:10.1108/S1530-353520230000023011

INTRODUCTION

The Philippines is one of the world's top labor-exporting countries. Millions of OFW are deployed annually, including new hires and rehires, and land-based and sea-based workers in various countries around the world, wherein the primary destination is the oil-rich Gulf countries (Asis, 2013; PSA, 2022). The stock estimate of the Commission of Filipino Overseas (CFO, 2013) shows that over 10 million Filipinos work or reside abroad. This translates to around 10–11 percent of the total Philippine population. The number of OFW was estimated at 1.77 million in 2020, which was lower than the 2.18 million reported in 2019 (PSA, 2022).

Family welfare has been the driving force of the decision to work abroad, where the families left behind are the principal beneficiaries (Asis, 2013). Lack of job opportunities, irregular employment, and low wages still dominate the reasons for migration. Hence, economic benefits have continuously fueled the attraction to leave home. The families benefited economically from overseas employment, allowing them to improve the quality of their life in terms of home ownership, increased amenities, and improved education of their children (Medina, 2001). With the concern for economic advancement, many have chosen to accept the consequences of temporary separation despite psychological and emotional costs (Go & Postrado, 1986). Thus, temporary separation from parents is a common condition for some Filipino youth because their parents work as OFW. At the same time, the perceived "social costs" of migration to families have also raised significant concerns, wherein mother's migration is seen to tear families apart (Acedera & Yeoh, 2020).

The literature on transnational family relationships in Asia proliferated in recent years, particularly in studying the effects of transnational migration on mothers and their left-behind children (Acedera & Yeoh, 2020). This research agenda has been driven by moral panics concerning the future of left-behind children (Acedera & Yeoh, 2020). Most of the studies dealing with labor migration focused on how the impact of parental absence affects the children left behind in terms of academic performance and health status. The economic benefits had also been comprehensively documented. However, there were few studies on the effects of marital infidelity of the spouse of the OFW husband or OFW wife on the children left behind.

Transnational migration has altered significant familial relationships, including marital relationships (Acedera & Yeoh, 2020). Medina (2001) noted that the temporary separation of spouses due to overseas employment has relevance to the marital relationship. Empirical inquiry into the transnational family is generally examined through the perspective of mothers, left-behind fathers, and left-behind children, to which this study aims to contribute to the discussion.

This study contributes to the understanding that labor migration is one of the factors that contribute to strained relationships between husband and wife, and the children of OFW were most affected when their parents got separated. The relationship between the child and the parent who committed infidelity has been significantly interrupted. Sevilla (1982) recommended that questions such as coping responses to parental conflicts and unhappy home situations, long-term effects of marital dissolution on children, and children's role in maintaining a healthy home life must be investigated. In this regard, this research addresses the need to examine the response of children, if not to parental conflicts but to the parent's infidelity and the effect of marital dissolution on them. The insights obtained in this study will enable family members to maintain harmonious family relationships, allowing parents to perform the different roles and functions in the child-rearing process and parental control over children's different activities and social relationships.

This study also adds knowledge to the present literature on parental absence (Asis, 2000, 2013; Dizon-Añonuevo & Añonuevo, 2003; Edillon, 2008; Parreñas, 2005; Taylor, 2008). It adds insights into the changes in the Filipino family, in particular, as a social institution. There are changing values and behaviors because of the increased participation of women in the labor force, which has affected the dynamics of family relationships. The changes in the family as a social institution are believed to affect the nature of society as a whole. Children who see the dissolution of their parent's marriage may become frustrated, hence might have difficulty in establishing their own personal relationships with others. The importance of finding out the effects of broken marriages on their children cannot remain to be ignored, as these children are growing up to establish their own families in the future, which may be affected by the difficulty they experience in dealing with the changed family situation.

This study was based on empirical data from research conducted from 2014 to 2015 among OFW children. The study seeks to determine the response of OFW children when they find out about the infidelity of his/her migrant father or migrant mother or his/her parent-left and to know how the overseas worker's children cope with the changed family situation. It provides a topic for discussion about Filipino migrant families with changed family situations from the experiences of the children that are relevant to the present situation of Filipino migrant families. Insights from this study will help OFW parents to know the views of their children regarding their changed family situation.

LITERATURE REVIEW
Social Cost of Parental Absence of OFW Parents

The increasing feminization of migration continues to influence values and ideologies while reshaping the Filipino family (Acedera & Yeoh, 2020). Migration has the peculiarity of reshuffling the family's internal structure, which in "breaking it up" physically, takes an emotional toll on individual members because of the impact it has on the family roles and responsibilities and the relationships of its immediate members (Asis et al., 2004). Collision of values among transnational families becomes more visibly amplified, with social ties becoming reorganized, deviating from what is traditionally acceptable (Acedera & Yeoh, 2020). Thus, changes in family structural arrangements can be observed. The impact of migration ranges from the economic benefits of the family left and the country at large through its remittances to the welfare of the family left in general. But a general concern is how the parental absence of OFWs leaves an impact on the children left behind (Reyes, 2009). Even after the migrant has returned to the family, their children, other than their family members, take time to readjust to the reconfigured family and restore their relationships (Asis et al., 2004).

Several researches in the Philippines were conducted to show how the impact of parental absence affects the children left behind. (1) The trend in international migration in Asia and the observed changes and emerging family-related issues in Asian families, including the Filipino family, are identified by Asis (2000). The discussion about the social consequences of migration was mainly drawn from the data from the Philippine experience (Asis, 2000). (2) Dizon-Añonuevo and Añonuevo (2003) assessed the impact of migration on migrants, their families, and their communities. The significant findings were categorized into three areas of concern: the situation of migrant women, the social cost of the feminization of migration, and the possibilities of reintegration. The study notes that:

> Physical separation from their husbands and strained relationships due to marital infidelity and irresponsibility of husbands had led to an increasing number of cases of extramarital affairs and lesbianism among migrant women. (Dizon-Añonuevo & Añonuevo, 2003, p. 470)

> Some have been bold in expressing their emotional and sexual needs and have engaged in extramarital affairs and lesbian relationships. (p. 471)

> Children are the most vulnerable to the physical separation and the family adjustments made in the absence of their mothers. (p. 473)

> A number of OFW returnees had a hard time coping with their estranged relations with their children and husbands. Some expressed their resistance to assuming the role they had before migration, which was that of being an unemployed, dependent, and submissive wife. The majority of the migrant returnees interviewed said that they had difficulty adjusting to their families and communities. Failed business endeavors push them to work abroad again. (p. 474)

(3) Edillon (2008) determines how the extent to which the rights pertaining to survival, development, participation, and protection of the children are affected by the parent's migration. (4) Parreñas (2005) examines the division of labor in transnational families with migrant mothers by looking at the work of the fathers, migrant mothers, eldest daughters, and extended kin to show that caring practices preserve the conventional gender norms in the family as it specifically shows that the migrant mothers' work at home and abroad maintain transnational families. Furthermore, it establishes that the migration of women does not result in a more egalitarian division of labor in the family. Lastly, (5) parenting within Filipino overseas families was analyzed by Taylor (2008) as perceived by adult children. Being parented in a transnational family, almost all children know and understand the reason why their parents left – for their benefit (Taylor, 2008). Interviews revealed the challenges of growing up in an OFW family and the

resiliency of these children in addressing the difficulties of the situation and being able to recognize their strengths to succeed in a non-traditional family structure (Taylor, 2008). The study also presented that children were able to adapt to balancing the role of assuming adult responsibilities and, at the same time, taking the leadership role whenever their migrant parent was home to visit or back home to retire (Taylor, 2008).

Separation of Parents

The separation brought by labor migration posed a threat to marriages and parent–child relationships (Asis, n.d.). However, the impacts of labor migration on children left behind are the focus of the majority of the studies about labor migration than the impacts on marital relationships (Asis, n.d.). Perceived fragility and subsequent breakdown of marriages among couples separated by overseas work are comprehended as among the "social cost" of migration (Aguilar et al., 2009). As Go (1993) has observed, by the early 1990s, there emerged

> a general hypothesis in the literature that overseas employment has generated a number of social problems, such as marital infidelity among wives, marital dissolutions, and various forms of delinquency among the youth.

Concerns about the stability of the family unit have been raised due to long periods of separation brought about by migration. One of the consequences often cited of the extended absence of migrants from the family is marital instability and consequent break-up of the family unit (United Nations Economic and Social Commission for Asia and the Pacific (UNESCAP), 2008). A study by Dizon-Añonuevo and Añonuevo (2003) found that the physical separation from the husbands and strained relationships due to marital infidelity and their irresponsibility have resulted in an increasing number of cases of extramarital affairs and lesbianism among migrant women.

In a study by Cabigon (1995), while some husbands remain faithful and even stop working to take care of the children and perform domestic tasks, others are reported to be womanizing, frequenting beer houses, and gallivanting. There are even cases where the husband lives with another woman to whom his wife's remittances and appliances sent are given (Cabigon, 1995). Thus, the infidelity of the husband left behind is the problem of the female migrant worker. On the other hand, marital breakdown seldom occurs primarily due to the determination and efforts of the wives with their tolerance, perseverance in their work, and prayers to keep the family intact. Furthermore, children help bind the marriage by encouraging harmonious settlement between their parents (Cabigon, 1995).

Research has cited (Sevilla, 1982) some of the reasons for the weakening of family and marriage bonds while the worker is away: inadequate emotional and psychological preparation for the husband or father's long absence, mainly due to the prevailing economic motive; little community support in terms of behavior control and moral example; and lack of training in appropriate income management and investment.

An ethnographic study conducted by Aguilar et al. (2009) revealed that different circumstances actually bring couples together and set them apart physically. Through genealogy and key informant interviews conducted, of the 224 marriages conducted in Barangay Paraiso, 17 unions (7.6 percent) ended in dissolution. Of the 17 failed unions, 11 unions involved at least one partner who was a migrant worker (Aguilar et al., 2009). The 11 failed marriages represent 11 percent of the total in terms of the 100 marital unions involving at least one overseas migrant (Aguilar et al., 2009).

Data from Barangay Paraiso (Aguilar et al., 2009) suggest that couples living apart because of overseas migration have a somewhat higher rate of marital dissolution than couples who are not physically separated by overseas work. Separated females account for 5.4 percent of the total female migrant population, while separated migrant males represent 6.1 percent of the entire male migrant population in Barangay Paraiso. In at least 8 of the 17 failed marriages, or close to half, infidelity was a factor in the separation: in five cases, the husband was unfaithful, and in three cases, it was the wife. About 14 of the 17 couples had children by the time their marriage ended. Most of the children were very young when their parents separated (Aguilar et al., 2009).

A study by Acedera and Yeoh (2020) examined how migrant wives and left-behind husbands deal with the dissolution of their marriages due to infidelities. More than a third of the participants reported infidelity, of which five left-behind husbands and three migrant wives self-reported having extramarital affairs, while four migrant wives reported finding out about their partner's infidelities (Acedera & Yeoh, 2020). Such instances cannot deny the fact that labor migration has been affecting the marital relationships of Filipino couples and, as such, had an impact on left-behind children.

Effects of Infidelity on Children

The effect of marital infidelity on children is an intensive subject that touches millions of homes, yet it is rarely discussed (Nogales, 2009). A child, whatever age he is, when their parents have been unfaithful to each other, has been left with psychological issues that can affect him for the rest of his life (Nogales, 2009). These children often react with intense feelings of anger, anxiety, guilt, shame, sadness, and confusion. They also might act out, regress, or withdraw (Nogales, 2009). However, they may also feel pressured to win back the love of the parent who committed infidelity or to become the caretaker of the betrayed parent (Nogales, 2009).

Nogales (2009) revealed that the core responses experienced by sons and daughters of every age once they found out that one or both of their parents has been unfaithful include: loss of trust, shame, confusion, anger, and ambivalence toward the betraying parent, resentment toward the betrayed parent and acting out.

It has been said that when children learn about their parent's infidelity, they find it difficult or impossible to trust that someone they love will not lie, reject, or abandon them. A child may also feel that the infidelity is a shame for himself and for the rest of the immediate family (Nogales, 2009). There is also confusion about the meaning of both love and marriage since children draw the conclusion that marriage is not what it appears to be when their parent's marriage involves infidelity (Nogales, 2009). The children also experience feelings of anger and yearning; they perceive the one who used to be their parent as deserving of their love and hate the one who committed infidelity (Nogales, 2009). In the same manner, Siguan et al. (2021) examined the experiences of adult Filipino children who are aware of the infidelity occurring or that occurred within their family. The authors (Siguan et al., 2021) believe that parental infidelity influences the quality of the parent–child relationship, the adult child's relationship with friends, and their future endeavors with romantic relationships.

Experience of Separation

A study about the experiences of children of parental separation was conducted in the UK, where results revealed that the experiences of parental separation are different in every child, and it was impossible to conclude that separation was either a positive or a negative experience (Hogan et al., 2002). A total of 60 children were interviewed, consisting of two age groups, 8–11 and 13–17 years old. The research was conducted with interviews with children and a brief questionnaire about family background, which was completed by their parents (Hogan et al., 2002).

A study by Siguan et al. (2021) revealed that children perceived infidelity as a shared challenge of the family, and some evaluated the situation negatively. The participants acknowledged the loss of communication between members of their family and the loss of connection even with extended family members.

Children experienced separation as both event and a process. The former is usually marked by one parent moving out of the house, and the latter involves adjustment over time and experiencing further changes in family structure (Hogan et al., 2002). Most children were told about the separation by their parents when the decision had been made. They are usually shocked to learn that their parents are separating. Some were not told about the separation, only to find out that separation occurred when a parent left home and did not return (Hogan et al., 2002).

Furthermore, children were better able to adapt to family changes when they were able to understand their parent's decisions, and it was crucial to children that there is communication between them and their parents (Hogan et al., 2002). Communication was important not only at the time of separation but over time since families underwent further changes (Hogan et al., 2002).

METHODOLOGY

In order to address the gaps in the current literature, the research employed a qualitative method and focused on identifying themes within the participant's understanding.

Selection of Participants

The following were the criteria used by the researcher for selecting the participants:

(1) The children are at least 14–25 years old as the participants since the condition of these children is a good indicator of how they handle the changes in their family situations. Adolescents may have a different way on how to handle such situations since many factors are at work (like physical and psychological changes and peer pressure). Those who are aged 20–25 were still considered to be part of the study since it can be assumed that they were still adolescents when the separation of their parents occurred. Hence, it can also be considered that they have a longer time to cope with the changed family situations and re-lationships.

(2) The children who are the participants of the study whose parents are working abroad should not be limited only to the children with OFW fathers; hence the study shall also consider children with OFW mothers since there might be differences in the situations of children with OFW mother and that of OFW father. The researcher also considers the fact that the remaining spouse in the country was the one to commit marital infidelity rather than the OFW spouse.

(3) The parents of the children should be separated. The separation will be con-ceptualized as a result of marital infidelity and strained marital relationships, which is a consequence of labor migration. Hence, separation may refer to any of the following:
    (a) Officially living separately (not under one roof), that is, after the sepa-ration, one of them decided to continue working abroad.
    (b) Separated by mutual consent or separated by legal separation.
    (c) Separation by an informal arrangement that one of the spouses left the other.

Data Collection

Snowball sampling was employed by the researcher since the OFW children with separated parents are considered to be a hidden population. Key informants were first identified by the researcher and were asked to help her locate the possible participants in this study.

Before the researcher proceeded to the interview proper, the participants were given an informed consent. For the participant who is a minor, the parent/guard-ian was informed about the study.

In-depth interviews were conducted with the use of an interview guide to pro-vide a comprehensive and more detailed account of the participants' experiences.

Ethical Considerations

Participation in the study was voluntary and based on free consent. The par-ticipants were informed of the nature and purpose of the research before their engagement in the study. The participants were given informed consent to provide them the background, the purpose, and how the interview will be conducted. The interviewer asked the participants for permission to record the interview. Recording the interview is essential since note-taking alone may not fully account for the participants' stories.

The participants were assured of the confidentiality of any information they shared. Pseudonyms were used and no names of the participants were divulged in the chapter to ensure anonymity and guarantee the confidentiality of their identity. The participants were assured that they had the right to withdraw from the study or decline to answer if the questions had caused them distress. If questions have caused them distress, they were free to decline to answer any or all questions, and they can terminate their involvement at any time if they choose. No risks and harm were encountered in doing this study.

Analysis of Data

The data gathered were transcribed carefully by the researcher. The recorded interviews were transcribed in a verbatim manner. Thematic analysis was used to make significant deductions from the data collected since thematic analysis "focuses on identifiable themes and patterns of living and/or behavior" (Aronson, 1994). This method of data analysis also requires identifying and naming themes based on the participant's response. Themes will be pieced together, thus forming a comprehensive picture of the participant's collective experience (Aronson, 1994).

RESULTS

This qualitative study explored the responses and ways of coping of children of OFWs when they found out about marital infidelity and the marital separation of their parents. A brief profile of the participants is presented in Table 11.1. Pseudonyms were used to ensure the confidentiality of participants' identities.

Table 11.1. Summary of Participant's Profile.

Name	Sex	Age	Birth Order	No. of Siblings	Parent Abroad	The Parent Who Committed Infidelity
Amy	Female	18	1st	0	Both	Father (abroad)
Benjie	Male	23	2nd	2	Both	Father (abroad)
Gelli	Female	20	1st	1	Mother	Father (parent-left/used to work abroad)
Pia	Female	20	3rd	3	Both	Mother (parent-left)
Gwen	Female	18	1st	2	Father	Mother (abroad) Father (parent-left)
Abi	Female	20	4th	3	Father	Mother (parent-left)
Jade	Female	17	1st	4	Mother	Mother (abroad)
Markus	Male	18	1st	2	Father	Father (abroad)
Kylie	Female	18	1st	2	Mother	Father (parent-left/used to work abroad)

This section of the study presents the themes drawn from the narratives of nine participants. The analysis is divided into two domains: response to the infidelity of the parent and the ways of coping of overseas workers' children with the changed family situation (Table 11.2).

First Domain: Response to the Infidelity of Parent

This domain analyzes the response of the participants to the infidelity of their parents. The emotions felt by the participants include feelings of hurt, hatred, and sadness. They disclosed that they were told by family members (mother, sister, and auntie) about the infidelity of their parents. Subsequently, the participants thought that their parent's marriage would lead to separation. The decision for separation was found to come from either the parent who had an affair with other man/woman or the parent who did not have an affair with other man/woman. Upon separation of their parents, participants felt hatred and sadness. Eventually, the decision for their parent's separation was accepted by the participants.

Finding Out the Infidelity of Parent

Five of the participants found out about the infidelity of their parents from their family members. They were gathered as a family or were personally told about it. Others knew the infidelity of their parent through "signs" which they either saw and observed at home (belongings of the other woman or conversation with the other woman on a cellphone) or heard from conversations of adults. Amy, 18, shared, *Sinabi ng mommy ko. Sana daw maintindihan ko. Sana hindi daw ako madisappoint sa kanila.* [My mom told me about it. She said that they hope I will understand the situation and I will not be disappointed with them.] Thorson (2013) revealed that the most frequent way of learning about a parent's infidelity was from a family member. However, the family member who shared this information with them was not their parent who engaged in infidelity. Instead, they learned it from a grandparent, sibling, or parent who was not involved in the extramarital. The same is true for Pia, 20, who narrated, *Ang unang nagsabi sakin*

Table 11.2. Two Domains and Their Themes.

Domain	Themes
Response to the infidelity of parent	Finding out about the infidelity
	Emotions felt toward parent's infidelity
	Thoughts of the separation of parents
	From whom the decision for separation came from
	Children's involvement in the separation
	Emotions felt toward parent's separation
	Acceptance of the separation
Ways of coping with the changed family situation	Friends as the primary support system
	Acceptance of the parent's relationship that caused the family's dissolution
	Seeing separation as the gradual process
	Maintaining a positive outlook despite the changed family relationship

ay ang aking nakakatandang kapatid na babae. [My older sister was the first who told me about it.]

Emotions Felt After Knowing the Infidelity

Parental infidelity can incite feelings of fear, anxiety, shock, worry, guilt, depression, and aggression in children (Lusterman, 2005; Platt et al., 2008). Nonchalant would define how some participants feel about the infidelity of their parent as others reasoned out that it already happened, and at first, they thought that it only happens in *teleseryes,* not even imagining that it could happen to them.

Hurt would justify how Amy and Gelli were disappointed by how their family ended up being broken, while hatred would define how Pia and Gwen felt while thinking of what other people will think of their family and how they will be affected as children. Pia and Kylie also felt sadness as their family would never be the same again. The two male participants in the study, Benjie and Markus, started questioning what their father had done.

The feelings of hatred and sadness felt by the participants are consistent with the findings of Nogales (2009), wherein children often react with intense feelings of anger, anxiety, guilt, shame, sadness, and confusion. Pia, 20, expressed, *Malungkot at "depressing." Meron ding halong galit at takot.* [It was sad and depressing. There is also a mixed feeling of anger and fear.]

Thought About Their Parents' Marriage after Knowing the Infidelity

Seven participants perceived that their parents' marriage would lead to misunderstanding and eventually to separation. However, two participants said their father had been a womanizer before. As for one of the participants whose mother was the one who is unfaithful, she thought that it would be a compromise between her mother and father. She said that what happened was her father was willing to give her mother a second chance and forgive her because before, her father was a womanizer. Pia, 20, shared, *Sa tingin ko, maghihiwalay na ang mga magulang ko, immediately.* [I think that my parents will get separated immediately.]

From Whom the Decision for Separation Came From

Three of the participants said that the decision for the separation came from their parent who had an affair with other man/woman. The mother of one of the participants had filed for separation. At the same time, another parent's separation took over a phone call. Amy, 20, said, *Sa Daddy ko, sya kasi ang nagsabi sa Mommy ko na hindi na nya mahal... .* [It was from my Dad. He told my Mom that he no longer loves her.]

Three participants said that the decision came from their parents, who did not have an affair with other man/woman. At the same time, two of them said that the decision was mutual. Benjie, 25, said, *Sa Mama ko.* [It was from my Mom.]

Children's Involvement in the Separation
Children were asked if they had a role in making decisions when their parents separated. Five of the participants said that their parents did not consider them in the decision made about the separation. They said that their parents' decision was final when they knew it. They were not asked for their opinion about it. This is consistent with the study of Hogan et al. (2002), wherein most children were told about the separation when the decision had been made. Some were not told about the separation and were usually shocked to learn that their parents were separating (Hogan et al., 2002).

One of the participants said that her parents had a formal conversation when they decided on the separation from her uncles and auntie, but they were not included in that conversation. She said they were asked if it was fine for them that her parents would be separated, but for her, it seemed that her mother's question was already leading to a final decision to be separated. *Feeling ko, actually hindi. Kasi, wala, hindi naman nila kami tinanong kung ano bang gusto namin,* Kylie, 18. [I think we're not considered. They do not ask us what we wanted.]

For the other participant, his mother's decision seems to be irrevocable, for she already filed a case to counter her husband's call for their annulment. *Ginather kami para sabihin na, ito yung decision ko, wala na kayong magagawa, wala na kayong say, wala akong pakialam kung may say kayo, basta ito yung mangyayari,* Markus, 18. [We were gathered and were told that "This is my decision. I don't care if you have anything to say. This is what will happen."]

Emotions Felt After the Separation
Two participants said they feel hatred toward their parents who had a relationship with another man/woman. They also said that nobody wants to have a broken family. Some also admitted that they felt sad about their parent's decision to be separated. Amy, 18, recounted, *Sa daddy ko ako nagalit nun. Eh syempre, sino ga namang anak na may ayaw ng buong pamilya?.* [I was angry at my Dad. No child would like not to have a complete family.]

Acceptance of the Decision for Separation
Six of the participants eventually accepted the separation of their parents. Two participants said that accepting their parents' separation was a process. One participant said it took her a year to finally accept that her parents' marriage could not be saved anymore. One of them also saw her parents as better off without each other. Meanwhile, another participant agreed to her parents' separation since her mother already has a boyfriend. Kylie, 20, said, *Oo. Kasi parang wala na ring way, parang kahit ako naniwala ako na wala na, hindi na talaga... it took me a year to finally accept na wala na, it's broken beyond repair.* [Yes, because there seems to be no other way. I also believe that there is no chance. It took me a year to accept that it's finally over. It's broken beyond repair.]

Second Domain: Ways of Coping with the Changed Family Situation

This domain analyzes how the children cope with their changed family situation. They related that friends were an essential source of support to whom they first tell about their parent's separation and the first to whom they tell their problems. Meanwhile, accepting their parent's relationship with other men/women was a gradual process. In the same manner, accepting their parents' separation was considered a gradual process, with the participants being mature in dealing with the changed family situation. Moreover, the participants said they keep a positive outlook in dealing with the problems arising from their changed family situation.

Friends as the Primary Source of Support

Friends were a particularly important source of support for children with separated parents, most especially their peers whom they have significant relationships with (Butler et al., 2002). Hogan et al. (2002) noted that friends help in two ways: first, by listening/understanding. In cases where children mentioned friends as a source of support, they referred to either their very close friends or friends who had a similar experience in their family. And second, by being available for activities that take the children's minds off their parents' separation. Their friends played the role of the means for children to enjoy themselves outside their families.

Six participants first told the separation of their parents to their close or circle of friends. While three of the participants first talked about the separation of their parents with their family members. Pia, 20, shared, "My friends, because I trust them, and I know that they will be very supportive." While Jade, 17, said, *Siguro ang una ko talagang sinabihan ay yung circle of friends ko talaga, hanggang sa utay-utay na ding nalaman.* [I think the first person I told are my friends until others already find out about our situation.]

The six participants said that these friends helped them by being their support system. Pia, 20, shared that she felt that by telling the story to her friends, the emotional burden was lifted from her. "Yes, they helped me in a sense that by just telling all my worries and problems to others, it felt like a huge emotional baggage has been lifted off my shoulder." One of them also said that it feels good when she is able to tell their changed family situation to her friends, who then remind her always to be optimistic.

Apart from being their support system, the participants also found their friends to be the first to share their problems with. Eight of the participants have a good relationship with their closest friends. Since their parents' separation, their friends had been the persons with whom they shared their problems other than family members. Jade and Kylie said that it feels good to know that their friends know their family situation so that they understand what they feel and the problems they have been through. While Amy, Benjie, Abi, and Gwen find it more comfortable to share their problems with their closest friends than with their family members. Benjie, 20, narrated, *Kaibigan, kaibigan talaga. Mas komportable ako sa kaibigan kesa sa Mama at kapatid ko. Ganon nga ata pag broken family, parang mas komportable sila sa kaibigan.* [Friends, it is really to my friends. I am more comfortable sharing problems with my friends than with my mom and siblings. I think that's really the case when you are from a broken family; it is more comfortable to share stories with your friends.]

Their friends served as a good influence on them, gave them pieces of advice, helped to adapt socially to their situation, helped them cope with problems in their family, and served as their support system. Gwen, 18, shared *Kailangan mo ding humanap yung alam mo yung level ng pagkakaintindi mo ng ibang bagay, hahanap ka ng ka-age mo, para maki-cope din sa'yo.* [You need to look for friends of the same age group to help you cope with the situation.] On the contrary, a study by Butler et al. (2003) reported that some children do not tell anyone because they were ashamed or embarrassed about what was happening and feared of being teased or rejected by friends, or they feared of becoming upset if they talked about it.

Accepting the Relationship of Their Parent with His/Her Man/Woman
Three of the participants said that they had learned to accept the relationship of their parent with other man or woman at the right time. Benjie, 23, recalled that there came a point when he could not do anything since it had already happened until he had accepted it. He shared, *Hindi ko masabi kung paano, basta dumating yung point na, wala ka nang magawa eh, parang andun na yun, kahit ano namang gawin mong pakiusap eh kung sila naman yung may gusto nuon, wala ka nang magagawa so natanggap ko na lang din, natanggap na lang din namin.* [I cannot actually tell how, and it's just that I came to a point where I cannot do anything. It was already there that even if you talk to them, but they already want to be separated, you cannot do anything about it until eventually, I came to accept it – we accepted it.]

In another case, Gelli, 20, noted that accepting the relationship of her father with other woman is a gradual process. She said that it became easier for her to accept it since she had confirmed the relationship with her father through some signs she saw in their house. And also that it was not told to her directly, which she thinks would be difficult to accept if ever it was said to her. Gelli said, *Natanggap ko naman. Eventually, step by step. Kasi hindi naman nga biglaan eh, parang may mga signs naman bago ko naconfirm.* [I was able to accept it. Eventually, it was step by step, since it was not sudden, there were signs actually before I was able to confirm it.]

And for Pia, 20, talking to her mother about their family situation had helped her. There had also been disclosure and self-reflection, and she was able to accept it through time. This supports the findings of Hogan et al. (2002) study, where children were better able to adapt to family changes when they were able to understand their parent's decisions. The study also noted that it was vital to children when there was communication between them and their parents (Hogan et al., 2002).

> Through self-reflection and talking to my mother about the situation. The disclosure also helped me accept our circumstances. I guess with time, I learned to forgive her and trust her again, Pia, 20.

Accepting the Separation of Their Parents
Lee and Bax (2000) noted that most adults and children are able to adapt effectively to new family dynamics and structures following separation. Seven

participants accepted their parents' separation, saying it takes time. Being used to their family situation allowed them to accept their parents' separation. Amy said that she was disappointed in having a broken family and that during meetings at their school, her friend's mother was the one attending for her since both of her parents were abroad. But little by little, she now understands their family situation and has become mature in dealing with it.

For Benjie and Gelli, it was about getting used to the situation that helped them accept their parents' separation. Gelli, 20, mentioned that her parents are better off without each other. For Benjie, 23, the separation of his parents had already appeared to be normal since they were living with the other woman in the same house, wherein the relationship between his parents was already strained.

Abi, 20, shared that accepting her parents' separation is a gradual process, and she does not let it affect her. Kylie, 18, said it took her a year to finally accept that her parent's marriage could not be saved anymore as there was no reconciliation between her parents. Kylie shared, *Nung una mahirap, nung una ayaw ko. Umaasa ako na maaayos pa to. They would talk things out; they would understand na magiging okay, magiging okay. Yun talaga yun thinking ko nun. Then after a year na walang reconciliation na nagaganap, I accepted na, hindi na talaga, it's hopeless.* [At first, it was difficult, and I didn't want them to be separated. I am hoping that it will be fixed and that they will talk things out. That they would understand that it will be okay. That was my thinking then. Then after a year, there is no reconciliation; I accepted that it could not be saved; it's hopeless.]

Dealing with the Changed Family Situation
Although many children initially found their parent's separation to be upsetting, most experienced adaptation and coping over time (Hogan et al., 2002). All participants have a positive outlook on facing the problems that resulted from their parent's separation. The ways mentioned include praying, having a positive mindset, trying to make efforts to arrive at solutions to problems, acceptance of what their family had become and its consequences, and dealing with the problem itself.

> I stopped denying and stopped lying to other people. When people ask me about my family situation, I tell them right away. In the beginning, I was always worried about what other people think of me after hearing my stories, but then with time, I just came to the realization that whatever happened to my family is a huge part of me, and there should be nothing to be ashamed of. My past actually helps me become stronger in life, Pia, 20.

DISCUSSION

The magnitude of today's labor migration has affected familial relationships over time. The increased incidence of international labor migration raised concerns about Filipino children growing up without fathers, mothers, or both parents, and consequences of labor migration on marital relationships, and the stability of Filipino families being the basic social unit of the society, and as the most important institution in the Philippines.

Overseas employment of Filipino workers was intended to be temporary, but it has become a permanent feature of the country's economy. Transnational labor migration is now commonly accepted as a form of livelihood strategy, and overseas employment continues to serve as a vehicle for many families' social mobility. Working overseas is now becoming an option for most unemployed Filipinos searching for "greener pastures." In the belief of economic advancement, many have chosen to accept the consequences of temporary separation, including its social and emotional costs.

This study tries to explain the experiences of OFW children with separated parents due to marital infidelity as a consequence of labor migration. Although there has been much concern about how marital stability was affected by temporary labor migration, reports on the subject have tended to be impressionistic and to lack a basis for adequate data (Zlotnik, 1995). He noted that separation or divorce is more likely to occur due to strains associated with migration. It is difficult for some married couples to keep a healthy relationship because working abroad requires physical separation from their spouse and decreased day-to-day interaction, which can lead to marital strains.

Exploring family dynamics is essential when understanding the family. These family dynamics may be impacted by parent–child relationships, parents' relationships, relationships with extended family members, and marital strains to name a few. This study provides an insight that overseas employment does not just affect the relationship of the parent and children through temporary separation but extends to the marital separation of husband and wife that leads to family dissolution, which cannot be ignored.

This study suggests that children were the most affected by the parent's strained marital relationship resulting from infidelity committed while a spouse works abroad. The situation was first seen as an upsetting event for the children, mainly because the changed family situation can be displayed as a process starting with finding out about the parent's infidelity, learning about the separation, and adjusting to the new family relationship.

With their parents' separation, children can develop a perception of how they will be accepted in their future relationships, given that they came from a broken family. This gives the impression that the relationship between husband and wife plays an important model in their children's perception of their future relationships.

Finally, the findings point out that the separation of parents is different for every OFW child – this is primarily because of the differences in who is the parent who committed infidelity. Children view infidelity as an incident that will eventually lead to separation. They also found that their parents' separation was something they had to accept and deal with.

With this, the study offers a conceptual framework of how OFW children respond and cope with their parent's separation (Fig. 11.1).

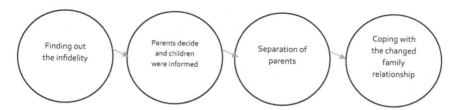

Fig. 11.1. Conceptual Framework of how OFW children respond and cope with their parent's separation.

CONCLUDING INSIGHTS

Although this study adds to the knowledge and understanding of the experiences of OFW children with separated parents because of marital infidelity as a consequence brought by labor migration, it also shows limitations that might have influenced its findings. First, there were only two male participants in the study. There were differences in their experiences and coping patterns from the female participants in the study; hence, few themes were identified between the two male cases. Since it was the father of the male participants who had committed infidelity, there should also be male participants whose mother had committed infidelity to compare the experiences of the male and female participants when it was their mother who committed infidelity. Additionally, the study only deals with children. The reason for the infidelity of parents was not explored in the study. Only the children's response to the infidelity was the focus of the study. It is also important to know the context of the infidelity and separation from the parent's perspective to establish a better relationship between the labor migration and its consequences affecting the married couple when one decides to work abroad.

Succeeding research must be done to fully contextualize the experiences of OFW children with separated parents as a result of marital infidelity due to labor migration. Hence, the author offers several recommendations for further study. Future studies should consider the number of participants in the study. The researcher recommends having an equal number of participants whose OFW mother committed infidelity, whose OFW father committed infidelity, whose father-left committed infidelity and whose mother-left committed infidelity, to come up with a comparative research of the experiences of OFW children according to whose parents had committed infidelity. In addition to this, given that there were only two male participants in the study, the researcher recommends that future studies should increase the number of male participants because they have different experiences, perceptions, problems, and coping patterns with having separated parents that have resulted from marital infidelity.

Furthermore, it is equally important to know the context of infidelity from the parents; hence the reason for infidelity should also be explored. The predisposing factors that lead to the infidelity committed by the parents [migrant parent or parent-left] – number of years abroad, physical separation from husband/wife, inadequate emotional preparation, and working conditions should further be examined. Future studies can pose the question of how they deal with their spouse's infidelity and separation. The experiences of the OFW children can also be verified by interviewing their friends, parents, siblings, and extended family. It can be done using the triangulation method to cross-check information. This study recommends that future researchers interview the parent who committed infidelity, either the migrant parent or the parent-left and any of their children, and the parent who does not commit infidelity, which is either the migrant parent or the parent-left and any of their children.

REFERENCES

Acedera, K. A. F., & Yeoh, B. S. A. (2020). 'Until death do us part'? Migrant wives, left-behind husbands, and the negotiation of intimacy in transnational marriages. *Journal of Ethnic and Migration Studies, 14*(16), 3508–3525. https://doi.org/10.1080/1369183X.2019.1592414

Aguilar, F. V., Peñalosa, J. E. Z., Liwanag, T. B. T., Cruz, R. S., & Melendrez, J. M. (2009). *Maalwang Buhay, family, overseas migration and cultures of relatedness in Barangay Paraiso.* Ateneo de Manila University Press.

Aronson, J. (1994). A pragmatic view of thematic analysis. *The Qualitative Report, 2*(1), 1–3.

Asis, M. M. B. (2013). Looking after the left-behind families of overseas Filipino workers: The Philippine experience. *QScience proceedings, 2013*(1), 8. https://doi.org/10.5339/qproc.2013.fmd.4

Asis, M. M. B. (2000). Imagining the future of migration and families in Asia. *Asian and Pacific Migration Journal, 9*(3), 255–272.

Asis, M. M. B. (n.d.). *The social dimensions of international migration in the Philippines.* Scalabrini Migration Center. http://smc.org.ph/MAPID/MAPID%20CD/Philippines%20pdf%20file/1.2.3%20The%20Social%20Dimensions%20of%20International%20Migration.pdf

Asis, M. M. B., Huang, S., & Yeoh, B. S. A. (2004). When the light of the home is abroad: Unskilled female migration and the Filipino family. *Singapore Journal of Tropical Geography, 25*(2), 198–215.

Butler, I., Scanlan, L., Robinson, M., Douglas, G., & Murch, M. (2003). *Divorcing children.* Jessica Kingsley.

Butler, I., Scanlan, L., Robinson, M., Douglas, G., & Murch, M. (2002). Children's involvement in their parents' divorce: Implications for practice. *Children & Society, 16*(2), 89–102. https://doi.org/10.1002/chi.702

Cabigon, J. V. (1995). Filipino wives in foreign lands. *Philippine Social Science Review, 52*(1–4), 63–75.

Commission of Filipino Overseas. (2013). *Stock estimate of Filipino overseas.* http://www.cfo.gov.ph/images/stories/pdf/StockEstimate2013.pdf

Dizon-Añonuevo, E., & Añonuevo, A. T. (2003). Women, migration and integration. *Transactions National Academy Sciences & Technology Philippines, 25*(2), 467–481.

Edillon, R. (2008). *The effects of parent's migration on the rights of children left behind.* United Nations Children's Fund (UNICEF), Policy, Advocacy and Knowledge Management (PAKM), Division of Policy and Practice.

Go, S. P. (1993). *The Filipino family in the eighties.* Social Development Research Center, De La Salle University.

Go, S. P., & Postrado, L. T. (1986). Filipino overseas contract workers: Their families and communities. In F. Arnold & N. M. Shah (Eds.), *Asian labor migration: Pipeline to the Middle East* (pp. 125–145). Westview Press, Inc.

Hogan, D., Halpenny, A. M., & Greene, S. (2002). *Children's experiences of parental separation.* The Children's Research Centre, University of Dublin.

Lee, C. M., & Bax, K. A. (2000). Children's reactions to parental separation and divorce. *Paediatrics & Child Health, 5*(4), 217–218. https://doi.org/10.1093/pch/5.4.217.

Lusterman, D. (2005). Helping children and adults cope with parental infidelity. *Journal of Clinical Psychology, 61*(11), 1439–1451. https://doi.org/10.1002/jclp.20193.

Medina, B. T. G. (2001). *The Filipino family* (2nd ed.). University of the Philippines Press.

Nogales, A. (2009). *How children are impacted by marital infidelity.* www.ananogales.com/htmls_en/colleagues/Children_%20Infidelity_Article_9_09.pdf

Parreñas, R. S. (2005). The gender paradox in the transnational families of Filipino migrant women. *Asian and Pacific Migration Journal, 14*(3), 243–268.

Philippine Statistics Authority. (2022). *2020 overseas Filipino workers.* https://psa.gov.ph/sites/default/files/attachments/hsd/specialrelease/2020%20SOF%20Special%20Release.pdf

Platt, R. L., Nalbone, D. P., Cassanova, G. M., & Wetchler, J. L. (2008). Parental conflict and infidelity as predictors of adult children's attachment style and infidelity. *American Journal of Family Therapy, 36*, 149–161. https://doi.org/10.1080/01926180701236258.

Reyes, M. M. (2009). *Migration and Filipino children left-behind: A literature review.* United Nations Children's Fund (UNICEF). http://www.unicef.org/philippines/mediacentre_10202.html

Sevilla, J. C. C. (1982). *Research on the Filipino family: Research and prospects.* Development Academy of the Philippines.

Siguan, A., Ong, M. F. T. & Cañete, S. I. M. (2021). The impact of infidelity on Filipino family dynamics and young adult Filipino's self-concept. *MALIM: Jurnal Pe Pengajian Umum Asia Tenggara, 22*(2021), 14–37. https://doi.org/10.17576/malim-2021-2201-02

Taylor, A. R. (2008). *Parenting in Filipino transnational families* [Theses and Dissertations, Paper 265]. University of North Florida. http://digitalcommons.unf.edu/etd/265

Thorson, A. (2013). Adult children's discovery of their parents' infidelity. *Qualitative Communication Research, 2*(1), 61–80. https://doi.org/10.1525/qcr.2013.2.1.61

United Nations Economic and Social Commission for Asia and the Pacific. (2008). *Key trends and challenges on international migration and development in Asia and Pacific.* http://www.un.org/esa/population/meetings/EGM_Ittmig_Asia/BGpaper_ESCAP.pdf

Zlotnik, H. (1995). Migration and the family: The female perspective. *Asian and Pacific Migration Journal, 4*(2–3), 253–271.

CHAPTER 12

THE FAMILY AS A FARM INSTITUTION: CASES IN JAPAN AND THE PHILIPPINES

Carlo S. Gutierrez

ABSTRACT

This chapter deals with family/household relevance as a stakeholder institution in rural (farm) communities. The data collection approach is qualitative. Families in Japan and the Philippines' rice-cultivating communities were the subjects of the study. Results revealed that households in the two sites were experiencing a unique ontological crisis vis-á-vis farming communities. The crisis pointed to the problem of farm families' relegation as secondary stakeholders in the farming sector. Despite the struggle for survival in the farm sector, farm families were differently adaptive and enduring in dealing with the modern development – that is, selective technology adoption, farmland redefinition, struggle and resistance against farm policies, and community group accommodation, to name a few. This endurance contributes to farm family persistence as a relevant institution in Japan and the Philippines.

Keywords: Institutions; family/household; farm sector; smallholding; agriculture; comparative study

INTRODUCTION

This study situates the family as an institutional actor in society. Moreover, farm families are a significant part of the familial institution, albeit differing in sectoral

Resilience and Familism: The Dynamic Nature of Families in the Philippines
Contemporary Perspectives in Family Research, Volume 23, 205–225
Copyright © 2023 by Emerald Publishing Limited
All rights of reproduction in any form reserved
ISSN: 1530-3535/doi:10.1108/S1530-353520230000023012

or livelihood characteristics to that of, say, for instance, non-farm families or households. The term "institution" in this regard, is defined based on the sociological tradition – as a social structure with hierarchical form, with actors, roles, functions, and inter-generational latency or transmission (Abdelnour et al., 2017; Fürstenberg, 2016; North, 2016). Thus, the family in this study is viewed as a social setup relevant to contemporary times.

Family is explicitly adaptive based on popular theories – for example, game theory (provides meaning), functional structuralism (social harmony), and social agency theory (Parsons & Mayhew, 1982; Searle, 1995; Von Neumann & Morgenstern, 2004). The family is guided and defined by the rules of marriage and marital union. The family draws legitimacy from other institutions via these rules – that is, the church, the state, and others. The sexual division of labor within the family framed the roles and functions of family members. More importantly, various forms of families are active members of the community and have roles in shaping development policies or projects of society. Families are stakeholders even in farm society.

However, in recent development and institution-related studies, the position of the family as a primary social institution has been questioned. Some researchers considered the family as a passive actor in the development process that needs targeting or programmatic consideration (e.g., Dawe & Peter Timmer, 2012; Timmer, 2005). Some even suggested that a family is merely an organized group embedded within a larger institution of the state/government and the economy (Rogers, 2017).

In *The Agrarian Question* – in two volumes, Kautsky (1988) claimed that farm families, in general, were culturally maladaptive. He explained this by comparing urban to rural development during the industrial revolution in Europe. Kautsky explained that rural families lack the physical, educational, and cultural capacity to manage and organize farms efficiently. He believed that farm industrialization emanating from within the family [institution] is impossible as they lack the capacity for capital exploitation. He explained that state-initiated development will fail if the family was left to implement projects on the farm independently. Kautsky advised the forced appropriation of land in farm industrialization, undermining the family.

Kautsky's stance relied on Marx's worldview. His perspective perceived a unitary institutional world where the state dominates all aspects of life. Those who followed in the footsteps of Kautsky were optimistic about farm productivity changes benefitting the family – that is, Djurfeldt (1981) and Hyden (2005). Nevertheless, thinkers adhering to the agrarian question seem to tolerate the disregard of the family as an agency for development. Farm family, in this view, is never legitimately considered a productive part of society.

Neo-institutionalism even went to the extent of suggesting that the family is not an institution. The family is a normative organization based on neo-institutionalism. Rogers (2017) explained that from neo-institutionalism, the family should not be regarded as an institution but rather as an organization embedded in a larger institution. What is that larger institution? Rogers never expounded. The idea that the family resembles an organization is new and challenging. Rogers, in the same way, hinted at the family's contemporary irrelevance. Unfortunately, it puts the ontology of the family as something consciously designed and dependent on rationally created goals. Rogers' idea of the family as a purely rational organization is misleading.

Equating the family as an [rational] organization implies that it serves specific purposes – for example, for growth, development, and efficiency, among others (Clemens & Cook, 1999; Rutherford, 1994; Selznick, 1996). Institutional theories boxed the family into the category of the *homo economicus* – one governed by material production and consumption. The neo-institutionalist's view of the family failed to consider it a complex agent of development or change. In the context of my research, external and internal factors, not limited to economic ones, influenced the family.

This chapter has five parts: (1) Conceptual Framework, (2) Ethical Compliance and Methodology, (3) Data and Results, (4) Discussion, and (5) Conclusion. The data in this chapter were from face-to-face interviews among farm household heads in Japan and the Philippines sites, supplemented by demographic statistics related to farming.

CONCEPTUAL FRAMEWORK

The term "institution" is polysemic – it has multiple meanings and is context or field-dependent. The institution may refer to any of the given: (1) a form of standard, (2) a state of high status, (3) a social group structure, and (4) a repetitive and taken-for-granted habit, among others. Family-based in this chapter is framed along the social context and should be read as a complex social grouping – similar to (3) above.

Not all social collectives or groups/organizations are institutions. Although, some collectives can become an institution in time. The institution, in this research context, is a form of social construct or relationship with discernible material or social ramifications – that is, perceivable or interpretable structure, a gathering of people, to name a few. The institution I am referring to is a social institution – with an emphasis on the social or the people. A *social institution* is any form of a social collective with a domain, organized with social interactions, guided, and legitimized by rules and rituals. It is responsible or forced to produce and distribute collective goods, capable of self-reproduction, and interacting with other institutions through symbolic exchanges in the circular economy of collective goods. The definition is specific, but some aspects need clarification – social domains, collective goods, rules and rituals, and symbolic exchanges. No social arrangements or social relationships are definable as institutions without the given aspects.

The concept of *institutional domain* is lesser known but a classical term in sociology; it draws connections from the work of Durkheim on *the Division of Labor in Society*. Durkheim explained that the division of labor resulted in specialization, segmentation, and social system formation in society. In "Developing the Concept of Society: Institutional Domains, Regimes of Inequalities and

Complex Systems in a Global Era," Walby (2020) explained that institutional domains are symbolic markers of social institutions. Institutional domains refer to the outcome of structural differentiation resulting in an institution with a specific function (and social niche). Institutional domains are arenas of relations of inequality (Turner, 2010; Walby, 2020). There are domains in the works of Turner referencing past sociologists: polity, economy, civil society, violence, family or kinship, and others. Domains are characterized by relations of inequality,[1] or more aptly, difference.

Collective goods are the rationale for institutional endurance and existence. Collective goods are goods, services, or functions that institutions produce and distribute to other institutions necessary for society's welfare and survival. In *The Moral Foundations of Social Institutions: A Philosophical Study*, Miller (2009, p. 56) identified the properties of collective goods:

> (1) they are produced, maintained, or renewed using the joint activity of members of organizations or systems of organizations, that is, by institutional actors, (2) they are available to the whole community, and (3) they ought to be produced (or maintained or renewed) and made available to the whole community because they are desirable goods and ones to which the members of the community have an (institutional) joint moral right.

Production and distribution of scarce resources (public goods) are the collective goods of the economic or business institutions. The provision of infrastructure to produce public goods and the maintenance of order are the collective goods of the polity. These are goods produced within the collectivity or the social context. More importantly, this separates an institution from an organization. The private domain, where the personal and kinship relationship occurs, is the domain of the family.

Set of rules and rituals separate institutions from one another. We can mention North's institutional typology for a simple explanation. There are general institutions in society: political bodies (political parties, the senate, a city council, and a regulatory agency); economic bodies (firms, trade unions, family farms, and cooperatives); social bodies (churches, clubs, and athletic associations); and

Table 12.1. Generalized Symbolic Media of Institutional Domains.

Institution/Domain	Symbolic Media
Family/kinship	*Love/loyalty*, or the use of intense positive affective states to forge and mark commitments to others and groups of others
Polity/state	*Power* or the capacity to control the actions of others
Civil society	*Solidarity/freedom*, the ability to express one's personal interest in a community, based on voluntary will and social mobilization
Economy	*Money*, or the denotation of exchange values for objects, actions, and services by the metrics inhering in money
Religion	*Sacredness/piety*, or the commitment to beliefs about forces and entities inhabiting a non-observable supranatural realm and the propensity to explain events and conditions by references to these sacred forces
Others	Technology, health, knowledge, competitiveness, influence, and aesthetics, among others

Source: Based on Abrutyn and Turner (2011).

educational bodies (schools, colleges, and vocational training centers) (North, 2016). Rules can be formal (written) or informal (unwritten).

Formal rules governed organization within institutions. For instance, rational-legal or the law (constitution) rules most political bodies' affairs. The church observes a combination of written and unwritten rules. Rules connect to some institution-unique rituals that mark the entry to an institution. Rules, likewise, control social behaviors. For example, an oath of office is necessary before a person's government career. A church or civil wedding marks the start of a family and others. These rules and rituals are unique to a specific institution. In time, these rules and practices turned normative or "sacred" that they become the desire or goal for those who wish to enter family or government.

Institutions are involved in constant symbolic exchanges. Institutional stakeholders interact with other stakeholders through the symbolic exchange. In "The Old Institutionalism Meets the New Institutionalism," Abrutyn and Turner, building on the works of Parsons and Smelser (1956), explained that institutions connect with other institutions. "Generalized symbolic media are exchanged among actors and between diverse institutional domains" (Abrutyn & Turner, 2011, pp. 285–286) (see Table 12.1). For instance, exchanges or interactions by the family are mediated by love/loyalty and power, while interactions within the school happen by technology and learning. All institutions possess symbolic media in varying degrees. Likewise, all institutions differentially exchange a proportion of symbolic media depending on the institution and its domains.

Only groups that produce collective goods and are durable (able to survive inter-generational transition) and capable of self-reproduction can be called

Table 12.2. Relevant Institutions in Farm Communities.

Institution	Domain	Level of Social Structure	Dominant Symbolic Media	Collective Goods/Primary function	Rules and Rituals
State/ Government	Public polity	Macro-level	Power	Order wealth production/ distribution	Law and policy
Civil society (groups)	Associational space community	Meso-level	Freedom and Solidarity	Social mobilization and inter-institutional linkages	Agenda and *Laissez faire*
Economic institutions	Market economic domain	All levels	Money	Production/ distribution of public goods and services	Capitalism, efficiency, and profit
Family	Private kinship	Micro-level	Love and Loyalty	Household economy and reproduction of society	Marriage and socialization

Source: Based on Rosenblum and Post (2002).

institutions.[2] Only those institutions that satisfy this qualification can experience inter- and intra-institutional interaction through symbolic exchanges. However, old institutionalism provided a list of institutions for analysis. New institutionalism offers a limited choice – often limited to political-economic ones.

The above definition of the institution and the inclusion of the farm family is necessary based on two relevant factors. These factors are (1) collective goods production by farm households – farm outputs and labor force, and (2) intergenerational transmission – continuity of farming in society. These are the main factors that give legitimacy to an institution in society (Gregorio, 2020; Gutierrez, 2021). Collective goods connect the family to other institutions and, thus, enable it to do multiple exchanges (collective goods and symbolic media) (see Table 12.2).

The ability of the family to remain within the livelihood base and reproduce itself (socially and biologically) adds to its institutional legitimacy. If farm families are incapable of producing future farmers, farm families will cease to exist. Thus, the two factors are significant gauges of institutional relevance. Moreover, the aspects in question in this chapter are related to the two factors discussed earlier: *are farm families in Japan and the Philippines able to contribute to the goods provision of their respective countries, and are farm families capable of reproducing the next generation of farmers?* These are questions of institutional legitimacy from the context of social institutionalism.

ETHICAL COMPLIANCE AND METHODOLOGY

The activities relating to the data collection for this research were allowed under the NUS-IRB guidelines. I was permitted data gathering related to this research through a 2016 approval following all ethical stipulations and restrictions. This research's data collection scheme is qualitative. The methodology employed in this research included participant observation among farmers at the sites, face-to-face interviews, and others. Permissions for entry were inquired about and approved by the local and municipal heads of the communities. Participants in the research were personally asked for consent through direct contact, assisted by locals in the farm communities. Opt-out options at any point of the data gathering are available for those who wish to withdraw their participation in the study. There are few cases of participation refusal in Japanese communities. In contrast, withdrawal of consent in the Philippines is negligible and accounted for less than 10% of the total invitations.

Locales of the Study

This research is a multi-site study. Each country had one site, selected purposively. Communities devoted to rice planting were the locales for the data collection. The choice of farmers devoted to rice farming is strategic and logical since more than a third of all farmers in Asia and Africa (Freiner, 2018; Hayami, 1978; Mariano et al., 2012; Misiko & Halm, 2016) were devoted to rice production. Likewise, this means that the situation of rice family farmers represented farmers in general (Roche, 1997). The sites are Izumi-ward, Sendai City, Miyagi Prefecture in Japan, and Barangay Talangka in Sta. Maria, Laguna, Philippines.

Japan Data Collection Site

The farm community of Izumi-ward in Sendai City, Miyagi Prefecture, is the locale in Japan. Miyagi is in the northeast region of Japan, known as the Tohoku *chihou* (region). It is more than 600 km away from the capital city of Tokyo. Sendai is the capital city of Miyagi. Miyagi Prefecture, according to the MAFF annual reports and the official website (of the local government of Miyagi), is a prefecture of multiple industries.

Izumi-ward is inland, located more than 10 km away from coastal areas. It has smallholding farms (an average of 1–3 hectares). However, in contrast to Gen et al.'s (in Thompson et al., 2019) description of a Japanese farm community as *san-chan*, the Izumi farm was predominantly characterized by single-generation farmers. The *san-chan* (*obaasan, ojiisan, and okaasan*) was conspicuously absent. Rice farming, at least in the case of Izumi-ward, is done by the single-generation head(s) of the family – either the mother (*okaasan*) and father (*otoosan*) or by the grandmother (*obaasan*) and grandfather (*ojiisan*).

Philippine Data Collection Site

Laguna is a multi-industry province in the south of Manila. In 2020, it was home to special economic zones, manufacturing hubs, fisheries, and farming industries. Sta Maria municipality in Laguna prides itself as the "Rice Granary" of the province. The data-gathering phase among farm households (in Laguna) happened through a year-long community immersion and face-to-face interviews with farm households in Sta Maria.

Sta Maria is a fourth-class farming municipality. Rice and upland (fruit) farming are sources of income in the area. Sta Maria is among the remotest areas of Laguna and is nearer to the Province of Quezon than to Manila. The municipality was accessible by an occasional jeepney or serviced van plying to and from the Manila area (in the pre-COVID-19 period).

Based on the statistical census of 2020 and as manifested in the official website of the Philippine Statistical Authority (PSA) and the Department of Health (DOH), Sta Maria's population stood at 33,965 with a population density of $313/km^2$ ($812/mi^2$). The total population of the municipality spreads across 25 Barangays or villages. Household interviews for this research commenced in Barangay Talangka.

Data Collection Scheme

The data in this study were part of the broader interrogation of the smallholding persistence phenomenon. The data collection scheme was eclectic and qualitative. Izumi-ward (Japan) and the town of Sta Maria, Laguna (Philippines) were farm communities chosen for comparison. The criteria for the site selection include strategic access, geographic similarities, crops cultivated (both are rice communities), and proximities to the urban centers.

Japan and the Philippines were nation-states for comparison due to their historical (farm) intersections. The rice crisis of 2007–2009 put these two nations

Table 12.3. Summary of the Collected Data.

Site/Locale	Institutions	Data Collection Approach	Data Collected
Japan	Household	Interview Existing primary data on family	5 household heads[a] MAFF survey reports on family and household income
Philippines	Household	Interview Existing primary data on family	35 household heads Micro-economic data

[a]There is a lopsided household representation based on in-depth interview respondents. There was difficulty in the access to family households due to the unwillingness of the community. The COVID-19 pandemic only exacerbated this difficulty. To supplement this lack of more representation, annual white paper reports pertaining to farm households from the Ministry of Agriculture, Forestry and Fisheries of Japan (1998–2020) were utilized in the study.

intricately connected in the political economy of rice and agriculture (Alavi et al., 2011; Davidson, 2016; Dawe, 2010; Menelly, 2016).

The data gathered were from 2018 to 2021. Family-related data came from ethnographic community immersion, in-depth interviews with family heads, and supplementary statistical reports in Japan and the Philippines. Table 12.3 summarizes the collected family-related data. During in-depth interviews, a questionnaire served as a guide for conversation. The questionnaire has the following information: (1) social, economic, and demographic aspects of the family and farming, (2) nature of farming and land ownership, (3) heir to the land and livelihood, and (4) other farm-related issues.

I will focus on the current and historical state of the farm in Japan and the Philippines (farm size) and the demographic realities that are facing the farm families. The notion of aging among farmers and inter-generational farm transmission are salient points that remained problematic in the farming sector for both countries, and these require context.

DATA AND RESULT

There have been problems with distributive development and the demographic nature of agriculture. The farming sector has been losing areas of arable farmlands, despite an increasing number of farm-dependent households becoming dependent on farming (Rigg et al., 2018), particularly in the Asian region. Andriesse (Thompson et al., 2019) and Timmer (2005) pointed out that farmers, in general, are the poorest sector of society despite occupying a pertinent role in the food sector. This aspect of small farm size, contributing to dismal economic productivity, and demographic concerns (of aging and family size) through the years reflect the current conditions of farm households in this study. The presentation of data based on the survey (and supplemental statistics) are as follows: (1) socio-economic and demographic data, (2) farm household landholding categories, (3) farm inter-generational transmission through land inheritance, and (4) civil society group membership.

Izumi and Talangka Household's Relevant Social Characteristics

In both the Philippines and Japan study sites, farmers' and farm households' characteristics are dynamic and complex. Sex or gender division of labor characteristics seems to indicate equal gender responsibility. A pressing issue is the aging farm workers in both countries.

Though the interviewed household heads in Japan were comparatively fewer than that in the Philippines, insights were discernible about the farmers in Japan and the Philippines based on Table 12.4. Females were as involved in farming as males in the rice farm sector. Rice farmers were overwhelmingly household-based, with most farmers being married. Only two respondents are single at the time of the interview. However, these single farmers were economically supporting their nuclear families (family of birth).

The average age of respondents in Izumi and Talangka reflected the national trends for both countries; farmers in the two sites were considered old. At 64.3 years old (Japan) and 56.16 years old (Philippines) average age, respectively, farmers in the study were comparable to retired employees in the non-farm sector. Moreover, the average age mirrored the national trend of national and global aging of farmers. The farm sector seems unable to attract younger workers to replace existing food producers. In 2020, Japan's average farmer was 67 years old, and farmers in the Philippines were 60 years old nationally (see Fig. 12.1).

Farmers' educational attainment was interpretable as varied and complex. More than half of the respondents in Japan and the Philippines were non-college graduates. That is, despite agriculture as a higher education area for both countries for centuries now. Notwithstanding that, it is not proper to assume that farmers have a low level of educational attainment. More than half of Izumi farmers were high school graduates, while the rest were college (level) educated. Talangka farmers have varying degrees of educational attainment as well. Almost 30% of the farmers (10) interviewed were college degree holders.

The gender division of labor, the average age, and educational attainment of farmers can be indications of complex farm dynamics. At least from this survey, the two communities involved in the study were dominated by almost retired age

Table 12.4. Socio-economic Status and Demographic Data.

SES Category	Japan ($n = 5$)	Philippines ($n = 35$)
Sex		
Male	2	18
Female	3	17
Education		
Elementary	–	16
High school	3	9
College (level)	2	10
Marital status		
Single	–	2
Married	5	33
Average age of farmers	64.23	56.15

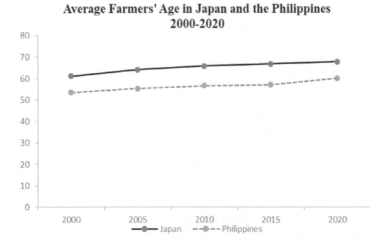

Fig. 12.1.   Aging of Farmers in Japan and the Philippines.

farmers. Further, women were as much involved in the farm operations as males were. More importantly, current rice farmers cannot be reduced as the "less edu-cated" sector. Farmer's education in this study was evidently diverse. I have not encountered a farmer in Izumi or Talangka who has not attended any formal education. Thus, it is acceptable to suggest that in terms of social factors, rice communities involved in this study are relatively diverse. If this reflects the whole farming sector, then we can assume diversity in farm labor participation but with demographic graying problems looming on the horizon.

Farm Household Landholding Categories

Landholding, or farmland ownership, is a primary input in food production. It defines the socio-political relationship of farmers in the community. The ability to invest in farming depends on access to arable land. However, this simple rela-tionship to land access is not as simple as farmers owning the land (possessing the land title) or not.

Based on the respondents, the average size of farms in the communities in this study was around less than 3 hectares. Japan's rice field is slightly big-ger by area. This size falls into the definition of smallholding farms (Graeub et al., 2016; Hazell & Rahman, 2014; Netting, 1993; Thompson et al., 2019). This farm size average is not just an Asian phenomenon. Smallholding is a global phenomenon seen in countries with high population density and devoted to staple crops.

In ownership typology, Japan is unique as it has institutionalized family own-ership of land. This uniqueness was evident in the 100% (5 households) farm-land family ownership. Landholding in Japan has clear corresponding legal status. According to other past sources, farming is a state-regulated livelihood.

Table 12.5. Nature of Farm Ownership.

Land-Related Category	Japan ($n = 5$)	Philippines ($n = 35$)
Average size of farm	2.5 hectares	1.78 hectares
Length of farm experience		
Less than 10 years	–	3
11–20 years	1	9
More than 20 years	4	23
Farmland holding type		
Family owned	5	10
Tenancy (by state)	–	14
Renting (by landlord)	–	4
Others (e.g., land is pawned)	–	7
Source of household income		
Rice only	–	4
Rice and fruit crops	–	10
Rice and livestock	–	7
Rice and vegetables	1	1
Rice production and non-farm works	4	13

Farmland ownership is permitted, historically, only among households who have been tilling the land (McDonald, 1997). The Philippines, on the other hand, had a more convoluted landholding condition than Japan (see Table 12.5).

Several farmers in Talangka privately purchased their land (10 households). Nevertheless, more than half of those interviewed have been farming under tenancy arrangements (18 household heads). There are, at present, two types of tenancy arrangements: (1) agrarian reform beneficiary, and (2) landlord tenancy arrangement in Barangay Talangka. The government closely monitors the agrarian reform tenancy. It is with stipulations on the amount of land tax to be levied (20% of the harvest). The state required a single heir for a land tenancy transfer. There is a preferable purchase by the farmer in cases where the landlord wishes to divest from the land. Additionally, land sale of the land is only permitted upon concurrence by the tenant. Landlord tenancy, on the other hand, relied heavily on the benevolence of the landowner, who is often with blood relations to the renting farmer.

Household income sources among rice farmers in this study reflected the limitation of farming as a sustainable source of revenue for the household. All respondents in Izumi belonged to multiple-income farm households. In Barangay Talangka, barely 15% of those interviewed relied solely on rice cultivation. Farmers in the Philippines and elsewhere were involved in pluriactivity or multiple activities for income (Netting, 1993; Thompson et al., 2019). More than half (18 households) of respondents surveyed in the Philippines incorporated livestock and horticulture to augment income. Finally, a third of those surveyed in the Philippines relied on non-farm income to ameliorate rice-farm revenue – for example, remittance from abroad, support from city-dwelling relatives, and carpentry, among others.

Farm Inter-generational Transmission

A farm family shall remain a stakeholder if continuity or continuous collective goods production in society is guaranteed. That means a household that stopped producing crops (or labor) ceases to become a farm household. The term "farm household" is not just a marker of what it does for their livelihood. It is a mark of cultural and symbolic importance in the community.

A farming household is not just earning money from the farm. These families create a whole cultural industry that marks the characteristics of that community. For instance, particular crops usually determine the products and culture that develop therein – for example, the culinary industry, wine and spirits production, and horticultural tourism, among others. Thus, the continuity of farm families (and the industry they spawn and support) corresponds to the continuity of the community. What is the situation of farm continuity among farmers in Izumi-ward and Barangay Talangka?

The Japanese respondent's average family size was 3.75 persons. That means that farmers interviewed have at least 1–2 children at the time of the interview. The presence of a qualified heir raises the hope that farmers will have successors once they are incapable of tilling the land. However, respondents in Japan were unsure of the prospect of the land (see Table 12.6).

All family heads had children involved in non-farm work in or outside the community. The absent adult children on the farm were not unique to Izumi, though. Abandonment of farmland due to the lack of a qualified heir or the unwillingness of the heir to take on the land is a serious problem in Japan (Ito et al., 2016; Jentzsch, 2017). This problem is an off-shoot of economic affluence and the decreasing fertility rate observed in developed economies. The national family size among respondents in Izumi-ward was even higher than the national average in 2020 (2.27 persons). Small family size is problematic as farmers' average family size fell below the replacement rate of 4 per household (see Fig. 12.2).

Table 12.6.   Inter-generational Transmission of the Farm.

Land-Related Category	Japan ($n = 5$)	Philippines ($n = 35$)
Average size of the family	3.75	4.85
Number of children		
None	–	2
1–3	5	13
4 or more	–	20
Current type of land inheritance (by law)		
One heir	Yes	No
Equal inheritance by all children	No	Yes
Farmland transmission status		
Presence of clear heir (single heir)	–	11
Kids do not want to farm	4	–
Unsure if kids will be willing to farm but willing to take on the land	1	3
Land will be divided to heirs	–	11
Others (e.g., owner's decision)	–	10

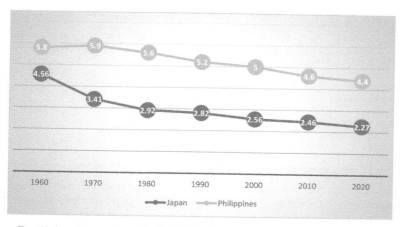

Fig. 12.2. Average Family Size in Japan and the Philippines 1960–2020.

Among respondents in Barangay Talangka, the average size of the family (4.85 persons), a high number of children (3–6 kids on the average), and ambivalence among heirs were among salient issues. The problem of farm continuity in the Philippines is multi-factor in this regard. Internally, high competition among heirs often resulted in the division of land (for titled farmland). Since equal inheritance is culturally and legally acceptable among privately owned land, in the future, land division among title-holding households is likely. This inheritance rule, most likely, will result in the division of an already small parcel of land. Externally, development exposure (or demand) by the community for state services (collective goods) will result in a land conversion. All of these can impact the persistence of farm households in the community.

Civil Society or Farm Group Engagement

The production of public and collective goods by an institution involves the active engagement of the family with other institutions. Institutions, such as the farm family, have the autonomy to decide on the operation of their resources. However, much of what they needed was beyond this autonomy. No institution is completely autonomous. The state, the family, the civil society, and other institutions are locked in a relational existence (Rosenblum & Post, 2002). The farm community (or the family), as a part of society, exchanges its resources (collective goods and symbolic media) with other institutions. The exchanges involved are indispensable even in the farm communities studied.

In the Japanese farming system, access to farm inputs and the produce market would only be allowed for households registered in a cooperative(s). The government channels resources on planned production guidelines and R&D through these cooperatives. Thus, membership in the central cooperative of Japan (JA Zenchu) is a requirement before farming. The cooperative acts as a quasi-government (Esham et al., 2012; Freiner, 2018; Klinedintlt & Sato, 1994) entity as viewed by some researchers.

Table 12.7.   Farm Group and/or Civil Society Group Participation.

Civil Society Participation	Japan ($n = 5$)	Philippines ($n = 35$)
Membership in Farm Group		
Cooperative	5	–
Irrigators' association	–	21
Women's group	–	2
Other groups	–	5
No membership	–	7
Mode of Membership in Groups		
Mandatory	Yes	No
Voluntary	No	Yes

In the Philippines, there is no mandatory farm group membership by the state. Participation in the multiple groups existing in the community of Talangka was purely on a volitional term. However, most of the surveyed farmers were involved in one or more civil society organizations (CSOs) on the farm (28/35). Almost 80% of the farmers actively participated in organizational activities involving their farms. Respondents explained that these organizations provided information that helps or promotes their farm, synchronized their farm to the whole community, provided access to other farm needs, and gave alternative livelihood access (see Table 12.7).

DISCUSSION

The issue of farming's inability to catch up with industrial development was not new. The slow farming development started with the industrial revolution (Kautsky, 1988). The responsibility of catching has been relegated among farm families who are de facto owners and operators of farmlands. In institutionalism, family (institutional) continuity relates to the ability of the family to produce and exchange collective goods (e.g., biological and social reproduction, provision of the labor force, and production of farm goods, among others). Additionally, the ability to endure for generations (the presence of heirs or the next farmers) is equally important. Collective goods production was complicated by the dilemma of aging among farmers, decreasing fertility in the world, and the lack of interest in farming by the children of farmers.

Despite ascending to the developed economy status, Japan has not produced an industrial-scale farm. This inability was due to multiple reasons. First, the lack of farm expansion in Japan was attributable to the progressive demographic aging of the farm communities (Robertson, 1988). The aging phenomenon has extended to all parts of Japan – even in major cities (Traphagan & Knight, 2003). All farmers in the Japanese village of this study fell into this demographic tier – the retired age group. Size expansion through investment may not be an attractive option for the technically "retired farmers." In Japan, older people invest in stocks, market portfolios, or savings as insurance for old-age emergencies and prospects (Robinson, 2017) but not in farming.

Buying land property in old age, with the lack of a viable heir to pass over the property, is problematic and not a productive move for farmers. By 2020, the average size of a farm family was 2.27 in Japan. With this family size, there was an increasing likelihood that farm households in Japan lacking in viable heirs. Many families do not have children; the lack of heirs only made a family investment in the land even less appealing. In Japan, even among farm households with children, there is no assurance of farm continuity as young adults prefer city-related jobs.

Second, if interest in expanding one's farm is present, there is no more vacant farmland to acquire. The lack of free lands for acquisition emanated from the post-war land reform laws. The law allowed for the distribution of land to as many farm families. In 2010–2020, family farmers owned more than 98% of farmland in Japan (see Gen et al. in Thompson et al., 2019), with an average size of 1.1 hectares (Organisation for Economic Co-operation and Development (OECD), 2016). There were restrictions preventing land consolidation for large-scale farming by a single household. These restrictions are the lack of available land for purchase, the limit set by law for land consolidation by one farmer or a family (3–5 hectares), and the broader demographic pressure on land (factories are slowly encroaching on Izumi-ward farmland).

Third, farms remained cultivated. An average farm household is a petty property owner and a seasonal cultivator. Despite the intensive labor requirement of farms (with or without machines), the seasonality of rice farming allowed for pluriactivity. Pluriactivity refers to the involvement of farmers in non-farm employment during farm off-season. Non-farm jobs can augment the income derived from the farm. In effect, the multi-income nature of rice farming added to the viability of the farm and the household. Thus, pluriactivity reduced the prospect of additional time spent on the farm (in case of farm expansion). As the income earned in non-farm work became more dependable, farm-related development in the household stagnated. Household farming became cyclical but multi-income.

Japan's agricultural technology is modern and probably up to date compared to other modern nation-states – as far as rice farming is concerned. The initial intention of the pre-war government was to establish an industrial type of food production that employed large machinery, new agricultural inputs, and adaptive farm practices (Anderson, 1988; Hayami, 1975; Kuroda, 2013a, 2013b; Organisation for Economic Co-operation and Development (OECD), 1995). Industrial agriculture using a large-scale production setup could only be implemented in Hokkaido – that is, where land-geographic endowment and demographic factors were conducive for industrial-type food production. The rest of Japan followed small-scale production due to land availability limitations and demographic restrictions.

Farm households have a predictable farming environment due to the state-to-CSO relation or accommodation. This direct channel to farmers reduced inputs and transaction costs, adding to the profitability and viability of the small farms – that is, easy access to farm inputs and a direct market for output. The connection between CSO and the farm households aligned the interests of the two institutions surrounding landholding. That is, unwittingly, the transformation of small-holdings into economically viable farms. Viable farms were coincidentally small by land reform laws' intentions.

The Philippines' case is unique in its challenges but equally problematic to Japan. One of the critical problems the Philippines faced during the time of President Benigno Aquino III (2010–2016) was overpopulation. Additionally, uncontrolled population growth has repercussions in easing the poverty rate – large families tend to be poorer (United Nations & Department of International Economic and Social Affairs, 1991). The poorest of the poor are the farmers and fisherfolks (Andriesse, 2018; Timmer, 2005) in the Philippines.

Since the 1980s, researchers expressed that the average size of families in the Philippines (and across Southeast Asia) was to decrease. The fertility rate among women followed the same decreasing trend (Rigg, 2012; Rigg et al., 2018). In the Philippines' case, the average family size among farmers dropped from approximately six persons per family in 1960 to around 4.4 persons per family in 2020. This trend for smaller families is [expected] to linger in the decades to come in the Philippines.

The more pressing concern, however, was the presence of multigenerational families in the rural communities. Multigenerational families accounted for a higher population and higher population density. This is relevant to Barangay Talangka, Sta Maria. The population density of Sta Maria, based on the 2020 census, was around 320/km², near the national rate of 365/km². With this demographic development, the state promoted the modernization of farming and the manufacturing sector for job creation in the Philippines. These previous priorities of the government mitigated the effects of job competition in the farm sector – some adults are forced to look for a job elsewhere.

Some members of farm families must leave the community to look for occupations. There were not enough jobs on the farm; there were just too many farmers. Population explosion in the Philippines from the 1960s, or more poignantly after World War II, has created crowded rural communities. Densely populated farms partly explain why some farmers must move out of Talangka. High competition for limited jobs and the increasing modernization of farm techniques forced the adult population of the farm out to cities. More families meant higher competition for farmland. The erosion of excess labor toward the cities added to the likelihood of maintenance of the farm. Surreptitiously, internal competition for jobs resulted in farming continuity, to some degree.

All policies related to agrarian reform emanated from the state up to the point of implementation. Unlike in Japan, contentions or conflicts in the Philippines concerning land rights, especially those that involved farmers, end up in court. Conflict intermediaries in the Philippines happened through political patrons or the court and never through CSOs. CSOs were, historically, seen as anti-establishment and anti-elite. Japan's pathway for landholding conflict resolution [to reiterate] is through CSO channels – with serious developmental (or protectionist) consequences.

In Talangka, farmland rights are accessible in two ways – both were sanctioned by the state – through private purchase and land tenancy. The first manner of the acquisition was through the private-ownership path. A family can purchase land based on the prevailing market price. There was no legal prohibition on the size of land accumulated through private purchase. Land purchase is subject to the availability of land for sale and the capability of farmers to pay. The inheritance of land through this setup is subject to the dynamics of family relations. There is a legal provision in the Philippines that dictates instances of problematizing the terms of land inheritance in the absence of a written will. All property of the family shall be divided equally among the remaining heirs. Equality rule became the usual pattern of property inheritance even in farmlands.

The second path to farmland acquisition is through tenancy rights. A tenancy is an arrangement when farmers cultivate the land owned by others. That refers to tenancy relations. Upon the request or intention of the farmer/tenant, Department of Agrarian Reform (DAR) will call the attention of the landowners for a formal meeting and contract signing. Several respondents in Talangka, who entered into this tenancy agreement, explained that the usual landowners were either blood relatives or absentee landlords residing in another municipality or city. There was no hacienda system in Talangka. However, there were old haciendas in other barangays, and they were all subjected to agrarian reform laws – that is, all large swathes of lands with tenants had been re-distributed by DAR.

Farms in the town of Talangka were small – a reflection of the national trend among rice farms in the Philippines – typically around 1–5 hectares. From the point of view of families on the farm, this was a result of the post-war population boom. The increasing population of the Philippines, reaching 100 M in 2018, had a corresponding need for land space. Cities of the Philippines were expanding to the rural vicinity for housing, public services, and development expansion. As a result, some rural lands slowly converted to private subdivision housing.

Population and family size in the farm community expanded more than in the cities. This rapid population growth resulted in increasing competition for farm-related jobs. The dramatic repercussion is the need of farmers themselves for land space for housing. Lands cut off by the state's road project were eventually transformed into housing areas by families. The land area devoted to rice cultivation has been decreasing in Talangka for a combination of reasons – prominent of which is the demographic problem of the farm community itself. However, there was no reason to assume that farmlands were disappearing and soon will be gone in Talangka – tenanted lands through DAR will persist expectedly.

Farming endures as the whole family seldom abandons the community for good – that includes the farmland. Despite the high labor erosion due to the dwindling availability of jobs on the farm, farm families in Talangka remained. A family member cultivating the land shares the harvest with family members – even to those who reside outside the community. In return, these families receive some financial support from family members in the upkeep of the farm. This support system added to the endurance of the family farm as it can be difficult to part ways with the land without the whole family's consensus.

More importantly, families under tenancy contracts are obligated to cultivate the land. In exchange for the land right extended to them by the state through agrarian-reform tenancy, families are expected to be productive on the farm. Legal restrictions for land sale and land-use conversion (from farming to non-farming) were in place for DAR-monitored land. The farm households were encouraged to be productive to a point where they could purchase the (tenanted) land in the future. When that time comes, some restrictions by the land reform laws shall be lifted. In the meantime, DAR-monitored farmlands will remain small. In communities where farmers are under tenancy contracts, the Irrigators' Association (IA) served as the vanguard of water infrastructure. In societies where the community spirit is intact (conflict, cooperation, and negotiations were alive), smallholding will persist through the CSO's assistance.

CONCLUSION

Farm households are primary players in food production all over the globe, at least for the non-corporate arrangement. Typically, small family farms performed other relevant roles in the community – that is, ecological maintenance, disaster and fire prevention, and community interaction sites, among others. Recently, the ability of farm families to continue their biological and social reproduction collective goods function was under scrutiny.

Farm households have demographic qualities that can be a complex dilemma in the farm communities. The aging population and the absent farmland heir have been complicating the landholding issues in Japan. I believe these reasons contribute to the frequent farm abandonment in rural Japan. Rural areas remotely located visá-vis the regional city centers were prone to this land fallowing. While farmers in Izumi-ward considered farmland valuable – economically, historically, and culturally (retirement haven). Forward-looking, family farm continuity prospect is bleak due to the demographic situation.

Japan and the Philippines have high population densities. Hing population density presented a heightened competition for farmland usage. However, this was more dramatic in the Philippines' case. In 2020, the fertility rate for the Philippines stood at 2.53 births per woman. However, according to the official website of the PSA, rural women have a higher fertility rate than urban women. Rural women gave birth to almost two children more than urban women, despite the decreasing national fertility average. The higher fertility rate among farm women means that the demand for land space due to settlement, public services, schools, health care, and other related infrastructure will considerably be higher in rural areas in the coming years.

For [both] Japan and the Philippines, the differing demographic issues posed limits on how they interact with other stakeholders on the farm. In both countries, industrial encroachment-imposed pressure on the size of farmlands. Some farmlands have been converted to other uses away from farming. Japanese farmers feared the farmlands handed to them through generations were in danger of being lost. Family lands can be lost once farm industrialization begins in their community. This concern will cause challenges to the prospect of farm industrialization in the future, more so when the community size stagnates and dwindles, resulting in land abandonment.

In the Philippines, the absence of an effort by the state for a farm industrialization project led to primarily family-based farming. The divergent demographic dilemma of Japan and the Philippines converged on the smallholding survival.

The achievement of the economic viability of small farms contributed to the persistence of farm households in Japan and the Philippines.

Finally, families in the farm communities remained instrumental in rural society. Despite the numerous challenges – that is, demographic, economic, political, and others – families contribute to the social reproduction of farm and non-farm institutions. The endurance of the family as an institution can happen through an array of adaptive strategies. These strategies include, as manifested in the data presented, inter-institutional accommodation, pluriactivity of livelihood, selective technological accommodation, farmland redefinition, and subtle resistance to policies and development, among others, within the farm.

NOTES

1. Turner (2010) used the term inequality to denote that there is differential access to resources by members of specific institutions and that not all members have the same degree of access to resources. I am referring to his idea that institutions have a hierarchical origin, at least theoretically.

2. I will interchangeably use the terms institutions and social institutions within this research. However, I wish to clarify that the term institution I am employing here is with reference to people and social collectivity. Thus, when I mentioned institution, it is in reference to the social groupings and not the broader definition of the institution which may include tangible objects, rules, and conventions, among others. The emphasis here is social groupings as institutional forms only.

REFERENCES

Abdelnour, S., Hasselbladh, H., & Kallinikos, J. (2017). Agency and institutions in organization studies. *Organization Studies*, *38*(12), 1775–1792. https://doi.org/10.1177/0170840617708007

Abrutyn, S., & Turner, J. H. (2011). The old institutionalism meets the new institutionalism. *Sociological Perspectives*, *54*(3), 283–306. https://doi.org/10.1525/sop.2011.54.3.283

Alavi, H. R., Htenas, A., & Kopicki, R. (2011). *Trusting trade and the private sector for food security in Southeast Asia*. World Bank Publications. https://doi.org/10.1596/978-0-8213-8626-2

Anderson, K. (1988). *Japan's agricultural policy in international perspective*. Research School of Pacific Studies, Australian National University.

Andriesse, E. (2018). Primary sector value chains, poverty reduction, and rural development challenges in the Philippines. *Geographical Review*, *108*(3), 345–366. https://doi.org/10.1111/gere.12287

Clemens, E. S., & Cook, J. M. (1999). Politics and institutionalism: Explaining durability and change. *Annual Review of Sociology*, *25*, 441–466. https://doi.org/10.1146/annurev.soc.25.1.441

Davidson, J. S. (2016). Why the Philippines chooses to import rice. *Critical Asian Studies*, *48*(1), 100–122. https://doi.org/10.1080/14672715.2015.1129184

Dawe, D. (Ed.). (2012). *The rice crisis: Markets, policies and food security*. Routledge.

Dawe, D., & Peter Timmer, C. (2012). Why stable food prices are a good thing: Lessons from stabilizing rice prices in Asia. *Global Food Security*, *1*(2), 127–133. https://doi.org/10.1016/j.gfs.2012.09.001

Djurfeldt, G. (1981). What happened to the agrarian bourgeoisie and rural proletariat under monopoly capitalism? *Acta Sociologica*, *24*(3), 167–191. https://doi.org/10.1177/000169938102400303

Esham, M., Kobayashi, H., Matsumura, I., & Alam, A. (2012). Japanese agricultural cooperatives at crossroads. *American-Eurasian Journal of Agriculture & Environmental Science*, *12*, 943–953. https://doi.org/10.5829/idosi.aejaes.2012.12.07.1759

Freiner, N. L. (2018). Japan Agriculture (JA): The Role of the Agricultural Cooperative: The Loss of a Traditional Lifestyle. In *Rice and Agricultural Policies in Japan* (pp. 81–105). Palgrave Macmillan. https://doi.org/10.1007/978-3-319-91430-5_4

Fürstenberg, K. (2016). Evolutionary institutionalism. *Politics and the Life Sciences*, *35*(1), 48–60. https://doi.org/10.1017/pls.2016.8

Graeub, B. E., Chappell, M. J., Wittman, H., Ledermann, S., Kerr, R. B., & Gemmill-Herren, B. (2016). The state of family farms in the world. *World Development*, *87*, 1–15. https://doi.org/10.1016/j.worlddev.2015.05.012

Gregorio, V. L. (2020). *Farm and familialism in Southeast Asia: Gender and generational relations in Malaysian and Philippine villages* [Thesis]. https://scholarbank.nus.edu.sg/handle/10635/188061

Gutierrez, C. S. (2021). *Institutional interactionism and farm landholdings in Japan and the Philippines*. National University of Singapore. https://scholarbank.nus.edu.sg/handle/10635/224568

Hayami, Y. (1975). *A century of agricultural growth in Japan its relevance to Asian development*. University of Minnesota Press.

Hayami, Y. (1978). *Anatomy of a peasant economy: A rice village in the Philippines*. International Rice Research Institute.

Hazell, P. B. R., & Rahman, A. (Eds.). (2014). *New directions for smallholder agriculture*. Oxford University Press. https://doi.org/10.1093/acprof:oso/9780199689347.001.0001

Hyden, G. (2005). *The agrarian question*. Cambridge University Press.

Ito, J., Nishikori, M., Toyoshi, M., & Feuer, H. N. (2016). The contribution of land exchange institutions and markets in countering farmland abandonment in Japan. *Land Use Policy*, *57*, 582–593. https://doi.org/10.1016/j.landusepol.2016.06.020

Jentzsch, H. (2017). Abandoned land, corporate farming, and farmland banks: A local perspective on the process of deregulating and redistributing farmland in Japan. *Contemporary Japan*, *29*(1), 31–46. https://doi.org/10.1080/18692729.2017.1256977

Kautsky, K. (1988). *The Agrarian question*. Zwan.

Klinedintlt, M., & Sato, H. (1994). The Japanese cooperative sector. *Journal of Economic Issues*, *28*(2), 509–517. https://doi.org/10.1080/00213624.1994.11505564

Kuroda, Y. (2013a). *Production structure and productivity of Japanese agriculture: Volume 1: Quantitative investigations on production structure*. Palgrave Macmillan.

Kuroda, Y. (2013b). *Production structure and productivity of Japanese agriculture: Volume 2: Impacts of policy measures*. Palgrave Macmillan.

Mariano, M. J., Villano, R., & Fleming, E. (2012). Factors influencing farmers' adoption of modern rice technologies and good management practices in the Philippines. *Agricultural Systems*, *110*, 41–53. https://doi.org/10.1016/j.agsy.2012.03.010

McDonald, M. G. (1997). Agricultural landholding in Japan: Fifty years after land reform. *Geoforum*, *28*(1), 55–78. https://doi.org/10.1016/S0016-7185(97)85527-3

Menelly, S. (2016). A lesson in mismanagement: The global rice crisis of 2008. *Harvard International Review*, *37*(3), 44–47.

Miller, S. (2009). *The moral foundations of social institutions: A philosophical study*. Cambridge University Press. https://doi.org/10.1017/CBO9780511818622

Misiko, M., & Halm, E. (2016). ABCs of diversifying information resources among rice smallholders of Ghana. *Journal of Agricultural Education and Extension*, *22*(3), 271–289. https://doi.org/10.1080/1389224X.2015.1038281

Netting, R. M. (1993). *Smallholders, householders*. Stanford University Press.

North, D. C. (2016). Institutions and economic theory. *The American Economist (New York, N.Y. 1960)*, *61*(1), 72. https://doi.org/10.1177/0569434516630194

Organisation for Economic Co-operation and Development (OECD). (1995). *Agricultural policy reform and adjustment in Japan*. Organisation for Economic Co-operation and Development.

Organisation for Economic Co-operation and Development OECD. (2016). *Agricultural policy monitoring and evaluation*. Organisation for Economic Co-operation and Development.

Parsons, T., & Smelser, N. J. (1956). *Economy and society: A study in the integration of economic and social theory* (Vol. 4). Routledge & K. Paul.

Rigg, J. (2012). *Unplanned development: Tracking change in South-East Asia*. Zed Books.

Rigg, J., Salamanca, A., Phongsiri, M., & Sripun, M. (2018). More farmers, less farming? Understanding the truncated agrarian transition in Thailand. *World Development*, *107*, 327–337. https://doi.org/10.1016/j.worlddev.2018.03.008

Robertson, J. (1988). Furusato Japan: The culture and politics of nostalgia. *International Journal of Politics, Culture, and Society, 1*(4), 494–518. https://doi.org/10.1007/BF01390685

Robinson, G. (2017). Pragmatic financialization: The role of the Japanese post office. *New Political Economy, 22*(1), 61–75. https://doi.org/10.1080/13563467.2016.1195347

Roche, J. (1997). *The international rice trade*. Elsevier Science.

Rogers, P. (2017). Family is NOT an institution: Distinguishing institutions from organizations in social science and social theory. *International Review of Sociology, 27*(1), 126–141. https://doi.org/10.1080/03906701.2016.1235214

Rosenblum, N. L., & Post, R. C. (2002). *Civil society and government*. Princeton University Press.

Rutherford, M. (1994). *Institutions in Economics: The old and the new institutionalism*. Cambridge University Press. https://doi.org/10.1017/CBO9780511625879

Searle, J. R. (1995). *The construction of social reality*. Free Press.

Selznick, P. (1996). Institutionalism "old" and "new." *Administrative Science Quarterly, 41*(2), 270–277. https://doi.org/10.2307/2393719

Thompson, E. C., Gillen, J., & Rigg, J. (2019). *Asian smallholders in comparative perspective*. Amsterdam University Press.

Timmer, P. (2005). *Agriculture and pro-poor growth: An Asian perspective* (SSRN Scholarly Paper ID 984256). Social Science Research Network. https://papers.ssrn.com/abstract=984256

Traphagan, J. W., & Knight, J. (2003). *Demographic change and the family in Japan's aging society*. State University of New York Press.

Turner, J. H. (2010). The dynamics of institutional domains. In J. H. Turner (Ed.), *Theoretical principles of sociology, Volume 1: Macrodynamics* (pp. 105–151). Springer. https://doi.org/10.1007/978-1-4419-6228-7_4

United Nations & Department of International Economic and Social Affairs. (1991). *World urbanization prospects 1990: Estimates and projections of urban and rural populations and of urban agglomerations* (Vol. 121). United Nations.

Von Neumann, J., Morgenstern, O. (2004). *Theory of games and economic behavior*. Princeton University Press.

Walby, S. (2020). Developing the concept of society: Institutional domains, regimes of inequalities and complex systems in a global era. *Current Sociology, 69*(3), 315–332. https://doi.org/10.1177/0011392120932940

CHAPTER 13

PARENTAL LIVELIHOOD PREFERENCE FOR CHILDREN AMONG MUNICIPAL FISHING FAMILIES IN SOUTH NEGROS, PHILIPPINES

Enrique G. Oracion

ABSTRACT

Livelihood preference for children is anchored in the aspiration of parents for a better life for them with due consideration of their capacities given available resources and opportunities from inside and outside the community. Given the data from an earlier survey I conducted, this chapter examines the fisheries management issues as contexts and the time factors that may have influenced the livelihood preference for children of parents, primarily fathers. Twenty-five percent of parents or 30 out of the 120 non-probability samples of municipal fishing families surveyed in South Negros in the Philippines preferred fishing for their children. For a comparative analysis, 30 parents were also randomly drawn from the remaining samples who preferred other livelihoods for their children away from fishing. As a male-dominated industry, evident in the fishing history of families, the tradition may have already declined among most parents as non-fishing livelihoods were perceived to offer family resilience to ecological and socioeconomic changes. The projected decrease in new families engaged in fishing would also mean a pressure reduction on municipal fisheries; thus, opportunities for non-fishing livelihoods must be accessible through full

Resilience and Familism: The Dynamic Nature of Families in the Philippines
Contemporary Perspectives in Family Research, Volume 23, 227–246
Copyright © 2023 by Emerald Publishing Limited
All rights of reproduction in any form reserved
ISSN: 1530-3535/doi:10.1108/S1530-353520230000023013

scholarships for college or technical-vocational education. Meanwhile, basic education sciences should infuse lessons in responsible or right fishing practices to expose children to sustainable fisheries at a young age if they pursue fishing livelihoods when they become adults.

Keywords: Fishing livelihoods; municipal fishing; parental preference; children; South Negros; Philippines

INTRODUCTION

Fishing livelihood is not all the same and the people engaged in fisheries do not enjoy similar economic status and benefits because they do not own and employ the same resources and technology (de la Peña, 2016; Neri, 2016; Toring, 2017; Turgo, 2017; Ushijima & Zayas, 1994). In the Philippines at present, there are three major types of fisheries reported by the Bureau of Fisheries and Aquatic Resources (2021): aquaculture, municipal capture fisheries, and commercial capture fisheries. Of the 4.40 million metric tons (MT) fisheries production of the Philippines in 2020, aquaculture contributed more than half of the total amount (52.79%) with the commercial capture fisheries (25.05%) and municipal capture fisheries (22.16%) following closely with each other. In terms of the cash value of the total production for the same year which amounted to Php 273.5 million, the share of municipal capture fisheries was the least (22.34%) while aquaculture was the highest earner (41.82%) with the commercial capture fisheries (35.84%) in the second place. At the local level, fishing-dependent households around Philippine lakes engaged in aquaculture also showed significantly higher income compared to those in the capture or open fishing (Palanca-Tan, 2020; Palanca-Tan & Bongat-Bayod, 2021).

The national fisheries production in 2020 had actually decreased when compared with the 2019 data, particularly in aquaculture and municipal capture fisheries, but the total loss was covered up by the commercial capture fisheries (Bureau of Fisheries and Aquatic Resources, 2021). Comparatively speaking, while the decrease in fisheries production and income was higher in municipal capture fisheries compared to aquaculture, it is likewise interesting to note that the commercial capture fisheries substantially enjoyed an increase despite being also into captive production like those fishers confined in municipal waters. Improved fishing technology and increased investments may be the reasons, but the intrusion of commercial fishing vessels in municipal waters may be another possibility of the reported increase in production. However, the intrusion puts the "municipal fishing grounds under siege" (Mayuga, 2021) that deprived the municipal fishers of their major source of livelihood and protein food in the absence of enough social and economic capital (Ramos, 2017).

Therefore, the significant decline in fish stocks was not only due to the accumulated impacts of climate change, but also the result of the persistence of illegal, unreported, and unregulated (IUU) fishing to feed a growing population, particularly with the intrusion of large commercial fishing vessels in municipal waters mentioned earlier (Anticamara & Go, 2016; Fabinyi & Barclay, 2022). The severe damage to the marine environment caused by IUU fishing creates long-term havoc on fishing livelihoods that ultimately results in a critical loss of economic revenue to the government (Chapsos & Noortmann, 2019). Moreover, the degradation of the broader ecosystems in the coastal zones and upland areas due to indiscriminate infrastructure development, domestic and industrial waste disposal, shipping, and agricultural runoff has worsened for poor fishing households (Fabinyi & Barclay, 2022; Neri, 2016; Toring, 2017). Thus, the increasing efforts of the government and conservation organizations to regulate access to fisheries and reduce pressures to harvest fisheries (Malayang et al., 2020) may be good in the long term, but these also appear unfavorable to small fishing households without alternative livelihood sources.

So, the question is asked. Could the uncertainty of fishing amid climate change, the associated risk at sea, the fishing restrictions enforced, and the poor income have already discouraged small fishers from preferring fishing livelihoods for their children? The answer to this question makes it also interesting to know how some of the fisheries management issues may have influenced their livelihood preference for their children when the latter will have their own respective families. Furthermore, the reasons of those parents who did not prefer fishing and fishing-related livelihoods for their children are worthy of analysis as bases for addressing the concerns of parents that may have destined themselves as families of small fishers. With this aim, the fishing and fishing-related livelihood history of these two families was pursued to identify further the time factors that had influenced the preference and non-preference of parents for fishing and fishing-related livelihoods.

LITERATURE REVIEW

One of the pressing issues in fisheries management that persisted since the passing of the Philippine Fisheries Code of 1998 or Republic Act 8550 as amended by Republic Act 10654 is the enforcement of fisheries laws in curtailing IUU fishing activities (Catedrilla et al., 2012). Bribery by wealthy offenders and political interventions to get away with criminal prosecution and their ability to pay fines and penalties if they were apprehended likewise contribute to the persistence of IUU fishing that threatens fisheries sustainability in the Asian region like in the Philippines (Fernandez, 2009) and Indonesia (Chapsos & Noortmann, 2019). To satisfy the greed for profit and take advantage of the growing seafood market, because they already have much compared to the poor, are reinforcing reasons for violating fisheries laws (Fabinyi, 2009). On the other hand, poverty is also cited as one of the significant reasons why fisheries law violations remain a considerable threat to Philippine fisheries (Catedrilla et al., 2012).

The small fishers have exclusive use of the municipal waters to protect their rights to food and survival. These waters cover 15 km of the waters off the shoreline according to the provisions of the Philippine Fisheries Code (Ramos, 2017). The city or municipal local government units have jurisdiction over these marine areas, including streams, lakes, and inland bodies of water. They have the power to enforce fisheries laws, rules, and regulations within the municipal waters (Anticamara & Go, 2016). Theoretically, substantial compliance with the exclusivity of the municipal waters and the observance of fisheries laws could have helped sustain fisheries and fishing livelihoods. These laws include using the proper fishing gear, reporting fish catch for management purposes, securing fishing gear registration and licenses, and observing close and open fishing seasons. And the least complied law, as reported by municipal fishers, is the temporal restriction on fishing, suggesting the absence of other livelihood sources if fishing would stop for specific days or months (Oracion, 2020).

With fish scarcity being a usual experience now in the Philippines, importation is a strategy to prevent exorbitant fish price increases driven by the huge consumer demand, according to a government official (Lagare, 2022). This strategy also mitigates the seasonal closure of fishing grounds for particular species and the damage to fishing boats and equipment during natural calamities. Rola et al. (2018) confirmed the positive impact of the closed fishing season policy for sardines on the general welfare of fishers and fish factory workers in the case of the Zamboanga Peninsula in the Philippines. But this situation is probable only when there are ready alternative livelihoods during the seasonal closure of fishing. However, the variations in geography and social structure in fishing across regions in the Philippines bring different experiences to fishers differentiated by their capital access to combat temporal fishing restrictions (Fabinyi & Barclay, 2022).

The increasing number of fisheries law violations will go on if the municipal fishers have no other ways to earn amidst the deteriorating quality of the marine ecosystems. It is a struggle between ensuring the survival of their families and complying with all the regulations and restrictions imposed by authorities but without providing them with better options. They are in a dilemma to prioritize, given the pressure from within and outside the family. Although some may have already understood the positive results of right or responsible fishing according to legally and ecologically allowed, voluntary or intrinsic compliance is still challenging to achieve with the high economic pressure on the families of poor municipal fishers. Thus, enforcement may not be the only solution, and there is truth to this assumption. In one province in the Philippines, the improvement in fisheries law enforcement operations was associated with the increasing number of apprehensions of violators and cases filed in courts (Catedrilla et al., 2012).

Fisheries managers collaborating with local fishers who spend most of their time in the community may help promote voluntary compliance and upscaling and sustaining fisheries management. Aligning management policies to local dynamics and building goodwill activities would increase fisheries law compliance, resulting in improved ecological health (Warner & Pomeroy, 2012). If properly motivated and provided the right incentives to get actively involved in fisheries management, the local fishers who have direct knowledge about illegal and irresponsible fishing activities can suggest ways to prevent or report these to proper authorities for appropriate actions (Chapsos & Noortmann, 2019). Similarly, women and youth have significant contributions if given enough space and voices in the management process. Increasing transparency, opening communication, promoting co-management, and integrating local knowledge in decision-making will favor a meaningful collaboration (Anticamara & Go, 2016).

The preceding fisheries management issues and concerns may be perceived and appreciated differently by the commercial and municipal fishers. They are assigned to different fishing grounds, use different types of fishing technologies, have different needs and priorities, enjoy different income levels, etc. Municipal fishers are miserably experiencing low fish catch and income due to depleted fisheries. They use less capital-intensive gears such as hooks and lines and nets that are manually operated compared to commercial fishers operating larger vessels and fishing equipment (Turgo, 2014). The municipal fishers directly fish for a living with the use of small fishing vessels, either engine- or paddle-powered, while the commercial fishers are for a business that hires others to do the actual fishing in the deep seas and are paid from the share of the catch (de la Peña, 2016; Fabinyi & Barclay, 2022).

Traditionally, municipal fishing in the Philippines is a family affair and gendered (Fabinyi & Barclay, 2022; Israel-Sobritchea, 1994; Turgo, 2017). Husbands go out to fish while wives (Oracion, 1998a) and children (Oracion, 1998b) participate during the different phases of the fishing operation. Before going to the sea, the wives assist in preparing for the needs of their husbands, while in extreme cases, some join their husbands in actual fishing, even on deep seas (Pastor, 2016). Generally, after the trip, the wives would take charge of trading fish to middle buyers or in the neighborhood while the male children help clean the boat and repair the fishing nets if they are not in school. Mature and physically abled children also accompanied their fathers in fishing – a form of socialization (e.g., Castillo, 1979, for farming families) – not only as additional family labor, but also to prepare them of their anticipated role in a coastal community. The exposure to fishing explains the emergence of younger fishers in families where adult fishers have retired or left for better livelihoods (Knudsen, 2016). This development happens when children cannot finish school and find better jobs or the family does not shift to another livelihood. One major obstacle is the lack of savings or capital to move away from fishing (de la Peña, 2016).

But parents may not also prefer fishing livelihood for their children given the circumstances that make difficult the life of municipal fishing families. So, if they foresee better alternatives with greater probabilities for their children to earn more, perhaps away from home, they would work hard to direct the livelihood preference of their children. This phenomenon among rural families was also investigated by Gregorio (2020) but in farming communities in the Philippines and Malaysia. She identified four parenting typologies to explain various strategies employed by parents to break the intergenerational transmission of poverty. From an investment perspective, these strategies include preparing children to work outside the community by sending them to school, urging them to seek city-based employment if they cannot finish school, allowing them to experience farm work while also attending school, and imparting farming knowledge which they can also use to manage their own in the future. This parent–child interaction as regards to future livelihood will be further examined in the case of municipal fishing families.

METHODS

The data used in this chapter come from the fishing regulations perception survey of municipal fishers in South Negros, which I did in 2020 for the Silliman University USAID Fish Right Program. The program, which promotes the ecosystem approach to fisheries management (EAFM), covers two other sites in the Philippines, namely, the Visayan Sea and Calamianes Island Group and Silliman University is the local partner academic institution that handles the program activities in South Negros (Kotowicz et al., 2022). Specifically, the covered sites in South Negros included 11 local government units clustered into three for sampling purposes. In Negros Oriental, the first cluster covered Dumaguete City, Bacong, Dauin, Zamboanguita, and Siaton, while the second cluster covered Sta. Catalina, Bayawan City, and Basay. The third cluster was in Negros Occidental, composed of Hinobaan, Sipalay City, and Cauayan (Fig. 13.1).

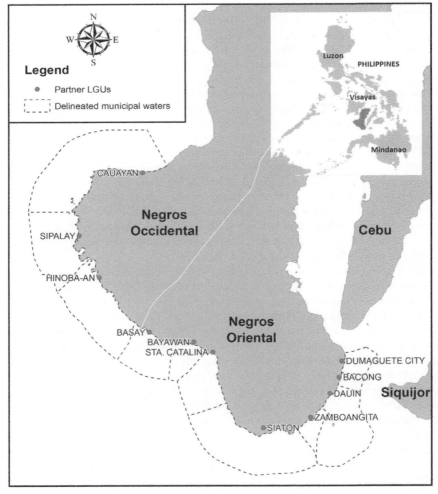

Fig. 13.1.   Map of South Negros Project. *Source*: USAID Fish Right Program.

The investigation covered the experiences of 60 families of municipal or small fishers identified from the original 120 samples included in the survey and equally distributed among the three clusters. The survey covered 23 coastal barangays randomly sampled from the list of barangays in all three clusters where the families of municipal fishers resided. Interviewed was the father or the mother present during the survey. Only 30 parents among those interviewed preferred to have their children pursue fishing and fishing-related livelihoods when they would already establish their own families. To better understand the contexts and factors that influenced their decisions, 30 randomly sampled families from among those who did not prefer fishing for their children served as a comparison.

The Silliman University Research Ethics Committee approved the research proposal for implementation. The interview always started with the information about the purpose behind the conduct of the survey. The respondents were assured of their privacy rights and the confidentiality of information they would share before asking about their willingness to participate. They were also informed that they could discontinue the interview if they felt uncomfortable with some of the questions asked. Moreover, they were asked to question and express their sentiments if they had some doubts. Replacements were immediately made for those who refused to participate or discontinued the interview. And before the interview ended, they were debriefed and assured that the information they shared would be solely for the fisheries conservation program planning as the primary goal and for future publications to share some lessons from their experiences.

Data were processed and presented using descriptive statistics such as mean, frequency, and percentage distribution. The chi-square test and *t*-test were used to measure significant differences in the fisheries management issues stances and demographics of respondents, respectively, classified according to their fishing livelihood preference for their children.

RESULTS

Family of municipal fishers. The plan was to interview either the father or the mother, whoever was available and willing to be interviewed. But the mothers tended to ask the fathers to answer because of the topics covered in the interview. Traditionally, fishing livelihood is a masculine matter (see Israel-Sobritchea, 1994), in which the father and mature male children, who already go out fishing, have the expertise and direct information. Therefore, fathers who are assigned to go out and fish, rather than the mothers, are more familiar with issues related to fisheries management, particularly fisheries law enforcement and compliance. It was not unusual that about 82% ($n = 49$) of the respondents were fathers compared to 18% ($n = 11$) mothers. Although the mothers would agree to the interview, they often only relayed what they had observed or heard from the fathers. Nonetheless, few mothers who were into actual fishing were enthusiastic about sharing their experiences.

The fathers were older (50.97 years old) than the mothers (46.31 years old). They have been married for 23 years already with four children. The couples resided where they were interviewed for almost 21 years, suggesting that some may have lived somewhere after marriage. Moreover, the fathers were already fishers before having families because they had been into fishing for the past 26–27 years. Based on multiple responses, almost 92% of the fathers were into actual fishing in municipal waters, 10% were into fishing-related activities, and 22% were also engaged in non-fishing activities. The data suggest that several fathers had multiple livelihood sources to support the needs of their families since almost 50% or 30 of the wives did not have sources of cash income. And of the distribution of mothers based on multiple responses who reported to be economically productive, which excludes those as housewives only but were most likely underrated, only 20% were involved in actual fishing, 33% in fish trading, and 53% in non-fishing livelihoods (Table 13.1).

Table 13.1.   Fishing and Non-Fishing Livelihood Involvement of Fathers and Mothers.

Parents	Actual Fishing (%)	Fishing-related (%)	Non-fishing (%)
Fathers ($n = 60$)	55 (91.67)	6 (10.00)	13 (21.67)
Mothers ($n = 30$)	6 (20.00)	10 (33.33)	16 (53.33)

Multiple Responses

Generally, the husbands brought more cash income to the family than the wives. But the wives have also either directly or indirectly contributed in terms of their unpaid labor in fishing livelihood. As mentioned earlier, the wives, and their abled children, assisted the husbands in their fishing activities. Three out of the ten mothers were engaged in non-fishing livelihoods such as tending a *sari-sari* or variety store, working with the local government unit, and others. They did bring cash income, and the number may increase due to the declining income of fathers from fishing. Perhaps with limited entrepreneurial skills, the mothers who admitted to being non-earning in terms of cash income did not have the opportunities and access to capital to start a business at home. The observations here on the economic contribution of fathers and mothers in fishing families are similarly described in other studies (de la Peña, 2016; Pastor, 2016).

Although 78% of the respondents were members of fishers' associations, the economic benefits of being members come in the form of livelihood or relief assistance provided by the local government units. About 76% were also members of cooperatives where they can apply for loans during emergencies. During the study period, the miserable conditions of fisheries require that municipal fishing families have safety nets or networks that they can depend upon when nothing can prevent the worst scenario. They assessed that the condition of stocks of fish species they usually catch during the study period had better conditions 10 years ago. The community assessment validated this perception about the status of fish stocks and the incidence of IUU fishing in South Negros (Oracion et al., 2021).

Fishing involvement and livelihood preference for children. Twenty-one families, or 35% of the 60 families included in this report, had a total of 33 male children in actual fishing during the study period. The respondents from these families, either father or mother, were further classified into those who preferred their children to continue or pursue fishing livelihoods in the future and those who wished they could have other livelihood sources. Parents who chose fishing livelihood for their children represented 14 families (46.67%) and had 21 children in actual fishing. Meanwhile, parents who were against having their children engaged in fishing represented seven families (23.33%) with 12 children in actual fishing. Therefore, the parents who favored fishing livelihood for their children had more children already engaged in the fishing industry during the study period.

But why would parents not want their children to go into fishing and fishing-related livelihoods? Out of the 30 parents who held this position, 36% explained that they wanted their children to finish school or earn a college degree so they could find a better job. They had an appreciation for schools as the means to have access to employment opportunities away from the dangers associated with fishing. Twenty percent feared children being exposed to risk every time they went out at sea, particularly during sudden unfavorable weather conditions. There are also parents who would leave the decision to their children despite the associated dangers of fishing (10.00%). Admittedly, other parents had observed that the children had not shown interest at all in fishing as a future livelihood (10.00%).

Meanwhile, about 13% of the parents had the following combinations of reasons why fishing is no longer attractive: fishing is not a permanent or stable livelihood, fish stocks are already depleted, farming is a better option, and having female children. About 10% of the parents did not cite their reasons. Thus, how parents assessed some fisheries management issues presented to them, among several others, may help in understanding what livelihood they prefer for their children. Incidentally, no significant differences existed in the stances between parents who preferred and did not prefer fishing livelihoods for their children (see Table 13.2). So, only the general results are discussed with the assumption that these issues are either temporary or permanent constraints in their fishing activities depending on how they impact their economic well-being.

Municipal waters and marine protected areas (MPAs). Two major fisheries management issues pertaining to the declaration of municipal waters and the establishment of MPAs. The respondents were asked if they agreed with the present size declared as municipal waters inclusive for the small or subsistence fishing and restricted from large commercial fishing vessels. Although 15 km offshore comprised the municipal waters, the amended Philippine Fisheries Code (RA 10654) provides that small to medium-sized commercial fishing vessels may operate within 10.1–15 km but not in depths less than 7 fathoms. However, certain conditions and processes have to be met before these commercial fishing vessels are allowed (see Mayuga, 2021; Ramos, 2017). One of these requirements is prior consultation with various stakeholders before passing a local ordinance to this effect. The city or municipal Fisheries and Aquatic Resources Management Council (FARMC) must hold public hearings. However, allowing commercial fishers to fish nearer the coast would increase competition over dwindling municipal fisheries to the disadvantage of the municipal fishers, given their limited capital and fishing technology.

Table 13.2. Comparison of Stances on Fisheries Management Issues of Parents According to Their Fishing Livelihood Preference for Children.

Fisheries Management Issues	Fishing Livelihood for Children		All Parents (%)
	Preferred (%)	Not Preferred (%)	
Fishers should collectively take an active role in fisheries management	30 (100.00)	30 (100.00)	60 (100.00)
Women seeking significant roles in fisheries management should be supported	29 (96.67)	28 (93.33)	57 (95.00)
Youth should be given active roles in promoting fisheries conservation	29 (96.67)	29 (96.67)	58 (96.67)
The present size declared as municipal water is enough	25 (83.33)	29 (96.67)	54 (90.00)
The establishment of MPAs should be supported	25 (83.33)	28 (93.33)	53 (88.33)
There is a need to increase the existing size of MPAs	13 (43.33)	16 (53.33)	29 (48.33)
The present fines and penalties stop violators of fisheries laws	11 (36.67)	14 (46.67)	25 (41.67)
The importation of fish every time there is scarcity in the Philippine market is acceptable.	14 (46.67)	8 (26.67)	22 (36.67)

Note: Chi-square test results at 0.05 level of significance do not show significant differences in the responses per issue of respondents between parents who preferred or did not prefer fishing livelihoods for their children.

Ninety percent of the respondents agreed with the size of water areas presently declared as municipal waters, and this also means they recognized the arrangement where large commercial fishing vessels are restricted (see Table 13.2). Meanwhile, allowing small- to medium-sized commercial fishing vessels to fish within the prescribed area given certain conditions set by law is not valid in all local government units. But municipal fishers like the owners of *payaw* (fish attracting devices) also benefited from the latter arrangement when they allowed commercial fishers to cast nets in these devices. The former got a share of the catch of commercial fishers. Other municipal fishers assisted in tracking or attracting schools of fish using lights. They do not own bigger boats and fishing nets, so they learned to work with commercial fishers.

One-third of the respondents who agreed with the exclusivity of municipal waters explained that municipal fishers, given their limited fishing technology, must be allotted enough area to fish for their food and income. Others said that delineating the area to particular fishing types prevents conflict and mitigates the fast depletion of fish stocks. However, a few of the respondents lamented the poor enforcement of this provision of the fisheries laws.

Meanwhile, the possible expansion of the size of MPAs in their respective communities would reduce their favored fishing grounds and already diminishing fish catch. The contested issue about MPAs is between the goal of sustainable fisheries production in the long-term and providing the immediate needs for food and income of small fishers without alternative livelihood sources (Oracion, 2017).

The above fisheries management issues affect the fathers, mothers, and children of families engaged in municipal fishing. Depending on the outcomes and new opportunities opened up by successful MPAs may influence the livelihood decisions of families, which is either to continue fishing or to move to the tourism industry (Pedju, 2017). Eighty-eight percent were supportive of the establishment of MPAs as conservation tools while 48% agreed to increase the size to maximize fisheries impacts and benefits (see Table 13.2).

Participation in fisheries management. The third issue focuses on the participation in fisheries management of the local government units of fishers, including women and youth, who should be involved as stakeholders and stewards (Kotowicz et al., 2022). The fact that a majority of the respondents were members of fishers' associations, 100% agreed when asked if they should collectively take a more active role in the governance of their fisheries by being involved in rule-making than leave this to the authorities (see Table 13.2). Authentic participation is evident only among fishers' associations that get involved through their leaders in analyzing fisheries issues, looking for solutions, planning for actions, formulating policies and regulations, and implementing these through their associations. Among the local government units in South Negros, the fishers' associations, through their federation officials, were represented in the FARMC in drafting or amending their fisheries ordinances.

On the other hand, 95% agreed to support women seeking significant roles in fisheries management, while 97% favored giving the youth active involvement in promoting marine biodiversity conservation (see Table 13.2). The women could become leaders of community organizations or become members of *bantay dagat* (sea wardens). Involving the youth in fisheries management decisions and actions would prepare them to assume a more active role when they become adults and fishers for livelihood or fisheries managers working with government or academic institutions. These sentiments may be linked to the five people they identified with from a list to have influenced their decisions to support sustainable fisheries programs in their communities. As a whole, 43% pointed to family members and relatives as most influential on top of the fishers' association leaders (40.00%), barangay captains (38.33%), and mayors (25.00%). Meanwhile, 37% also included their friends and neighbors as influencers. Therefore, fisheries management projects and activities must work around kinship networks and not only through legal authorities or local government officials to be successful.

Fines and penalties to restrain violations. The fines and penalties related to violations of fisheries laws are the fourth fisheries management issue being re-examined if these had indeed restrained IUU fishing. Incidentally, 58% observed that these did not stop violators in contrast to the 42% who positively noted the effects because there were still fish to catch (see Table 13.2). The persistence of IUU fishing was raised as evidence of the failure of fisheries laws to be effectively enforced and of the authorities to punish irresponsible fishers engaged in municipal and commercial fisheries. According to the respondents who were optimistic about the effects of fisheries law enforcement, the amount for fines was already huge and enough to prevent violators. A few even commented that fish stocks had already improved in areas with better enforcement, but only 32% were aware of apprehensions of violators. Meanwhile, the unsatisfied respondents reported that IUU fishing still existed, which implied the failure to consistently impose fines and penalties on violators. They suggested increasing the fines and confiscating the fishing boats and paraphernalia of violators.

Fish scarcity and importation. While the fish stock decline is a persistent phenomenon because of the deteriorating quality of marine habitat, fish scarcity is seasonal but proportionate to the percentage decline in fish stock every year or every five years. Fish scarcity for a particular period is also due to conservation measures imposed both at temporal and spatial scales. The enforcement of seasonal closure of fishing for certain species is an example of a temporal scale. The establishment of MPAs is an example of spatial restriction which reduced traditional but critical fishing grounds. Weather conditions, lunar position, and other natural events also influence the seasonality of fish catch. But fish scarcity now is seriously felt compared to the past, making fish importation a coping measure to control excessively high fish prices in the market. Fish importation as a fisheries management measure, also as an issue, allows critical fishing grounds and fish species to rehabilitate and restock, respectively, but this draws mixed reactions among consumers and fishers.

Table 13.2 shows that only about 37% of the respondents agreed with importation every time fish scarcity hits the Philippine market. Fear was a primary reason for their resentment. A plurality who disagreed with importation suspected that the fish from other countries might be contaminated or have excessive chemicals that keep the fish fresh (42.42%). Others were apprehensive that the imported fish would be more expensive because they come from outside the country (21.21%). Moreover, they believed that there was no urgency to import because fish stocks would not be depleted, although supplies were scarcer at a certain period (21.21%).

In contrast, other respondents believed that fish prices would drop when imported fish would flood the market, putting the local fishers at a disadvantage and should not be allowed to happen (15.16%). Meanwhile, all the respondents who agreed on fish importation explained that this measure is necessary to meet the need and cushion the negative impact of scarcity on the protein requirements of Filipinos. This contention alludes to the low-income families who could only afford fish but those of lower quality.

Family fishing history. The saying in Cebuano Visayan that goes *ang pagpang-isda gadagan sa dugo* (fishing runs in the blood) suggests that fishing livelihood has been the survival mode of particular families. The family's fishing history could be traced from grandparents to grandchildren, both the sides of father and mother. A bilinear kinship system explains why Filipinos trace their consanguinity or blood relatives both along paternal and maternal lines. One line may be more influential than the other depending on geographic proximity or when the paternal or maternal relatives reside in the same community (Oracion, 2006). Fishing livelihood influence on children is more decisive when the relatives are exposed to the same resources and with limited opportunities for outside employment. Thus, relatives residing in coastal communities most likely subsisted in actual fishing or any fishing-related livelihoods than their relatives in farming communities far from the coasts.

The respondents who preferred and did not prefer fishing livelihood for their children were asked if their respective fathers, mothers, brothers, and sisters had a history of fishing involvement, particularly in municipal fisheries. Fifty-five percent of parents who favored their children to pursue fishing livelihoods had fathers with a history of fishing involvement compared to the 49% who said they want their children to find other sources of income. Meanwhile, 47% who had brothers involved in fishing preferred their children to have a fishing livelihood when they would have their own families compared to the 43% who had opposite plans. Compared to the fathers, the percentage of mothers was lesser in fishing-related activities. Only 17% of the respondents considered fishing livelihood, such as fish processing and trading, as better for their children than the 12% who felt that fishing was not profitable given the worsening state of fisheries. Meanwhile, 10% of each cluster of respondents had sisters engaged in fishing-related activities.

Fishing experience and livelihood preference. The families of municipal fishers who preferred fishing livelihood for children have more fathers who opted for it (86.67%) than fathers of families that desired other livelihood options (76.67%). Therefore, more mothers admitted to driving their children toward non-fishing livelihoods (27.33%) than mothers who considered fishing as good enough for their children (13.33%). Although the noted difference in parental preference is not statistically significant, there appears to be a tendency for fathers to expect their children to continue their trade compared with mothers who aspire for something better with lesser risks involved (Table 13.3).

Comparatively speaking, the fathers who preferred their children to remain or engage in the fishing industry were, on average, older (53.76 years old) compared to fathers who aspired their children to be in other types of livelihoods (48.07 years old). The difference is significant at 0.05 level (t-test = 2.024 and p-value = 0.048). Although the difference in the case of the mothers is not statistically significant, the results imply that, on average, older mothers (48.18 years old) preferred fishing livelihood for their children compared to those younger (44.43 years old).

Overall, younger parents exposed to the crisis in fisheries must have anticipated a more difficult life for their children if they still rely on fishing, as informed by their own experiences. Fathers of families who preferred fishing livelihood for their children have spent, on average, about 31 years in the industry compared to 22 years for those who wished for other livelihoods for their children. The difference in the number of years the fathers engaged in the fishing industry classified

Table 13.3. Comparison of Livelihood Preference for Children of Fathers and Mothers.

Parents	Livelihood Preference		All (%)
	Fishing (%)	Non-fishing (%)	
Fathers	26 (86.67)	23 (76.67)	49 (81.67)
Mothers	4 (13.33)	7 (23.33)	11 (18.33)
Total	30 (100.00)	30 (100.00)	60 (100.00)

Note: Chi-square = 0.445, p-value = 0.5046, not statistically significant at 0.05 level.

according to fishing livelihood preference for children is significant at 0.05 level (t-test = 2.283 and p-value = 0.026). As assumed earlier, the data confirm that older parents who had spent long years fishing may have already adjusted to its nature and are aware of the limited opportunities available to their children outside of the community. Perhaps the hope for an improvement in fisheries has a better chance of realization given the various initiatives of local government units and private conservation organizations in sustainable fisheries management programs involving fishing communities and several stakeholders.

DISCUSSION

The families of municipal fishers described that the fish stocks in South Negros some 10 years ago from the conduct of the survey already showed a severe decline, and the various foreign-funded fisheries management programs here (Cabral et al., 2015; Pomeroy et al., 1997; White et al., 2006) could have only slowed down the destruction of the marine environment and fisheries. The problem is very complex and requires EAFM that guides the most recent conservation initiative in South Negros of the Fish Right Program. This approach aims to avert further ecological catastrophe as the destruction of the terrestrial areas has also significantly impacted the marine environment. Since environmental damage does not recognize political boundaries, EAFM promotes intergovernmental action to protect and conserve fisheries by ensuring that various local government units and government agencies coordinate their efforts and pool their resources to achieve these goals.

Anchored also on the EAFM lens, this investigation focuses on how family dynamics like intergenerational livelihood expectations are likewise affected by the conditions and management of fisheries. More specifically, the data demonstrated how the livelihood preference of parents for their children has to be viewed as valuable management information in fisheries to reduce fishing pressure when parents discourage their children from the fishing industry. The increase in the number of fishers could be significant if the present families with at least two children will also go for a fishing livelihood when they establish their own families. The possibility is high when they are not educationally equipped and with no better options. Thus, the presence of diverse and stable livelihood opportunities could reduce fishing pressure as more families would be willing to exit the fishing industry (Slater et al., 2012).

Sociologically, the livelihood preference for children by parents is a decision actually anchored on cost and benefit calculations for the family as a whole which suggests familialism or familism that prioritizes the welfare of immediate family members, particularly of young children. This cultural value may be still present, particularly in rural communities, but slowly dwindling as members are subsequently allowed to make decisions away from what the family upholds that the parents may have decided upon (Gregorio, 2020). About four decades ago, rural sociologist Gelia T. Castillo (1979) observed the traditional notion about children as investments who could provide additional financial support and security to older parents as the latter also strongly influenced the major decisions of the former.

Although the traditional parent–child relationship which shows subservient children has already changed due to modernization as has been taught in introductory Sociology course in the Philippines, "parents still feel ... that their age and experience better qualify them to judge what is best for the children, especially in the selection of careers" (Hunt et al., 1994, p. 217). The children in municipal fishing families, in particular, who are made to inherit or reject the fishing legacy of their parents are informed by the opportunities as well as the challenges awaiting them within and outside the community. In this case, the parent–child relationship in livelihood selection is propelled not only according to the anticipated monetary gains but also by a complexity of factors such as the associated risk in fishing, perceived results of fisheries law enforcement and management, family fishing history, and age and fishing experience of fathers.

The parents who preferred fishing livelihood for their children as the only option and those who aspired to secure them away from what they perceived as a risky and unstable source of income have equally good reasons behind their decisions. Generally, they agreed on the size declared as municipal waters and supported the establishment of MPAs. Despite the persistent non-compliance of fisheries laws due to poor enforcement, there was a general feeling that these spatial measures may help reduce fishing pressures for the benefit of municipal fishers. Thus, they wanted to be actively involved in fisheries management as they also endorsed the women and the youth to have significant roles in the program.

Meanwhile, the municipal fishers felt that the fisheries laws violator's existing fines and penalties did not effectively prevent IUU fishing. This observation was consistent with their assessment of poor enforcement, which they perceived to be due to political intervention. Moreover, the amounts of fines and the degree of the penalty imposed on violators are lesser than the benefits enjoyed in IUU fishing. There is a need to revisit existing fisheries ordinances of local government units if the provisions on fines and penalties are responsive to the current situation and the actual value of money.

While the law-abiding municipal fishers felt shortchanged in fisheries law enforcement, they also severely perceived the negative economic impact of fish importation when the Philippine fish market is scarce. The already disadvantaged municipal fishers, due to the depleted fisheries and increased cost of fishing, suffered more because the low-priced imported fishes competed with locally captured fishes in the market. This strategy may be good for the consumers but not for the municipal fishers if no safety nets are ready to save them. Thus, seven out of every ten parents who perceived more economic difficulties and associated risks in fishing did not prefer this livelihood for their children.

The families of municipal fishers that still consider fishing as a viable livelihood option, particularly for male children, had a broader fishing history, evident in the comparative distribution of fathers and brothers of the respondents engaged in fishing. Fishing knowledge and skills were internalized through observations and apprenticeships when sons tagged along with their fathers at sea (Fernandez, 2017). On the other hand, the trend in the distribution of mothers and sisters engaged in fishing-related livelihoods must have been determined by the activities they shared. The daughters were socialized through the mothers to become economically productive. Some women who participated in fish processing and trading and actual nearshore fishing felt they had economically contributed to family income. Although the differences were not statistically significant, perhaps due to the small sample size, more parents who preferred that their children pursue fishing livelihoods had more members of their families of orientation in the fishing industry than those who aspired for other livelihoods.

The shift away from fishing livelihood to land-based livelihood like farming, driving motorcycles for passengers, carpentry works, and others (de la Peña, 2016; Neri, 2016) may reduce fishing pressure to allow fish stocks to regenerate but only with the success of the fisheries management programs. However, those examples of land-based jobs cannot assure a better life for the children when they become adults with families to raise. I had documented more than 15 years ago the children in Apo Island who said, for example, that they would have "better life chances if they had college degrees and found employment outside ..." (Oracion, 2006, p. 66). But the cost involved is a major challenge to poor parents who may be unwilling to invest in it if the chances of getting a college education are lesser (Hedges et al., 2016). Although tuition fees are free in state universities and colleges, other related costs will be an additional burden to poor families, especially when children have to study away from home (Bawagan, 2015).

Concurrently, the parents' age and years of experience in the fishing industry influenced their fishing livelihood preference for their children. The assumption is that the older the person is, and with more years of experience in actual fishing and fishing-related livelihoods, the better their adaptability and resiliency to the changes in the conditions of the marine environment and fisheries. Subsequently, they feel better about the industry's future that had influenced their livelihood preference for their children. However, this contention does not overlook how their assessment of the present conditions of fisheries has persuaded them to make the most out of these or anticipate the better outcomes of fisheries management programs. Otherwise, they could quickly drive their children away from the fishing industry for their livelihood (Slater et al., 2012).

In synthesis, the foregoing experiences of municipal fishers in South Negros also approximate those of other Filipino poor rural families who equally aspire, similar to farming communities in Davao del Sur (Gregorio, 2020) and indigenous communities in Mindoro (Bawagan, 2015), a better life for their children but are restricted by limited social and economic capital. While fishing is perceived now as risky and hard because of the accumulated impacts of climate change and the persisting problem of IUU fishing, it is always a ready option for the livelihood of their children if they would fail to get quality education and secure better employment opportunities.

CONCLUSION

The two groups of parents identified from families of municipal fishers – the first preferred fishing for their children and the second opted for any livelihood outside of fishing – did not significantly differ in their stances on fisheries management issues. They shared similar appreciation and assessment of the relevance of some fishing-related policies and interventions. But their livelihood preferences for children significantly differed when comparing fathers by their age and years of experience in actual fishing. Older fathers who had spent long years in the fishery sector were confident about their children's abilities to overcome challenges based on their industry knowledge. Their stances on certain fisheries management issues as to how these would contribute to or expose to risk the economic well-being of municipal fishers must have likewise influenced their decisions. But family dynamics has changed now that permits older children to decide what is good for themselves, like getting away from fishing, if they could have the opportunity to prepare educationally for it with support from the government or private organizations.

Although having most parents wished their children would exit the fishing industry would disrupt family fishing history and tradition, the livelihood change would have helped them get away from intergenerational poverty as this movement will also significantly reduce the pressure on fisheries (Kotowicz et al., 2022). It is easy to project this scenario as the possible outcome of the non-fishing livelihood preferences of parents, but this depends on the capacity of parents to shoulder the total cost of education for their children. State universities and colleges offer free tuition fees; however, there are other needs of students, especially if they go to schools away from home. Parents have to worry about these as they also face difficulties in their daily subsistence unless they are willing to borrow money from the cooperatives where they are members.

The probability of success in earning a college degree or acquiring vocational skills, given the resources available and accessible to parents, is what makes the non-fishing livelihood preference of children a significant indicator of fishing pressure reduction in the future. Among other things being equal, the more children get out of the fishing industry through education, the greater the probability of reducing the number of fishers in a particular coastal community. Thus, the non-fishing livelihood preference for children is a piece of vital information for designing an intervention to reinforce existing harvest control measures.

The recommendation is for the government to also provide full scholarships and financial support for other school needs to qualified children of municipal fishing families. These items must be components of a fisheries management program with a sufficient budget. After all, every parent wants to give a beautiful life to their children. The preference of the majority of these parents for non-fishing livelihood shows such aspiration at this period when Philippine fisheries are under continuous threats of climate change impacts and abusive human activities that need massive restoration through an ecosystem approach. Meanwhile, basic education sciences should infuse lessons about responsible or right fishing practices

(Patron et al., 2020; Picardal et al., 2020; Romagos et al., 2020) to expose children to sustainable fisheries at a young age if they pursue fishing livelihoods when they become adults.

ACKNOWLEDGMENTS

The data used in this chapter were from the perception survey I conducted involving municipal fishers on fishing regulations in South Negros. Silliman University is a consortium partner in South Negros of the BFAR-USAID Fish Right Program under Cooperative Agreement number 72049218CA00004, awarded on March 30, 2018, to the University of Rhode Island. But the views expressed and opinions contained in this chapter are mine and are not intended as statements of policy of either USAID or the cooperating organizations.

REFERENCES

Anticamara, J. A., & Go, K. T. B. (2016). Spatio-temporal declines in Philippine fisheries and its implications to coastal municipal fishers' catch and income. *Frontiers in Marine Science, 3*, 21. https://doi.org/10.3389/fmars.2016.00021

Bawagan, A. B. (2015). Three generations of Iraya Mangyans: Roles and dilemmas in the modern world. In A. T. Torres, L. L. Samson, & M. P. Diaz (Eds.), *Filipino generations in a changing landscape* (pp. 9–26). Philippine Social Science Council.

Bureau of Fisheries and Aquatic Resources. (2021). *Philippine fisheries profile of 2020*. Bureau of Fisheries and Aquatic Resources, Quezon City. Retrieved July 21, 2022, from https://www.bfar.da.gov.ph

Cabral, R. B., Mamuag, S. S., & Aliño, P. M. (2015). Designing a marine protected areas network in a data limited situation. *Marine Policy, 59*, 64–76. http://dx.doi.org/10.1016/j.marpol.2015.04.013

Castillo, G. T. (1979). *Beyond Manila: Philippine rural problems in perspective*. IDRC.

Catedrilla, L. C., Espectato, L. N. Serofia, G. D., & Jimenez, C. N. (2012). Fisheries law enforcement and compliance in District 1, Iloilo Province, Philippines. *Ocean & Coastal Management, 60*, 31–37. doi:10.1016/j.ocecoaman.2012.01.003.

Chapsos, K., & Noortmann, M. (2019). Involving local fishing communities in policy making: Addressing illegal fishing in Indonesia. *Marine Policy, 109*, 103708. https://doi.org/10.1016/j.marpol.2019.103708

de la Peña, L. (2016). Shifting livelihood and intensification of fishing effort in a Visayan Island. *Aghamtao, 25*(1), 120–134.

Fabinyi, M. (2009). *Fishing for fairness: Poverty, morality and marine resource regulation in the Philippines*. The Australian University Press.

Fabinyi, M., & Barclay, K. (2022). *Asia-Pacific fishing livelihoods*. Palgrave: Macmillan: Switzerland.

Fernandez, A. J. (2017). Whale shark (*Rhincodon typus*) watching and tourism in Barangay Tan-awan, Oslob, Cebu: Ecological insights from local knowledge. *Aghamtao, 25*(2), 307–331.

Fernandez, P. (2009). The sea around the Philippines: Governance and maintenance for a complex coastal ecosystem. *Environment, 51*(3), 36–51. www.environmentmagazine.org

Gregorio, V. L. (2020). *Farm and familialism in Southeast Asia: Gender and generational relations in Malaysian and Philippine villages* [Ph.D. dissertation in sociology]. National University of Singapore.

Hedges, S., Mulder, M. B., James, S., & Lawson, D. W. (2016). Sending children to school: Rural livelihoods and parental investment in education in northern Tanzania. *Evolution and Human Behavior, 37*, 142–151.

Hunt, C. L., Espiritu, S. C., Quisumbing, L. R., & Green, J. J. (1994). *Sociology in the Philippine setting: A modular approach*. SIBS Publishing House Inc.

Israel-Sobritchea, C. (1994). Gender roles and economic change in a fishing community in Central Visayas. In I. Ushijima & C. N. Zayas (Eds.), *Fishers of the Visayas, Visayan anthropological studies: 1991–1993* (pp. 279–304). University of the Philippine Press.

Knudsen, M. (2016). Poverty and beyond: Small-scale fishing in overexploited marine environments. *Human Ecology, 44*, 341–352. https://doi.org/10.1007/s10745-016-9824-y

Kotowicz, D. M., Torell, E., Castro, J., Oracion, E. G., Pollnac, R., & Ricci, G. (2022). Exploring influences on environmental stewardship of fishing communities in fisheries management in the Philippines. *Environmental Management, 69*(6), 1102–1117. https://doi.org/10.1007/s00267-022-01645-4

Lagare, J. B. (2022). Let that sink in: Agri chief details reasons to import fish. Retrieved April 26, 2022, from https://newsinfo.inquirer.net/1543122/let-that-sink-in-agri-chief-details-reasons-to-import-fish#ixzz7Q7J5F1am

Malayang, B. S., Oracion, E. G., Bomediano, M. R., Calumpong, H. P., Abesamis, R. A., & Montebon, R. D. (2020). Opportunities and challenges to fisheries policy in the Philippines. *Today Journal of Environmental Science and Management, 23*(1), 111–126. https://doi.org/10.47125/jesam/2020_1/11

Mayuga, J. L. (2021). Municipal fishing grounds under siege. *Business Mirror*. Retrieved August 13, 2022, from https://businessmirror.com.ph/2021/05/16/municipal-fishing-grounds-under-siege/

Neri, D. J. C. (2016). Part fishers, part farmers: Livelihood strategies and diversification in a frontier community. *Aghamtao, 25*(1), 85–119.

Oracion, E. G. (1998a). Exchange transaction of Apo Island with the mainland: From the perspectives of wives involved in fish trading. *Silliman Journal, 39*, 34–53.

Oracion, E. G. (1998b). The little fisherfolks: Involvement and stories of children in the local fishing industry. *Convergence, 4*, 30–39.

Oracion, E. G. (2006). Are the children willing? Intergenerational support for marine protected area sustainability. *Silliman Journal, 47*(1), 48–74.

Oracion, E. G. (2017). Revisiting tensions and successes of marine protected areas in a Visayan Municipality. *AghamTao, 25*(2), 285–306.

Oracion, E. G. (2020). Fishing regulation knowledge, attitude and practices: A perception survey of municipal and commercial fishers in Southern Negros. BFAR-USAID Fish Right Program, Silliman University, Dumaguete City.

Oracion, E. G., Bomediano, M. R., Alpuerto, J. B., & Beronio, R. D. (2021). *Community assessment of illegal, unreported and unregulated fishing in South Negros oriental*. BFAR-USAID Fish Right Program, Silliman University.

Palanca-Tan, R. (2020). Economic vulnerabilities of fishing-dependent households around Laguna Lake, Philippines. *Philippine Journal of Science, 149*(3-a), 815–831.

Palanca-Tan, R., & Bongat-Bayod, S. (2021). Fishing and rural livelihood: A Philippine context. *Open Journal of Animal Sciences, 11*, 84–95. https://doi.org/10.4236/ojas.2021.111007

Pastor, J. (2016). *Ang mga kababayen-an sa kabaybayon* (Women of the coast): Life histories of deep-sea women fishers in Governor Generoso, Davao Oriental. *Aghamtao, 25*(1), 45–84.

Patron, M. J. T., Picardal, R. B., Romagos, Y. M., & Oracion, E. G. (2020). *Impacts on fisheries of right fishing*. Aquatic Biodiversity Conservation Learning Augmentation Material for Grade 5 Science. USAID Fish Right Program. Institute of Environmental and Marine Sciences, Silliman University.

Picardal, R. B., Patron, M. J. T., Romagos, Y. M., & Oracion, E. G. (2020). *Mga Kaayohan sa Tawo sa Eksaktong Pagpangisda*. Aquatic Biodiversity Conservation Learning Augmentation Material for Grade 3 Science. USAID Fish Right Program. Institute of Environmental and Marine Sciences, Silliman University.

Pedju, F. M. K. (2017). *Stakeholders' perceptions of the impacts of marine protected areas tourism on the social and ecological system resilience in Bali, Indonesia* [Ph.D. research project]. Auckland University of Technology.

Pomeroy, R. S., Pollnac, R. B., Katon, B. M., & Predo, C. D. (1997). Evaluating factors contributing to the success of community-based coastal resource management: The Central Visayas Regional

Project-1, Philippines. *Ocean & Coastal Management*, *36*(1–3), 97–120. https://doi.org/10.1016/S0964-5691(97)00016-1

Ramos, J. L. (2017). *Primer the fisheries code of the Philippines (RA 8550, as amended by RA 10654)*. Oceana Philippines International.

Rola, A. C., Narvaez, T. A., Naguit, M. R. A., Elazegui, D. D., Brillo, B. B. C., Paunlagui, M. M., Jalotjot, H. C. & Cervantes, C. P. (2018). Impact of the closed fishing season policy for sardines in Zamboanga Peninsula, Philippines. *Marine Policy*, *87*, 40–50. https://doi.org/10.1016/j.marpol.2017.09.029

Romagos, Y. M., Patron, M. J. T., Picardal, R. B., & Oracion, E. G. (2020). *Promoting sustainable fisheries*. Aquatic Biodiversity Conservation Learning Augmentation Material for Grade 11 Science. USAID Fish Right Program. Institute of Environmental and Marine Sciences, Silliman University.

Slater, M. J., Napigkit, F. A., & Stead, S. M. (2012). Resource perception, livelihood choices and fishery exit in a coastal resource management area. *Ocean and Coastal Management*. https://doi.org/10.1016/j.ocecoaman.2012.11.003

Toring, R. J. (2017). The dynamics of fish trade in Cebu City. *Aghamtao*, *25*(2), 231–254.

Turgo, N. N. (2014). Redefining and experiencing masculinity in a Philippine fishing community. *Philippine Sociological Review*, *62*, 7–38.

Turgo, N. N. (2017). "*Amoy isda*": The middle-class life of fishmongers. *Aghamtao*, *25*(2), 201–230.

Ushijima, I., & Zayas, C. N. (1994). *Fishers of the Visayas: Visayas maritime anthropological studies I, 1991–1993*. College of Social Sciences and Philosophy Publications Office and the University of the Philippines Press.

Warner, T. E., & Pomeroy, R. S. (2012). Creating compliance: A cross-sectional study of the factors associated with marine protected area outcomes. *Marine Policy*, *36*, 922–932.

White, A., Deguit, E., & Jatulan, W. (2006). Integrated coastal management in the Philippine local governance: Evolution and benefits. *Coastal Management*, *34*, 287–302. https://doi.org/10.1080/08920750600686687

REPRESENTATIONS OF THE FILIPINO FAMILY

CHAPTER 14

SELF, FAMILY, AND DEMOCRACY: INDIVIDUALISM AND COLLECTIVISM IN TWO CONTEMPORARY FILIPINO FAMILY FILMS

Janus Isaac V. Nolasco

ABSTRACT

Analysis of Philippine society has largely turned on the collectivist/individualist binary. Taking off from this dualism and from the notion and practice of siblingship (Aguilar, 2013). This chapter looks at two contemporary Filipino family films – Kung Ayaw Mo, Huwag Mo! (If You Don't Want, So Be It) and Four Sisters and a Wedding. These films articulate and resolve the tensions, ambivalences, and conflicts between self and family, autonomy and dependence, and individualism and collectivism. This chapter also shows how the collectivism–individualism binary has broader political resonance, touches on the relationship between family and democracy, and proposes the family as a complementary point from which to theorize democracy in the Philippines.

Keywords: Democracy; family; Filipino films; politics; collectivism; individualism

Resilience and Familism: The Dynamic Nature of Families in the Philippines
Contemporary Perspectives in Family Research, Volume 23, 249–265
Copyright © 2023 by Emerald Publishing Limited
All rights of reproduction in any form reserved
ISSN: 1530-3535/doi:10.1108/S1530-353520230000023014

THE FAMILY IN PHILIPPINE SOCIETY

As Article 149 of the Philippine Family Code declares (Executive Order 209, 1987), the family is the "foundation of the nation." Such is its importance that "no custom, practice or agreement destructive of the family shall be recognized or given effect." Eighty percent of businesses in the Philippines are "family owned and controlled" (Go, 2018; cf. Kaelin, 2012, p. 140). Indeed, as a seminal work put it,

> the family ....demands his interest and loyalty more than any other institution in the larger
> society ....It pervades every aspect of his life, be it social, political, religious, or economic.
> Community life is organized around the family. (Medina, 2015, p. 12)

Unsurprisingly, the family figures prominently in Philippine popular culture. From literature to cinema, it is the subject and setting of many a plot, and the background of any narrative, from comedy and romance to drama or action. Regardless of genre, stories on families, especially in mainstream productions, generally affirm the value of the institution. It is easy to take this ubiquity for granted. A concern with family, after all, is not unique to Philippine cinema. Yet, this pervasiveness obscures how the Filipino family film touches on no less than the problem of democracy in the Philippines? Indeed, might not these narratives of arguments and reconciliation between and among family members have a broader political resonance? Although dysfunctional families permeate world literature and cinema, what specific issues does the Filipino family film address?

THE ARGUMENT AND ORGANIZATION

In a Filipino family film, members of a family comprise the main characters – either protagonists or antagonists – and function as such (as a father, brother, son, etc.). Second, their relationships with each other constitute the conflict and its eventual resolution.[1] Analyzing two such movies, *Kung Ayaw Mo, Huwag Mo!* (1998) and *Four Sisters and a Wedding* (2013), this chapter shows that the contemporary Filipino family film articulates and manages the tensions between the demands of the self (autonomy and self-determination) and its obligations to the family (collectivism and siblingship). The genre illustrates how the family stifles its members' identity and/or independence and seeks to accommodate autonomy while preserving and affirming the communalism of the family.[2]

The chapter will discuss the individualism–collectivism binary as a frame for analyzing Philippine society and culture. Next, it projects this dualism as a spectrum along which the two films can be plotted. The chapter then summarizes *Kung Ayaw Mo, Huwag Mo!* and *Four Sisters and a Wedding* and shows how each film illustrates the argument and resonates with broader trends in Philippine society. Concluding the chapter is a meditation on the political valence of the films, particularly the link between family and democracy. Drawing on the feminist critique of liberalism, it suggests the need to think of the family as a complementary starting point to think about, and build, liberal democracy.

INDIVIDUALISM AND COLLECTIVISM IN PHILIPPINE SOCIETY AND FILM

Individualism and collectivism are concepts by which cultures or countries are described in psychology, sociology, and anthropology (e.g., Darwish & Huber, 2010). Filipino psychologists note that

> in individualist cultures, the self is defined as an independent identity. In collectivist cultures, the self is defined in terms of primary ingroups or relationships...such as the family, tribe, work group, or nation .... (Macapagal et al., 2013, p. 31)

The Philippines is said to fall in the latter camp (Hofstede Insights, n.d.).

The individualism-collectivism binary has dovetailed with postwar national-ist sentiment in the Philippines; it is often deemed a dividing line between the West and the East. The former is thought of as individualist, which lamentably intrudes into a more communal indigenous ethic of the latter (de Guia, 2005, p. 366; cf. Enriquez, 1994). This collectivism has also shaped the postwar (self-) image of Philippine society. In the 1970s, for instance, a seminal work in political science alleged the communal nature of the modern postwar state, which is said to be characterized by the *pangulo* regime (from the word, "ulo," meaning "head" and "leader").

> The pangulo regime includes as an integral part of the system the value of organic hierarchy, which prescribes that the pain suffered by the humblest member is also suffered by the entire barangay ....Everyone must share with, care for, or love the others...the pangulo regime is not a mere system .... It is a properly communal pangulo regime. (Agpalo, 1996, p. 200)

Meanwhile, Aguilar (2013) and others have shown how migrant families embody communalism through the notion and practice of siblingship.

> The sibling set is characterized by a persuasive commonality and equality, particularly as idea-tionally they are deemed as sharing the same substance of life in being *magka-dugo*. Indeed, sib-lings share a unique "blood" (*dugo*) that is different from the individual "blood" of the parents, which are "mixed" in the child .... One does not possess siblings; rather, one is an integral part of a sibling group. (Aguilar, 2013, p. 356)

In this arrangement, siblings ought to help and care for one another. Older children defer or sacrifice their own plans for the sake of their younger brothers or sisters, who can and do reciprocate in various ways.

Despite its limitations,[3] the binary between individualism and collectivism can still guide the analysis of two contemporary Filipino family films, *Kung Ayaw Mo, Huwag Mo!* (1998) and *Four Sisters and a Wedding* (2013). For the conflicts they portray are framed precisely in its terms (though the films certainly do not use "individualism" or "collectivism"), and they also portray siblingship in action. The binary doubles as a *spectrum* along which any family movie can be plotted. To what extent does a film lean toward or away from communalism and indi-vidualism, self and family, autonomy and dependence, or perhaps even reject the entire binary? The two films must be seen only as two possible locations on a con-tinuum, with other movies staking different positions therein. Furthermore, both portray the relationships of only what seems to be typical middle-class families.

As such, they should not necessarily be taken as representative across regions (rural areas, for instance) and throughout Philippine history.

Like most concepts, individualism has a rich linguistic, social, and political history (Lukes, 1973), not least its connection to liberal democracy. Aware of this background, and for the purposes of its analysis, this chapter equates individualism with self-determination: the capacity of a person to decide for herself with or without the need for the approval of their, say, parents or siblings. Used interchangeably with autonomy and self-affirmation, it entails the pursuit of one's own desires, plans, and interests. It also refuses to subordinate the self to the communal, collectivist domain of the family, which dictates who people can marry (*Four Sisters and a Wedding*) or whether they can have a boyfriend (*Kung Ayaw Mo, Huwag Mo!*). Collectivism or communalism, by contrast, comes in the form of enforcing or accepting family influence or obligations, as in siblingship.

THE FILMS

Kung Ayaw Mo, Huwag Mo! (Sineneng, 1998) and *Four Sisters and a Wedding* (Garcia-Molina, 2013) are produced by Star Cinema, which started in 1993 and is the "foremost Filipino film production and distribution outfit" (Star Cinema, n.d.). It is "committed to producing family-oriented stories" (ABS-CBN News, 2018). The analysis will focus more on the dialogue, which embodies the problématique best. All quotations in English are my translations from Filipino and are represented by time stamps. Needless to say, this analysis contains spoilers.

Kung Ayaw Mo, Huwag Mo!

Released in February 1998, *Kung Ayaw Mo, Huwag Mo!* features the Cabantog sisters, Doris (Maricel Soriano) and Ditas (Jolina Magdangal). Both their parents are dead, and Doris, the elder, has also become a mother figure for Ditas, a college student. Strict yet loving, Doris forbids Ditas to date until she graduates from university. Ditas, however, eventually, enters a relationship with Nico (Marvin Agustin), a young taxi driver whom Doris had hired earlier to chauffeur Ditas to and from school. The couple keeps their relationship a secret, but Doris discovers it anyway and feels betrayed. The sisters argue, Ditas runs away, but they eventually reconcile.

The tight relationship between the sisters is established in the opening scene. They tease each other and joke around, but Doris forbids Ditas to have a boy-friend until she finishes college. Meant to be taken lightly and comically, this scene signifies their intimacy, but it also establishes the hierarchy in their relationship. The rest of the film sets up how Doris and Ditas meet Nico. Ditas first hates Nico, who apparently has a crush on her. Their relationship develops, and they hide it from Doris. They do want to tell her, but defer doing so, deciding to confess after Ditas' debutante party. Events overtake them, and Doris inadvertently discovers the relationship during the gathering.

The sisters have a dialogue at home. Their exchange showcases the tensions, ambivalences, paradoxes, and equivalences between self and family, autonomy and dependence, self-determination and sacrifice. The dialogue shifts to and from each pole, and at times blurs them altogether. The debate starts off with Doris's lament.

> Is what I've done still not enough? What else haven't I given? Are my sacrifices for you still insufficient? I worked so that I can send you to a good school, so that somehow, you can be equal to your classmates. Even if I was sick, I did not lie down. Even if I was shaking ... I couldn't lie down. There are times when I want to buy something for myself, but what do I do? I just close my eyes. Because I know I have to prioritize your needs. And then this? Tell me, where did I fall short? (Sineneng, 1998, 1:24:36–1:25:50)

Power Dynamics

Doris is invoking the reciprocal nature of siblingship: since she gives, sacrifices, and does so much for her younger sister, she expects obedience, and takes issue with the exercise of one's autonomy, which Ditas defends later on in another round of discussion.

> [...] I just want you to know that we like different things. That even though we're sisters, we're still different. But...for all my life, you're always the one in charge. Even if I do not want it, but if you say so, I follow anyway, right? (1:33:59–1:34:14)

Doris doubles down, however. "Because I know what's right and wrong for you. Because don't you forget, I'm still the one who takes care of you [literally, giving you life]" (1:34:15–1:34:22). This exemplifies the power dynamic between siblings where giving, providing, and self-sacrifice express love but also establish status, hierarchy, and control. Ditas speaks out against it.

> I didn't ask that of you. I also did not ask and want you to spend all your time raising me ... And like you ..., you also did not ask and want your life to be like this .... Thus, I'll forever owe you a debt of gratitude for raising me .... And forever will I also regret that you did not live for yourself because of me. (1:34:26–1:35:08)

Obligations, Sacrifice, and Self-determination

These lines and the next showcase a related tension. On the one hand, Ditas recognizes how obligations militate against independence. On the other hand, she moves away from the language of obligation and recognizes the need for autonomy and self-determination ("living for oneself"). However, Doris replies, "But I wanted that because you're my sister. I love you" (1:35:15–1:35:19). This is an interesting response, for it expresses the former in terms of the latter. The obligation to care for a sibling ceases to be so if it is willingly and lovingly embraced. Conversely, individual agency transforms into a kind of determinism, a sociobiological imperative ("because you're my sister!").

At the same time, if *Kung Ayaw Mo, Huwag Mo!* critiques the obligations, it also affirms them. Ditas commits to her duties in the very act of criticizing them. She may chafe against the imposition, but she also does so precisely because she cares for Doris. Ditas wants her older sister to live a life for herself. In this respect, there is an intimate connection and tension between self-sacrifice and self-determination. Self-sacrifice denies one's autonomy and one's dreams, yet it enables others to be self-determining. Similarly, such autonomy is also aware that

independence is only possible because of a more fundamental dependence, which
Ditas acknowledges.

> [...]you're the one who taught me everything. You're the one who taught me how to stand on
> my own. But you don't want to let me go so I can walk on my own. You're the one who taught
> me how to fight and to be strong. You're also the one who taught me to hide and lie because
> I feared you... I did not really want to hurt you, but I did not know how to tell you the truth.
> (1:35:35–1:36:05)

Thus, while Ditas acknowledges the imbrication of dependence and self-determination, she also recognizes how the dependence that underpins their sisterhood
also damages it. It generates fear and distance, to say nothing of the hierarchy
and inequality, that mark their otherwise intimate relationship.

At this point, Doris still does not see how Ditas is actually affecting a reconciliation between self-determination and family obligation. Doris asks if Ditas
prefers that she, the elder, leave her and Nico alone. Given the chance to do what
she wants, Ditas backtracks and promises to obey her sister, "I can turn my back
on Nico just for you" (1:36:20–1:36:24). Yet, even as she bows down yet again to
a family obligation, Ditas reiterates her autonomy anew while promising to finish
her studies, as Doris wants.

Yet Doris still insists on absolute obedience, at which point, Ditas proceeds to
pack her bags and runs away. This act ultimately signifies a rejection of siblingship
and family obligations. But the film – and Doris herself – cannot countenance a full-
blown separation. The family must be affirmed again and at once. And so the next
sequence – partly composed of flashbacks – sees Doris alone, looking back at the
happy times she had with Ditas. Doris later asks Mike (Doris's boyfriend) whether
she was wrong, and he tells her it's not a mistake to love per se, only if one overdoes it.

This is also a belated recognition and refusal of the power dynamic that gov-
erns siblingship, as well as a gradual accommodation of self-determination within
the communal obligations to the family. Doris and Ditas eventually reconcile,
but there is a deeper reconciliation here. That the sisters are sharing their views
and debating already hints at a shift in their relationship. The film no longer
reveals it, but Doris will presumably allow Ditas to continue her relationship
with Nico. In this happy ending, family obligations no longer mean abandoning
one's autonomy.

Four Sisters and a Wedding

A similar dynamic takes place in *Four Sisters and a Wedding* (henceforth, *Four
Sisters*), which was released in 2013. The film chronicles the relationships within
the Salazar family: the mother, Grace (Connie Reyes), and her four daughters,
Teddie (Toni Gonzaga), Bobbie (Bea Alonso), Alex (Angel Locsin), Gabbi
(Shaina Magdayao), and the youngest, CJ (Enchong Dee).

Three of the sisters have left the nest. Teddie works in Spain, Bobbie in New
York, and Alex is renting an apartment. Only CJ and Gabbi live at home with
their mother. The Salazars are a typical and happy middle-class family, at least at
the start of the film. Much of the drama ensues after CJ announces that he will
be marrying Princess (Angeline Quinto) in a few weeks' time. All of the Salazar

siblings come home to meet their parents, and the four sisters plan to sabotage the wedding. Over the course of the film, the Salazar siblings fight, but everything ends on a happy note.

Clash

Several instances showcase the clash between self and family. First is CJ's relationship with his four sisters who oppose his wedding. At a family dinner, they feel he has not thought about it, and that he is rushing into the marriage. CJ, they add, has known Princess for just four months. Only Alex insists that CJ is old enough to make his own decisions (which CJ reiterates elsewhere). CJ walks out and the sisters apologize, insisting that they are only interfering out of love and concern, and want to make sure he is not doing this on impulse.

Things would be resolved at that point, but the sisters proceed to stop it anyway. But matters come to a head after Teddie seeks to expose the Bayags' spa and massage business, which she thinks is a cover for prostitution services. But the business is wholesome, and Teddie is caught in the act by Princess' mother, Jeanette (Carmi Martin), whose husband (Boboy Garrovillo) threatens (but does not push through) legal action. Back home, this leads to another angry confrontation between CJ and his sisters. Yet again, he rages against their meddling, and Teddie and the others only insist that they, as their elder siblings are protecting him, the youngest, out of love. Taking offense at his anger, they say that he ought to consider their concern and respect their seniority before he raises his voice. Yet CJ fights back, insisting on his independence.

The most emblematic of the tension between self and siblingship is the relationship between Bobbie and Alex. Bobbie had a boyfriend, Chad, who proposed to marry her. Their relationship falls apart, and Chad later courts Alex, and they become a couple six months after he and Bobbie broke up. Bobbie feels that Alex is the reason that Bobbie and Chad are separated. Alex counters that they had already done so when she, Alex, came into the picture and that they broke up only because Bobbie left for the United States. Defending herself, Bobbie says "that was for our future" (1:21:35–1:21:37), to which Alex responds that Bobbie was just really ambitious and career-driven. Their argument circles back to Chad. Alex argues that she did inform Bobbie that Chad was putting the moves on her and that she had asked for Bobbie's blessing. And though Bobbie said yes, she insists that Alex should have "read between the lines" (1:22:02–1:22:03) and should not have pursued the relationship. "If you [Alex] had any amount of decency in your body, you would not have asked in the first place" (1:22:06–1:22:09). Bobbie was only asking for "responsibility and respect for our relationship as sisters" (1:22:30–1:22:33).

Alex says she did try to resist Chad's advances out of respect for Bobbie. Alex knew that she'd hurt her sister for entertaining Chad, but Alex did so because it "felt so good if someone appreciates you"(1:48:18–1:48:21) and because she had lost her "best friend," Bobbie, who "understood" and "accepted"(1:48:35–1:48:43) her for who she was. Alex adds that she was hurt when Bobbie got angry at her, because she, Alex, felt that "she had no right to be happy" (1:48:58–1:49:00), and that "I had no right to be loved because Chad was my sister's ex" (1:48:58). Here, siblingship takes precedence over and clashes with, one's "right to be happy." And the tension weighs heavily on Alex. She later apologizes to Bobbie, acknowledging that pursuing her own happiness hurt the latter.

Compatibility
The concern for the self and the demands of siblingship in Alex's case are not simply opposites, however. Seeking one's happiness at the expense of a sister arises only precisely because of her absence, as Alex shares. Self-concern seems to arise strongly only when sibling relations and mutual support have disappeared. There would have been no problem had Bobbie not left for New York (the impact of migration). At the same time, Bobbie's case also shows the compatibility between self and family. On the one hand, she is the epitome of the self-made individual. She is confident and speaks her mind, unlike many Filipinos who find it hard to say what they mean, and who equate being straightforward with arrogance. Bobbie knows that's how she comes across. Embodying the individualist ethos, she tells Alex "not to give comments about my personal life because I don't give comments about yours" (1:04:22–1:04:26). The line establishes their identities as separate individuals, which is anathema to the demands of siblingship. It is no coincidence that the film has her working in an ultra-individualist society, the United States.

On the other hand, Bobbie's drive to succeed and pursue her career turns out to have been motivated by the financial needs of the family: school, migration fees, hospital expenses, and the like. Also, Bobbie tells us she simply learned to be tough and independent because she was not a favored child by her mom or dad. For her toughness and assertiveness, she apologizes and confesses.

> Maybe that's what I really am. Because I chose to be that way. I needed to be that way. Especially when I went to New York .... Maybe my career is important to me, but I know I did not do that just for myself.... Even though I wanted to go home so badly, because it was so lonely, so difficult to be alone, and I missed all of you so much. But I stuck it out. I steeled myself. I toughened up because I needed to. But that I am tough does not mean I have no feelings anymore. (1:42:05–1:43:36)

As with Alex, the implication is that self-determination seems to arise and resonate only in the absence of family. At any rate, the passage also shows the limitations and vulnerability of the self-made individual and illustrates the link between and among siblingship, sacrifice, and self-determination. Bobbie's "sacrifice" – going to New York – enabled her siblings to pursue their own careers/plans.

Balancing Act
Four Sisters affirms and critiques both individualism and collectivism, siblingship and self-determination. This balancing act is evident in several ways. First, the film shows Grace longing for the time when her children were happy and were getting along, an idyll that has been damaged by self-determination. A conflict between siblings arises precisely because one sister, Alex, placed her interests

above that of her sibling (Bobbie), or one's older sisters oppose one's decision to get married. Indeed, the househelp (Vangie Labalan) attributes the conflicts to their having "their own beliefs, opinions, and principles" (1:17:02–1:17:08).

However, individualism is not solely to blame. The conflicts also have to do with family obligations, since they justify meddling and impede the pursuit of individual happiness (CJ and Alex) and weigh someone down (Teddie as a failure and her fear of disappointing her mother). Faced with this conflict between autonomy and family, the househelp tells Grace that despite having their own beliefs and opinions, they are nevertheless bound by their ties as sisters. "But if you are worrying they might drift apart, that won't happen because their lives are connected, connected by your love for them" (1:17:09–1:17:18).

In *Four Sisters*, siblingship eventually prevails and entails a recognition and acceptance of each one's autonomy, including their respective grievances. In this regard, the three poignant cases involve Teddie and her mother, Alex and Bobbie, and Bobbie and her mother. Teddie confesses her predicament (she was a failure in Spain), which her mother and a few of her siblings do not know of, and feels a sense of liberation and acceptance afterward. Next, after Bobbie tells her mother how she struggled with her mother's favoritism, Grace says, "I'm sorry... I didn't know you felt that way" (1:43:50–1:43:52), and seems surprised when she learns that she apparently favored CJ and Teddie (but she does explain her favoritism). Lastly, Bobbie tells Alex that she, Bobbie, was so focused on her own hurt that it blinded her to Alex's pain.

THE SOCIAL CONTEXT OF THE CONTEMPORARY FILIPINO FAMILY FILM[4]

In articulating and reconciling the tensions between self and siblingship, between family obligations and individual autonomy, *Four Sisters* and *Kung Ayaw Mo, Huwag Mo!* register certain trends in Philippine society, from shifting demographics to the expression of individualism. This is not to say that the Filipino family changed only recently, or that Filipino family films began to showcase individualism, or chafed against the family, only from the late 1990s.[5] It is only to argue that these films resonate in the context of these developments, regardless of the latter's historicity.[6]

Changing Demographics

Morillo and Capuno (2013, p. 7, note 25) speak of "evolving family values away from traditional ones" as well as "shifting family structures and dynamics." These include adolescents "growing up in households with one parent ... and another quarter with neither parent" (Alampay, 2014, p. 118); commuter marriages, where couples live apart (Gregorio, 2020); "family nuclearization" at the expense of "extended family coresidence" (Chen et al., 2016, p. 2), which is partly indicated by the decrease in household size, from 4.6 in 2010 to 4.1 in 2020 (PSA, 2022); increasing rates of "divorce, separation and cohabitation" (Abalos, 2017). In the Philippines and Thailand, "between 20–40% of women of women 20–24 years old and more than 10% of men 25–29 years old are cohabiting" (Jeung, 2022, p. 12).

Migration has also affected and created new, family dynamics. Many Filipino children grow up sans either or both parents, with damaging social (Jimenez, 2019) and psychological costs (Arellano-Carandang et al., 2007; Garcia, 2012; Parreñas, 2006), a reality to which Filipinos are nevertheless adjusting (Asis, 1994, 2006) via communication technologies (Acedera & Yeoh, 2022). Alarms over these and other changes have been sounded. "Labor migration," a lawyer remarked, "destroys the Filipino nation ..." (Jimenez, 2019). Few academic studies examine this panic, but there seems to be a general sense that traditional family ties are being eroded and need to be renewed (Pangilinan, 2018). Writing about "the evolving Filipino value system," a psychiatrist notes with relief that "it was indeed heartening to learn that majority of these families still possess the core Filipino family values." She then insists that "these values need ... to be nurtured by the family and its social environment" (Halili-Jao, 2018). Indeed, a noted psychologist does acknowledge the changing demographics, but says that the jury is still out on their impact on "family roles and dynamics" (Alampay, 2014, p. 118).

Individualism

The trends that the two films reflect most clearly are the discourse on autonomy and the acknowledgment of the darker side of family obligations. This individualism is reinforced partly by migration, which "open[s] up possibilities for children's agency and independence" (Asis, 2006, p. 45). But a clearer sign of this self-determination lies in recent affirmations of the self. Few scholarly studies or statistics explicitly account for, or even measure, this phenomenon, but its expressions are readily evident in the following: a new generation of romance films (Nolasco, 2021); the growth of "new media" that "generates a sense of individualism" (Pertierra, 2012, p. 33); celebrations of singlehood (Reyes, 2020; Trinidad, 2021), which partly dovetails with the growth of the single population in the Philippines (PSA, 2020); and the rise of "adulting" (Estrada, 2016) and "living solo," which in turn has been enabled, or at least capitalized on, by a real estate boom (Brittany, n.d.). There also have been affirmations of the self in the context of romantic relationships (Manarang, 2019) and in the growing phenomenon of self-care.

Toxic Families

Though the family remains highly valued in Philippine society, a discourse on "toxic Filipino culture" has emerged online, much of which pertains to family life and involves suppressing any hint of autonomy. This notion of toxicity somewhat resembles the concept of "poisonous parenting" (Dunham & Dermer, 2011), but however it is called, scholarly attention on the topic has been relatively sparse, if nonexistent in the Philippine context. Yet, the discourse of family toxicity is undeniably real. The problem seems to be pervasive enough to have its own page in Reddit Philippines (Reddit, n.d.), where members share applicable experiences. Elsewhere, a millennial has complained that:

The hierarchical structures of our families also make our relationships feel a lot less democratic. It is considered rebellion to speak up and voice an opinion toward an elder; submission to patriarchs is an expectation. (Baylosis, 2019)

Echoing the sentiment, a freelance writer (Pieraz, 2020) has also bemoaned the five "toxic expectations of the Filipino family."

There is a love/hate relationship we all have with our families. We've all experienced the struggle of doing and saying what we know is expected from us versus what we personally feel we should do or say....I have kept my mouth shut in conversations with family members just because it is someone older on the opposing opinion. I have helped out more than I wanted just because it's "for family."

This kind of toxicity does not appear in *Kung Ayaw Mo, Huwag Mo!* and *Four Sisters*, but it is somewhat evident in the relationship between Doris and Ditas, and between CJ and her older siblings.

Indeed, both films do not fully reflect each of these social trends, but they do betray an awareness and anxiety that family life has changed, if not broken down, and that certain adjustments need to be made. In *Four Sisters*, Grace longs for the good old days.

I'm just sad.... I was hoping that when they came home, they'd get along well again, just as they did when they were kids. I wish they stayed as children, huh? So that there will only be laughter. They may fight, but make up soon enough. (1:16:29–1:16:54)

Furthermore, migration changed, and was shaped by, the dynamics of the Salazar family; it affirmed and damaged the ties among the siblings and their parents, leading to conflict and tension. Bobbie had to migrate to help her family and also learned to be independent in the process, and her absence partly led to an estrangement with Alex, who said that her departure for the United States deprived her, Alex, of sisterly support. Similarly, in *Kung Ayaw Mo, Huwag Mo!*, Doris has dinner with her boyfriend, Mike, after Doris runs away. Mike tells Doris that Ditas is all grown up and that "You [Doris] can no longer stop what your sister is feeling" (1:28:55–1:28:58). The autonomy of the individual must be accounted for.

PHILIPPINE DEMOCRACY VIA THE FAMILY

Though it's more pronounced in the latter, *Kung Ayaw Mo, Huwag Mo!* and *Four Sisters* project the family as a communal space that reconciles autonomy and obligations to kin. What can be construed as typical drama – siblings argue, fight, and shout – can be seen as agonistic deliberation.[7] This is not to say that all sibling conflict has a utopian, democratic dimension. But in the films, the family comes together; each member airs grievances, shares regrets and intentions, and admits failings. They speak up, and are heard, eliciting forgiveness, empathy, mutual respect, and understanding. Each one opens up to, and accounts for, the other. Reckoning with another self, the siblings develop fellow-feeling and renew a sense of togetherness. This can certainly be read as a typical family reconciliation and the affirmation of interdependence, but it also dramatizes a key democratic value: the recognition of different points of view. In this respect, the much-vaunted Filipino "shared sense of self" carries a democratic, deliberative potential.

It is easy to dismiss the foregoing since in theory, individualism and collectivism need not clash. After all, our growth as individuals depends on our dependence on, and relationships with, others (Enriquez, 1994; Grimshaw, 1986, p. 170; Jordan, 2011). But for *Kung Ayaw Mo, Huwag Mo!* and *Four Sisters*, this compatibility is not a given. The characters in both films have to struggle – plenty of tears, shouting matches – for that modus vivendi. And then no explicit or triumphant individualist ethos emerges from the films. It is something to beg and apologize for. Ditas pleads with Doris, and Alex has to apologize for asserting her own happiness over Bobbie, who likewise has to rationalize her pursuit of a career over her family.

That this is the case already hints at the precarious status of, and the narrow space for, democratic values in the Philippines. Whatever else their faults, *Four Sisters* and *Kung Ayaw Mo, Huwag Mo!*, if not the contemporary family film itself, betray a political sensibility. They seek a space for, and address the lack of, democratic values in a collectivist, family-oriented society. In so doing, the two films offer a springboard with which one can reconsider the relationship between the family and democratization.

An agent of socialization, the family is an arena where (political) values are formed and contested. "Filipino parents hold predominantly traditional and authoritarian childrearing attitudes" (Alampay & Jocson, 2011, p. 3), which are informed by the "expectations that children obey adult authority and submit to parental directives … that are consistent with the prevailing, well-entranced sociocultural values of respect and obedience towards elders" (p. 7). Furthermore, "disiplina, or discipline, is a dominant theme of Filipino childrearing" (Alampay, 2014, p. 111).[8] Thus, when pro-government Filipinos tell critics of the state's pandemic response to "sumunod ka na lang" (Just obey), or when the state invokes "discipline" in enforcing the law, one detects a resonance of family matters in public policy.

The family undeniably shapes the Filipinos' political imaginary. President Ferdinand Marcos Sr. saw himself and his wife, First Lady Imelda Marcos, as the father and mother, respectively, of the nation (Adel, 2017). Scholars speak of "kinship politics" (Roces, 2011) or "an anarchy of families" (McCoy, 1993). President Duterte was called "Tatay (Father) Digong," while more recently, Vice Presidential candidate Leni Robredo came to be known as "Mama (Mother) Leni." The entanglement of the family in politics is not just a matter of invoking the institution in, say, rhetoric. Nor is it just a case of state policy on, among other things, family planning. Rather, this pertains to the family as a literal terrain of political life. Its ubiquity resonates with the novels of Jane Austen, which "concern the social history of the landed gentry. Jane Austen did not write about the family rather than society; on the country, the family in her day was society" (Eagleton, 2004, p. 115).

Similarly, in the Philippines, "the values governing familial life are extended and modified as applied to the wider society" (Kaelin, 2012, p. 139). Thus, to explore the family is to grapple with politics in its broader sense (e.g., not just limited to the state), as much feminist work has shown. More specifically, to dramatize the demands of the self and its tensions with family – as *Four Sisters* and *Kung Ayaw Mo, Huwag Mo!* do – is to touch on the status of liberal democratic values (self-determination and autonomy) in a collectivist society. It also invokes the debate on the relationship between liberalism/individualism and collectivism/communitarianism (cf. Eagleton, 1998, p. 298ff; Eichner, 2010; Eliot, 1910; Held, 1993, pp. 160–191; Pennock, 1979, pp. 59–120).

Given the family's centrality, it is strangely absent in the theorizing and building Philippine democracy. This is perfectly understandable. The family has a bad rap in political theorizing: it serves to reproduce state power (Ferguson, 2012, p. 7; Lewis, 2022, p. 7). In the Philippines, it is the source of political dynasties. It exemplifies a particularistic politics that needs to be transcended in the name of, say, the nation or the common good (Rappler, 2022). The family has also been generally associated with authoritarianism (Cooper, 2017; Koganzon, 2021), not least in the propaganda of President Ferdinand Marcos Sr. (Crisol, n.d. cited in McCoy, 1993, p. 16).

Without discounting these associations, ignoring the family in democratic theorizing overlooks a key insight of feminist political thought. Thinking about Philippine democracy must recognize that citizens are not (just) atomized individuals with rights who then relate to the state. They are also citizens embedded in social relations, not least of them ties among kin. This perspective exemplifies a feminist corrective to liberalism, which obscures the dependence of the liberal democratic subject – often the male breadwinner – on the family from which he obtains "care and replenishment" (Held, 1993, p. 163). Accordingly, paying attention to the family returns political theorizing to its proper starting point. "[I]t is clear that the family, and not the adult individual, is the basic political unit of liberal as of non-liberal philosophers" (Okin, 1979, p. 282 cited in Held, 1993, p. 163).

Even so, it is not clear how exactly the family can help build a democratic society. But complex though its links are to larger political institutions, this attention to the family is animated by hope. The connection is not iron-clad, but the literature does suggest that families can be a "space in which children can become committed to the democratic process … and learn how to speak and listen in a deliberative matter" (Gastil, 2014, p. 147). Citing empirical studies like Chaffee, Jack, and Wackman (1973), Gastil (2014, p. 148) adds that "children from families with the more deliberative orientation developed higher levels of political knowledge and involvement; a deliberative child is more likely to become a deliberative adult." After all, "a democratic workplace, a democratic university, and a democratic university are as much part of a democratic society as is a democratic state" (Wright, 2019, p. 16).[9] One could add democratic families to the list. Indeed, can a society be democratic if families are bastions of authoritarian parenting? Can we preach democratic values in the "public" sphere while perpetuating authoritarian, non-participatory practices at home, school, or at work?

Certainly, the family is no magic bullet for democracy, but given its pervasiveness in the Philippines, it's reasonable to argue that democratization cannot proceed without somehow taking the family into account. Answering if, how, and to what extent democratic families contribute to democratization in the Philippines simply reckons with the "facts on the ground."

But much needs to be addressed and accounted for, including the politically negative role and reputation of the family (see above). In the meantime, a starting point is to ground gender quality at home (Gornick & Meyers, 2009), and to look at Filipino family dynamics anew (e.g., Aguilar, 2009; Cruz, 2019; Kibiten, 2016) and consider their implications for democratization (or otherwise). Conversely, the family – as examined in Philippine sociology, psychology, and anthropology – should now be taken up in political science beyond questions of political dynasties. Indeed, there is a need to untangle the "undertheorized and underresearched" (Ginsborg, 2013, p. 17) relationship among the family, civil society, and the state. This chapter has teased out the matter somewhat, but Kaelin (2012) has already taken much larger steps in this direction.

CONCLUSION

Using the individualist–collectivist binary and Aguilar's (2013) notion of siblingship, this chapter has analyzed two Filipino family films, *Kung Ayaw Mo, Huwag Mo!* and *Four Sisters and a Wedding*. It argues how both films articulate and manage the tensions between self and family, autonomy and dependence, and individualism and collectivism. This tension resonates within the changing dynamics of the Filipino family, and with the contemporary discourse of individualism. In showing the political valence of films, the chapter proposes the family as a complementary starting point for theorizing and practicing democracy in the Philippines.

NOTES

1. This is my own working definition. It seeks to specify how the genre differs from others which also feature the family.
2. Nolasco (2021) has a similar problematique.
3. Zialcita (1999) has examined the merits of the individualist–collectivist binary, as do Voronov and Singer (2002).
4. This section draws on Nolasco (2021, pp. 175–176).
5. As Cooper (2017, p. 7) notes, "The history of the family is one of perpetual crisis."
6. It would be interesting to compare the two films analyzed here with earlier portrayals of the Filipino family.
7. Filipinos do not readily air their views, and generally avoid confrontations. Thus, tensions and resentments are suppressed, and left to fester. Perhaps this helps explains why many Filipino family films (or TV shows) place so much premium on dramatic confrontations, where the characters let it all out.
8. This does not mean that Filipino families are all militaristic, authoritarian spaces with no room for emotional warmth and support. For an overview of the literature on Filipino parenting, see Ochoa and Torre (2014).
9. Attending to the family by no means abandons prodemocracy civil society movements, or eschewing the need for, say, institutional reforms.

REFERENCES

Abalos, J. B. (2017, July 10). The rise of divorce, separation, and cohabitation in the Philippines. *N-IUSSP*. https://www.niussp.org/family-and-households/the-rise-of-divorce-separation-and-cohabitation-in-the-philippines/

ABS-CBN News. (2018, June 13). *Growing family: ABS-CBN Films no longer just Star Cinema*. ABS-CBN News. https://news.abs-cbn.com/entertainment/06/13/18/growing-family-abs-cbn-films-no-longer-just-star-cinema

Acedera, K. F., & Yeoh, B. S. A. (2022). The intimate lives of left-behind young adults in the Philippines: Social media, gendered intimacies, and transnational parenting. *Journal of Immigrant & Refugee Studies, 20*(2), 206–219. https://doi.org/10.1080/15562948.2022.2044572

Adel, R. (2017). *Malakas and maganda: The art of deception.* PhilStar Global. https://newslab.philstar.com/31-years-of-amnesia/malakas-at-maganda

Agpalo, R. E. (1996). *Adventures in political science.* University of the Philippines Press.

Aguilar, F., Jr. (2009). *Maalwang buhay: Family, overseas migration, and cultures of relatedness in Barangay Paraiso.* Ateneo de Manila University Press.

Aguilar, F., Jr. (2013). Brother's keeper? Siblingship, overseas migration, and centripetal ethnography in a Philippine village. *Ethnography, 14*(3), 346–368. https://doi.org/10.1177/1466138113491674

Alampay, L. P. (2014). Parenting in the Philippines. In H. Selin (Ed.), *Parenting across cultures: Childrearing, motherhood and fatherhood in non-western cultures* (pp. 05–21). Springer.

Alampay, L. P., & Jocson, R. M. (2011). Attributions and attitudes of mothers and fathers in the Philippines. *Parenting Science and Practise, 11*(2–3), 163–176. https://doi.org/10.1080%2F15295192.2011.585564

Arellano-Carandang, M. L. G., Sison, B. A., & Carandang, C. (2007). *Nawala ang Ilaw ng Tahanan [The light of the home is gone]: Case studies of families left behind by OFW mothers.* Anvil Publishing.

Asis, M. M. B. (1994). Family ties in a world without borders. *Philippine Sociological Review, 42*(1–4, January–December), 16–26. https://www.jstor.org/stable/41853660

Asis, M. M. B. (2006). Living with migration: Experiences of left-behind children in the Philippines. *Asian Population Studies, 2*(1), 45–67. https://doi.org/10.1080/17441730600700556

Baylosis, M. (2019, August 23). Toxic Filipino culture? *Inquirer.* https://opinion.inquirer.net/123484/toxic-filipino-culture

Brittany. (n.d.) *Why living solo is on the rise for young adults.* https://www.brittany.com.ph/blogs/why-living-solo-is-on-the-rise-for-young-adults/

Chaffee, S., Jack, M., & Wackman, D. B. (1973). Family communication patterns and adolescent political participation. In J. Dennis (Ed.), *Socialization to politics: A reader* (pp. 349–364). John Wiley and Sons.

Chen, F., Bao, L., Shattuck, R. M., Borja, J. B., & Guiltiano, S. (2016). Implications of changes in family structure and composition for the psychological well-being of Filipina women in middle and later years. *Research on Aging, 39*(2), 275–299. https://doi.org/10.1177%2F0164027515611181

Cooper, M. (2017). *Family values: Between neoliberalism and the new social conservatism.* Zone Books.

Crisol, J. (n.d). *Towards the restructuring of Filipino values.* Office of Civil Relations, Philippine Army.

Cruz, R. (2019). An inheritance that cannot be stolen: schooling, kinship, and personhood in post-1945 central Philippines. *Comparative Studies in Society and History, 61*(4), 894–924. https://doi.org/10.1017/S0010417519000240

Darwish, A.-F. E., & Huber, G. L. (2010). Individualism vs collectivism in different cultures: A cross-cultural study. *Intercultural Education, 14*(1), 47–56. https://doi.org/10.1080/1467598032000044647

de Guia, K. (2005). *The self in the other: Worldviews and lifestyles of Filipino culture-bearers.* Anvil Publishing.

Dunham, S. M., & Dermer, S. B. (2011). Poisonous parenting. In S. M. Dunham, S. B. Dermer, & J. Carlson (Eds.), *Poisonous parenting: Toxic relationships between parents and their adult children* (pp. 1–24). Routledge.

Eagleton, T. (1998) [1994]. The right and the good: Postmodernism and the liberal state. In S. Regan (Ed.), *The Eagleton reader* (pp. 294–303). Blackwell Publishers, Inc.

Eagleton, T. (2004). *The English novel: An introduction.* Blackwell Publishing.

Eichner, M. (2010). *The supportive state: Families, government, and America's political ideals.* Oxford University Press.

Eliot, C. W. (1910). *The conflict between individualism and collectivism in a democracy.* Charles Scribner's Sons.

Enriquez, V. G. (1994). *From colonial to liberation psychology: The Philippine experience.* De La Salle University Press.

Estrada, O. (2016, January 13). *8 things to remember when living alone for the first time.* Preen.ph. https://preen.ph/21132/8-things-to-remember-when-living-alone-for-the-first-time.

Executive Order 209. (1987, July 6). The family code of the Philippines. https://www.chanrobles.com/executiveorderno209.htm#.Y1Ec8PxBy3B

Ferguson, K. (2012). *All in the family: on community and incommensurability*. Duke University Press.

Garcia, F. A. (2012). *Pamilya, Migrasyon, Disintegrasyon*. C&E Publishing.

Garcia-Molina, C. (Director). (2013). *Four sisters and a wedding* [Film]. Star Cinema. https://www.youtube.com/watch?v=rVkg-3Pifig&t=4579s

Gastil, J. (2014). *Democracy in small groups: Participation, decision-making, & communication* (2nd ed.). New Society Publishers.

Ginsborg, P. (2013). Uncharted territories: Individuals, families, civil society and the democratic state. In J. Nautz, P. Ginsborg, & T. Nijhuis (Eds.), *The golden chain: Family, civil society, and the state* (pp. 17–42). Berghahn Books.

Go, V. J. (2018, July 24). Most businesses are family business. *The FreeMan*. https://www.philstar.com/the-freeman/cebu-business/2018/07/24/1836287/most-businesses-are-family-business.

Gornick, J., & Meyers, M. (2009). *Gender equality: Transforming family divisions of labor*. Verso.

Gregorio, V. L. (2020). Isolation and immunity within the family: Commuter marriages in Southeast Asia. *Current Sociology, 70*(2), 703–719. https://doi.org/10.1177/0011392120972143

Grimshaw, J. (1986). *Philosophy and feminist thinking*. University of Minnesota Press.

Halili-Jao, N. (2018, July 29). *The evolving Filipino value system*. PhilStar Global. https://www.philstar.com/lifestyle/allure/2018/07/29/1837596/evolving-filipino-family-value-system

Held, V. (1993). *Feminist morality: Transforming culture, society, and politics*. University of Chicago Press.

Hofstede Insights. (n.d.). *Philippines*. https://www.hofstede-insights.com/country/the-philippines/#:~:text=In%20Individualist%20societies%20people%20are,and%20their%20direct%20family%20only.&text=The%20Philippines%2C%20with%20a%20score,extended%20family%2C%20or%20extended%20relationships.

Jeung, W.-J. J. (2022). *Demographic and family transition in Southeast Asia*. Springer.

Jimenez, J. B. (2019, September 3). *How labor migration destroys the Filipino family*. PhilStar. https://www.philstar.com/the-freeman/opinion/2019/09/03/1948504/how-labor-migration-destroys-filipino-family.

Jordan, J. (2011). Disconnection and parenting: A relational-cultural perspective. In S. M. Dunham, S. B. Dermer, & J. Carlson (Eds.), *Poisonous parenting: Toxic relationships between parents and their adult children* (pp. 145–162). Routledge.

Kaelin, L. (2012). *Strong family, weak state: Hegel's political philosophy and the Filipino family*. Ateneo de Manila University Press.

Kibiten, G. P. (2016). *The politics of clan reunions: Ritual, kinship, and cultural transformation among Kankanaeys of Northern Luzon*. Ateneo de Manila University Press.

Koganzon, R. (2021). *Liberal states, authoritarian families: Childhood and education in early modern thought*. Oxford University Press.

Lewis, S. (2022). *Abolish the family: A manifesto for care and liberation*. Verso.

Lukes, S. (1973). *Individualism*. Basil Blackwell.

Macapagal, M., Elizabeth, J., Ofreneo, M. A., Montiel, C. J., & Nolasco, J. M. (2013). *Social psychology in the Philippine context*. Ateneo de Manila Press.

Manarang, E. (2019, March 12). *Sa Ngayon, Ako Muna*. BoilingWaters.ph. https://boilingwaters.ph/sa-ngayon-ako-muna/

McCoy, A. (Ed.). (1993). *An anarchy of families: State and family in the Philippines*. Ateneo de Manila University Press.

Medina, B. T. G. (2015). *The Filipino family* (3rd ed.). University of the Philippines Press.

Morillo, H., & Capuno, J. J. (2013). Views and values on family among Filipino: An empirical exploration. *Asian Journal of Social Science, 41*, 5–28. https://doi.org/10.1163/15685314-12341278

Nolasco, J. I. (2021). Hello, love, liberal democracy: The politics of the contemporary Filipino romance film. *Pelikula: A Journal of Philippine Cinema, 6*, 169–180. https://58686479-5e42-4048-b1f7-e91523ee7fbc.filesusr.com/ugd/e760e1_f7948d3e3bfb4429a47f4ab7dec1f979.pdf

Ochoa, D. P., & Torre, B. A. (2014). Parenting research in the Philippines: a review of the literature from 2004–2014. Pambansang Samahan ng Sikolohiyang Pilipino and the Philippine Educational Theater Association.

Okin, S. M. (1979). *Women in western political thought*. Princeton University Press.

Pangilinan, E. S. (2018, October 7). Reviving the fading Filipino values. *Sunstar Pampanga*. https://www.pressreader.com/philippines/sunstar-pampanga/20181007/281706910630025

Parreñas, R. S. (2006). *Children of global migration: Transnational families and gendered woes*. Ateneo de Manila University.

Pertierra, R. (2012). *The new media, society, and politics in the Philippines*. fesmedia Asia. https://library.fes.de/pdf-files/bueros/asia-media/09241.pdf

PSA (Philippine Statistics Authority). (2020). *Single population in the Philippines (results from the 2015 Census of Population)*. https://psa.gov.ph/content/single-population-philippines-results-2015-census-population.

PSA (Philippine Statistics Authority). (2022). *Household population, number of households, and average household size of the Philippines (2020 Census of Population and Housing)*. https://psa.gov.ph/population-and-housing/node/166426

Pennock, J. R. (1979). *Democratic political theory*. Princeton University Press.

Pieraz, A. (2020, December 11). The toxic expectations of the Filipino family. *Wonder*. https://wonder.ph/life/toxic-expectations-of-the-filipino-family/

Rappler. (2022, March 28). *Hindi family business ang demokrasya natin [Our democracy is not a family business]* [EDITORIAL]. Rappler. https://www.rappler.com/voices/editorials/philippine-democracy-political-dynasties-not-family-business/

Reddit. (n.d.). *TOXIC Filipino family culture*. Reddit. https://www.reddit.com/r/Philippines/comments/j1sdsx/toxic_filipino_family_culture/

Reyes, T. (2020, February 14). These Filipino women have never had boyfriends and they couldn't be happier. *Vice*. https://www.vice.com/en/article/5dmy7z/single-filipino-women-no-boyfriend-since-birth-nbsb.

Roces, M. (2001). *Kinship politics in postwar Philippines: The Lopez family, 1946–2000*. De La Salle University Press.

Sineneng, J. L. (Director). (1998). *Kung Ayaw Mo, Huwag Mo!* [Film]. StarCinema. Digitally restored version.

Star Cinema. (n.d.) *About*. https://starcinema.abs-cbn.com/about

Trinidad, B. (2021, September 5). The perks of being single. *L!fe: The Philippine Star*. https://philstarlife.com/self/591330-perks-single

Voronov, M., & Singer, J. A. (2002). The myth of individualism-collectivism: A critical review. *The Journal of Social Psychology, 142*(4), 461–480. https://doi.org/10.1080/00224540209603912

Wright, E. O. (2019). *How to be anti-capitalist in the twenty-first century*. Verso Books.

Zialcita, F. (1999). Is communitarianism uniquely Asian? A Filipino's perspective. *Sojourn: Journal of Social Issues in Southeast Asia, 14*(2), 313–331. https://www.jstor.org/stable/41056999

CHAPTER 15

TUNAY NA LALAKI/TRUE MANHOOD IN THE PHILIPPINES: HISTORICAL DEVELOPMENT, IDENTITY FORMATIONS, AND FAMILY CONTEXTS

A. M. Leal Rodriguez

ABSTRACT

The rise of "strong man" politics in the Philippines brings attention to manhood narratives. Machismo remains a strong presence in the upper echelons of society, despite gender equality initiatives and a strong feminist movement. With Rodrigo Duterte portraying the "father-figure" of the nation, one questions what this type of manhood means for the Filipino family.

This study traces the construction of Filipino manhood in relation to the country's strongest unit of the family. Utilizing a systematic review of seminal outputs on masculinity, this piece explores the definition of Filipino manhood using texts from various Filipino gender and development scholars. Sikolohiyang Pilipino or Indigenous Filipino Psychology frames the identified themes that surround the image of a Tunay na Lalaki *or True Man. The* labas *(outer world) and* loob *(inner self) are then framed in relation to Filipino men's roles. Intersections between one's peer group, socio-economic class, and the situation in the global migration context inform the formation of one's labas (outer self/ identity). The findings indicate that Filipino manhood traits, as seen in one's* loob *(inner self) contextualize one's understanding of manhood's construction*

Resilience and Familism: The Dynamic Nature of Families in the Philippines
Contemporary Perspectives in Family Research, Volume 23, 267–284
Copyright © 2023 by Emerald Publishing Limited
All rights of reproduction in any form reserved
ISSN: 1530-3535/doi:10.1108/S1530-353520230000023015

as familial. By unearthing the nuances of manhood in the archipelago, this chapter showcases masculinities from the subaltern and purports possible ways of decolonizing "from below."

Keywords: Filipino; masculinity; family; brotherhood; fatherhood

ANG *TUNAY NA LALAKI* – THE TRUE MAN: AN INTRODUCTION

The complicated colonial history of the Philippines makes it easy to assume the Filipino identity is *pinagtagpi-tagpi* – a patchwork of different colonial and indigenous values. The country survived 400 years of colonization under the Spanish, Americans, and Japanese. Despite the European and American domination of the Philippines' culture, language, and tradition, Filipinos are more "Asian in consciousness and aspiration" (Cullinane et al., 2020) sharing values such as strong family ties with their South-East Asian neighbors while "Filipinizing" traits from the colonizers' cultures (Abinales & Amoroso, 2005).

The Philippines does not have a single, monolithic culture with a centuries-old history (Tiongson, 1983, p. 83), but a collection of values that creates a diverse nation with differing cultures and interests. Values from the country's colonizers intertwine with pre-Philippine or supposedly *indigenous* Filipino values, creating contradictions in Philippine identity. The lack of a unified culture means there is no one uncontested archetype of Filipino masculinity. I posit that the Filipino identity is more like a *banig* – a woven mat. Rather than quilting scraps, the *banig* is created by folding strips of dyed and treated rattan or palm leaves into a complex geometrical pattern. Traditional *banigs* use few colors, yet there are endless possibilities for the patterns created. Indigenous groups in the Philippines make the *banig*, but it is more strongly associated with one's socio-economic class: the *banig* is placed on the floor and used as a place to sleep or eat. One can extend this image when understanding the rich tapestry of Filipino masculinity – different threads which represent different values or ideas plaited to form the *Tunay na Lalaki* or "True Man" idea in the Archipelago. Given the slipperiness of Filipino masculinity's definition, the *Tunay na Lalaki* or "True Manhood" serves as a core ideal for Filipino manhood. The older generation saw true men as emotionally strong and independent (Aguiling-Dalisay et al., 2000), the leaders and patriarchs of the family (Alcantara, 1994). The family remains the base unit of Filipino identity, with fatherhood and service to the family remaining a core feature for Filipino men. Yet migration patterns (Angeles, 2001; Margold, 1995) that feminized the export of labor indicate a shift in these ideals. With Filipino masculinity so deeply intertwined with the idea of fatherhood and family, how do aspects of masculinity related to family impact notions of Filipino manhood? I explore the history of the re-indigenization movement of the Philippines, which frames our understanding of the *Tunay na Lalaki* image. Utilizing a systematic review of seminal outputs on masculinity, I explore the definition of Filipino manhood using texts from various Filipino gender and development scholars. The identi-fied themes that surround the image of a *Tunay na Lalaki* or True Manhood will be framed through *Sikolohiyang Pilipino* or Indigenous Filipino Psychology. This piece then highlight the *labas* (outer self/world) and *loob* (inner self) relating to Filipino men's roles. Intersections between one's peer group, socio-economic class, and the situation in the global migration context inform the formation of one's *labas* (outer self/identity). The findings indicate that Filipino manhood traits, as seen in one's *loob* (inner self) contextualize our understanding of man-hood's construction as familial.

CONTEXTUAL FRAMEWORK: SIKOLOHIYANG PILIPINO

Formal descriptions of Philippine manhood were developed alongside the "filipinization" and re-indigenization movement of various disciplines in the Philippine education sector. The critical gaze cast on Philippine masculinity occurred in conjunction with two movements – the Philippine women's move-ment and the cultural revalidation of Filipino identity through indigenizing Filipino disciplines.

Sikolohiyang Pilipino (roughly translated as Philippine Psychology) resulted from the country struggling to find a national identity in light of social unrest, student protests, workers' strikes, a growing communist insurgency movement, and eventually martial law. Virgilio Enriquez, one of the pioneers of this move-ment, countered the dominant image of the Western gaze often imposed on the Filipino people. The framework he developed explained Philippine realities using a Filipino perspective, which includes the nuances of Filipino values and char-acteristics often overlooked by Western lenses (Enriquez, 1992). The movement started during the early 1960s and focused on defining the Filipino's core iden-tity and contributed to Filipinos' struggle "to assert their national and cultural identity" (Pe-Pua & Protacio-Marcelino, 2000, p. 49). Alongside other discipli-nal shifts such as the *Pantayong Pananaw* (us/our view) for Philippine history (Guillermo, 2009), *Sikolohiyang Pilipino* called for reflections on the internal val-ues, practices, and beliefs of the Filipino people. In its call to assess the country's history, language, and Filipino characteristics from this perspective, the move-ment hoped for "indigenisation from within" or a "cultural revalidation" that "fostered a national identity and consciousness" (Enriquez, 1992; San Juan, 2006). Different factors contributed to this stance, including a psychology of lan-guage and culture which pushed for social involvement from numerous disciplines. These were buoyed by the Philippine Studies Program (PSP) at the University of the Philippines. Founded by former president-dictator Marcos, the PSP encouraged faculty interest in cultural nationalism in the History, Psychology, and Anthropology Departments, which would greatly expand Filipino as their medium of instruction (Gaerlan, 1998, p. 11), overcoming the American English which dominated Philippine academic circles and reinvigorating the idea of a Filipino academic lens.

The development of a Filipino identity coincided with reimagining gender roles. Scholars argued that the current patriarchal system of the Philippines resulted from the widespread conversion of pre-colonial Filipinos to Christianity, creating a shift in the country's colonial gender systems (Alcantara, 1994; Brewer, 2004; Eviota, 1992). Interactions between a sex-gender system and the economy remain deeply embedded in Philippine life (Eviota, 1992). Thus, local understandings of the Philippines' gendered culture, such as Eviota's (1992) "Political Economy of Gender," saw the upheaval of patriarchal systems through the subversion of the gendered division of labor along sexual lines (Alcantara, 1994; Eviota, 1992). The Philippine women's struggle was borne from both the fight for democracy during the country's Martial Law era (1972–1981) that coincided with the International Decade for Women (1975–1985).

The boom of women's organizations in the post-Martial Law era of the Philippines (the 1980s onwards) identified women's oppression to be rooted in three factors: "gender inequality, class domination and national subservience to foreign interests" (Torres, 1987, p. 326). During this period, Filipino women found themselves battling the international development projects that reinforced the Filipina-as-homemaker stereotype (Torres, 1987). Both government, non-government, and academic groups outlined the supposed traits of men and women to foreground the dismantling of these gender roles (Eviota, 1994).

Filipino men's gender roles were defined in conjunction with understanding Filipinos' place in the global migration chain. The feminization of particular industries had roots in the country's colonial history, with women placed in industries that mirrored their work at home. The Labour Export Policy of 1974 (Maca, 2018) led to a mass migration of skilled and unskilled Filipino workers abroad, the ripples of this policy extending well beyond the Marcos dictatorship during Martial Law, inciting shifts in the patriarchal gender order of society. The feminization of labor deployment became pronounced in the 1990s.

More women went abroad to work in gender-based occupations such as domestic workers, entertainers, and factory work (Ofreneo & Samonte, 2005). These women became the primary income earners of their families, leaving the care of their children to their husbands. Filipino men who remained in the country shifted from their roles as husbands, fathers, and family providers (Angeles, 2001) to caregivers. Filipino men who worked abroad contended with different, hegemonic identities outside the familiarity of their Filipino identity. The gendered nature of overseas work had adverse effects on men, as the male overseas Filipino workers were emasculated due to their lower ranks, falling victim to abuse, racism, and xenophobia (Margold, 1995). The shifting of gender roles due to labor migration became an opportunity to reimagine imposed gender roles.

Consequently, the demand of the feminist movement to reform the patriarchal society of the Philippines (Aguiling-Dalisay et al., 1995) highlighted the importance of analyzing men's roles, specifically their role in the family. Philippine gender advocates of the 1990s called for a reimagining of gender roles in the family due to trends in globalization and labor migration issues (Tadeo-Pingol, 2001a). This troubling of gender roles (Aguiling-Dalisay et al., 1995; Alcantara, 1994; Margold, 1995) became critical to dismantling oppressive patriarchal structures in the home (Angeles, 2001; Eviota, 1994). From this, the analysis of Filipino manhood came to be. Conceptions of *Tunay na Lalaki* (True Manhood) along-side *Ganap na Lalaki* (Whole Man) using *Katanginan* (traits) helped identify these transitions (Aguiling-Dalisay et al., 1995).

The seminal text of Jane Margold (1995) introduced the experience of male Filipino workers and tackled their issues as a gender beyond the family context. She identified a "crisis of masculinity" through her interviews with Filipino men, mainly from the North of the Philippines or Ilokano, who worked in Saudi and other Gulf states. Experiences of constant "assaults on their manhood," includ-ing beatings and the fear of homosexual rape (p. 276), were highlighted, and were shown to have affected their iterations of manhood after their reintegration into Philippine society. The Filipino man's identity manifests as the other in the dias-pora, as he faces a foreign, oppressive male identity. The theme of Filipino man versus foreign man helps frame Filipino manhood as marginalized in the global setting. This us–them and outer–inner dynamic becomes imperative to under-standing the in-group culture which I expound on when understanding Filipino homosociality.

Studies reclaiming academic disciplines utilize the concepts of *loob* (inside) and *labas* (outside) to understand Filipino culture. While the depth and mean-ing of these two concepts cannot be translated as an inside–outside dynamic, the rich inner world of *loob* may describe the Filipino identity and core personality (Alejo, 2018). It can be extended to include sexual orientation and identity along-side social roles (Garcia, 1996), extending to and influencing the *labas* or outer roles and gender expression through behavior and appearance (Garcia, 1996). This idea of *loob* and *labas* further frames the trends in Filipino studies on gen-der, specifically masculinity. Using the us–them and inner–outer binary, I delve into the factors that contribute to the rich tapestry of Filipino masculine identity.

DISCUSSION

The Loob and Filipino Traits

Identifying one singular definition for Filipino manhood can be challenging, given the diversity that exists across the Archipelago. Despite this, many still attempt to identify the parameters of Filipino manhood. Another binary frames Filipino manhood: the distinct separation of manhood and womanhood. "Filipino society still seems to be rooted in a masculinity–femininity understanding and applica-tion of gender that is bipolar in nature" (Valledor-Lukey, 2012, p. 29), with much of the country's laws adhering to the male–female gender binary. Gender roles and ideologies become the lens that informs the understanding of men's everyday practice, taking center stage in studying masculinities in the Philippines through gender role construction (Valledor-Lukey, 2012). In understanding men's gender roles, one can see what values and characteristics distinguish Filipino men from other groups and survey the development of Filipino manhood and its influences.

Filipino studies that attempt to categorize Filipino masculinity focus on individ-ual men's capacities and the roles they play in their homes. The *Filipino Adherence to Masculinity Expectations (FAME) Scale,* developed by Rubio and Green (2011), takes masculine ideology and identifies male role norms that cut across the 77 ethnolinguistic groups of the Philippines to create an emic definition of Filipino manhood. Unlike previous literature that focused on the Filipino Diaspora in the United States of America, Rubio and Green's work focuses on Filipino men in the Philippines and includes more non-Western masculinities in the Critical Studies of Men and Masculinity movement. Describing masculine ideology as "an individual's internalisation of cultural belief systems and attitudes toward masculinity and men's roles" (Pleck et al., 1993, p. 88, quoted in Rubio & Green, 2011), the study creates a frame for understanding traditional Filipino masculine ideology. The study identifies seven traits of Filipino masculinity: responsibility, family-orientedness, respectful deference to spouse, women, and the elderly, integrity, intelligence and academic achievement, strength, and a sense of community (Rubio & Green, 2011).

The FAME scale becomes a significant measure of individual men's stress when one fails to adhere to prosocial ideas of Filipino masculinity. These dimensions of masculinity may be what Filipino men unconsciously idealize, serving as the standard of their masculinity (Cabrera, 2017). While the traits in the FAME scale are idealized, the effects of adapting to these traits are very real. Traits, such as deference to spouse and wife or family-orientedness in the FAME, indicate the heteronormativity present in Philippine society. Institutions such as the Roman Catholic Church perpetuate these notions of what "real" men, women, and families aspire to be (Brewer, 2004; Valledor-Lukey, 2012), which are imbibed and reproduced by individuals.

However, these traits are also internalized by homosexual and bisexual men "for reasons that include social pressures, pleasing one's parents, acquisition of material inheritance, and concealment of one's sexual identity" (Lee, 2002, p. 37). The lack of conformity causes gender role strain and negatively affects potential mental health (Agbayani et al., 2018). The original conception of role strain can link back to the feminization of labor migration in the country (Margold, 1995). Having a mother earning dollars overseas removed the title of primary income earners from their husbands (Tadeo-Pingol, 2001a), shifting the identified masculinity dynamic. The psychological health of gay men in the Philippines (Rubio & Green, 2009) could be affected by non-conformity, while adherence to positive traits can bolster health-seeking behavior in men with occupational stresses (Agbayani et al., 2018).

The gender traits of masculinity from previous scholars are well documented and validated by Valledor-Lukey (2012) and Rubio and Green (2011). Descriptions of Filipino men include traits such as strength (physically, emotionally, and therefore incapable of having close ties to men), being capable (being the providers for their family or responsible for their family), and virile (having a "healthy" libido), as well as superior to women (Aguiling-Dalisay et al., 1995). While these traits are constructed as positive markers of Filipino masculinity, their connections with positive assertions of masculinity yield negative traits as well. Men were said to be emotionally unavailable and independent (Aguiling-Dalisay et al., 1995). Studies on Filipino manhood show commonalities such as the fear of feminization or femininophobia (Turgo, 2014, p. 23) as a continuing marker of masculinity.

Loob (inner) characteristics can be seen as threads formed by the country's colonial history. While these traits of masculinity can be considered positive, they are not representative of all notions of masculinity. Ideal masculinity and deviations from these images are different from actual experiences of masculinity. Masculinity construction involves power relations between and within genders (Connell, 2005, p. 71). While the FAME scale offers a more global perspective of men and masculinity research, including cross-cultural masculinity ideologies, the FAME scale has significant correlations to the Masculinity Attitudes, Stress, and Conformity (MASC) Questionnaire. The MASC Questionnaire was constructed in the North American context. However, similarities between the MASC and FAME scales can be attributed to the Philippine's colonization under America. Rubio and Green (2011) note that American colonizers imbibed Americans into the Filipino school system, influencing these traits (Rubio & Green, 2011). Despite similarities, differences still exist.

Studies on Filipino manhood focus on the description of embodied "masculine" traits and characteristics, leading to a totalizing and contradictory view of the *Tunay na Lalaki* or True Man archetype in the Archipelago. However, Filipino masculinities are multiple masculinities (White, 1997). Authors of the FAME scale recognized the limitations of their instrument as one that focuses mostly on Northern Filipino men. The FAME scale (Rubio & Green, 2009, 2011) comes from a psychological lens that highlights individual characteristics in lieu of the systems that creates them. Similarly, those who embody the traits in this FAME scale may not be considered as "powerful." Which men are the mold for hegemonic masculinity? The disparate geography of the country makes the conception of hegemonic masculinity context-specific. There is no one monolithic and unmoving masculinity in the Philippines. However,

> masculinity can be understood as an aspect of personhood that requires some external acknowledgment from, and continuous engagement with, the broader social institutions that work to shape and maintain it. (Waling, 2017, p. 431)

Who dictates what traits men should follow to be considered "true men?" Given the external environment's influence on masculinity, one can turn to the *labas* or outer environment to see which non-Filipino groups shape masculinity. The following sections look into the concept of the Filipino man concerning the *labas,* and external influences that shape and mold masculinity.

The Labas: Systems that Form Filipino Manhood

Notions of the *labas* often concern the external characteristics of one's identity (Valledor-Lukey, 2012), but here it describes systems that produce Filipino men, both formal and institutional organizations, and the less formal, cultural ties create parameters for masculine identities. The *querida* (mistress) and *barkada* (posse) systems (Angeles, 2001, p. 12) are two informal systems that can be condensed into the themes of homosociality and sexuality. Homosocial relations in the *barkada* phenomenon appear consistently in existing masculinity studies due to their role in behavior regulation. The theme of sexuality becomes the standard method to prove one's manhood, especially for those considered "marginalized" in their context. Homosociality and sexuality inform the discourse on Philippine masculinity, both traits that relate to family and family-orientedness.

Much literature exists on homosocial interaction. In place of romantic relationships, the "bromance" (Robinson et al., 2019) or intimate and platonic male bonding becomes essential to the formation of men. The male *barkada* is akin to "brotherhood," a "peer group" that is an "egalitarian orientation emphasising mutual caring, loyalty, and friendship that often tends to run deeper than blood relationships" (p. 120). While the term can be gender-neutral, the male *barkada* serves as a safe space of "masculine solidarity ... a form of escape from the daily grind of work and family" (Angeles, 2001, p. 13). It also affirms and polices one's masculine identity (Lasco, 2018). The next section explores the barkada as a bonding and binding force, including institutionalized homosocial groups such as Philippine fraternities.

Homosociality Through Barkada and Brads
The *barkada* concept links peer socialization to the formation of masculine identities. Originally a slang term, the word barkada was said to have originated from the Spanish word *barcada*, a derivative of the word *barco*, or boat. During the Spanish Colonial Period (pre-1989), offenders of grave crimes who could not be convicted in their community's rudimentary jails were sent via *barcos* to Manila. "*Barcada*" referred to a "boat-load" of these heavy offenders. The convicts were said to have formed bonds in their "*barcada*," having spent time in transport with only their fellow convicts for company. Furthermore, after their release and settlement in the Tondo area (near the Manila harbor where these boats moored), these "*barcada*" ties *were used* to re-establish their lives (Dumont, 1993).

Currently, the *barkada* become family in the absence of actual family, with masculine intimacy and camaraderie (Dumont, 1993; Fabinyi, 2007) that exist in these groups and often remain beyond adolescence. These groups compensate for the lack of support from social structures such as family and formalized institutions like schools or government services. These informal mechanisms become especially important for lower-income groups (Lasco, 2014, 2018), serving as social capital and social protection. Existing in this peer group becomes vital in forming manhood, as being with male peers teaches one about masculine identity.

The *barkada* exists as an informal peer group, yet the unspoken rules have both beneficial and harmful effects on one's identity. Self-regulation in these informal groups come from the *loob* (inner self) as the *barkada* defines the parameters of acceptable manhood through inciting loyalty and moral conformity, creating different microcultures that young men embody and reproduce (Dumont, 1993; Lasco, 2018). Conformity avoids rocking the boat and promotes *pakikisama* (oneness). Peer group socialization contributes to a machismo culture that highlights "strength, sexual aggression, physique and independence" (Acaba, 2014, p. 1) and uses sex with women as an initiation right to the group. Peer groups structure the moral world and gender ideology that mitigates or promotes risk-taking as a feature of masculinity (Lasco, 2018). Young men from low-income groups can have sex with men for money, as long as their *barkada* affirms their manhood (Acaba, 2014; Lasco, 2018). The *barkada* becomes a form of social street capital in the diaspora – with overseas Filipino workers and Filipino immigrants using the barkada to define their masculinity; male friendship becomes a form of intimacy that serves as a survival mechanism abroad (Alsaybar, 1999; Margold, 1995). *Barkadas* manifest the importance of kinship in the Philippine identity, which is essential to Filipino life. What happens when these microcultures of in-group loyalty groups become formalized? Philippine fraternities show the result of institutionalized male *barkadas* (Gutierrez, 2019) that exist in highly competitive areas of university life.

Fraternities are all-male groups that merit study in the homosocial bonds they foster. Studies on fraternities focus on higher education in the Global North context, contrasting with the Philippine's post-colonial experience. Fraternities often exist in the higher education context and have a history of violence (ABS-CBN News Investigative and Research Group, 2017; Zarco & Shoemaker, 2012), a problem so prevalent that the country has two laws banning hazing as an initiation right (R. A. 8049, 1995; R. A. 11053, 2018). Fraternities' connection to violence can be seen in various schools, including the country's top university –

[…] no other type of UPD (University of the Philippines, Diliman) student organisation – recreational or academic and not even a Greek-letter sorority – is associated with the extent and level of violence that is linked with fraternities. (Gutierrez, 2019, p. 245)

The masculinity tied to these fraternities is elite, as its members often occupy positions in the upper echelons of society (McCoy, 2000). While violent initiation rites are not unique to the country, colonial forces play a hand in the history of hazing that informs current understandings of Filipino masculinity and homosociality.

Violent initiation rites in fraternities have undeniable links to the American occupation of the Archipelago. Filipinos were considered the "little brown brothers" of American colonists (Kramer, 2006), justifying the benevolent assimilation of the Philippines through three images of Filipino men: Filipino men as savage and thus needed to be tamed, Filipino men as child-like and needed guidance, and Filipino men as feminine (Hoganson, 1998).

The military, economy, and education were significant themes present during the American Colonial era and promoted the American colonizers' masculinist imperial agenda for conquest (Rafael, 2018). "Warfare was the mother of a new masculinity propagated globally through colonial armies, boys' schools, and youth movements" (McCoy, 1995, p. 696). American colonists consciously used education and military pursuits to mold men's minds (Constantino, 1966), rapidly expanding the reach of higher education. Focus existed on creating "a professional civil service, public education to unify the country and build capacity, and the formation and training of a Philippine Constabulary to keep the peace" (Abinales & Amoroso, 2005, p. 119). The first teachers and school chaplains were military officers and volunteer soldiers (Musa & Ziatdinov, 2012), foreshadowing the connection between a Filipino's American education and the military.

The university became the vessel for America's military interests through the Philippine Military Academy (PMA) and the Military Reserve Corps. The American colonials barred Filipinos from entering the military, removing Filipino military leaders from their position to suppress threats of an insurgency. Young Filipinos no longer had the revolutionary movement to serve as their initiation right. The Americans capitalized on the emasculated young Filipinos by promoting entry into military institutions. Filipino men could enroll in the American-run PMA, while male college students were mandated to join the Military Reserve Corps, as it was part of the University of the Philippines curriculum. The PMA served "as a social laboratory, a crucible for casting a new form of Filipino masculinity" (p. 331), adapting Western manhood practices into the Philippine context. These academies and the reserve corps co-opted the "near-universal folk ritual of male initiation to make military service synonymous with the passage to manhood" (McCoy, 2000, p. 315). This male initiation took the form in hazing

> a harsh initiation ceremony that "welcomes" newcomers through harassment, humiliation, and physical abuse, is part of the rite of passage of cadets' transformation to becoming "real men" and true brothers-in-arms. (McCoy, 1995, p. 29)

The adaptation of America's West Point hazing became a "transformative trauma" that signaled the transition of boyhood to manhood, creating a cult of masculinity that fostered group solidarity and brotherhood (McCoy, 1995, 2000).

This culture of indoctrination and male initiation played into the kinship values of Filipinos. The institutionalized hazing of plebes to socialized men to become *closer than brothers* (McCoy, 2000), an essential feature of kinship that had often been undermined during the Spanish colonial period. PMA cadets formed lifetime bonds (McCoy, 2000) through blood and shared suffering. Ironically, this ownership of a colonial initiation right served as a form of liberation from colonial emasculation, reshaping the gender roles of the country.

The current fraternity system still uses brotherhood, such as the *kuya* (older brother) system, to incite loyalty. Mentorship occurs between the younger and older members or influential alumni who serve as their *kuya*. Fraternity men call each other – *brad* (short for brother). Fraternities link neophytes with successful, accomplished alumni, where the benefit of powerful connections outweigh the violence of initiation rites: The bonds of fraternities extend past university life into one's professional life. "This view corresponds to the contemporary demands of a precarious global job market where Filipinos must compete for employment opportunities locally and potentially overseas" (Gutierrez, 2019, p. 250), becoming a commentary on the neo-liberal education system.

Fraternities serve as a powerful system that reproduces and reinforces elite masculinity. It is elite in its selectiveness and exclusiveness. With the historical origins of fraternities linked to violence and power, fraternities "present themselves as training grounds for young men who want to a face *battle* in whatever form" (Gutierrez, 2019, p. 250). If one survives the violent hazing, one is assured academic success, job security, and relative protection under the law. Current fraternities would seek men who were the cream of the crop and served as a space to negotiate manhood, free from other authority figures that police its gateways (Gutierrez, 2019, p. 247).

I posit that *pagbabarkada* (having a *barkada*) serves to incorporate principles of family in masculinity formation. In the absence of one unified identity, the *labas-loob* (outer-inner) dynamic and us-versus-them mentality become a marker of Filipino identity. For cadets, the absence of a concrete nation and unified identity meant familial ties forged in the reputation of the institution. In undergoing a shared experience, their bond became a brotherhood.

In place of one solid nation, pockets of community through "brotherhood" exist. However, with every in-group culture created, stark distinctions between them and the "other" are formed. Instead of the aggrieved entitlement (Kimmel, 2013), Filipino men focus on in and out-group mentality, created to resist marginality. What does this say about masculinity and those who are marginalized? The following section details the intersections of sexuality and marginalized masculinities in the Archipelago.

The Bragging: Sexuality and the Marginalized Filipino Man

A recurring topic in Filipino masculinities studies involves marginalized men claiming power. Case studies focusing on working-class Filipino men (Fabinyi, 2007; Fajardo, 2007, 2008; Turgo, 2014; Yea, 2015) dominate the field's literature. Studies on Philippine masculinities center on context-specific masculinities (Fabinyi, 2007, 2012; Fajardo, 2008; Turgo, 2014) that embodies or subverts their milieu's hegemonic masculinity (Yea, 2015). Marginalized and context-specific masculinities highlight the neo-liberal and globalized economy's influence on Filipino masculinity. However, hegemonic masculinity may not exist in postcolonial societies as the constant push and pull of colonial and global forces emasculate indigenous and native men constantly (Margold, 1995). Filipino masculinity becomes a form of marginalized masculinity on the global stage. While homosociality plays a vital role in Filipino manhood, sexuality and family become the overarching narrative that guides masculine identity. In the absence of social capital and power, Filipino men enforce their masculinity through sexual relations or duty to their families. This section discusses marginality and sexuality and how these two are tied together.

The feminization of Filipino men is part of the greater imperial discourse of American colonial forces (Fajardo, 2008; Hoganson, 1998). Feminization as a strategy of colonization signaled the colonized country as "weak." The feminization of labor abroad brought the erosion of the "Father-as-breadwinner" and contributed to this shift in "traditional" gender roles. The lack of a strong and unifying Filipino identity and masculinity left room for exploitation. Colonial forces eventually filled the "masculine" gap. Even now, the international arena serves as a point of interest insofar as it allows Filipino men to define themselves against those who hold the position of the hegemon – the strongmen in this globalized, neo-colonial setting. Hegemonic masculinity then would be the Western, non-Filipino men in a neo-liberal economic state.

The focus on global masculinities explains the abundance of research on overseas Filipino men as workers in low-income occupations (Arguillas et al., 2018; Fajardo, 2007, 2008; Margold, 1995; Mckay & Lucero Prisno, 2012). Filipino seafaring and fishing have become popular topics in men and masculinity studies due to a large number of Filipinos abroad, and as it is a space dominated by men offering a space to "highlight a more masculine occupation and image of the Philippines and its people" (Fajardo, 2008, p. 404). Despite the lack of financial power, the ability to provide for one's family needs overshadows the exploitative working conditions "and transform the fruits of his labor into recognisable trappings of masculine prestige" (Mckay & Lucero Prisno, 2012, p. 31). For Filipino men robbed of power in their own country, compensation happens through subversion of stereotypes, where men own traditionally feminine roles and turn them masculine (Tadeo-Pingol, 2001b; Turgo, 2014). Feminization can be overlooked for the sake of providing for one's family (Turgo, 2014) and transcending a demoralized state. Despite the lack of power, these marginalized men take pride in their status of providing for their families, despite possible detrimental outcomes (Yea, 2015). As Owen (1999) notes, to be a "man" is congruent "not just with physical masculinity, but with social class" (p. 27). For the poor with no economic power, the *Tunay na Lalaki* sacrifices for his family.

Romantic relationships and sexual conquests serve as tangential markers for Filipino manhood. Unlike other cultures that may place a premium on sexuality, sex is discussed more for the youth despite the *querida* (mistress) culture (Angeles, 2001) adopted from the Spanish colonial period. Despite this mistress culture, men joke about the wife being a *boss* or *kumander* (commander), husbands being *macho-machunurin sa asawa* (macho but obedient to their wives) or *under the saya* ("under the skirt" or subservient to his wife) (Angeles, 2001). A dynamic exists wherein men are taught to respect their peers, but low-status women can be bought (Gutierrez, 2019), the practice of prostitution reinforced by certain fraternities.

Images of sacrifice and sexuality may be focused on heterosexual Filipino men. There are multiple studies on queer masculinity just because of their deviance from the norm. This serves as an alternative lens to view masculinity because the non-adherence to masculine norms, hegemonic or not, causes distress (Cabrera, 2017; Rubio & Green, 2009). LGBT literature on Filipino manhood mentions femininity as a marker against true manhood (Garcia, 1996). The term *bakla* refers to homosexual men but connotes more feminine ways of enacting this sexuality (Remoto, 2002). In a country where one's sexual orientation is closely tied to one's sex (Valledor-Lukey, 2012), gender binaries are constantly reinforced. Even a "real man" can have sex with a *bakla*, as long as he does not become *bakla* himself (Lasco, 2018). Even Filipinos in the diaspora utilize strength, seen in the glorification of the boxer Manny Pacquiao, to "challenge U.S. colonial policies in the Philippines, and to remake definitions of Filipino heterosexual masculinity" (Arnaldo, 2019, p. 4). While physical markers of homosexual men, such as femininity, are changing, the narrative of Filipino men as heads of the family and providers still exists.

Tatay Digong and the Filipino Family
The Philippines does not have a single, monolithic culture with a centuries-old history (Tiongson, 1983, p. 83), nor does it have a monolithic form of manhood, as the formulation of gender becomes context-specific (Beasley et al., 2012).

Tunay na lalaki or "True Manhood" serves as a core ideal for Filipino manhood, a man who is emotionally strong and independent (Aguiling-Dalisay et al., 1995), a leader and patriarch of his family (Alcantara, 1994). Familial relations remain at the core of one's Filipino identity, with fatherhood and service to the family as core traits for Filipino men. Former president Rodrigo Duterte's positioning as the Philippines' father becomes a familiar archetype for the Filipino people.

Current studies show how Filipinos' notions of fatherhood influence the construction of masculinity and are embedded in Filipino identity and nationhood. While Philippine elite masculinity becomes synonymous with the country's national identity (Owen, 1999), this ideal is not representative of masculinity in the archipelago. Philippine President Rodrigo Duterte built his campaign around being anti-elite. With his *bastos pero medyo maginoo* [a vulgar man who is sometimes a gentleman] identity (De Chavez, & Pacheco, 2020), Duterte posed as the everyday man and father of the nation. Duterte embodied all dimensions of Filipino manhood (Rubio & Green, 2011). Duterte's aggressive patterns of speech and rhetoric showcased during his violent war on drugs showed assertiveness and dominance. Filipinos perceived his family-orientedness and sense of community through his positioning as a *haligi ng tahanan* (pillar of the home), a provider for his family – the Filipino people. Duterte played into the strong sense of community Filipinos have, Filipino man versus foreign man, by speaking against the International Criminal Court and the United Nations. His election into the highest political position in the country, the presidency, validated one's perception of his sense of responsibility, academic abilities, and integrity. He sang praises for beautiful women highlighting his "respect for women." He enacted Filipino manhood traits of virility (having a "healthy" libido) and superiority to women (Aguiling-Dalisay et al., 1995) with comments that sexualized and demeaned women, with former Vice President Leni Robredo being his favorite target. His description of his opponents as *bakla* (homosexual) shows his association of homosexuality with weakness and femininity, a trait he distances himself from constantly. This fear of feminization can be associated with a kind of masculinity that was re-emphasized after the feminization of Filipino men during the American Colonial Era (Hoganson, 1998). Duterte's identity as *Tatay Digong* (Father Digong) successfully positioned him as a "Tunay na Lalaki" whose election into the presidency legitimized his speech and action.

Duterte brings the idea of "masculine solidarity" (Angeles, 2001) to the political sphere. His fulfillment of the current "Tunay na Lalaki" scripts and overemphasis on manhood (Parmanand, 2020) exemplify Filipino in-group culture and homosociality, often associated with the male *barkada* and the family. The *barkada* remains a vital peer group in forming manhood, defining acceptable manhood and moral conformity (Dumont, 1993; Lasco, 2018). The upbringing of Filipino men plays a role in their easy acceptance of his rhetoric. Specifically, Filipino father–child relationships in lower-income households contain themes of authority, restriction, obedience, and control "with children showing greater submission and deference to fathers than mothers" (Alampay, 2014, p. 117). When the most powerful man in the country allows violent speech and sexual deviance, marginalized men who may not have access to his powerful networks or resources may copy his speech and actions as a form of being "in," and therefore gaining power. Through this, one can both please their *ka-barkada* (posse) and their *tatay* (father). While Duterte's rhetoric, speech and action become problematic, one can forgive him if it's for the greater good of the family – the Filipino people.

Filipino Manhood and the Family: A Conclusion

This study goes beyond the men-as-the-problem discourse and highlights inter-sections of ethnicity, class, religion, region, sexuality, and age that color a man's identity (Fabinyi, 2007) alongside the systems that perpetuate domination. Men suffer due to their gender but still benefit from gender inequality (White, 1997). Filipino men suffer due to their class position as well as their subjugated position in the global arena. Filipino's marginalized masculinity (Connell & Messerschmidt, 2005) creates the in-group versus out-group mentality of the Filipino. Through the descriptions of masculinity formation centering on family concepts, one sees how in-group culture serves as a coping mechanism for Filipino men's marginalization while maintaining dominant and oppressive gender structures.

Manhood is created by the family and more extensive kinship networks, be it through formal or informal groups, as men fit with the expectations of this group, including that of gender traits and roles (Jocano, 1998). While more positive images of masculinity such as pakiki-isa (oneness) exist, one can see how pakiki-isa can turn harmful when placed in specific contexts such as violent hazing rites and Duterte's oppressed traditional masculinity (De Chavez & Pacheco, 2020). The challenge in understanding men and masculinity in the Philippines involves unpacking the nuances of this culture from institutions that form men.

Rather than focus on the individual, one must go beyond the idea that men oppress women. This piece explore patterns outside of men's particular traits and private stories. While these are essential, oppression is so intricately woven into various systems and must be studied with care. The election of Duterte shows the strong desire for a leader who is an "everyday man," *Tunay na Lalaki* and a father figure, further highlighting the country's patriarchal nature. His election into office shows that while there is no one uncontested archetype of Filipino masculinity, the current Filipino public values rhetoric plays on machismo, family values, and homosociality. I acknowledge there is no one way to be a man in the archipelago. However, the masculine ideology that underpins our current context cannot be overlooked. *Sikolohiyang Pilipino's* conceptions of *labas–loob* (in-group/out-group) can enhance our understanding of Filipino families, specifically the importance given to fatherhood and brotherhood. Through this, one can further explore the formations of Filipino manhood. By understanding this *banig* of Philippine masculinity, one can dissect how differ-ent facets of manhood are woven together to further the country's machismo, one that pervades different powerful institutions. The *banig* shows the impor-tance of an emic approach to gender equality. Shifts must be made to this nar-rative. only then can the outer environment or *labas* foster or bring out a more inclusive *loob*.

ACKNOWLEDGMENTS

I express my gratitude to my supervisors, Dr David Mayeda and Dr Kirsten Locke for supporting my scholarly work.

REFERENCES

Abinales, P. N., & Amoroso, D. J. (2005). *State and society in the Philippines.* Rowman & Littlefield Publishers.

ABS-CBN Investigative and Research Group. (2017, October 3). *Deaths caused by Hazing.* ABS-CBN News. https://news.abs-cbn.com/news/multimedia/infographic/09/27/17/deaths-caused-by-hazing

Acaba, J. (2014). Tropa: Masculinity and power in sexual health-seeking behaviors among male youth gangs. *Asia Pacific E-Journal of Health Social Science, 1*(1), 1–3.

Agbayani, B. E. M., Villaflor, P. I. A. T. M., Villaret, N. P. B., & Hechanova, M. R. M. (2018). The role of Filipino masculine ideology on the adaptive coping, psychological well-being and vicarious trauma of first responders. *International Journal of Culture and Mental Health, 11*(4), 753–762. https://doi.org/10.1080/17542863.2018.1561736

Aguiling-Dalisay, G., Heugten, L., & Sto Domingo, M. (1995). Ang Pagkalalaki ayon sa mga Lalaki: Pag-aaral sa Tatlong Grupong Kultural sa Pilipinas. *Philippine Social Science Review, 52,* 143–166.

Alampay, L. P. (2014). Parenting in the Philippines. In H. Selin (Ed.), *Parenting across cultures: Childrearing, motherhood and fatherhood in non-western cultures* (pp. 105–121). Springer. https://doi.org/10.1007/978-94-007-7503-9_9

Alcantara, A. N. (1994). Gender roles, fertility, and the status of married Filipino men and women. *Philippine Sociological Review, 42*(1–4), 94–109.

Alejo, A. (2018). Loob ng Tao. *Social Transformations Journal of the Global South, 6*(1), 5–28.

Alsaybar, B. D. (1999). Deconstructing deviance: Filipino American Youth Gangs, "party culture," and ethnic identity in Los Angeles. *Amerasia Journal, 25*(1), 116–138. https://doi.org/10.17953/amer.25.1.p5274h67q1l1077k

Angeles, L. C. (2001). The Filipino male as macho-Machunurin: Bringing men and masculinities in gender and development in the Philippines. *Kasarinlan Journal of Third World Issues, 16*(1), 9–30.

Arguillas, F. O., Williams, L. B., & Arguillas, M. J. B. (2018). Men's changing productive and reproductive roles in transnational Filipino families. *Journal of Comparative Family Studies, 49*(2), 179–201.

Arnaldo, C. R., Jr. (2019). 'Undisputed' racialised masculinities: Boxing fandom, identity, and the cultural politics of masculinity. *Identities, 27*(6), 1–20. https://doi.org/10.1080/10702 89X.2019.1624068

Beasley, C., Brook, H., & Holmes, M. (2012). *Heterosexuality in theory and practice.* Routledge. https://doi.org/10.4324/9780203103920

Brewer, C. (2004). *Shamanism, Catholicism and gender relations in colonial Philippines 1521–1685.* Ashgate.

Cabrera, R. (2017). Gender role strain and the psychological health of Filipino gay men. *Issues IAFOR Journal of Psychology & the Behavioral Sciences, 3*(2), 35–51.

Connell, R. (2002). *Gender.* Blackwell Publishers.

Connell, R. (2005). *Masculinities* (2nd ed.). University of California Press.

Connell, R. W., & Messerschmidt, J. W. (2005). Hegemonic masculinity: Rethinking the concept. *Gender & Society, 19*(6), 829–859. https://doi.org/10.1177/0891243205278639

Constantino, R. (1966). *The Filipinos in the Philippines: And other essays.* Filipino Signatures.

Cullinane, M., Hernandez, C., & Borlaza, G. C. (2020). Philippines. In *Encyclopedia Britannica.* https://www.britannica.com/place/Philippines

De Chavez, J. C., & Pacheco, V. (2020). Masculinity in the age of (Philippine) populism: Spectacle, hypermasculinity, and Rodrigo Duterte. *Masculinities & Social Change, 9*(3), 261. https://doi.org/10.17583/mcs.2020.5157

Dumont, J. -P. (1993). The Visayan Male "Barkada": Manly behavior and male identity on a Philippine Island. *Philippine Studies*, *41*(4), 401–436.

Encinas-Franco, J. (2022). The presidential kiss: Duterte's gendered populism, hypermasculinity, and Filipino migrants. *NORMA*, *17*(2), 107–123. https://doi.org/10.1080/18902138.2022.2026107

Enriquez, V. (1989). *Neo-colonial politics and language struggles in the Philippines*. Rapid Lithographic.

Enriquez, V. (1992). From colonial to liberation psychology. The University of the Philippines Press.

Eviota, E. U. (1992). *The political economy of gender women and the sexual division of labour in the Philippines*. Zed Books.

Eviota, E. U. (1994). *Sex and gender in Philippine society: A discussion of issues on the relations between women and men*. National Commission on the Role of Filipino Women.

Fabinyi, M. (2007). Illegal fishing and masculinity in the Philippines: A look at the Calamianes Islands in Palawan. *Philippine Studies*, *55*(4), 509–529.

Fabinyi, M. (2012). Fishing in marine protected areas: Resistance, youth and masculinity. In *Fishing for fairness: Poverty, morality and marine resource regulation in the Philippines*. ANU Press.

Fajardo, K. (2007). Working-class Filipino masculinities. *American Quarterly*, *59*(2), 451–458. https://doi.org/10.1353/aq.2007.0040

Fajardo, K. (2008). Transportation: Translating Filipino and Filipino American Tomboy masculinities through global migration and seafaring. *GLQ*, *14*(2–3), 403–424.

Gaerlan, B. (1998). *The politics and pedagogy of language use at the University of Philippines: The history of English as the medium of instruction and the challenge mounted by Filipino*. ProQuest Dissertations Publishing. http://search.proquest.com/docview/304424871/

Garcia, J. N. C. (1996). *Philippine gay culture: The last 30 years: Binabae to bakla, Silahis to MSM*. University of the Philippines Press.

Guillermo, R. (2009). Pantayong Pananaw and the history of Philippine political concepts. *Kritika Kultura*, *13*, 107–116. https://doi.org/10.3860/kk.v0i13.1209

Gutierrez, F. C. (2019). Violence and hypermasculinity in university fraternity initiations: Situating the reproduction of masculinity in the Philippines. *The Journal of Men's Studies*, *27*(3), 243–264. https://doi.org/10.1177/1060826518815147

Hoganson, K. L. (1998). *Fighting for American manhood*. Yale University Press. www.jstor.org/stable/j.ctt32bht5

Jocano, F. L. (1998). *Filipino social organization: Traditional kinship and family organization/F. Landa Jocano*. Punlad Research House.

Kimmel, M. (2013). *Angry White men: American masculinity at the end of an era*. Nation Books.

Kramer, P. A. (2006). *The blood of government: Race, empire, the United States, and the Philippines*. University of North Carolina Press.

Lasco, G. (2014). Pampagilas: Methamphetamine in the everyday economic lives of underclass male youths in a Philippine port. *International Journal of Drug Policy*, *25*(4), 783–788. https://doi.org/10.1016/j.drugpo.2014.06.011

Lasco, G. (2018). Call boys: Drug use and sex work among marginalized young men in a Philippine port community. *Contemporary Drug Problems*, *45*(1), 33–46. https://doi.org/10.1177/0091450917742052

Lee, R. (2002). Psychosocial contexts of the homosexuality of Filipino men in heterosexual unions. *Journal of Homosexuality*, *42*, 35–63. https://doi.org/10.1300/J082v42n04_03

Maca, M. (2018). Education in the 'New Society' and the Philippine labour export policy (1972–1986. *Journal of International and Comparative Education*, *7*(1), 1–16. https://doi.org/10.14425/jice.2018.7.1.1

Margold, J. A. (1995). Narratives of masculinity and transnational migration: Filipino workers in the Middle East. In A. Ong & M. Peletz (Eds.), *Bewitching women, pious men: Gender and body politics in Southeast Asia* (pp. 274–298). Berkeley.

McCoy, A. W. (1995). "Same Banana": Hazing and honor at the Philippine Military Academy. *The Journal of Asian Studies*, *54*(3), 689–726. https://doi.org/10.2307/2059448

McCoy, A. W. (2000). Philippine commonwealth and cult of masculinity. *Philippine Studies*, *48*(3), 315–346.

McKay, P. S. C. (2007). Filipino Sea Men: Constructing masculinities in an ethnic labour niche. *Journal of Ethnic and Migration Studies, 33*(4), 617–633. https://doi.org/10.1080/13691830701265461

Mckay, S., & Lucero Prisno, D. E., III. (2012). Masculinities Afloat: Filipino seafarers and situational performance of Manhood. In Mi. Ford & L. Lyons (Eds.), *Men and masculinities in Southeast Asia* (pp. 20–37). Taylor and Francis. https://www.worldcat.org/title/men-and-masculinities-in-southeast-asia/oclc/956673380

Musa, S., & Ziatdinov, R. (2012). Features and historical aspects of the Philippines educational system. *European Journal of Contemporary Education, 2*(2), 155–176.

Ofreneo, R. E., & Samonte, I. A. (2005). *Empowering Filipino migrant workers: Policy issues and challenges.* International Labour Office. https://public.ebookcentral.proquest.com/choice/publicfullrecord.aspx?p=359432

Owen, N. (1999). *Masculinity and national identity in the 19th century Philippines.* Illes I Imperis Estudios De Historia De Las Sociedades En El Mundo Colonial Y Post Colonial. https://www.academia.edu/27033736/Masculinity_and_National_Identity_in_the_19th_century_Philippines

Parmanand, S. (2020). Duterte as the macho messiah: Chauvinist populism and the feminisation of human rights in the Philippines. *Review of Women's Studies, 29*(2), 1–30.

Pe-Pua, R. (1989). Pagtatanong-tanong: A cross-cultural research method. *International Journal of Intercultural Relations, 13*(2), 147–163. https://doi.org/10.1016/0147-1767(89)90003-5

Pe-Pua, R., & Protacio-Marcelino, E. (2000). Sikolohiyang Pilipino (Filipino psychology): A legacy of Virgilio G. Enriquez. *Asian Journal of Social Psychology, 3*(1), 49–71. https://doi.org/10.1111/1467-839X.00054

R. A. 8049. (1995). *An act regulating hazing and other forms of initiation rites in fraternities, sororities, and other organizations and providing penalities therefor (1995).* https://elibrary.judiciary.gov.ph/thebookshelf/showdocs/2/3818

R. A. 11053. (2018). *Anti-hazing act of 2018.* https://www.officialgazette.gov.ph/2018/06/29/republic-act-no-11053/

Rafael, V. L. (2018). Colonial contractions: The making of the modern Philippines, 1565–1946. In *Oxford Research Encyclopedia of Asian History.* Oxford University Press. https://doi.org/10.1093/acrefore/9780190277727.013.268

Remoto, D. (2002). *Gaydar.* Anvil Pub.

Robinson, S., White, A., & Anderson, E. (2019). Privileging the bromance: A critical appraisal of romantic and bromantic relationships. *Men and Masculinities, 22*(5), 850–871. https://doi.org/10.1177/1097184X17730386

Rubio, R., & Green, R. -J. (2009). Filipino masculinity and psychological distress: A preliminary comparison between gay and heterosexual men. *Sexuality Research & Social Policy, 6*(3), 61. https://doi.org/10.1525/srsp.2009.6.3.61

Rubio, R., & Green, R. -J. (2011). Filipino men's roles and their correlates. *Culture, Society and Masculinities, 3*, 77–102. https://doi.org/10.3149/CSM.0302.77

San Juan, E. (2006). Toward a decolonizing indigenous psychology in the Philippines: Introducing Sikolohiyang Pilipino. *Journal for Cultural Research, 10*(1), 47–67. https://doi.org/10.1080/14797580500422018

Tadeo-Pingol, A. (2001). *Remaking masculinities: Identity, power, and gender dynamics in families with migrant wives and househusbands.* UP Center for Women's Studies.

Torres, A. T. (1987). The Filipina looks at herself: A review of women's studies in the Philippines. *Transactions of National Academy of Sciences & Technology (Philippines), 9*, 307–330.

Tiongson, N. (1983). *What is Philippine drama.* Philippine Educational Theater Association.

Turgo, N. N. (2014). Redefining and experiencing masculinity in a Philippine fishing community. *Philippine Sociological Review, 62*, 7–38.

Valledor-Lukey, V. V. (2012). *Pagkababae at Pagkalalake (Femininity and Masculinity): Developing a Filipino Gender Trait Inventory and predicting self-esteem and sexism* [Child and Family Studies – Dissertations]. Syracuse University.

Waling, A. (2017). "We are so pumped full of shit by the media": Masculinity, magazines, and the lack of self-identification. *Men and Masculinities, 20*(4), 427–452. https://doi.org/10.1177/1097184X16652654

White, S. C. (1997). Men, masculinities, and the politics of development. *Gender & Development, 5*(2), 14–22. https://doi.org/10.1080/741922357

Yea, S. (2015). Masculinity under the knife: Filipino men, trafficking and the black organ market in Manila, the Philippines. *Gender, Place & Culture, 22*(1), 123–142. https://doi.org/10.1080/0966 369X.2013.832657

Zarco, R. M., & Shoemaker, D. J. (2012). Report on student organization conflicts, University of the Philippines, Diliman, 1938–2000. *Philippine Sociological Review, 60*, 19–69.

CHAPTER 16

THE ELDERLY IN THE FILIPINO FAMILY

Belen T. Medina and Maria Cecilia T. Medina

ABSTRACT

A review of the literature on the Filipino elderly reveals that social and cultural expectations of filial duty and obligations are still strong in the Filipino family. Filial piety based on the concept of "utang na loob" or debt of gratitude to parents, and respect for age are important traditional Filipino values as evident in the support given by children to their parents, and in the words and practices showing deference to the older generation. Studies have shown that the most common living arrangement of the elderly is co-residence with children or to have at least one child living close by in the neighborhood. With the generally poor economic well-being of the elderly, they rely heavily on their children both in the Philippines and abroad for support. Caregiving of the elderly is family-based with the children, particularly the daughters, as major providers of care and assistance to maintain their physical well-being. Studies have also shown the importance of intergenerational solidarity for the social well-being and mental health of the elderly through constant communication and visits, with a two-way flow of economic and emotional support between parents and children. Institutionalization of the elderly appears to be a last resort to complement rather than replace the welfare function of the family.

For future research, it is recommended that government laws benefitting the elderly and their implementation be analyzed, including the most effective way to reach those in remote areas in order to disseminate information on their benefits. Studies should also be done to develop programs for caregiving training and incentives, on ways to uphold standards and monitor the quality of

Resilience and Familism: The Dynamic Nature of Families in the Philippines
Contemporary Perspectives in Family Research, Volume 23, 285–299
Copyright © 2023 by Emerald Publishing Limited
All rights of reproduction in any form reserved
ISSN: 1530-3535/doi:10.1108/S1530-353520230000023016

facilities of private retirement homes, to establish more government homes or
home-care services for the indigent who needs long-term care. It is also recom-
mended that studies on geriatric centers and facilities be done to ensure high-
quality of elderly care.

Keywords: Filipino family; elderly; care; filial piety; aging; well-being

A review of the literature on the Filipino elderly reveals that social and cultural
expectations of filial duty and obligations are still strong in the Filipino family.

The vast literature on the elderly today is a result of increased scientific interest
and concern for older people which started in 1982 when the United Nations des-
ignated it as The Year of the Elderly. Prior to this, there was practically no social
research conducted locally on the topic.

One possible reason for the slow development of scientific interest in the study
of the elderly is that, from the Filipino cultural viewpoint, older people are not
considered a burden, and are not perceived as posing any critical problem to society because of the assumption that the family is to take care of its welfare.

Another possible reason for the slow development of scientific interest in the
elderly is because they compose only about 7–8 percent of the total population
according to the 2020 Census of Population and Housing (Philippine Statistics
Authority, 2020). Because of the fertility decline and increased life expectancy, however, the proportion of elderly people in the population has grown
faster than the total population, and has increased from 6.3 million in the 2010
Census (Philippine Statistics Authority, 2010) to 8.2 million in the 2020 Census
(Philippine Statistics Authority, 2020). In fact, according to United Nations estimate, the Philippines has the highest growth rate of the elderly population in
the whole of Asia and the Pacific (Paquio, 1994). Due to the improvement in
health and medical science, life expectancy at birth has increased from 60.9 years
in 1975 (Economic and Social Commission for Asia and the Pacific, 1997) to
71.7 years for both sexes, 75.9 years for females, and 67.7 years for males in 2020
(Philippines Demographics, 2020).

Consequently, there are now many studies on the elderly, not only for theoretical but also more especially for social planning and policy purposes. What
stands out in the literature on the aged is that social and cultural expectations
of filial duty and obligations are still strong as discussed under the following
headings.

FILIAL DUTY AND RESPECT FOR AGE

One of the most important traditional Filipino values imparted to children early
in life is filial piety and respect to parents, grandparents, and elderly relatives.
Children not only feel that they owe their parents respect, obedience, and love
but they also feel eternally grateful for having been brought up and supported
by them. This filial piety is based on the concept of "utang na loob" or debt of

gratitude. Filipino culture heavily subscribes to the notion that one owes his life and everything to his parents (Medina, 2015, p. 248).

Filial piety coincides very well with the traditional Filipino respect for age. Filipino society is organized on the basis of generation and the concept of seniority which involves deference to and respect for older persons regardless of gender (Jocano, 1988, pp. 137–138).

A traditional and polite way to speak to the elderly person is to use "po" or "ho," and to use the plural form of the second person "kayo" instead of the singular form "ikaw" or "ka" for "you." Another sign of respect is to address an elderly person who belongs to one's grandparents' generation as "Lolo" (grandfather) or "Lola" (grandmother) without regard to real or direct consanguineal or affinal relations. If the elderly person belongs to one's parents' generation then he is addressed as "Tiyo" or "Tata" or "Tito" (uncle) for the male, or "Tiya" or "Nana" or "Tita" (aunt) for the female, again irrespective of actual blood ties. Within the same generation, the older person among the Tagalogs is addressed as "Kaka" or "Ka" followed by the first name such as "Ka Pedro." Among the Ilokanos, it is "Manong" for the male and "Manang" for the female. A young person may not address an older one, much less an aged person, by his first name only (Medina, 2015, p. 243).

The "mano" tradition in which the young person kisses the hand of the elderly is also another way of showing respect. Instead of kissing the hand, however, the more common way now is for the younger person to just touch his forehead on the hand of the older person, as in asking for the latter's blessing. Today, especially in the urban areas, these practices are not often followed anymore.

Respect is shown in other ways, like kissing an elderly on the cheek, bowing, offering a seat, or extending a helping hand. The polite way of speaking to an elderly, including the use of respectful terms, however, is still widely observed (Medina, 2015, pp. 243–244).

LIVING ARRANGEMENTS

Care and support for elderly parents are being manifested in the living arrangements. Data from the 1996 Philippine Elderly Survey and the 2007 Philippine Study on Ageing by the UP Population Institute and Demographic Research and Development Foundation show that the most common living arrangement of the elderly is co-residence with children (Cruz et al., 2016). This is also confirmed by the 2018 Longitudinal Study of Ageing and Health in the Philippines where 60 percent of older people are found to be co-residing with at least one child. Findings also show that, of the 13 percent of older people who live alone, 61 percent have children living in the same barangay (Cruz & Cruz, 2019, p. 36). Thus, these older persons are not really alone because there is at least one child living in the neighborhood.

This co-residence pattern has continued to be the norm and is the preferred living arrangement by both older people and their children. Data taken from a sample survey of households drawn at random from selected rural, urban, and Metro

Manila communities, and stratified by socioeconomic status (Medina et al., 1996, p. 48) reveal that aged parents prefer to live with their children for security and to have somebody close to take care of them. Other reasons for wanting to live with their children are: "for happiness," "for the love that children provide," "it is the obligation of children to care for them," and "to provide parental guidance."

Children reside with their parents as a filial and normative obligation to show love and affection, and to set an example to their own children of the value of caring for the elderly. Thus, there is hardly any "empty-nest" stage in the life cycle of the Filipino family.

Many families have devised creative solutions in which proximity to the elderly and independence is both maintained. For instance, it is not unusual for families to build extensions or to divide a house into several units by way of doors and walls to achieve both proximity and privacy (Domingo & Asis, 1995). This kind of living arrangement which was found also in a small urbanizing community, is referred to as "talaba"-style or oyster-like extension of the house, and is designed to enable the elderly to be close by but at the same time maintain a certain amount of independence (Domingo, 1999). Moreover, adult children who have their own homes assist their elderly by sending food or money, or by sending their children to run errands for their grandparents. Therefore, through these special arrangements, the flow of support between family members is maintained.

The daughter is usually the preferred co-resident by the elderly because females are believed to be more capable of providing care, attention, and love; the unmarried daughter is the first choice followed by the married daughter (Domingo & Asis, 1995; Medina et al., 1996). The 1996 Philippine Elderly Survey, however, notes that the elderly, especially the old women, prefer to live with a married child, usually a daughter, which explains the presence of children-in-law and grandchildren in the household.

The latest survey on the elderly, the 2018 Longitudinal Study of Ageing and Health in the Philippines confirmed that 73 percent of older people prefer a daughter as co-resident, which is significantly more so among females than males. This shows the prevalence of the belief in traditional gender roles (i.e., men should work for the family while women should stay home and take care of the household). This preference to live with a daughter instead of a son is the highest among the 80 years old and above. Only a small proportion reported living with a son as the ideal arrangement, with more males than females preferring to live with a son (7 percent) than with a daughter (5 percent). The least preferred arrangement is rotating residence among the children (Cruz & Cabaraban, 2019, pp. 122–124).

In general, the choice of a co-resident child is guided by the quality of the relationship with the elderly parent, as seen in relational factors such as compatibility, closeness, and the presence of a special bond. Other considerations are the health and economic status of the elderly, as well as the preference and economic status of the children. In the end, especially when the elderly person is ill, family members decide on the basis of sentiment and practicality (Domingo & Asis, 1995).

There are older people, however, especially those belonging to the more affluent classes who opt for an independent life because they can afford to live separately and retain their dignity. In a sample survey of households in rural, urban, and Metro Manila communities (Medina et al., 1996, p. 48), a large proportion of the rich (17.9 percent) would prefer to live separately from their children for reasons like "less problems in being alone," "to have privacy in their own house," "do not like to be a burden to their children," and "to avoid problems with in-laws." Moreover, many older people, for sentimental reasons, wish to stay in the same house where they have lived for so long. They just prefer to be visited by their children and grandchildren regularly.

ECONOMIC WELL-BEING AND SUPPORT

The elderly in the Philippines have generally poor economic well-being. Although they own the houses they live in, they have generally low levels of income, assets, and resources. Their income sources are their children (59 percent), pension (42 percent), earnings from work (34 percent), income from the farm (23 percent), and remittances from their children abroad (15 percent); 22 percent of the elderly have liabilities, 43 percent of which are mostly loans from moneylenders such as pawnshops, credit unions, and cooperatives, and 22 percent of which are personal loans (Cruz, 2019, p. 106).

The male elderly, compared to the female, are more likely to work for a living, except for the well-to-do who can live comfortably without working, and except for the emigrant retirees who have returned to the Philippines ("balikbayan") and whose foreign pension, when converted into pesos, is more than enough for their basic needs. Many of the male elderly, however, are in the rural areas, working on the farm, so they do not qualify for pension benefits of the Government Service Insurance System or Social Security System. Despite multiple income sources, the elderly continue to work for a living despite their advanced age (Cruz et al., 2009). The males, particularly, work until they fall into poor health because they are the expected breadwinners (Natividad et al., 2014).

In the 2018 Longitudinal Study of Ageing and Health, it was found that only 5 percent have savings in the bank. When asked about the adequacy of their house-hold income, 38 percent said their income was just enough for their daily expenses, 43 percent reported some difficulty in meeting household expenses, and 14 percent said they had considerable difficulty in meeting expenses. Of those who had consid-erable difficulty in meeting expenses, 46 percent said that their main source of funds to meet the shortfall of income was money from their children while 26 percent borrow from relatives and/or friends. Findings, therefore, confirm that the family, particularly the children, is the traditional source of economic support for older Filipinos. Older females, particularly, rely heavily on children as their main source of income, 10 percent of them claiming remittances from children abroad as their most important source of income (Cruz, 2019, pp. 110–113).

The contribution of remittances from children abroad as a filial obligation is significant, considering that a quarter of older people have at least one child living or working abroad (Cruz et al., 2014). This dependence on remittances from abroad increases with advancing age, especially among the female elderly and urban residents compared to the male elderly and rural residents (Cruz & Laguna, 2009). With millions of households receiving financial assistance from family members working overseas, the monthly remittance to the Philippines, estimated at USD 24.5 billion in 2012 makes the Philippines the world's third highest net remittance recipient after India and China (Pernia et al., 2013).

PHYSICAL WELL-BEING AND CAREGIVING

Physical well-being is measured in terms of functional ability in activities of daily living (ADL) such as walking, eating, putting on clothes, taking a bath, standing up from the bed or chair and sitting down, going around the house, and using the toilet (Cruz et al., 2009). Older people find it more and more difficult to do these simple tasks and activities as they age.

In the case of those who are not yet extremely old and are still functionally able to cope with ADL, difficulties with respect to instrumental ADL (IADL) may be experienced. These activities include preparation of meals, doing housework, using the telephone, using transportation, shopping, and taking medicines (Ogena, 2007). One who used to be very active and solicitous over the children and grandchildren by cooking their favorite meals, taking them to the mall, and catering to all their desires now may feel useless due to physical restraints.

Findings from the 2018 Longitudinal Study of Ageing show that most elderly Filipinos assess themselves to be of average or better than average health, and the percentage of those who considered themselves as very unhealthy increases with age. However, this self-rating was done using their own judgment without their being given any referents with which to compare themselves. Among the self-reported diseases included in the survey, the most commonly diagnosed illnesses are hypertension, arthritis, cataracts, diabetes, angina and heart disease, and renal and urinary tract illness, in that order (Natividad, 2019, p. 68).

Because of the increase in the number of elderly persons, there is a growing demand for caregivers in the family. There is an increased need for the elderly to be assisted in performing some daily activities such as standing up from the bed or chair, using the toilet, and taking a bath. The need for caregivers becomes even more urgent in case of severe disability which necessitates bed confinement. This has tremendous implications for long-term care and rehabilitation.

Just as childcare is generally done by women, the caregivers of the elderly are usually women. For the married elderly, the most likely caregiver is the spouse, more often the wife, who has the advantage of longer longevity, rather than the husband. The daughter or daughter-in-law usually takes care of the parents. This is confirmed in the 2018 Longitudinal Study of Ageing where about a third of the respondents named the spouse as the one who takes care of them when they are sick. Although 6 in 10 men reported that their major caregiver is their spouse, only 18 percent of the women said the same. Women most commonly reported a daughter as their major caregiver (38 percent), while only 14 percent of the men are taken care of by a daughter. As age increases, the percentage taken care of by the spouse progressively decreases while the percentage taken care of by a daughter increases, thus, in the long run, caregiving of the elderly is mostly a female role (Natividad, 2019, pp. 96–97). This is especially true for long-term care or care over an extended period, most commonly due to dementia or being bed-ridden because of a stroke, a fall, or both. Among the respondents surveyed in the 2018 Longitudinal Study of Ageing, more daughters (37 percent) than spouses (33 percent) are long-term caregivers, and when asked for their preferred caregivers, most preferred are daughter, spouse, and son, in that order. Other preferred caregivers all fall within the same close family circle, including daughter-in-law and grandchild. None of the respondents mentioned hospitals or nursing homes, an indication that the provision of long-term care in the future remains a female-dominated family responsibility (Natividad, 2019, pp. 100–101).

Even among the small percentage (7 percent) of the elderly in the same study who have primary caregivers, the daughter form the bulk of primary caregivers (40 percent), followed by the spouse (29 percent), and daughter-in-law (9 percent), most of whom are co-residents, or if not, they reside next door or in the same barangay (Laguna, 2019, pp. 177–179). According to the same study, the average age of the primary caregivers is 51 which suggests that they have also their own families to attend to as parents or spouses, implying that the double burden of caring is heavier on Filipino women. Moreover, it was found that the caregivers provide more assistance in household tasks than in the personal care of the elderly, implying that caregiving duties are seen as part of the normative household duties of women. It was also found that this gendered pattern of car-egiving is replicated in succeeding generations where granddaughters are more involved in caring for their grandparents than grandsons. The son's caregiving is even passed on to their wives; thus next to daughters, the daughters'-in-law act as caregivers (Laguna, 2019, pp. 183–190).

On the whole, caregiving in the Philippines is family-based and family-ori-ented. As in other Asian countries, caring for older people is governed by cultural values and norms such as filial piety and familism. Children are the major pro-viders of parental care in old age; caregiving is unpaid and voluntary, a form of repayment for the good parenting the children received early in their lives.

SOCIAL WELL-BEING AND MENTAL HEALTH

Social well-being is largely understood in the context of intergenerational soli-darity (Cruz et al., 2009). This is because parent–child relations are a primary source of mutual emotional support. The Life-Span Attachment Theory helps explain this persistence of the parent–child relationship up to later life. Older people and their children have developed strong bonds based on a long history of family interaction, so that the attachments thus formed encourage them to con-tinue interaction throughout the family life cycle (Brubaker, 1985). Attachment is manifested by psychological closeness through constant interaction and com-munication, and physical contact through close residential proximity or regular visits. Contact may also be maintained by means of telephone and letters or mes-sages sent through other people. This attachment theory applies to families in all societies. Even in the Western world, research and national surveys have demonstrated that elderly persons are in regular contact with their families, especially adult children, and are neither isolated nor ignored by their kin (Heinamann, 1983, p. 128).

One indicator of intergenerational solidarity is the frequency of visits and communication between parents and children. Results of studies reveal a high level of intergenerational exchange of visits and communication between the Filipino elderly and their children. Data from the 1996 Philippine Elderly Survey and the 2007 Philippine Longitudinal Study of Ageing by the UP Population Institute show that most older people are in constant communication with their children, with 52 percent daily visits, 77 percent at least weekly visits, and 8 percent on special occasions or at least yearly visits; and that about 8 out of 10 elderly have an active exchange of communication with their children at least weekly through phone calls, text messages, letters, and e-mail (Cruz et al., 2009).

The 2018 Longitudinal Study of Ageing likewise show close communication between adult children and their aging parents, with the majority (66.2 percent) of non-co-resident adult children visiting their aging parents daily, about 20.5 percent visiting at least once every few days, and about 8 percent paying weekly visits. Looking at the other direction of the exchange, more than half (53.8 percent) of the adult children had daily visits from their parents, 22 percent were visited every few days, 7.7 percent were visited every week, and only 8 percent were never visited by their aging parents in the year before the survey. With regards to communication by phone, social networking sites like Facebook, and other social media platforms, 17 percent of the children communicated with their parents daily, 8 percent communicated every few days, 4 percent communicated as the need arises, and the majority or two out of three children have not communicated in the past month. (Cabaraban et al., 2019, pp. 198–200).

Another indicator of intergenerational solidarity is the intergenerational flow of support. Past studies have found that 92.9 percent of older people receive support from their children, mostly in terms of financial assistance (91 percent), help with food and meals (73.4 percent), and material goods (47 percent) such as clothes, medicines, and other gifts, as well as non-material support such as companionship (25.5 percent) and advice (11.6 percent) in connection with problems they encounter (Cruz et al., 2009).

The latest survey, the 2018 Longitudinal Study of Ageing, shows that 64 percent of adult children financially supported their parents in the month before the interview, with 21 percent of them giving monthly support of about P500. When asked if their other siblings also give financial support, 24 percent reported that all their siblings do, 71 percent said only some of their siblings do, 3 percent said no other siblings are giving support, and 2 percent said they have no siblings so they are the only ones supporting their parents (Cabaraban et al., 2019, pp. 201–202).

There is a two-way flow of support between elderly parents and their children, both co-resident and non-co-resident. Older people claim that they also provide support to their children, mostly in terms of advice, guidance, and consultation. They usually own the house where their co-resident children live, and many of them, especially the better-off, claim to provide their children with financial assistance. Thus, elderly parents are not just recipients but also providers of support to their children. This is confirmed in the 2018 Longitudinal Study of Ageing where two in five children received financial support from their parents in the month before the interview, although only 9 percent of them receive this support every month with about P500 as the median amount. The proportion of children who receive support decreases as the elderly parents' age increases (Cabaraban et al., 2019, pp. 203–204).

Other forms of support the elderly give to their children include emotional support, mostly in terms of advice, guidance, and consultation, as well as personal care and help with the household chores. The elderly mother is a domestic consultant to her daughter or daughter-in-law, supervisor of the house-helpers, or the real housekeeper. Moreover, many elderly mothers are so close to their married daughters who live abroad such that they make a trip every time the latter gives birth, in order to assist for one or two months, considering the non-availability of house help in a foreign land (Medina, 2015).

The familial web of relationships is not only between parents and children but is multigenerational, that is, it also includes grandchildren. Aging parents usually serve as caregivers of their grandchildren. They delight in experiencing once more the old familiar task of changing the baby's diapers, singing lullabies, and telling fairy tales to their grandchildren. They are so close to their grandchildren that they pamper them with toys, clothes, money, etc. Thus, spoiled or pampered grandchildren are referred to as "laki sa Lola" (brought up by grandmother). Many grandchildren perceive their grandparents to be more loving, more caring, and more understanding than their own parents. On the other hand, many grandparents feel that their love for their grandchildren is stronger than their love for their own children. They usually intervene for their grandchildren when they are scolded or confronted by their parents. In fact, misunderstandings sometimes occur between grandparents and adult children, arising from differences in opinion on the rearing and disciplining of grandchildren (Salvador, 1999).

Grandparents play an important role in child care also for their non-co-resident children. The babies and kids of the non-co-resident children are brought to the grandparents' house in the morning to be cared for and picked up later after work. This pattern of child care extends to the Filipino emigrants abroad who send for their parents across the miles to have someone watch the house and the grandchildren while they work as breadwinners. For many Filipino contract workers abroad, their children are left behind in the care of their grandparents (Medina, 2015).

Thus, the Filipino elderly is highly involved in various forms of mutual and reciprocal economic and emotional support with their children and grandchildren. They are also involved in a high level of exchange of visits and communication through letters, telephone calls, or text messages with both co-resident and non-co-resident children. This strong intergenerational solidarity through frequent visits and communication, as well as the two-way flow of economic and emotional support has helped the Filipino elderly enjoy a high level of social well-being. Thus, the results of the 2018 Longitudinal Study of Ageing show a low level of loneliness and feeling of social isolation among the elderly. The majority rarely or never felt a lack of companionship, felt left out, or felt isolated from others. The traditional filial piety dictates that the elderly is assured of access to children for companionship and assistance when needed. Thus, an overwhelming majority (94 percent) of the elderly said that they are very or somewhat satisfied with their lives (Ogena, 2019, pp. 146–147).

INSTITUTIONALIZATION OF THE ELDERLY

Because of this traditional filial responsibility and obligation to care for elderly parents, the Philippines, compared to other ASEAN countries, exhibits one of the highest incidences of elderly who continue to live with at least one of their children. Thus, homes for the aged are slow to develop in the Philippines.

Statistics from the Department of Social Welfare and Development (2019) show that there are about 29 accredited non-governmental organizations or private social welfare agencies including religious or interfaith group-led home-care institutions. Some provide permanent residential and nursing care, but others provide only temporary shelter. Examples are the Camillus MedHaven Nursing Home run by a group of Catholic religious brothers and priests, Little Sisters of the Poor, located at the San Lorenzo Ruiz Home for the elderly in Pasay City and run by an international religious congregation, and Kanlungan ni Maria Home for the Aged Inc. (Wiki Answers, 2013).

There are about four government-owned facilities for the elderly (Paguirigan, 2019, p. 150). The largest is Golden Acres which stands on a lot in Bago Bantay, Quezon City, with about 200 elderly residents mostly abandoned and destitute with no known kin (Natividad, 2005).

In general, the institutionalization of the elderly appears to be a last resort, after exhausting all means to care for them at home. There is a stigma attached to the institutionalization of aged parents.

The idea of alternative living arrangements for older people who have independent means, however, is gaining acceptance and support. This is true among highly educated women or retired professionals who never married and are childless, or those whose children have settled down permanently abroad, or those who have opted not to stay with their locally-based children but have the means to afford monthly fees in retirement homes (Natividad, 2005). Thus, some retirement homes have been established such as Helping Hands Philippines, Mountain Crest Residential Care, and Tagaytay Residential Care, all located in Tagaytay City (Retirement Homes, 2013).

Findings of the 2018 Longitudinal Study of Ageing reveal that about 80 percent of the respondents, particularly the males, have a greater predisposition toward institutional living. They think that the home for the aged is beneficial for the elderly who do not have anyone to care for them, that their health will be better taken care of in such a facility, and that this setup gives them a better chance to socialize with people of their own age. Those who are opposed to the idea of having homes for the aged believe that the family should take care of the elderly, that the elderly will miss his/her family, that the elderly would not like to live with strangers, and that it is shameful for the family to place the elderly in nursing homes (Paguirigan, 2019, pp. 154–158).

Even if most of the elderly in the survey think that to have homes for the aged is a good idea, more than three-quarters of them do not want to live in such facilities themselves. Those who want to live in such a facility gave the following conditions: if the children do not want to take care of their parents, if the elderly is abandoned, if the children do not treat their parents well, if the conditions and treatment in the facility are good, or if the elderly is no longer comfortable living with the children (Paguirigan, 2019, p. 157). Thus, the social and cultural expectations of filial duty and obligation are still strong, and the elderly would not like to live in homes for the aged as much as possible if they can help it.

RECOMMENDATIONS FOR FUTURE RESEARCH ON THE WELFARE OF THE ELDERLY

On Government Laws Benefitting the Elderly

The government has been very supportive of the elderly by way of legislation but much more can be done in implementation. For instance despite the laws providing 20 percent discounts in medicine, fare, movies, etc. in the Senior Citizen Act of 1992 or Republic Act 7432 (Republic of the Philippines, 1992), the expanded senior citizen's Act of 2003 or Republic Act No. 9257 (Republic of the Philippines, 2004), and Senior Citizens Act of 2010 or Republic Act No. 9994 (Republic of the Philippines, 2010), the law benefit only the richer and more educated elderly rather than their poorer and less educated counterparts who are not aware of these laws.

There is a need to gather data on the proportion of elderly who are aware of these benefits, including privileges like free medical and dental services, free flu and pneumococcal vaccinations, and free medicine for hypertension and diabetes in government facilities, health centers, and rural health units. There is also a need to study how information on these benefits may be disseminated and what are the most effective means of reaching the elderly in the most far-flung barrios.

Another problem is that even if the elderly is informed about the system of discounts available for them, only the rich who have the means to purchase these items and services can benefit, compared to the poor who have no purchasing power. About 30 percent of the respondents in the 2018 Longitudinal Study of Ageing and Health in the Philippines, for instance, reported that they had an unmet need for medical attention mainly because of a lack of financial means (Cruz et al., 2019, p. 216).

There is a social pension scheme for indigent elderly at P500 a month as provided by the Senior Citizens Act of 2010 which has been doubled lately by Congress to P1,000 a month with the new law – Republic Act No. 11916 (Tan, 2022), but even this is insufficient to cover the most basic expenses of the elderly. Thus, there is a need to study how much is the most reasonable amount of pension to be given and how to better target the intended poorest recipients. There are many indigents who are not reached especially those who are in the most remote areas.

In 2016, Republic Act 10868 or the "Centenarian Act of 2016" was signed into law which provides for a cash gift of 100,000 pesos for Filipinos who reach the age of 100 (Rosario, 2022). While a number of Filipino centenarians have received the cash gift, this is only a one-time grant and will not sustain the elderly for long. Furthermore, last September 2022, it was reported that there were 662 Filipino centenarians still waiting to receive their pension since the Department of Budget and Management did not grant the request of 66.2 million pesos earmarked for distribution to them. In addition, the amount is not funded in the 2023 budget of the agency (Porcalla, 2022).

House Bill No. 10647, which sought to amend the Centenarian Act of 2016, was also approved on final reading by Congress providing for a cash gift of P25,000 to senior citizens who reach 80, 85, 90, and 95 years of age, as well as P1 million to those who reach 101 years of age (Cervantes, 2022). Again, this has to be provided for in the budget to be implemented and this is only a one-time grant.

Regarding health insurance, PhilHealth coverage is mandatory for indigent elderly (Republic Act No. 9994 or Senior Citizen Act of 2010) and to all Filipino citizens (Republic Act No. 11223 or Universal Health Care Act), but the benefits remain inadequate to cover the cost of health care, especially outpatient care. According to the findings of the 2018 Longitudinal Study of Ageing and Health in the Philippines, half of the respondents covered by PhilHealth claim that their children paid for most of the cost of their hospitalization while a fourth said that they themselves and their spouses paid for their medical expenses (Cruz et al., 2019, p. 217). Thus, there is also a need to study whether PhilHealth should be expanded to cover the full health insurance of the elderly.

On Caregiving

There is an increasing demand for caregiving arrangements for the elderly, especially long-term care. There has to be a study whereby the subject of aging and caregiving for the elderly can be integrated into the school curriculum together with other home economics subjects like cooking, sewing, and baby care. Local government units may also offer elderly caregiving training free of charge just like the Quezon City barangays offering free three months vocational skills courses such as Automotive Servicing and Bread/Pastry Training under the Manpower Barangay-based Skills Training Program of the Quezon City Social Services Development Department. Additionally, the Technical Education and Skills Development Authority may also provide short-term training for informal home-based caregivers to improve their caregiving skills and help them cope with the mental, emotional, and physical strain of caring for their elderly.

Another problem is the availability of caregivers for the elderly. Studies show the important role of female spouses and daughters in caregiving. This gendered pattern for caregiving tasks is also followed in the succeeding generation where granddaughters are preferred to grandsons. The son's caregiving duty is also passed on to their wives; thus next to daughters, the daughters-in-law assume the caregiving responsibility. However, with the increased participation of women in the labor force together with their increased rate of migration to the urban areas and abroad, the number of potential caregivers is greatly diminished. Thus, there is a need to study how to provide incentives for women to stay home and care for their old family members. There is also a need for counseling programs for the young to sustain positive attitudes toward the elderly. This is in line with the possible shrinking level of intergenerational support and waning filial piety as observed lately in Japan and Korea (Cruz et al., 2019, p. 224). Similar lower level of financial support was found in the 2018 Longitudinal Study of Ageing and Health in the Philippines compared to that of the 2007 Philippine Study on Ageing (Marquez, 2019, p. 170).

On Alternative Living Arrangements

It has been noted that there are elderly who have independent means and can afford monthly fees to pay for institutional living. Thus, retirement homes have been established to cater to these older people. There is a need to study how prevalent are these retirement homes and the quality of their facilities. There should be a standard set of requirements before these retirement homes are allowed to operate, and there should be close monitoring periodically to ensure that they are operating satisfactorily, with provision for high-quality medical personnel and services.

For those who cannot afford privately owned retirement homes, the government can establish a program whereby the indigent elderly who needs long-term care may be assisted either through home care services (includes daycare or night care services and visiting nurse services) or facility care services (includes the establishment of nursing homes, intermediary term or long-term care facilities) depending on the level of care needed. Thus, additional government homes for the aged would cater not solely to the destitute and abandoned as they are now doing, but most especially to the indigent who need long-term care, the senile, the mentally handicapped, those with Alzheimer's disease, and so on.

REFERENCES

Brubaker, T. H. (1985). *Later life families*. Sage Publications.

Cabaraban, M. K. S. I., Paguirigan, M. R. B., & Cruz, G. T. (2019). Children of older persons. In G. T. Cruz, C. J. P. Cruz, & Y. Saito (Eds.), *Ageing and health in the Philippines* (pp. 193–214). Economic Research Institute for ASEAN and East Asia and Demographic Research and Development Foundation Inc.

Cervantes, F. (2022, January 31). *House raises centenarian cash gift to P1-M*. Philippine News Agency. pna.gov.ph/articles/1166754

Cruz, C. J. P. (2019). Economic well-being. In G. T. Cruz, C. J. P. Cruz, & Y. Saito (Eds.), *Ageing and health in the Philippines* (pp. 105–116). Economic Research Institute for ASEAN and East Asia and Demographic Research and Development Foundation Inc.

Cruz, G. T., & Cabaraban, M. K. S. I. (2019). Generativity, attitudes and beliefs. In G. T. Cruz, C. J. P. Cruz, & Y. Saito (Eds.), *Ageing and health in the Philippines* (pp. 117–128). Economic Research Institute for ASEAN and East Asia and Demographic Research and Development Foundation Inc.

Cruz, C. J. P., & Cruz, G. T. (2019). Filipino older persons. In G. T. Cruz, C. J. P. Cruz, & Y. Saito (Eds.), *Ageing and health in the Philippines* (pp. 27–46). Economic Research Institute for ASEAN and East Asia and Demographic Research and Development Foundation Inc.

Cruz, G. T., Joefrey, B. A., Melissa, C. L., Josefina, N. N., & Yasuhiko, S. (2009). Changing social structures and well-being of the older Filipinos. *Transactions of the National Academy of Science and Technology (Philippines), 32*(2), 197–222.

Cruz, G. T., & Laguna, E. (2009). Overseas labour migration and well-being of older Filipinos. In E. N. Arifin & A. Ananta (Eds.), *Older persons in Southeast Asia: An emerging asset* (pp. 315–333). Institute of Southeast Asian Studies.

Cruz, G. T., Lavares, A. M. T., Marquez, M. P. N., Natividad, J. N., & Saito, Y. (2014). Gender and economic well-being among older Filipinos. In T.W. Demasayaham (Ed.), *Gender and Ageing: Southeast Asian Perspectives* (pp. 288–314). Institute of Southeast Asian Studies (ISEAS).

Cruz, G. T., Natividad, J. N., Gonzales, M. L., & Saito, Y. (2016). *Aging in the Philippines: Findings from the 2007 Philippine study on aging*. University of the Philippines Population Institute and Demographic Research and Development Foundation.

Cruz, G. T., Natividad, J. N., & Saito, Y. (2019). Discussion, conclusions, and recommendations. In G. T. Cruz, C. J. P. Cruz, & Y. Saito (Eds.), *Ageing and health in the Philippines* (pp. 215–226). Philippines Economic Research Institute for ASEAN and East Asia and Demographic Research and Development Foundation Inc.

Department of Social Welfare and Development. (2019). *Statistics of NGO/private social welfare development agencies (SWDAs) providing programs and services to older persons with registration and licensed to operate and/or accreditation issued by DSWD as of July 9, 2019 (Residential Care)*. DSWD Central Office.

Domingo, Ma. Fe A. (1999, November 18). Involvements in old age: Cruz-na-Ligas experience. In *Second national conference of the Pambansang Samahan sa Pag-aaral ng Pagtanda (PSPP)*, Mirriam College.

Domingo, L. J., & Asis, M. B. (1995). Living arrangements and the flow of support between generations in the Philippines. *Journal of Cross-cultural Gerontology, 10*(1–2), 21–51.

Economic and Social Commission for Asia and the Pacific. (1997). *Statistical yearbook for Asia and the Pacific*. Economic and Social Commission for Asia and the Pacific.

Heinamann, G. D. (1983). Family involvement and support for widowed persons. In T. H. Brubaker (Ed.), *Family relationships in later life* (pp. 127–148). Sage Publications.

Jocano, F. L. (1988). *Social organization in three Philippine villages*. Centro Escolar University Research and Development Center.

Laguna, E. P. (2019). Caring for older persons. In G. T. Cruz, C. J. P. Cruz, & Y. Saito (Eds.), *Ageing and health in the Philippines* (pp. 173–192). Economic Research Institute for ASEAN and East Asia and Demographic Research and Development Foundation Inc.

Marquez, M. P. N. (2019). Family support and intergenerational exchanges. In G. T. Cruz, C. J. P. Cruz, & Y. Saito (Eds.), *Ageing and health in the Philippines* (pp. 161–172). Economic Research Institute for ASEAN and East Asia and Demographic Research and Development Foundation Inc.

Medina, B. T., de Guzman, E. A., Roldan, A. A., & Bautista, R. Ma. J. (1996). *The Filipino family, emerging structures and arrangement*. Monograph Series I. Office of Research Coordination, University of the Philippines, University of the Philippines Press.

Medina, B. T. (2015). *The Filipino family* (3rd ed.). University of the Philippines Press.

Natividad, J. N. (2005). Gender and ageing in the Philippines. In K. Mehta (Ed.), *Untapped resources: Women in ageing societies across Asia* (pp. 161–168). Marshall Cavendish International Private Limited.

Natividad, J. N. (2019). Health status. In G. T. Cruz, C. J. P. Cruz, & Y. Saito (Eds.), *Ageing and health in the Philippines* (pp. 47–74). Economic Research Institute for ASEAN and East Asia and Demographic Research and Development Foundation Inc.

Natividad, J. N., Saito, Y., & Cruz, G. T. (2014). Work, retirement, and the gender divide in the Philippines. In T. W. Demasayaham (Ed.), *Gender and ageing: Southeast Asian perspectives* (pp. 315–388). Institute of Southeast Asian Studies (ISEAS).

Ogena, N. B. (2007). The low and slow ageing in the Philippines: Auspicious or challenging? In G. Sinigoj, G. Jones, K. Hirokawa, & S. Linhart (Eds.), *The impact of ageing: A common challenge for Europe and Asia* (pp. 105–124). LIT Publishing International.

Ogena, N. B. (2019). Activities, social isolation, and information technology. In G. T. Cruz, C. J. P. Cruz, & Y. Saito (Eds.), *Ageing and health in the Philippines* (pp. 129–148). Economic Research Institute for ASEAN and East Asia and Demographic Research and Development Foundation Inc.

Paguirigan, M. R. B. (2019). Services for older persons. In G. T. Cruz, C. J. P. Cruz, & Y. Saito (Eds.), *Ageing and health in the Philippines* (pp. 149–160). Economic Research Institute for ASEAN and East Asia and Demographic Research and Development Foundation Inc.

Paquio, B. B. (1994, February 5). RP has highest growth rate of elderly population in Asia. *Manila Bulletin*, B-13.

Pernia, E. M., Elena, E. P., Jackson, L. U., & Maria, R. S. P. (2013, September 1). *International migration, remittances, and economic development in the Philippines*. National Research Council of the Philippines.

Philippines Demographics. (2020). *Life expectancy in the Philippines*. Retrieved August 22, 2021 from https//www. worldometers.info>demographics>Philippines

Republic of the Philippines. (1992). *Republic Act 7432: Senior Citizens Act of 1992*. Retrieved October 20, 2022 from elibrary.judiciary.gov.ph/thebookshelf/showdocs/2/15066

Republic of the Philippines. (2003). *Republic Act 9257: Expanded Senior Citizens Act of 2003*. Retrieved October 26, 2022, from htpps://www.Officialgazette.gov.ph/2004/02/06/republic-act-no-9257/

Republic of the Philippines. (2010). *Republic Act 9994: Expanded Senior Citizens Act of 2010*. Retrieved October 10, 2022, from htpps://www.Officialgazette.gov.ph/2010/02/15/republic-act-no.9994/#:~;text=Section%201%20of%20Republic%20Act,"SECTION%201

Republic of the Philippines. (2016). *Republic Act 10868: Centenarian Act of 2016*. Retrieved October 30, 2022, from officialgazette.gov.ph/downloads/2016/06jun/20160623-RA-10868-BSA.pdf

Republic of the Philippines. (2019a). *Republic Act 11223: Universal Health Care Law of 2019*. Retrieved October 16, 2022, from lawphil.net/Statutes/repacts/ra2019/ra_11223_2019.html

Republic of the Philippines. (2019b). *Republic Act 11350: National Commission of Senior Citizen Act*. Retrieved August 20, 2022, from officialgazette.gov.ph/25/republic-act-no-11350/

Philippine Statistics Authority. (2010). *The age and sex structure of the Philippine population: Facts from the 2010 Census*. Retrieved January 6, 2022, from psa.gov.ph/content/age-and-sex-structure-philippine-population-facts-2010-census.pdf

Philippine Statistics Authority. (2020). *Census of population and housing*. Philippine Statistics Authority. Retrieved January 16, 2022, from psa.gov.ph/content/2020-census-population-and-housing-2020-cph-population counts-declared-official-president

Porcalla, D. (2022, September 8). *"DSWD: No funds for 662 pinoy centenarians' cash gift."* Retrieved October 30, 2022, from philstar.com/nation/2022/09/08/2208147/dswd-no-funds-662-pinoy-centenarians-cash-gift

Retirement Homes. (2013). *Philippine assisted living and senior living*. Retirement Homes. Retrieved July 24, 2013, from http://www.retirementhomes.com/homes/Assisted_Living/International/Philippines/index.html

Rosario, B. (2022, January 31). *Lower house Oks 25,000 for seniors aged over 80; 1 M for 101 year old centenarians*. Retrieved October 30, 2022, from mb.com.ph/2022/01/31/lower-house-oks-p25,000-for-someone-aged-over-80-p1-M-for-101-year-old-centenarians

Salvador, A. E. (1999, November 18). Exploring the relationships of three generational households. In *Second international conference of the Pambansang Samahan sa Pag-aaral ng Pagtanda (PSSP)*, Miriam College.

Tan, A. (2022, August 2). *Social pension for poor senior citizens increased to P1000 monthly with new law*. Business World Online. Retrieved September 5, 2022, from bworldonline.com

Wiki Answers. (2013). *List of nursing homes in the Philippines*. Wiki Answers. Retrieved July 24, 2013. http://wiki.answers.com/Q/List_of_nursing_homes_in_the_Philippines

INDEX